Jeremiah Jones

A New and Full Method of Settling the Canonical Authority of the

New Testament

Vol. 3

Jeremiah Jones

A New and Full Method of Settling the Canonical Authority of the New Testament
Vol. 3

ISBN/EAN: 9783744715478

Printed in Europe, USA, Canada, Australia, Japan

Cover: Foto ©Lupo / pixelio.de

More available books at **www.hansebooks.com**

A

NEW AND FULL

M E T H O D

OF SETTLING

THE CANONICAL AUTHORITY

OF THE

NEW TESTAMENT.

TO WHICH IS SUBJOINED

A VINDICATION OF THE FORMER PART

OF

ST. MATTHEW'S GOSPEL,

FROM MR. WHISTON'S CHARGE OF DISLOCATIONS.

———————

IN THREE VOLUMES.

———————

BY

THE REV. JEREMIAH JONES.

————

V O L. III.

————

OXFORD:
AT THE CLARENDON PRESS.
MDCCXCVIII.

A

METHOD

FOR

SETTLING THE CANON

OF THE

NEW TESTAMENT.

PART IV.

*A general Differtation, or Proof, concerning the Canonical Au-
thority of the Four Gofpels.*

BEFORE I enter upon the proof of the Canonical authority of each of the Gofpels in particular, it will be very
ferviceable to my defign to obferve and fhew, that *the primitive Chriftians have exprefsly acknowledged only four Gofpels ;
and thofe four Gofpels which we now receive under the names of
Matthew, Mark, Luke, and John, to be genuine and Canonical.* I fhall produce the feveral teftimonies which I have obferved, according to the order of time in which the writers
ved ; and among thefe it will not be amifs to place,

1. St. John.

I. The teftimony of St. John the Apoftle; concerning whom we are told by Eufebius [a], *That when the three Gofpels (of Matthew, Mark, and Luke) were publifhed and known to every body, St. John at length faw them, approved them, and confirmed the truth of them; but (owned) that they were defective as to the account of thofe things which were done by our Saviour at the beginning of his miniftry——For which reafon John, being defired by his friends, fupplied the defects of the three others, and wrote his Gofpel to inform us of that time, and the things which were done by our Saviour in it,* viz. *before the imprifonment of John the Baptift.* Now hence it follows;

1. That before St. John wrote his Gofpel, the Chriftians of that firft age owned and received no other than the Gofpels of Matthew, Mark, and Luke; although it is certain there were many other falfe Gofpels extant at that time, as I have elfewhere proved.

2. That thefe three were univerfally received and approved.

3. That they were with juft reafon fo approved, becaufe St. John alfo did approve them.

Befides this teftimony of Eufebius, I find in a very old book, intitled, Μαρτύριον Τιμοθέȣ τȣ̑ 'Αποςόλȣ, i. e. *The Martyrdom of Timothy the Apoftle,* of which we have an extract in Photius (Cod. ccliv.); "That when, after the death of Domitian, "Nerva became Emperor, John returned to Ephefus, from ".which place he had been banifhed by Domitian, he then "took the feveral books which contained the hiftory of our "Saviour's fufferings and miracles and doctrines, and were "now tranflated into feveral different languages, reviewed "them, rectified them, and joined himfelf to the former three "Evangelifts (by writing his Gofpel)." I confefs I cannot

---

[a] Τὼν προαναγραφέντων τριῶν εἰς πάντας ἤδη καὶ εἰς αὐτὸν Διαδεδομένων, ἀποδέξαςϑαι μέν φασιν ἀλήϑειαν αὐτοῖς ἐπιμαρτυρήσαντα· μόνον δὲ ἄρα λείπεςϑαι τῇ γραφῇ τὴν περὶ τῶν ἐν πρώτοις κ̀ κατ' ἀρχὴν τȣ̑ κηρύγματος ὑπὸ τȣ̑ Χριςȣ̑ πεπραγμένων διήγησιν — Παρακληϑέντα δὴ ἐν τȣ́τοις ἕνεκα φησὶ τὸν ἀπόςολον Ἰωάννην, τὸν ὑπὸ τῶν προτέρων εὐαγγελιςῶν παρασιωπηϑέντα χρόνον, καὶ τὰ κατὰ τȣ̑τον πεπραγμένα τῷ Σωτῆρι (ταῦτα δ' ἦν τὰ πρὸ τῆς τȣ̑ Βαπτιςȣ̑ καϑείρξεως) τῷ κατ' αὐτὸν εὐαγγελίῳ παραδȣ̑ναι. Hift. Eccl. l. 3. c. 24.

certainly

certainly determine the age of this book. There is a book extant, intitled *The Martyrdom of Timothy*, which goes under the name of Polycrates, a Bishop of Ephesus, in the latter end of the second century, out of which Photius seems to have made this extract; and if this be true, it makes the history more valid: but it must be owned that several learned men are of opinion this book was not made by Polycrates, into which it is not my business here to enquire.

2. St. POLYCARP.

II. The testimony of Polycarp, who, according to Irenæus [a], *was not only instructed by the Apostles, and acquainted with many who had seen Christ, but placed by the Apostles in Asia, as Bishop of Smyrna, whom*, says he, *I also saw when I was young.* He (Polycarp) expressly mentions together our four Gospels and their authors thus: " [b] It was not without " reason that the Evangelists began their Gospels different " ways; though the design of each of them was the same. " Matthew, because he wrote to the Hebrews, began with the " genealogy of Christ, that he might evidence Christ to be " descended of that family, which all the Prophets had foretold " he should descend from. John being fixed among the " Ephesians, who as Gentiles were ignorant of the law, be- " gan his Gospel with an account of the cause of our redemp- " tion, viz. that God would have his Son become incarnate

[a] Καὶ Πολύκαρπος δὲ οὐ μόνον ὑπὸ ἀποςόλων μαθητευθεὶς, καὶ συναναςραφεὶς πολλοῖς τοῖς τὸν Χριςὸν ἑωρακόσιν, ἀλλὰ καὶ ὑπὸ ἀποςόλων καταςαθεὶς εἰς τὴν Ἀσίαν ἐν τῇ ἐν Σμύρνῃ ἐκκλησίᾳ ἐπίσκοπος, ὃν καὶ ἡμεῖς ἑωράκαμεν ἐν τῇ πρώτῃ ἡμῶν ἡλικίᾳ. Adv. Hæres. l. 3. c. 3. et apud Euseb. l. 4. c. 14.

[b] Rationaliter Evangelistæ principiis diversis utuntur, quamvis una eademque evangelizandi eorum probetur intentio. Matthæus, ut Hebræis scribens, genealogiæ Christi ordinem texuit, ut ostenderet ab ea Christum descendisse progenie, de qua eum nasciturum universi Prophetæ cecinerant. Joannes autem ad Ephesum constitutus, qui legem tanquam ex Gentibus ignorabant, a causa nostræ redemptionis Evangelii sumpsit exordium; quæ causa ex eo apparet, quod filium suum Deus pro nostra salute voluit incarnari. Lucas vero a Zachariæ sacerdotio incipit, ut ejus filii miraculo nativitatis, et tanti prædicatoris officio, Divinitatem Christi gentibus declararet. Unde et Marcus antiqua prophetici mysterii competentia adventui Christi declarat, ut non nova, sed antiquitus prolata ejus Prædicatio probaretur.

" for

" for our falvation. Luke begins with the priefthood of Za-
" charias, that by the account of his fon's miraculous birth,
" and his being fo confiderable a preacher, he might evidence
" the divinity of Chrift to the Gentiles. Mark began his
" Gofpel with the explication of fome antient prophecies re-
" lating to the coming of Chrift, that his Gofpel might ap-
" pear no new thing, but the fame as had been of old." For
this fragment of Polycarp we are obliged to Feuardentius,
who in his notes on Irenæus, l. 3. c. 3. publifhed it with
fome other fragments of Polycarp out of a very antient manufcript of Victor Capuanus's Catena, upon the four Evangelifts, which Catena he there promifes to publifh; but whether
he did or no, I know not. Victor Capuanus lived, according
to Feuardentius, in the year of Chrift 480. Johan. Jacob.
Grynæus (Præfat. in Orthodoxographa) places him fooner,
viz. A. D. 455; but Bellarmine [a], and Dr. Cave [b], place him
near a hundred years later, viz. in the year 540, and 545, as
alfo does Dr. Mill [c].

3. TATIAN.

III. That there were only the four Gofpels of Matthew,
Mark, Luke, and John, received in the middle part of the fecond century, is evident from Tatian's Harmony, *which was
made about that time.* He was a fcholar of Juftin Martyr,
and συνάφειάν τινα καὶ συναγωγὴν ἐκ οἶδ' ὅπως τῶν εὐαγγελίων συνθεὶς, τὸ
διὰ τισσάρων τοῦτο προσωνόμασιν· ὁ καὶ παρά τισιν εἰσέτι νῦν φέρεται
(Eufeb. Hift. Eccl. lib. 4. c. 29.) *compiled a certain harmony
of the Gofpels, and called it,* The Gofpel of the Four; *which
is even to this day in the hands of fome.* The fame account is
alfo in Epiphanius, Hæref. 46. n. 1. There can be no reafonable doubt but that thefe four were the Gofpels of Matthew, Mark, Luke, and John; for not only the number
agrees, but thefe were the only four Gofpels that ever were
reduced to a harmony. Befides, if the above-mentioned Victor Capuanus is to be credited, the Harmony of Tatian is ftill
extant; for that which he publifhed in the fifth or fixth cen-

[a] Dr Scriptor. Ecclef. ad voc.   [c] Prolegom. in Nov. Teftam.
[b] Hift. Liter. tom. 1. p. 411.   §. 351.

tury, with a preface to prove it was wrote by Tatian, we have now printed among the *Orthodoxographa*[a]; and this contains our prefent four Gofpels, and no other. But I muft own that I queftion much, whether this be the work of Tatian, or no; for the genealogy of Chrift is in this Harmony of Tatian [b], which was not in the antient one under his name [c].

It may indeed be objected that Victor Capuanus, in his preface to that which he thought to be the Harmony of Tatian, fays, that *he gave his work the title of Diapente* [d]. *I find,* fays he, *by the hiftory of Eufebius, that Tatian, a very learned man and excellent orator of that time, compiled one Gofpel out of the four, to which he gave the title of Diapente, i. e.* of five; or, The Gofpel of Five: as though he had made his Harmony out of five Gofpels. Accordingly, I find that Grotius [e] has explained the word *Diapente*; *Tatian,* fays he, *when he made one Gofpel out of four, followed not only the Greek, but the Hebrew copies of Matthew; whence it came to pafs that his work,* which was commonly called Διὰ Τισσάρων, or The Gofpel of Four, *was by others called,* The Gofpel according to the Hebrews; *by others* Διὰ Πίντι, *or* The Gofpel of Five.

To this I anfwer, (1.) That though I queftion not but Tatian made ufe of the Hebrew copies of St. Matthew, yet he made ufe of them as what he looked upon to be the moft authentick and genuine, and fo made no ufe of the Greek, as of another or fifth Gofpel. This is what I have conjectured, and endeavoured to prove in the firft volume [f]; but all which can be concluded hence is, that by a miftake he made ufe of an interpolated corrupt tranflation of St. Matthew, in-

---

[a] Vol. 1. p. 659, &c.

[b] See chap. v. Orthodoxogr. p. 663.

[c] This I have obferved already, Vol. I. Part II. ch. xxxix. p. 390.

[d] Ex hiftoria quoque ejus (fcil. Eufebii) comperi, quod Tatianus, vir eruditiffimus, et orator illius temporis clariffimus, unum ex quatuor compaginaverit Evangelium, cui titulum Diapente impofuit. Or-

thodoxogr. p. 659.

[e] Puto autem Tatianum, cum ex quatuor Evangeliis unum concinnaret, fecutum in Matthæi verbis non Græcos tantum, fed et Hebræos codices, unde Evangelium illud quod vulgo Διὰ Τισσάρων, *per Quatuor,* ab aliis dictum *fecundum Hebræos,* ab aliis vero Διὰ Πίντι, *per Quinque.* Annot. in Titul. Matth.

[f] Loc. jam citat. p. 388, 389.

　　　　　　　　　　　　　　ftead

ſtead of the true Greek original, ſtill looking upon it as the work of that Evangeliſt, which is ſufficient to my purpoſe.

2. As to Grotius's conjecture, that it was called Διὰ Πίντι, or *The Goſpel of Five*, for the above-mentioned reaſon, it ſeems to me entirely to be founded upon a falſe reading; and that inſtead of Διὰ Πίντι we are to read in the preface of Victor Διὰ Τισσάρων, as is well conjectured by Mr. Fabricius[a]. My reaſons for this correction are,

1. That Victor in his preface ſays, he found the account which he gives in the Hiſtory of Euſebius; *but there is no ſuch thing to be found in Euſebius*; but on the contrary he ſaith, *Tatian gave his work the title of* Διὰ Τισσάρων, i. e. *The Goſpel of Four*. Either therefore Victor Capuanus was miſtaken, or elſe we muſt correct his words by thoſe of Euſebius, from whom he tranſcribed; i. e. for Διὰ Πίντι, muſt read Διὰ Τισσάρων; *The Goſpel of Four*, and not *The Goſpel of Five*.

2. If Victor Capuanus had thought any thing of five Goſpels being in Tatian's work, he would not have ſaid expreſsly, " Unum ex quatuor compaginaverit Evangelium," *He compiled one out of four Goſpels*.

3. Theodoret (who lived in or not long before the time of Victor Capuanus, viz. about the year of Chriſt 450.) tells us, *He compoſed a Goſpel* τὸ Διὰ Τισσάρων καλόμινον, i. e. which was called *The Goſpel of Four* [b].

Upon the whole then I conclude, there were but four Goſpels, viz. thoſe of Matthew, Mark, Luke, and John, in uſe in the Church in the time of Tatian, i. e. in the time of Juſtin Martyr, who was Tatian's maſter.

4. IRENÆUS.

IV. Irenæus, who was cotemporary with Tatian, has abundantly evidenced, that *there were no more than the four Goſpels*, which we now receive, *then received in the Church*.

---

[a] Cod Apoc. Nov. Teſt. tom. 1. P. 379.

[b] Hæretic. Fabul. lib. 1. c. 20. Beſides all I have ſaid on this head, it may not be amiſs to add the great Caſaubon's conjecture, or correction of this place, viz. That for Διὰ Πίντι we ſhould read Διὰ Πάντων, meaning that the title imported, The Goſpel of all the Four, or the whole entire Goſpel. Ad Baron. Annal. Ann. 31. N. 3.

He

He has wrote a large Chapter [a], intitled, *A proof that there can neither be more nor less than four Gospels*; out of all which I shall only observe these two things; (1.) That he says the very Hereticks owned them, and cited them [b]; (2.) He calls them vain, ignorant, and impudent, who assert, that there are either more or fewer than these four Gospels [c]. The fact therefore, which I am upon, being thus certain, I do not think myself obliged to say any thing concerning the allegorical arguments, which Irenæus makes use of to prove his point. Mr. Toland has bantered them [d], and Mr. Fabricius has shewn [e] that there is the like sort of reasoning upon that head in many of the antient Christian writers; but (as Du Pin says [f]) "These sort of allegories have no other foundation "but mere fancy; and it is in vain to seek for any other rea- "son of the number four, than God's own will."

5. TERTULLIAN.

V. Tertullian has expresly determined *the number of Gospels*, which were received by the Church in his time, *to four*. So (l. 4. *adv. Marcion.* c. 2.), "Nobis fidem ex Apostolis "Joannes et Matthæus infinuant, ex Apostolicis Lucas et "Marcus inftaurant;" i. e. *The credit of the Gospel-history is confirmed to us by two that were Apostles, viz. Matthew and John, and two that were Apostolick men (i. e. companions of the Apostles) Mark and Luke:* and in the same book, c. 5. speaking of the same four Gospels, and naming them, he says, "Eadem auctoritas Ecclesiarum Apostolicarum cæteris quo- "que patrocinabatur Evangeliis;" i. e. that *they were patronized or confirmed by the authority of the Apostolick Churches.*

---

[a] Adv. Hæref. lib. 3. c. 11. Oftensio quod neque plura, nec minus quam quatuor possunt esse Evangelia.

[b] Ut et ipsi hæretici testimonium reddant eis, & ex ipsis egrediens unusquisque eorum conetur suam confirmare doctrinam. Lib. 3. c. 11.

[c] Vani omnes, & indocti, & insuper audaces, qui frustrantur speci-em Evangelii, & vel plures quam dictæ funt, vel rursus pauciores inferunt personas Evangelii. Ad eund. loc.

[d] Amyntor, p. 50, &c.

[e] Cod. Apocr. N. T. tom. 1. p. 382, &c. et tom. 3. p. 555, &c.

[f] Hist. of the Can. vol. ii. c. 2. §. 2.

 6. CLE-

6. CLEMENS ALEXANDRINUS.

VI. Clemens Alexandrinus (not long after Irenæus) is the next, whose testimony I shall produce; he, disputing against Julius Caffianus, who had cited a paffage out of the Gospel of the Egyptians in favour of the doctrine of the unlawfulnefs of marriage, replies; *Firſt,* fays he, *I obferve this is not in either of the four Gofpels delivered to us, but in the Gofpel according to the Egyptians* '; by which he, who knows that Clemens continually cites the four Gofpels which we now receive, and no other, will be eafily induced to believe he here meant the fame four. See the place at large above, Vol. I. Part II. Chap. XVI. p. 199.

7. ORIGEN.

VII. Origen, the Scholar of Clemens Alexandrinus, has alfo confirmed the fame; viz. that *though there were many Gofpels forged by the Hereticks, which,* fays he, *we read, that we may not be thought ignorant,* Ecclefia quatuor habet E-vangelia, i. e. *the Church receives only four Gofpels* ᵇ; and a little after, Quatuor tantum Evangelia funt prolata, e quibus fub perfona Domini et Salvatoris noftri proferenda funt dog-mata: *There are only four Gofpels made ufe of, out of which the articles of our Religion as from Jefus Chriſt are to be propofed.* Once more a few lines after; In his omnibus nihil aliud pro-bamus nifi quod Ecclefia, i. e. quatuor tantum Evangelia re-cipienda; *Among all thefe Gofpels we approve none but thofe which the Church approves;* viz. that only the four Gofpels are to be received. It would be madnefs for any one, who ever faw Origen's works, to afk what four Gofpels he meant. Befides that, he elfewhere τὸν ἐκκλησιαστικὸν φυλάτων κανόνα, fpeak-ing of, or *reciting the Canon of the Church,* names thefe four Gofpels, ἃ καὶ μόνα ἀναντίῤῥητά ἐστι ἐν τῇ ὑπὸ τὸν οὐρανὸν ἐκκλησίᾳ τοῦ Θεοῦ, i. e. *which four alone are received without controverfy in the church of God, which is all over the world.* Comment. in Matth. apud Eufeb. H. E. l. 6. c. 25.

ᵃ Stromat. lib. 3. p. 465.   ᵇ Homil. in Luc. i. 1.

8. EUSE-

8. EUSEBIUS.

VIII. Eufebius (who lived in the beginning of the fourth century) exprefsly excludes all other Gofpels from the Canon befides thofe four which we now receive, but places them among the books which were without any controverfy received by the confent of the whole Church [a].

9. ATHANASIUS.

IX. In the Synopfis under the name of Athanafius, the author tells us, that all *the Gofpels which are read by any, are rather fit to be concealed than read, except the four alone which have been delivered to us.*

10. AMBROSE.

X. This Father in his preface to his Commentary on Luke has almoft tranfcribed Origen's words on the fame place ; accordingly he faith, *that though the Hereticks have many Gofpels, the Church hath only four, &c.* [b]

11. JEROME.

XI. In the preface to his Tranflation of the Gofpels he mentions fome falfe Gofpels, viz. thofe of Lucianus and Hefychius (fee above, Vol. I. Part II: Ch. XXII.), and promifes, *he will only be concerned with four, which,* fays he, *are in the following order, Matthew, Mark, Luke, and John* [c].

It would be endlefs to cite the many numerous proofs that may be eafily produced out of the Fathers of the fourth century. He that has a mind may fee farther proof of this matter, in the places of Epiphanius [d], Jerome [e], Chryfoftom [f], and Auftin [g], which are cited in the margin, and in the feveral

[a] Vid. Hift. Ecclef. l. 3. c. 24, 25. et alibi paffim.
[b] Procem. Comment. in Luc. in Init.
[c] Præfat. in Evang. ad Damafum.
[d] Hæref. 51. §. 4, &c.
[e] Præf. in Comm. in Matth. Comm. in Ezek. l. 10. et Epift. ad Paulin. de ftud. Scriptur. This laft Epiftle is commonly prefixed to the Vulgate.
[f] In Matth. i. N. B. Theophylaft has, according to his old cuftom, tranfcribed this of Chryfoftom concerning the four Evangelifts' agreement, which I refer to, into his preface on Matthew.
[g] De Confenf. Evangel. lib. 1. c. 2, 6. & Tract. 36. in Joan.

Catalogues of Origen, Eusebius, Athanasius, Cyril, that of the Council of Laodicea, Epiphanius, Gregory Nazianzen, Philastrius, Jerome, Austin, Ruffin, that of the third Council of Carthage, and the works of Dionysius the Areopagite, which I have collected in the first Volume, Part I. Ch. VIII p. 60, &c.

CHAP. I.

Who Matthew was. Heracleon, Origen, and Grotius, mistaken in supposing Matthew and Levi to be the Names of two Persons. He was a Jew. In what Countries he preached, and where he died: mentioned in the Talmud. The occasion of St. Matthew's writing his Gospel.

BEFORE I come to the Gospels themselves, and the proof of their authority, it seems to me necessary, that some account be given of the author. Accordingly, I shall now begin with some short relations or accounts concerning St. Matthew, the author of this Gospel. Besides what we have in the Canonical Gospels, there is not much that can be depended upon now left concerning him. The Popish legends, and the fabulous writers of later ages, will afford us accounts sufficiently particular; but disregarding all these, I shall only mention such things as seem to be more credible, and built upon better foundations. The account we have of him in his Gospel is, that *Jesus at Capernaum saw a man named Matthew sitting at the receipt of custom, and said unto him, Follow me; and he arose and followed him.* Matt. ix. 9. The other Evangelists (viz. Mark ii. 14. and Luke v. 27, 28.) relate the same history; only they, instead of Matthew, give him the name of Levi, which seems to have been his surname, or another name, by which he was as commonly called. It is a thing well known, that the Jews were wont to call a person

by

by more names than one ; *e. g.* Moſes's father in law is called
Jethro, Exod. iii. 1. and Num. x. 29. he is called Hobab;
and David's ſon, who is called 2 Sam. iii. 3. Chileab, goes
under the name of Daniel, 1 Chron. iii. 1. Simon was alſo
called Peter, Matt. x. 2. Lebbeus was ſurnamed Thaddeus,
ver. 3, &c. which ſurname, or ſecond name, ſeems to have
been added to diſtinguiſh them from others, who had the ſame
firſt name. I have mentioned this, becauſe ſome, both antient
and modern writers, have imagined Matthew and Levi to
have been two different perſons : thus Heracleon, an early
heretick of the ſecond century, and a remarkable perſon in the
ſchool of Valentinus, ſpeaking of thoſe diſciples of Chriſt,
who were not called to a publick acknowledgment or con-
feſſion of Chriſt (by Martyrdom), names Matthew, Philip,
Thomas, and Levi [a]; and Origen, diſcourſing particularly of
Chriſt's Apoſtles, firſt mentions Matthew the publican, and
afterwards names Levi the publican, but denies him to have
been an Apoſtle; Ἔϛω δὲ καὶ ὁ Λεῦης τελώνης ἀκολɣϑήσας τῷ Ἰησɤ̃,
ἀλλ' ὅτι γι τɤ̃ ἀριϑμɤ̃ τῶν ἀποϛόλων αὐτɤ̃ ἦν, εἰ μὴ κατά τινα τῶν ἀντι-
γράφων τɤ̃ κατὰ Μάρκον εὐαγγελίɤ [b], *Levi alſo the publican, who followed Jeſus, but was not of the number of his Apoſtles, unleſs
(we follow) ſome copies of Mark's Goſpel.* Among the moderns, Grotius is of this opinion [c]; but it is eaſy to refute it,
by obſerving not only that the *circumſtances of the fact are ſo
exactly the ſame as related* by the three Evangeliſts, but that
they agree preciſely as to the time, and all that which happened
immediately before and after his call by Chriſt, viz. all the
three Evangeliſts agree, that this call was as our Saviour was
going out of Capernaum immediately after the curing of the
paralytick; and the ſeveral hiſtories, which St. Matthew relates to have happened after his call by Chriſt (viz. that Chriſt
went *to eat with publicans and ſinners, the Phariſees cenſuring
him for it, his juſtification of himſelf, the diſciples of John coming to Chriſt with a queſtion about faſting, Chriſt's anſwer,
&c.),* are all related by St. Mark and St. Luke after the call

---

[a] Apud Clem. Alexand. Stromat. l. 4. p. 502.

[b] Adv. Celſ. l. 1. p. 48.
[c] Annot. in Matt. ix. 9.

of Levi; and this affords us the higheft evidence, that Matthew and Levi were the fame perfon. It is ftrange indeed that Heracleon and Origen fhould fall into fuch a miftake; but this is very rationally accounted for by Cotelerius[a] and Mr. Dodwell[b]; to whom, together with Dr. Whitby's[c] remarks on this opinion of Grotius, I refer the reader, who has a mind to examine farther into this matter.

The two names of this Evangelift, as alfo that of his father (viz. Alpheus, Mark ii. 14.), evince him to have been originally a Jew (it being certain that the Romans very frequently put the natives of the conquered provinces into fuch offices, under the principal officers who were generally Romans), although I obferve, that in two antient manufcripts which Cotelerius *(in Conftit. Apoftol.* l. 2. c. 63.) has publifhed out of the French King's library, Numb. 1789 and 1026, which recite the country and parents of the twelve Apoftles, there is the following account of Matthew, Ματθαῖος ὁ καὶ Λευὶς, τελώνης τὸ ἐπιτήδευμα, ἐκ πατρὸς Ῥύκε, μητρὸς δὲ Χαιροθείας, ἀπὸ τῆς Γαλιλαίας, *i. e. Matthew, called alfo Levi, a publican, whofe father was Rucus, and mother Chærotheia, born in Galilee*; both which are plainly Gentile names.

After he was called to be an Apoftle, he continued in that office till our Saviour's afcenfion in Judea; and if there be any credit to be given to the accounts of the antients, he continued there eight years afterward; whither he then went is not certain: Ruffin[d] affirms that he went into Ethiopia, and in this he is followed by the writers of fucceeding ages, Socrates, Simeon Metaphraftes, Abdias Babylonicus, &c. which laft has given us a very particular account of his preaching, miracles, and fuccefs in the converfion of multitudes there; his building a church there (viz. at Nadabbar, the capital city), and calling it the Refurrection, becaufe the raifing of the fon of King Æglippus from the dead was the occafion of it. [e]He preached Chrift in Hierapolis, a city of Syria, and fuffered

---

[a] Annot. in Conftit. Apoft. l. 8. c. 22.
[b] Differt. I. in Iren. §. 24.
[c] Annot. on Luke v. 27. See

alfo Dr. Mill on Mark ii. 14.
[d] Hift. Eccl. l. 1. c. 9.
[e] Vid. Abdiæ Hiftor. Certam. Apoftol. l. 7. per tot.

martyrdom

martyrdom there, according to a Greek manuscript under the name of Dorotheus, Bishop of Tyre (who lived in the beginning of the fourth century), which was transcribed by Mr. Dodwell, and by him given to Dr. Cave, who has published it with a Latin Version, and some Notes upon it [a]; though, according to the common editions of the Synopsis of Dorotheus, he died a natural death, and was buried with great honour at Hierapolis, a city of Parthia [b]; and this, viz. his dying without martyrdom, is plainly intimated in the passage of Heracleon above cited out of Clemens Alexandrinus. I have nothing farther to add under this head, but that which the Father last cited tells us of St. Matthew's great temperance and abstemiousness, viz. *that he eat no flesh, but that his usual food was acorns, seeds, and herbs* [c]; and that, according to Dr. Lightfoot [d], there is mention of him in the *Talmud Bab. Sanhedr. fol.* 43. 1. The Rabbins say, that Jesus had five disciples, which are there called by them מתאי נקאי נצר זבוני ותודה viz. Matthai (or Matthew), Nakai, Nezer, and Boni, and Thodah. These (they say there) were all punished with death. By these five disciples Dr. Lightfoot supposes they meant those disciples who were most conversant in Judea, viz. Matthew, who wrote his Gospel there, Peter, James, John, and Jude [e].

The cause or occasion of St. Matthew's writing his Gospel is generally agreed upon by the antient writers, who have made any mention of the matter, viz. that he *wrote it at Jerusalem for the sake of the convert Jews, who desired him to write it, when he was about to travel to the Gentile countries, to preach the Gospel.* So Origen [f]; "The first Gospel "was written by Matthew, first a publican, then an Apostle "of Jesus Christ, and published among the converted Jews in

---

[a] Hist. Lit. vol. i. p. 114, & 121.

[b] Doroth. de vit. ac mort. Prophet. et Apostol. Biblioth. Patr. vol. vii. ad voc. Matth.

[c] Pædagog. l. 2. c. 1. p. 148. Σπιγμάτων, καὶ ἀκροδρύων, καὶ λαχάνων, ἄνευ κρεῶν μιτιλάμβανιν.

[d] Hor. Hebr. in Matth. ix. 9.

[e] According to Abdias Babylonicus, lib. 7. cap. 14. he was run through the back in the Temple at Nadabbar in Ethiopia, by a soldier, by the order of the King Hyrtacus, whose marriage with Iphigenia, his brother's Daughter, St. Matthew opposed, she being a Nun.

[f] Exposit. in Matth. apud Euseb. Hist. Ecclef. l. 6. c. 25.

"Hebrew."

" Hebrew." Eusebius is more particular [a]; he tells us, " That
" the Apostles were not much inclined to write books.—
" That Paul wrote only a few short Epistles.—That of all
" our Lord's disciples Matthew and John only have left us
" any written memoirs, and it is said, they were compelled by
" some sort of necessity to write what they did; for Matthew
" having first preached to the Hebrews, when he determined
" to travel into other countries, published his Gospel in the
" language of his country, and left it with them to supply the
" want of his own presence among them." To the same purpose Jerome [b]; " Matthew, surnamed Levi, was the first who
" published a Gospel, and that in Judea, in the Hebrew lan-
" guage, principally for the sake of those Jews who were con-
" verted, and did not regard the truth of the Gospel (but ob-
" served the Law also), though the Law, as being but a sha-
" dow, was abolished."

CHAP. II.

*St. Matthew's Gospel of Canonical Authority. It is in all the
antient Catalogues of Sacred Books. It is cited by the primitive Fathers; viz. seven times in the Epistle of Barnabas,
twice in the first Epistle of Clemens Romanus to the Corinthians, eight times in the Fragment of the second, eight times
in the Shepherd of Hermas, six times in Polycarp's small
Epistle to the Philippians, twice in a Fragment of his Responsiones, and seven times in the Lesser Epistles of Ignatius.*

HAVING given some account of the Author of this Gospel, I proceed now to establish its authority, which I
hope will be effectually done by the following arguments.

ARG. I. St. Matthew's Gospel is of Canonical authority,
because *it is in all the Catalogues of Canonical books which we*

---

[a] Hist. Eccles. l. 3. c. 24.   [b] Præf. in Comm. in Matth.

have

have among the writings of the primitive Chriſtians. Prop. IV. Theſe Catalogues, viz. that of Origen, Euſebius, Athanaſius, Cyrill, the Council of Laodicea, Epiphanius, Gregory Nazi-anzen, Philaſtrius, Jerome, Ruffin, Auſtin, the third Council of Carthage, and the author of the books under the name of Dionyſius the Areopagite, I have collected them, Vol. I. Part I. Ch. VIII. and there referred to the ſeveral places where theſe Catalogues at large are to be found, and in every one of them the Goſpel of St. Matthew is enumerated.

Arg. II. The Goſpel of St. Matthew is Canonical, becauſe *it is cited as Scripture in the writings of the primitive Chriſtian Fathers.* Prop. V.

I have obſerved, Part I. Ch. V. p. 42. and Ch. IX. p. 65. that Mr. Dodwell [a], and from him Mr. Toland [b] have endea-voured in a good meaſure to rob us of this argument, by af-ſerting, "That the firſt writers of Chriſtianity had no certain "Canon, or collection of ſacred Scriptures of the New Teſ-"tament, which they cited; the Apocryphal writings being "bound in the ſame volume with the Apoſtles' writings; "that in Hermas there is not one place of the New Teſta-"ment quoted, nor in either of the other is any Evangeliſt "named: and if they do perhaps produce any places, which "are like ſome in our Goſpels, yet you will find them ſo "changed, and ſo much interpolated, that it is impoſſible to "know whether they took them out of ours, or ſome other "Apocryphal Goſpels. But it is certain they ſometimes "uſed the Apocryphal books, and cited what is not in our "Goſpels,—if they cite ſometimes any paſſages, which agree

---

[a] Sic autem vera Apoſtolorum Scripta cum Apocryphis in iiſdem voluminibus compingi ſolebant, ut nulla prorſus nota aut cenſura Ec-cleſiæ publica conſtaret, quæ qui-bus eſſent anteferenda. Habemus hodieque horum temporum Scrip-tores Eccleſiaſticos luculentiſſimos, Clementem Romanum, Barnabam, Hermam, Ignatium, Polycarpum —At Novi Teſtamenti in Herma ne quidem unum locum inveneris;

apud reliquos ne unum quidem E-vangeliſtam nomine ſuo compella-tum. Et ſi quos locos forte profe-rant, quibus ſimilia in noſtris le-guntur Evangeliis, ita tamen illos mutatos ut plurimum interpolatoſ-que reperies, ut ſciri nequeat, an e noſtris illos, an ex aliis produxerint Apocryphis Evangeliis, &c. *Diſ-ſert. in Iren.* 1. §. 39, &c.
[b] *Amyntor*, p. 69, &c.

" with

" with our Canonical Gospels, that was not done by any
" defign, fo as to evidence that they intended to confirm dif-
" putable points out of Canonical books; fo that perhaps thofe
" very paffages, which feem to be taken out of our Gofpels,
" were taken out of others, &c."

Dr. Grabe[a] and Dr. Mill[b] have adopted the fame fentiments into their fcheme, the defign of which, with a confutation of it, the reader may fee above in the firft Differtation
prefixed to this Part. The reafon of my mentioning it here,
is, becaufe I am now entering upon the particular proof of
their citing the books of our prefent Canon; and as I have
Vol. I. Part II. fhewn, that the primitive Chriftians have not
cited any Apocryphal books, fo I fhall endeavour now to fhew,
that they have cited and referred to thofe which we now receive, and for that purpofe fhall tranfcribe and fet down the
very words, with the manner of their being cited or introduced, together with the words of our Canonical books,
which I take to be referred to, in a parallel column.

N. B. I have fet down the citations at length only of thofe
which are called the Apoftolick Fathers, becaufe the citations in the other Fathers are fo plain and fo numerous,
that there can be about them no difpute; and though I do
not believe the writings under the names of Clemens Romanus, Barnabas, Polycarp, Hermas, and Ignatius, are all
genuine, and of that age to which they pretend; yet as they
are undoubtedly very antient, and referred to by fome of the
earlieft Fathers, I thought it proper to give them the firft
place in my collection.

* Spicileg. Patr. tom. 1. p. 322.
♭ Prolegom. in Nov. Teft. §. 138, &c.

A Cata-

A Catalogue of the several places of St. Matthew's Gospel, which are cited or referred to in the writings of the Apostolick Fathers.

St. MATTHEW's *Gospel.*

I. Ch. xxiv. 22. Κολοβω-
θήσονται αἱ ἡμέραι ἐκεῖναι: i. e.
Those days shall be shortened.

II. Ch. xx. 16. and xxii.
14. Πολλοὶ γάρ εἰσι κλητοὶ, ὀλίγοι
δὲ ἐκλεκτοί: i. e. *For many are
called, but few are chosen.*

III. Ch. ix. 13. Οὐ γὰρ ἦλθον καλέσαι δικαίους, ἀλλ' ἁμαρ-
τωλοὺς εἰς μετάνοιαν: *For I came
not to call the righteous, but
sinners to repentance.*

BARNABAS's *Epistle.*

I. Ch. iv. Dominus in-
tercidet tempora et dies; i. e.
*The Lord will shorten those
times and days.* That which
proves this a reference to St.
Matthew is, that the author
adds it upon a citation out of
Dan. ix. which is the very
same on account of which our
Lord is related by St. Matthew to have said it [a].

II. Ch. iv. Sicut scriptum
est, *Multi vocati, pauci electi* ;
i. e. as it is written, *Many
are called, but few are chosen.*

N. B. *The reason why these
two citations are put in
Latin, is, because we have
not the Greek of Barnabas
till the middle of the fifth
chapter.*

III. Ch. v. Ἵνα δείξῃ, ὅτι οὐκ
ἦλθε καλέσαι δικαίους, ἀλλὰ ἁμαρ-
τωλοὺς εἰς μετάνοιαν: i. e. *that he
might shew, that he came not
to call the righteous, but sinners to repentance [b].*

IV.

---

[a] Respiciunt hæc verba Domini.
Matt. xxiv. 2. Fell in loc.
[b] The preceding context in that

place of Barnabas plainly refers
also to this in St. Matthew; for
whereas it is there said, that when
Christ

St. MATTHEW's *Gospel.*

IV. Ch. xxvi. 31. Παταξω
τον ποιμενα, και διασκορπισθησεται
τα προβατα της ποιμνης : *I will
smite the shepherd, and the
sheep of the flock shall be scat-
tered abroad.*

BARNABAS's *Epistle.*

IV. Ch. v. Παταξω τον ποιμενα, τοτι σκορπισθησεται τα προβατα της ποιμνης : i. e. *I will
smite the shepherd, then the
sheep of the flock shall be scat-
tered abroad.*

If it be objected here, that
this author might take this, as
our Saviour did, out of Zechariah xiii. 7. and not out of
St Matthew's Gospel, I answer, that this cannot be supposed, because in the Hebrew
the verb הך is in the second
person, and the imperative
mood, and accordingly the
LXX. and all the Greek Versions have rendered it in the
imperative mood, *Smite the
shepherd*; whereas Barnabas
places that verb in the first
person of the future tense,
παταξω, *I will smite*, which
could only proceed from his
citing and following St Matthew, where we read παταξω,
I will smite. Hugo Menardus
(*in loc. Barnab.*) has made a
like observation upon the
word διασκορπισθησεται, viz. of
this author's following Matthew, which is yet more evi-

Christ chose his Apostles, he took
those who were exceeding great sinners, it must needs be that he refers
to the call of Matthew, and Christ's
being censured for going to his
house, and supping with him and

other sinners. See Orig. contr.
Celf. lib. 1. p. 49. and the Appendix to the first Volume, p. 412.—
See also Toland's Amyntor, p. 44.
and Richardson's Answer, p. 105,
106.

dent,

St. Matthew's *Gospel.*

Barnabas's *Epistle.*

dent, if our Cambridge edition of the LXX. be right, which has instead of that verb in the future tense, the verb ἰκστάσατι in the imperative mood.

V. Ch. xxvii. 54. 'Αληθῶς Θεῦ υἱὸς ἦν ὅτος : i. e. *Truly, this was the Son of God.*

V. Ch. VII. 'Αληθῶς ὅτος ἦν, ὁ τότε λέγων ἑαυτὸν υἱὸν Θεῦ ἀναι : i. e. *Truly this was he, who then said, he was the Son of God.*

The words in St Matthew are a confession of Christ extorted from the centurion at Christ's crucifixion, and the words in Barnabas are also a confession extorted from the Jews; so that there can be no doubt but he had read and referred to St Matthew here.

VI. Ch. xxii. 43, 44, 45. Christ proves himself to be the Lord from Psal. cx. 1. *The Lord said unto my Lord, sit thou, &c.* Εἰ ἦν Δαβὶδ καλεῖ αὐτὸν Κύριον, &c. *If then David calls him Lord, &c.*

VI. Ch. xii. This author cites the same words of the Psalmist, and concludes, 'Ιδ πῶς λέγει Δαβὶδ αὐτὸν Κύριον, &c. *See how David calls him Lord,* &c. Which is an argument so exactly agreeing with our Saviour's both in sense and words, that one cannot suppose but that this author took it from St. Matthew, or at least from St. Mark (xii. 36.) or St. Luke (xx. 42.).

VII. Ch. v. 42. Τῷ αἰτῦντί σι δίδυ : i. e. *Give to him that asketh thee.*

VII. Ch. xix. Παντὶ αἰτῦντί σι δίδυ : i. e. *Give to every one that asketh thee.*

St. Matthew's *Gospel.*

The *first Epistle of* Clemens Romanus *to the Corinthians.*

I. Ch. vi. 14. *If ye forgive men their trespasses, your heavenly Father will also forgive you.* Ch. vii. 1. *Judge not, lest ye be judged:* ver. 2. *With what measure ye mete, it shall be measured to you again.*

I. Ch. xiii. Forgive, that ye may be forgiven; as ye judge, so ye shall be judged; with what measure ye mete, it shall be measured to you again.

Clemens advises the Corinthians here, to remember these and other sayings of the Lord Jesus.

II. Ch. xviii. 6, 7. Ὃς δ' ἂν σκανδαλίσῃ ἵνα τῶν μικρῶν τύτων τῶν πιστευόντων εἰς ἐμὲ, συμφέρει αὐτῷ ἵνα κρεμασθῇ μύλος ὀνικὸς ἐπὶ τὸν τράχηλον αὐτῇ, καὶ καταποντισθῇ ἐν τῷ πελάγει τῆς θαλάσσης. Οὐαὶ τῷ κόσμῳ ἀπὸ τῶν σκανδάλων, &c. i. e. *But whoso shall offend one of these little ones, which believe in me, it were better for him that a millstone were hanged about his neck, and that he were drowned in the depth of the sea. Wo unto the world because of offences, &c.*

II. Ch. xlvi. Μνήσθητι τῶν λόγων Ἰησοῦ τῦ Κυρίυ ἡμῶν. Εἶπε γάρ· Οὐαὶ τῷ ἀνθρώπῳ ἐκείνῳ· καλὸν ἦν αὐτῷ εἰ ἐκ ἐγεννήθη, ἢ ἵνα τῶν ἐκλεκτῶν μυ σκανδαλίσαι· κρεῖττον ἦν αὐτῷ περιτεθῆναι μύλον, κ) καταποντισθῆναι εἰς τὴν θάλασσαν, ἢ ἵνα τῶν μικρῶν μυ σκανδαλίσαι: i. e. Remember the words of the Lord Jesus; for he said, *Wo to that man; it had been better for him if he had not been born, than that he should offend one of my elect. It were better for him that a millstone were put upon him (his neck), and that he were drowned in the sea, than to have offended one of these little ones.*

Cotelerius observes upon this place of Clemens, that he has here, according to the common practice of the antients,

St. MATTHEW's *Gospel.*

The first Epistle of CLEMENS ROMANUS *to the Corinthians.*

tients, joined several texts of Scripture together; and that he made use in this collection of the Gospels of Matthew, Mark, and Luke; and this is not improbable; however it is certain, that he makes use of another place of St. Matthew, (viz. xxvi. 24.) the words, *It had been better for him if he had not been born*, being there spoke of Judas Iscariot, and in neither of the three Evangelists speaking of offences.

St. MATTHEW's *Gospel.*

The second Epistle of CLEMENS ROMANUS *to the Corinthians.*

I. Ch. xviii. 11. Christ came σῶσαι τὸ ἀπολωλός : i. e. *to save that (or those) which were lost.*

I. Ch. i. Christ has done us this advantage, ἀπολλυμίνος ἡμᾶς ἴσωσιν : i. e. *He has saved us who were lost.*

II. Ch. ix. 13. Οὐ γὰρ ἦλθον καλίσαι δικαίυς, ἀλλ᾽ ἁμαρτωλὰς ιἰς μιτάνοιαν : i. e. *For I came not to call the righteous, but sinners to repentance.*

II. Ch. ii. Καὶ ἑτέρα δὲ γραφὴ λίγει· Ὅτι ἐκ ἦλθον καλίσαι δικαίυς, ἀλλὰ ἁμαρτωλύς : i. e. *And another Scripture saith, I came not to call the righteous, but sinners.*

III. Ch. x. 32. Πᾶς ἂν ὅςις ὁμολογήσει ἰν ἰμοὶ ἴμπροσθιν τῶν ἀνθρώπων, ὁμολογήσω κἀγὼ ἰν αὐτῷ ἴμπροσθιν τῦ πατρός μυ τῦ ἰν ὑρανοῖς : i. e. *Whosoever therefore shall confess me before men,*

III. Ch. iii. Λίγει δὲ καὶ αὐτός· Τὸν ὁμολογήσαιτά μι ἰνώπιον τῶν ἀνθρώπων, ὁμολογήσω αὐτὸν ἰνώπιον τῦ πατρός μυ : i. e. *For he himself saith, Whosoever shall confess me before men,*

St. MATTHEW's *Gospel.*

him will I confefs before my father, which is in heaven.

IV. Ch. vii. 21. Οὐ πᾶς ὁ λέγων μοι, Κύριε, Κύριε, εἰσελεύσεται εἰς τὴν βασιλείαν τῶν οὐρανῶν, ἀλλ᾽ ὁ ποιῶν τὸ θέλημα τῦ πατρός μυ τῦ ἐν οὐρανοῖς: i. e. *Not every one that faith unto me, Lord, Lord, fhall enter into the kingdom of heaven, but he that doth the will of my Father, who is in heaven.*

V. Ch. vii. 23. Οὐδέποτε ἔγνων ὑμᾶς· ἀποχωρεῖτε ἀπ᾽ ἐμῦ, οἱ ἐργαζόμενοι τὴν ἀνομίαν: i. e. *I never knew you; depart from me, ye that work iniquity.*

VI. Ch. x. 16, 26, 28. Ἰδῦ, ἐγὼ ἀποςέλλω ὑμᾶς ὡς πρόβατα ἐν μέσῳ λύκων.—26. Μὴ ὖν φοβηθῆτε αὐτύς·—28. Καὶ μὴ φοβηθῆτε ἀπὸ τῶν ἀποκτεινόντων τὸ σῦμα, τὴν δὲ ψυχὴν μὴ δυναμένων ἀποκτεῖναι· φοβήθητε δὲ μᾶλλον τ᾽ δυνάμενον καὶ ψυχὴν καὶ σῶμα ἀπολέσαι ἐν γεέννη: i. e. *Behold, I fend you forth as fheep in the*

The fecond Epiftle of CLEMENS ROMANUS *to the Corinthians.*

men, him will I confefs before my Father.

IV. Ch. iv. Λέγει γὰρ, Οὐ πᾶς ὁ λέγων μοι, Κύριε, Κύριε, σωθήσεται, ἀλλὰ ὁ ποιῶν τὴν δικαιοσύνην: i. e. For (the Lord) faith, *Not every one that faith unto me, Lord, Lord, fhall be faved, but he that worketh righteoufnefs.*

V. Ch. iv. Ὑπάγετε ἀπ᾽ ἐμῦ, ὐκ οἶδα ὑμᾶς, πόθεν ἐςε, ἐργάται ἀνομίας: i. e. *Depart from me, I know ye not whence ye are, ye workers of iniquity.*

This feems to be a citation, like that above out of the firft Epiftle, No. 2, if it was not taken out of Luke, (fee the Appendix to Vol. I. p. 412, 415.) the words πόθεν ἐςε being in Luke xiii. 27. and not in Matthew.

VI. Ch. v. Ἔσεσθε ὡς ἀρνία ἐν μέσῳ λύκων.—Μὴ φοβείσθωσαν τὰ ἀρνία τὺς λύκης μετὰ τὸ ἀποθανεῖν αὐτά· καὶ ὑμεῖς μὴ φοβεῖσθε τὺς ἀποκτείνοντας ὑμᾶς, καὶ μηδὲν ὑμῖν δυναμένης ποιεῖν· ἀλλὰ φοβεῖσθε τὸν μετὰ τὸ ἀποθανεῖν ὑμᾶς ἔχοντα ἐξυσίαν ψυχῆς καὶ σώματος, τῦ βαλεῖν εἰς γέενναν πυρός: i. e. *Ye fhall be as lambs in the midft*

St. MATTHEW's *Gospel.*

midft of wolves — 26. Fear them not therefore;— 28. And fear not them which kill the body, but are not able to kill the foul; but rather fear him, which is able to deftroy both foul and body in hell.

The fecond Epiftle of CLEMENS ROMANUS to the Corinthians.

midft of wolves :—Let not the lambs fear the wolves after death, and do not ye fear thofe who (can) kill you, and (afterwards) can do you no harm; but fear him who has power, after your death, to caft both foul and body into hell fire.

In the midft of this paffage there is a queftion of Peter to Chrift, viz. What if the wolves fhould tear in pieces the lambs? but concerning this, fee the Appendix to Vol. I. p. 413, 415.

VII. Ch. xvi. 26. Τί γὰρ ὠφιλεῖται ἄνθρωπⒶ, ἰὰν τὸν κόσμον ὅλον κερδέσῃ, τὴν δὶ ψυχὴν αὐτῦ ζημιωδῆ; i. e. For what is a man profited, if he fhould gain the whole world, and lofe his own foul?

VII. Ch. vi. Τί γὰρ τὸ ὄφιλος, ἰὰν τις τὸν ὅλον κόσμον κερδέσῃ, τὴν δὶ ψυχὴν ζημιώσῃ; i. e. For what will it profit a man, if he fhould gain the whole world, and lofe his own foul?

VIII. Ch. xii. 50. Ὅσις γὰρ ἂν ποιήσῃ τὸ θέλημα τῦ πατρός μυ τῦ ἰν ἐρανοῖς, αὐτός μυ ἀδελφὸς, καὶ ἀδελφὴ, καὶ μήτηρ ἰσίν: i. e. For whofoever fhall do the will of my Father which is in heaven, the fame is my brother and fifter and mother.

VIII. Ch. ix. Καὶ γὰρ εἴπεν ὁ Κύριος· ἀδελφοί μυ ὑτοί ἰσιν, οἱ ποιῦντις τὸ θέλημα τῦ πατρός μυ: i. e. For the Lord hath faid, They are my brethren, who do the will of my Father.

St. MATTHEW's *Gospel.*

I. Ch. v. 28. But I fay unto you, that whofoever looketh on a woman to luft after

The Shepherd of HERMAS.

I. Lib. I. Vif. i. §. 1. An non videtur tibi, viro jufto rem iniquam effe, fi afcenderit in

St. MATTHEW's *Gospel.*

her, hath committed adultery with her already in his heart.

N. B. The Greek of Hermas not being extant, but only a Latin Verſion, I judged there could be no neceſſity of inſerting St. Matthew's Greek.

II. Ch. x. 32, 33. *Whoſo-ever therefore ſhall confeſs me before men, him will I confeſs alſo before my Father which is in heaven : but whoſoever ſhall deny me before men, him will I alſo deny before my Father which is in heaven.*

III. Ch. xiii. 21, 22. *Yet hath he not root in himſelf, but dureth for a while; for*

The Shepherd of HERMAS.

in corde mala concupiſcentia ? i. e. Does it not ſeem to you to be a ſin, *for a good man to have luſtful inclinations in his heart ?*

He who conſiders that this is ſaid by a woman, who ex-preſsly in the words before charges Hermas with ſin a-gainſt God and her, not for fornication (for this he de-nies), but for having deſired or having in his heart luſted after her, will eaſily ſee there is a reference to Chriſt's words.

II. Lib. i. Viſ. ii. §. 2. Juravit enim Dominus per Filium ſuum: qui denegaverit filium et ſe, deſpondens vitam illius, et ipſe denegaturus eſt illum, in advenientibus die-bus. Ii autem qui nunquam denegaverint, ob nimiam mi-ſericordiam propitius factus eſt illis; i. e. The Lord hath ſworn by his Son, *that who-ſoever ſhall deny his Son and him, being afraid of his life, he will alſo deny him in the world to come; but thoſe who ſhall never deny him, he will then of his great mercy receive them into his favour.*

III. Lib. i. Viſ. iii. §. 6. Hi ſunt habentes quidem fi-dem, habentes autem et divi-tias

St. MATTHEW's *Gospel.*

when tribulation or perfecution arifeth becaufe of the word, by and by he is offended; he alfo that received the word among the thorns, is he that heareth the word, and the care of this world and the deceitfulnefs of riches choak the word, &c.

IV. Ch. xxvi. 24. *Wo unto that man—it had been good for that man if he had not been born.*

V. Ch. v. 28. *I fay unto you, that whofoever looketh on a woman to luft after her, hath committed adultery with her already in his heart.*

The Shepherd of HERMAS.

tias hujus feculi; cum ergo venerit tribulatio, propter divitias fuas et negotiationes abnegant Dominum; i. e. *They are perfons profeffing Chriftianity (i. e. who own the word), but having alfo the riches of this world, when tribulation arifeth (on account of the word), by reafon of their riches and worldly cares they deny the Lord, or (which is the fame) are offended.*

IV. Lib. i. Vif. iv. §. 2. Væ iis—melius erat illis non nafci; i. e. *Wo unto them— for it had been better for thefe men they had not been born.*

The phrafe is evidently borrowed from St. Matthew.

V. Lib. ii. Mandat. iv. §. 1. Non afcendat tibi cogitatio cordis de alieno matrimonio, aut de fornicatione; hæc enim parit peccatum magnum. —Si enim hæc cogitatio in cor tuum afcenderit tam mala, magnum peccatum facis; i. e. *Let not any purpofe be entertained in thy mind of committing adultery, or fornication, for even this purpofe produceth a great fin.—And if fuch evil purpofe be in thy mind, thou committeft great fin.* See above out of this book of Hermas, No 1.

VI.

St. MATTHEW's *Gospel.*

VI. Ch. xix. 9. *Whoso-*
ever shall put away his wife,
except it be for fornication,
and shall marry another, com-
mitteth adultery; and whoso
marrieth her which is put
away, doth commit adultery.
See Matt. v. 23.

VII. Ch. xxi. 22. *All*
things whatsoever ye shall ask
in prayer, believing (i. e. as
in ver. 21. not doubting), *ye*
shall receive.

The Shepherd of HERMAS.

VI. Lib. ii. Mandat. iv.
§. 1. Si permanserit in vitio
suo mulier—dimittat illam
vir, et vir per se maneat.
Quod si dimiserit mulierem
suam, et aliam duxerit, et ipse
mœchatur—propter hoc præ-
ceptum est vobis, ut cœlibes
maneatis, tum vir, tum mulier ; potest enim in hujus-
modi pœnitentia esse ; i. e.
If a wife shall persist in adul-
terous practices, a husband may
put her away, and live alone ;
but if he shall marry another
woman, he committeth adul-
tery—

Mr. Nye has in part ob-
served this place of Hermas,
and says, no doubt it was taken from St. Luke xvi. 18.
See his Defence of the Canon
against Amyntor, p. 48.

VII. Lib. ii. Mandat. ix.
Tolle a te dubitationem, et
nihil omnino dubites—pete
sine dubitatione—petitionem
animæ tuæ adimplebit—ex
omnibus petitionibus tuis nihil deerit tibi, si sine dubitatione petieris a Domino ; i. e.
Remove from thee all doubting,
and doubt not at all—ask with-
out doubting (or in faith), and
(God) will grant thy requests
—all things whatsoever thou
shalt ask shall be given thee, if
thou

St. MATTHEW's *Gospel.*

The Shepherd of HERMAS.

thou aſk them of the Lord without doubting (or in faith).

VIII. Ch. xxi. 33. *The parable of the vineyard.*

VIII. Lib. iii. Simil. v. §. 2. He ſeems to have borrowed the ſimilitude from the parable of our Saviour referred to in the oppoſite column.

IX. Ch. xvi. 18. *And upon this rock I will build my Church.*

IX. Lib. iii. Simil. ix. The Church is compared to a tower built upon a rock. See §. 2, 3, 12, 13, 14.

St. MATTHEW's *Gospel.*

The Epiſtle of POLYCARP *to the Philippians.*

I. See above under Clemens Romanus, Epiſt. I. No. 2.

I. Cap. ii. The words in Polycarp are near the ſame with thoſe referred to in the parallel column. I only obſerve, that he introduces them, Μνημονεύσαντες δὲ ὧν εἶπεν ὁ Κύριος διδάσκων: i. e. *Remember the things which the Lord ſaid in his teaching (or Sermon on the mount).*

II. Ch. v. 3, 10. Μακάριοι οἱ πτωχοὶ ἐν τῷ πνεύματι, ὅτι αὐτῶν ἐστιν ἡ βασιλεία τῶν οὐρανῶν. 10. Μακάριοι οἱ δεδιωγμένοι ἕνεκεν δικαιοσύνης, ὅτι αὐτῶν ἐστιν ἡ βασιλεία τῶν οὐρανῶν: i. e. *Bleſſed are the poor in ſpirit, for theirs is the kingdom of heaven.* ver. 10. *Bleſſed are they who are perſecuted for righteouſneſs ſake; for theirs is the kingdom of heaven.*

II. Cap. ii. Immediately after the preceding words he cites farther; Μακάριοι οἱ πτωχοὶ, καὶ οἱ διωκόμενοι ἕνεκεν δικαιοσύνης, ὅτι αὐτῶν ἐστιν ἡ βασιλεία τῶ Θεοῦ: i. e. *Bleſſed are the poor (in ſpirit), and they who are perſecuted for righteouſneſs ſake, for theirs is the kingdom of God.*

III. Ch. vi. 12. Καὶ ἄφις

III. Cap. vi. [Εἰ ὧ διόμεθα τῶ

St. MATTHEW's *Gospel.*

The Epistle of POLYCARP *to the Philippians.*

ἡμῖν τὰ ὀφιλήματα ἡμῶν, ὡς καὶ ἡμεῖς ἀφίεμεν τοῖς ὀφιλέταις ἡμῶν: i. e. *And forgive us our debts, as we forgive our debtors; and ver.* 14. *For if ye forgive men their trespasses, your heavenly Father will also forgive you.*

τῦ Κυρίυ, ἵνα ἡμῖν ἀφῇ, ὀφείλομεν καὶ ἡμεῖς ἀφιέναι: i. e. *If therefore we pray to the Lord that he would forgive us, we ought likewise to forgive others.*

IV. Ch. vi. 13. Καὶ μὴ εἰσενέγκῃς ἡμᾶς εἰς πειρασμόν: *And lead us not into temptation.*

IV. Cap. vii. Δεήσεσιν αἰτούμενοι τὸν παντεπόπτην Θεόν, μὴ εἰσενεγκεῖν ἡμᾶς εἰς πειρασμόν: *Earnestly praying to the all-seeing God, not to lead us into temptation.*

V. Ch. xxvi. 41. Τὸ μὲν πνεῦμα πρόθυμον, ἡ δὲ σὰρξ ἀσθενής; i. e. *The spirit truly is willing, but the flesh is weak.*

V. Cap. vii. Καθὼς εἶπεν ὁ Κύριος· Τὸ μὲν πνεῦμα πρόθυμον, ἡ δὲ σὰρξ ἀσθενής: i. e. *As the Lord hath said, The spirit truly is willing, but the flesh is weak.*

VI. Ch. v. 44. Προσεύχεσθε ὑπὲρ τῶν ἐπηρεαζόντων ὑμᾶς, καὶ διωκόντων ὑμᾶς: i. e. *Pray for them which despitefully use you and persecute you.*

VI. Ch. xii. Orate—pro persequentibus et odientibus vos; i. e. *Pray for those who persecute you and hate you.*

After these it will not be improper to add, that in the Fragments of the Responsiones of Polycarp, published by Feuardentius in Irenæus, lib. 3. c. 3. I find two places of St. Matthew's Gospel expounded, or paraphrased; viz.

1. Matthæus Dominum dixisse testatur, quod Moyses scribit Adam loquutum fuisse hoc modo; Hoc nunc os ex ossibus meis, et caro ex carne

1. Matthew testifies that our Lord said, *It was written by Moses, that Adam said thus; This now is bone of my bone, and flesh of my flesh; for this cause*

mea; propter hoc relinquet homo patrem et matrem, &c.

caufe fhall a man leave father and mother, &c. See Matt. xix. 5. and Gen. ii. 23, 24.

2. Calicem meum bibetis, &c. Per hujufmodi potum fignificat paffionem &c.

2. Matt. xx. 23. *Ye fhall drink indeed of my cup,* &c. by which cup he meant the martyrdom of thofe two Apoftles, John and James.

The Leffer, or thofe which are fuppofed the genuine Epiftles of IGNATIUS, *particularly;*

St. MATTHEW's *Gofpel.*

1. *The Epiftle of* IGNATIUS *to the Ephefians.*

I. Ch. xviii. 19. *If two of you fhall agree on earth, as touching any thing that they fhall afk, it fhall be done for them of my Father which is in heaven; for where two or three are gathered together in my name, there am I in the midft of them.*

I. Ch. v. Εἰ γὰρ ἑνὸς καὶ δευτέρου προσευχὴ τοσαύτην ἰχὺν ἔχει, &c. *For if the prayers of one or two be of fuch force,* &c. The larger Epiftle adds, Ὅτι τὸν Χριςὸν ἐν αὐτοῖς ἑςάναι, *as that Chrift will be in the midft of them.*

II. Ch. xii. 33. Ἐκ γὰρ τῶ καρπῶ τὸ δένδρον γινώσκεται: i. e. *For the tree is known by its fruit.*

II. Ch. xiv. Φανερὸν τὸ δένδρον ἀπὸ τῶ καρπῶ αὐτῶ: i. e. *The tree is known by its fruit.*

III. Ch. xxiii. 8, 10. Εἷς γάρ ἐςιν ὑμῶν ὁ καθηγητής: i. e. *For one is your mafter.*

III. Ch. xv. Εἷς ἐν διδάσκαλος: i. e. *One is (your) mafter.*

IV. Ch. ii. 2. Εἴδομεν γὰρ αὐτοῦ τὸν ἀςέρα: i. e. *We have feen his ftar.*

IV. Ch. xix. Ἀςὴρ ἐν οὐρανῷ ἔλαμψεν: i. c. *His ftar fhone in heaven.*

2. *The Epiftle to the* MAGNESIANS.

Ch. xxvii. 52, 53. *And the graves were opened, and*

Ch. ix. The Prophets expected Chrift, and when he came,

St. MATTHEW's *Gospel.*

many bodies of saints which slept arose, and came out of the graves after his resurrection, &c.

I. Ch. iii. 15. Πρέπον ἐςὶν ἡμῖν πληρῶσαι πᾶσαν δικαιοσύνην : i. e. *It becometh us to fulfil all righteousness.* Christ assigns this as a reason for his being baptized by John.

II. Ch. xix. 12. Ὁ δυνάμενος χωρεῖν χωρείτω : i. e. *He that is able to receive it, let him receive it.*

Ch. x. 16. Γίνεσθε ἂν φρόνιμοι ὡς οἱ ὄφεις, καὶ ἀκέραιοι ὡς αἱ περιςεραί : i. e. *Be ye therefore wise as serpents, and harmless as doves.*

2. *The Epistle of* IGNATIUS *to the* MAGNESIANS.

came, ἤγειρεν αὐτὸς ἐκ νεκρῶν, *he raised them from the dead.*

3. *The Epistle to the* SMYR-NEANS.

I. Ch. i. Christ was baptized by John, Ἵνα πληρωθῇ πᾶσα δικαιοσύνη ὑπ᾽ αὐτῦ : i. e. *That all righteousness might be fulfilled by him.*

II. Ch. vi. Ὁ χωρῶν χωρείτω : i. e. *He that can receive it, let him receive it.*

4. *The Epistle to* POLYCARP.

Ch. II. Φρόνιμος γίνυ, ὡς ὁ ὄφις, καὶ ἀκέραιος ὡσὶ περιςερά : i. e. *Be thou wise as a serpent, and harmless as a dove.*

Thus I have collected and produced at large several of those passages of St. Matthew's Gospel, which the Apostolick Fathers appear evidently to have cited or referred to; so that it will be henceforth manifest, by a bare cast of the eye upon the preceding tables, how much Mr. Dodwell and his followers have been mistaken in their famous notion, that none of our Gospels were cited by those Fathers.

CHAP.

CHAP. III.

St. Matthew's Gospel farther proved Canonical by the Citations out of it made by the Fathers next the Apostolick Age. Thirty-five places in Justin Martyr's Works produced, where it is cited. It is cited four Times in the small Treatise of Athenagoras; five Times by Theophilus Antiochenus; above two hundred and fifty Times by Irenæus, in nine of which Places he is named; seventy-three Times in the Works of Clemens Alexandrinus; and twenty-seven Times in his small Tract entitled, Quis Dives *salvetur? This Gospel proved Canonical, because it was read in the Christian Churches, and is in the Syriack Version.*

IT appearing thus, how particularly the apostolick Fathers have cited St. Matthew, I proceed now to shew, how the Fathers immediately succeeding the apostolick age have cited St. Matthew; not as above to produce all the several places at large, which would be almost to transcribe the Gospels, but only to lay down the several chapters and verses of the Gospel, with the particular places of those Fathers' works where they are cited; nor shall I think it needful to do this, with all the writers of the first four centuries, but such only as were the most early, and are the most considerable. It will be enough to shew instances in such as Justin Martyr, Athenagoras, Theophilus Antiochenus, Irenæus, Clemens Alexandrinus, &c. who lived in the second century, and to observe concerning the Fathers of the next centuries, such as Origen, Cyprian, Cyril, Austin, and others of and about their time, that they do in innumerable places cite this (as well as our other) Gospels; for the proof of which I would refer the reader, who will take no farther pains in the matter, to the Indexes of the Texts of Scripture, which are made and put at the end of their works by their editors. I proceed then to those early Fathers above-named, viz. Justin Martyr, Athenagoras, Theophilus Antiochenus, Irenæus, and Clemens Alexandrinus, whose

works

works I have with this view carefully examined, and find them very often to have cited or referred to this Gospel of St. Matthew.

I. *As to* JUSTIN MARTYR.

A Catalogue of several places which are cited out of St. Matthew's Gospel in the Works of Justin Martyr.

St. MATTHEW's *Gospel.*	JUSTIN MARTYR's *Works.*
1 Ch. i. 21.	1 Apolog. 2. pro Christo, p. 75.
2 Ch. ii. 11.	2 Dialog. cum Tryph. Jud. p. 315. et p. 334. *This he says he cited* ὡς γέγραπται ἐν τοῖς ἀπομνημονεύμασι τῶν ἀποστόλων αὐτῦ, from the Commentaries of Christ's Apostles.
3 Ch. iii. 1, 2, 3, 11.	3 Dialog. cum Tryph. Jud. p. 316.
4 ———— 11, 12.	4 Ibid. p. 268.
5 Ch. iv. 1, — 8, 9, 10, 11.	5 Ibid. p. 354. and p. 331. *This he says was written in the* ἀπομνημονεύμασι τῶν ἀποστόλων: i. e. in the Commentaries of the Apostles.
6 Ch. v. 20.	6 Ibid. p. 333. *This he says he learnt from the same books.*
7 Ch. v. 16, 22, 28, 29, 32, 36, 37, 39, 42, 44, 45, 46, 47; and Ch. vi. 2, 19, 20, 21, 26, 32, 33, 35, 45. viz. *a considerable part of our Lord's Sermon on the Mount in St. Matthew's words.*	7 Apolog. 2. pro Christian. p. 61, 62, 63.
8 Ch. v. 44.	8 Dialog. cum Tryph. p. 324.
Ibid.

St. MATTHEW's *Gospel.*	JUSTIN MARTYR's *Works.*
9 Ch. vii. 15.	9 Ibid. p. 253.
10 ———— 19, 21, &c.	10 Apolog. 2. pro Chrift. p. 64. et Dialog. cum Tryph. Jud. p. 301.
11 Ch. viii. 11.	11 Dialog. cum Tryph. Jud. p. 301, 349, 370.
12 Ch. ix. 13.	12 Apol. 2. pro Chrift. p. 62.
13 Ch. x. 28.	13 Ibid. p. 66.
14 Ch. xi. 12, — 15.	14 Dialog. cum Tryph. Jud. p. 271.
15 ———— 27.	15 Apol. 2. pro Chrift. p. 95. et in Dialog. cum Tryph. Jud. p. 326.
16 Ch. xii. 39, 40.	16 Dialog. cum Tryph. Jud. p. 334.
17 Ch. xiii. 3, 4, &c.	17 Ibid. p. 354.
18 Ch. xvi. 21.	18 Ibid. p. 302, et 327.
19 ———— 26, 27.	19 Apol. 2. pro Chrift. p. 62.
20 Ch. xvii. 10, 11, 12.	20 Dialog. cum Tryph. Jud. p. 269.
21 Ch. xix. 12.	21 Apolog. 2. pro Chriftián. p. 62.
22 ———— 16, 17.	22 Ibid. p. 63. et Dial. cum Tryph. Jud. p. 328.
23 ———— 26.	23 Ibid. p. 66.
24 Ch. xxi. 1, 2.	24 Dialog. cum Tryph. Jud. p. 272.
25 ———— 13.	25 Ibid. p. 235.
26 Ch. xxii. 16, 17, — 21.	26 Apol. 2. pro Chrift. p. 64.
27 ———— 30.	27 Dialog. cum Tryph. Jud. p. 308.
28 ———— 32.	28 Apol. 2. pro Chrift. p. 96.
29 ———— 36, &c.	29 Ibid. p. 63.

St. MATTHEW's *Gospel.*	JUSTIN MARTYR's *Works.*
30 Ch. xxiii. 23, 27.	30 Dialog. cum Tryph. Jud. p. 235, et 339.
31 Ch. xxiv. 24.	31 Ibid. p. 253.
32 Ch. xxvi. 26, &c.	32 Apol. 2. pro Chrift. p. 98. *This he says is delivered by the Apoftles,* ἐν τοῖς γινομίνοις ὑπ' αὐτῶν ἀπομνημονεύμασιν, ἃ καλεῖται εὐαγγίλια : i. e. in the Commentaries. or Books made by them, which are called Gofpels.
33 —— 39.	33 Dialog. cum Tryph. Jud. p. 326, et 331.
34 Ch. xxvii. 42, 43.	34 Ibid. p. 328.
35 —— 46.	35 Ibid. p. 326.

II. ATHENAGORAS.

He was a writer of the fecond century, either coeval with, or not long after Juftin Martyr; he wrote an excellent Apology for Chriftianity, which is infcribed to M. Aurelius Antoninus, and L. Aurelius Commodus, in which, though a fhort work, I have obferved the following references to St. Matthew's Gofpel.

St. MATTHEW's *Gospel.*	ATHENAGORÆ Legat. pro Chriftian.
1 Ch. v. 44, 45.	1 Page 11.
2 —— 46, 47.	2 —— 12.
3 —— 28.	3 —— 36.
4 Ch. xix. 9.	4 —— 37.

III. THEOPHILUS ANTIOCHENUS.

He lived under the fame Emperors, and was cotempo-rary with Athenagoras; he wrote three fmall treatifes, infcribed

inscribed to Autolycus, against the enemies of Christianity. He made use also of St. Matthew's Gospel,
as appears from the following places.

St. MATTHEW's *Gospel.*	THEOPHILUS ANTIOCHE- NUS.
1 Ch. xix. 26.	1 Lib. 1. p. 92.
2 Ch. v. 28.	2 Lib. 3. p. 126. *He cites under the name of* Εὐαγ- γελικὸς φωνή.
3 Ch. xix. 9.	3 Ibid.
4 Ch. v. 44—47.	4 Ibid.
5 Ch. vi. 3.	5 Ibid.

IV. IRENÆUS.

I proposed here, as in the former instance, to have produced all the several places in Irenæus, where St. Matthew's
Gospel is cited; but since that purpose, I find myself prevented
herein by the care and industry of Feuardentius: at the end of
his edition of Irenæus, there is an index already made with
great exactness, of most of the citations which that Father has
made of this Gospel; I have been at the pains carefully to examine every one of them, and do not find above ten or twelve
false references in the whole.   It will be enough therefore to
refer the reader to the index of Feuardentius, only adding two
observations which I have made, viz.

(1.) That Irenæus has at least two hundred and fifty times
cited or taken passages out of this Gospel.

(2.) That he does several times cite St. Matthew by
name; viz. in the following places.

    1 Lib. 3. adv. Hæref. c. 11. p. 259. citing those words,
      Matt. i. 1.

    2 Lib. 3. c. 18. p. 277. citing ch. i. 1,18—21.

3. Lib.

3 Lib. 3. c. 26. in init. collat. cum 25. in fin. citing ch. j. 18.

4 Lib. 3. c. 10. citing ch. ii. 2, &c.

5 Lib. 3. c. 9. citing ch. ii. 13.

6 Ibid. citing ch. iii. 3.

7 Ibid. citing ch. iii. 7.

8 Ibid. citing ch. iii. 9.

9 Lib. 3. c. 18. citing ch. iii. 16.

V. CLEMENS ALEXANDRINUS.

There is indeed a large collection of the texts of this Gospel cited by Clemens, prefixed to his works; but upon enquiry, I find this collection in many respects so inaccurate, so false, and defective, that as I could not depend upon it myself, so neither can I refer the reader to it. I have therefore made the following collection, which, though perhaps it does not contain all the places of St. Matthew's Gospel cited by Clemens, yet, I dare say, contains the far greatest part, without any one reference which is not fairly and justly made.

A Catalogue of the places of St. Matthew's Gospel, cited or referred to by CLEMENS ALEXANDRINUS.

St. MATTHEW'S *Gospel.*	The *Works of* CLEMENS ALEXANDRINUS.
1 Ch. iii. 7.	1 Pædagog. Lib. 1. c. 9. p. 123.
2 ———— 9.	2 Admonit. ad Gent. p. 3.
3 ———— 12.	3 Pædagog. Lib. 1. c. 9. p. 125.
4 Ch. v. 5.	4 Stromat. Lib. 4. p. 488.
5 ———— 8.	5 ———— Lib. 5. p. 548.
6 ———— 10.	6 ———— Lib. 4. p. 484.
7 ———— 13.	7 Pædagog. Lib. 3. c. 11. p. 257. et Stromat. Lib. 1. p. 290.

St.

St. Matthew's *Gospel.*	The *Works of* Clemens Alexandrinus.
8 Chap. v. 15.	8 Stromat. Lib. 1. p. 275.
9 ———— 20.	9 ———— Lib. 6. p. 696.
10 ———— 25.	10 ———— Lib. 4. p. 512.
11 ———— 27, 28.	11 Pædagog. Lib. 2. c. 6. p. 169. et Admonit. ad Gent. p. 68.
12 ———— 29.	12 Pædagog. Lib. 3. c. 11. p. 251.
13 ———— 36.	13 ———— c. 3. p. 223.
14 ———— 37.	14 Stromat. Lib. 5. p. 596.
15 ———— 39, 40.	15 Admonit. ad Gent. p. 68. et Pædagog. Lib. 3. c. 12. p. 262.
16 ———— 44, 45.	16 Stromat. Lib. 4. p. 511, 512. et Pædagog. Lib. 1. c. 8. p. 118, 119.
17 ———— 48.	17 ———— Lib. 4. p. 529.
18 Ch. vi. 1, 2, &c.	18 Ibid.
19 ———— 9.	19 Pædagog. Lib. 1. c. 8. p. 119.
20 ———— 24.	20 Stromat. Lib. 3. p. 436. et Lib. 6. p. 486.
21 ———— 25, 26, &c.	21 Pædagog. Lib. 2. c. 1. p. 148. et Lib. ejufd. c. 10. p. 197, 198. et Stromat. Lib. 4. p. 487.
22 ———— 34.	22 ———— Lib. 1. c. 12. p. 134. et ejufd. Lib. c. 5. p. 88.
23 Ch. vii. 6.	23 Stromat. Lib. 1. p. 297.
24 ———— 7.	24 ———— p. 295. et Lib. 2. p. 410. Lib. 3. p. 450. Lib. 5. p. 553.
25 ———— 12.	25 Pædagog. Lib. 3. c. 12. p. 260. confer Stromat. Lib. 2. p. 421.

St. MATTHEW's *Gospel.*	*The Works of* CLEMENS ALEXANDRINUS.
26 Chap. vii. 13.	26 Admonit. ad Gent. p. 63. et Stromat. Lib. 4. p. 476.
27 ———— 15.	27 Admonit. ad Gent. p. 3.
28 ———— 18.	28 Pædagog. Lib. 2. c. 5. p. 166.
29 Ch. viii. 12.	29 ———— Lib. 1. c. 10. p. 129.
30 ———— 20.	30 Stromat. Lib. 1. p. 280.
31 ———— 22.	31 ———— Lib. 3. p. 436.
32 Ch. x. 5.	32 ———— Lib. 3. p. 472.
33 ———— 23.	33 ———— Lib. 4. p. 504.
34 ———— 26.	34 ———— Lib. 1. p. 275.
35 ———— 27.	35 ———— p. 297.
36 ———— 32, 33.	36 ———— Lib. 4. p. 502, 503.
37 ———— 39.	37 ———— Lib. 2. p. 407. et Lib. 4. p. 484.
38 ———— 41.	38 ———— Lib. 4. p. 488.
39 Ch. xi. 3, 4. &c.	39 Pædagog. Lib. 1. c. 10. p. 129.
40 ———— 12.	40 Stromat. Lib. 4. p. 476. et Lib. 5. p. 553.
41 ———— 17.	41 Pædagog. Lib. 1. c. 5. p. 85.
42 ———— 18.	42 Stromat. Lib. 3. p. 448.
43 ———— 19.	43 Pædagog. Lib. 2. c. 2. p. 158.
44 ———— 25.	44 ———— Lib. 1. c. 6. p. 96.
45 ———— 27.	45 ———— p. 89. et c. 8. p. 119.
46 ———— 28, 29, 30.	46 Admonit. ad Gent. p. 75. et Pædagog. Lib. 1. c. 10. p. 129. et Stromat. Lib. 5. p. 560.

St.

St. MATTHEW's *Gospel.*	The *Works of* CLEMENS ALEXANDRINUS.
47 Ch. xii. 36, 37.	47 Pædagog. Lib. 2. c. 6. p. 169.
48 Ch. xiii. 11.	48 Stromat. Lib. 5. p. 586.
49 ———— 13.	49 ———— Lib. 1. p. 270.
50 Ch. xv. 9.	50 Pædagog. Lib. 1. c. 9. p. 121.
51 ———— 11.	51 ———— Lib. 2. c. 6. p. 168.
52 ———— 22.	52 Stromat. Lib. 6. p. 680.
53 Ch. xvii. 5.	53 Pædagog. Lib. 1. c. 11. p. 133.
54 Ch. xviii. 3.	54 ———— c. 5. p. 85.
55 ———— 21, 22.	55 ———— Lib. 3. c. 12. p. 261.
56 Ch. xix. 6, 8.	56 Stromat. Lib. 3. p. 446.
57 ———— 10, 11, 12.	57 ———— p. 447.
58 ———— 13.	58 Pædagog. Lib. 1. c. 5. p. 85.
59 ———— 21.	59 ———— Lib. 2. c. 3. p. 160. et Stromat. Lib. 4. p. 485.
60 Ch. xx. 16.	60 Stromat. Lib. 5. p. 554.
61 ———— 28.	61 Pædagog. Lib. 1. c. 9. p. 126.
62 Ch. xxii. 30.	62 ———— c. 4. p. 84.
63 ———— 37.	63 ———— Lib. 3. c. 12. p. 260.
64 ———— 37—40.	64 Stromat. Lib. 2. p. 391.
65 Ch. xxiii. 6.	65 Pædagog. Lib. 3. c. 12. p. 262.
66 ———— 9.	66 Stromat. Lib. 3. p. 463.
67 ———— 27.	67 Pædagog. Lib. 3. c. 9. p. 241.
68 ———— 37.	68 ———— Lib. 1. c. 5. p. 86. et c. 9. p. 121 et 123.

St. MATTHEW's *Gospel.*	*The Works of* CLEMENS ALEXANDRINUS.
69 Ch. xxiv. 13.	69 Stromat. Lib. 4. p. 503.
70 Ch. xxv. 34, &c.	70 Pædagog. Lib. 3. c. 12. p. 262. et Stromat. Lib. 2. p. 391, 392.
71 ——— 40.	71 Pædagog. Lib. 3. c. 4. p. 231.
72 Ch. xxvi. 23.	72 ——— Lib. 2. c. 8. p. 176.
73 ——— 26—28.	73 ——— c. 2. p. 158.

Befides the works of Clemens Alexandrinus, which are ufually found together, there is alfo a fmall tract extant, intitled, Τίς ὁ σωζόμενος πλούσιος; i. e. *What rich man can be faved?* publifhed laft by Bifhop Fell at Oxford, 1683; it feems to have full evidence of its genuinenefs, not only that Eufebius, Hift. Ecclef. l. 3. c. 23. cites a large piece of it as the work of Clemens under this fame title, but that Photius, Cod. cxi. fays, *The Stromata of Clemens Alexandrinus were in a very antient copy of that Father's works reckoned to be* eight; whereas now there are but feven: *the firft feven*, fays he, *had the fame title, but the eighth differed, being intitled in fome copies*, What rich man can be faved?—The treatife is very fmall, not making above fixty fmall pages in the Oxford duodecimo edition, but contains fuch numerous citations of this and other proofs of the New Teftament, that I thought it proper to collect them.

St. MATTHEW's *Gospel.*	*The Treatife of* CLEMENS ALEXANDRINUS, *intitled,* Quis Dives falvetur ?
1 Ch. v. 3.	1 Cap. xvi. p. 42. et c. xvii. p. 46. In this place St. Matthew is cited by name.
2 ——— 6.	2 Ibid.
3 ——— 13, 14.	3 Cap. xxxvi. p. 97.

St.

St. MATTHEW'S *Gospel.*	*The treatise of* CLEMENS A-LEXANDRINUS, *intitled,* Quis Dives salvetur ?
4 Ch. v. 25.	4 Cap. xl. p. 106.
5 —— 29.	5 —— xxiv. p. 65.
6 —— 39.	6 —— xviii. p. 49.
7 Ch. vi. 14.	7 —— xl. p. 105.
8 —— 19.	8 —— xiii. p. 34.
9 —— 21.	9 —— xvii. p. 45.
10 Ch. vii. 1, &c.	10 —— xxxiii. p. 90.
11 —— 21.	11 —— xxix. p. 81.
12 Ch. ix. 13.	12 —— xxxix. p. 102.
13 Ch. x. 22.	13 —— xxxii. p. 89.
14 —— 40.	14 —— xxxi. p. 82.
15 —— 41.	15 —— p. 85.
16 Ch. xi. 12.	16 —— xxi. p. 57.
17 —— 27.	17 —— viii. p. 21.
18 Ch. xii. 35.	18 —— xvii. p. 45.
19 Ch. xiii. 17.	19 —— xxix. p. 81.
20 Ch. xvii. 27.	20 —— xxi. p. 58.
21 Ch. xviii. 10.	21 —— xxxi. p. 82.
22 Ch. xix. 21.	22 —— x. p. 25.
23 —— 24.	23 —— ii. p. 6.
24 —— 27, 28.	24 —— xxii. p. 58.
25 Ch. xxii. 36, 37, &c.	25 —— xxvi. p. 74, &c.
26 Ch. xxiii. 12.	26 —— i. p. 5. Here this Gospel is called Θεῖος λό-γος, i. e. the word of God.
27 Ch. xxv. 36, &c.	27 Cap. xiii. p. 34.

ARG. III. The Gospel of St. Matthew is Canonical, *be-cause it was read as Scripture in the assemblies or churches of the primitive Christians,* by Prop. VI. I have above proved (Vol. I. Part I. Ch. X.) from Justin Martyr, Tertullian, Cyprian, &c. that it was the constant custom of the primitive churches to read the sacred Scriptures as part of their most solemn divine service ; I am now to prove that St. Matthew's
Gospel

Gospel was always among these books; and that will be evident;

1. From Cyril of Jerusalem; who, enumerating the books which ought to be read in the Churches, and which were read in the Churches, says, *Among the New Testament books there were only four Gospels, and that all others were spurious and hurtful*[a]. After reciting the other books of the New Testament, he adds a little below, *That all others were to be rejected, and as not being read in the church, were not to be read in private by his catechumen*—No one acquainted with Cyril's writing, and the other books of his time, can possibly question whether St. Matthew is included among the *four Gospels*, which he speaks of, as being read in the churches; especially considering that he frequently appeals to that Evangelist's Gospel, as sacred; and in one place[b] does appeal to him, as having *wrote a Gospel in testimony of the truth of Christianity, which ought to be credited*.

2. From the council of Laodicea, Can. LIX. where it is declared, *that no books which were not of the Canon should be read in the churches, and that those which were of the Canon and ought to be read*, were the Gospel according to St. Matthew, &c.[c]

3. From the testimony of Justin Martyr it seems not unfairly to be concluded, that *St. Matthew's Gospel was read in the primitive churches*. The proof I aim at, is as followeth: That Father tells us[d], that *on every Sunday there was an assembly of the neighbouring Christians*, and τὰ ἀπομνημονύματα τῶν Ἀποϛόλων—ἀναγινώσκιται, the Memoirs or Commentaries of the Apostles were read; under this word ἀπομνημονύματα were included

---

[a] Τῆς δὲ καινῆς διαθήκης τὰ τίσσαρα εὐαγγίλια· τὰ δὲ λοιπὰ ψευδεπίγραφα καὶ βλαβερὰ τυγχάνιι—τὰ δὲ λοιπὰ πάντα ἔξω κείσθω ἐν δευτέρῳ· καὶ ὅσα μὲν ἐν ἐκκλησίαις μὴ ἀναγινώσκιται, ταῦτα μηδὲ κατὰ σαυτὸν ἀναγίνωσκε. Catech. IV. §. 22.

[d] Catech. XIV. §. 8.

[c] Non oportet—libros in Ecclesiis legere, qui sunt extra Canonem, nisi solos Canonicos Novi et Veteris Testamenti. Quæ autem oportet legi, et in auctoritatem recipi, hæc sunt—Ic. Novi Testamenti Evangelium secundum Matthæum, &c.

[b] Apolog. 2. pro Christian. p. 58.

thoſe

thofe books which we now call *Gospels*, as is plain from what he faid immediately before, viz. ἐν τοῖς γενομένοις ὑπ᾽ αὐτῶν ἀπομνη-μονεύμασιν, ἃ καλεῖται εὐαγγέλια: i. e. *in the Commentaries made by the Apoſtles, which are called* GOSPELS: it follows therefore, that the Gospels, which were made by the Apoſtles, were read in the churches of Chriſtians in the time of Juſtin Martyr; and that St. Matthew's Gospel was among thefe is moſt appa-rently evident, becaufe Juſtin in many places of his writings, citing paſſages out of this Gospel, cites them as what he read in, and learnt from, thefe ἀπομνημονεύμασιν τῶν Ἀποϛόλων, i. e. from thefe *Commentaries or Gospels of the Apoſtles*; i. e. from St. Matthew's Gospel, where thofe words only are to be found.

ARG. IV. The Gospel of St. Matthew is Canonical, be-caufe *it is found among thofe which the churches of Syria re-ceived as fuch, and which they collected together, and tranſlated as Scripture in or near the Apoſtles' time*, Prop. XV. I ſhall only obferve farther, that the Author of this excellent verſion of the New Teſtament into Syriac (or fome one elfe) at the end of St. Matthew's Gospel has annexed the following teſtimony, which it will not be foreign to my purpofe to tranfcribe:

ܡܠܡ ܐܘܢܓܠܝܘܢ ܩܕܝ ܡܟܪܙܘܬܐ ܕܡܬܝ: ܐܝܟ ܕܐܟܪܙ: ܥܒܪܐܝܬ ܒܐܪܥܐ ܕܦܠܣܛܝܢܝ:

i. e. *The end of the Holy Gospel of the preaching of Matthew, which he preached in Hebrew in the land of Paleſtine.*

Thus I have endeavoured to eſtabliſh the Canonical autho-rity of this Gospel of St. Matthew by various arguments.

CHAP.

CHAP. IV.

*Other Arguments to prove the genuine Authority of St. Mat-
thew's Gospel. Bartholomew took it to preach in his Travels.
Papias and Hegesippus give Credit to it. The Manichees'
Objection against this Gospel. Faustus's Objection from St.
Matthew's oblique Way of Speech (ix. 9.) considered and re-
futed. Other Objections considered.*

BESIDES the preceding arguments, I have met with se-
veral other things, which seem to be no small proof of St.
Matthew's Gospel being of genuine and Canonical authority.
These are;

1. That St. Bartholomew, who was one of our Saviour's
twelve Apostles, when he went forth to preach and propagate
the Christian faith, *took along with him the Gospel of St. Matthew*; and particularly that *he preached according to this Gospel among the Indians, and left it among them at his departure
from them*: and that Pantænus afterwards, viz. in the second
century, *found this Gospel among them*; this is related both by
Eusebius [a], and Jerome [b], and seems clearly to prove that St.
Matthew's Gospel met with a suitable reception, and was
esteemed of the greatest authority even in the Apostles' time.

It may indeed be objected, that the Gospel which St. Bartholomew left among the Indians, is said by Eusebius to have
been written in Hebrew letters, and that I have elsewhere [c] attempted to prove that this very Gospel was that of the Nazarenes.

To which I answer, that as I have endeavoured largely to
prove, that St. Matthew's Gospel was originally written in
Greek [d], so I easily allow there was a very early version of it
made into Hebrew; and this as yet uninterpolated nor enlarged

---

[a] Hist. Eccl. lib. 5. c. 10.
[b] Catal. Vir. Illustr. in Barthol.
Pantæn.
[c] Vol. II. Part I. Ch. X. p. 172,
173.
[d] Vindication of St. Matthew's
Gospel against Mr. Whiston, ch.
17, 18, 19.

with

with the Nazarene additions, is what, I suppose, St. Bartholomew, who was a Jew, and preached (as the rest of the Apostles at this time) principally to those of his own nation, did take along with him in his travels.

2. That Papias, who was according to Irenæus [a] a disciple of John, and an acquaintance of Polycarp, intimates very clearly, that St. Matthew's Gospel *was in common use in his time* [b].

That Hegesippus [c], a writer of the second century, *wrote some dissertations upon the Gospel of the Hebrews, or the Gospel of St. Matthew, which the Nazarenes made use of.* Now these dissertations were wrote either upon the supposition, that this Hebrew Gospel was the true one of St. Matthew, or that it was not; if we say the *latter*, it is then evident they must be wrote with design to vindicate the authority of St. Matthew's true Gospel against the Nazarenes' copy; if the *former*, the authority of St. Matthew will be also thereby established, because all the credit, which the Nazarene Gospel had or pretended to, even among themselves, was founded upon the supposition of its being St. Matthew's; which, though false, yet shews the high opinion the primitive Christians did entertain of that Evangelist's writing.

The only persons (as far as I know) among the antients, who have made any objections against the authority of this Gospel, were the Manichees: the main and principal arguments which Faustus has made use of against it, are taken from the difficulties of the genealogy, Ch. I. But these fall not within my consideration, it being sufficient to my design to make it appear, that St. Matthew's Gospel was received as Scripture by the primitive Christians: one thing only I would observe, which seems more nearly to affect its authority, viz. [d] that Faustus undertakes to prove that this Gospel was not written by St. Matthew, because of *the oblique manner of ex-*

---

[a] Adv. Hæref. lib. 5. c. 33.
[b] Euseb. Hist. Eccl. l. 3. c. 39. in fine; ἑρμήνευσι δ᾽ αὐτὰ (i. e. Evangelium Matthæi) ὡς ἠδύνατο ἕκαστος.
[c] Ibid. lib. 4. c. 22.

[d] August. contr. Faust. Manich. l. 17. c. 1. Quis ergo de se ipso scribens dicat, Vidit hominem et vocavit Eum, et secutus est Eum, ac non potius dicat, Vidit Me, et vocavit Me &c.

preſſion (as it is called) which we meet with, Matt. ix. 9. *And as Jeſus paſſed forth from thence, he ſaw* a man *named Matthew, ſitting at the receipt of cuſtom, and he ſaith unto* him, *Follow me;* and He *aroſe and followed him:* " Matthew, ſays " Fauſtus, did not write that Goſpel, but ſome one elſe under " his name, as is plain by thoſe very words of the pretended " Matthew; for who, ſays he, writing concerning himſelf, " would ſay, he ſaw a MAN, and called HIM, and HE follow- " ed him; and would not rather ſay, He ſaw ME, and called " ME, and I followed him ?" But nothing can be more weak than this ſort of arguing, it being a thing undeniable, that this oblique way of writing is common in all ſorts of hiſtorians, and that they very frequently do ſpeak of themſelves not in the firſt, but in the third perſon. It is common (ſays Auſtin in his anſwer to[a] Fauſtus on this head) in ſecular or (what we call) profane hiſtories. It is always done by Moſes, and very frequently by our Saviour and his Apoſtles. The many inſtances which that Father produces, and which are every where to be met with, make it needleſs for me to produce any. He who has a mind may conſult the many places in Moſes's writings, where we find him ſpeaking in the third perſon of himſelf, or in this oblique way of ſpeech, viz. And the Lord ſaid unto Moſes, and Moſes did ſuch and ſuch things; and beſides theſe, the places both of the Old and New Teſtament referred to at the bottom of the page[b]. So that this argument will by no means prove what it is brought for, that Matthew did not write that Goſpel which goes under his name.

The German Anabaptiſts of the laſt and preceding century (perſons very different in their principles and practices from thoſe who now go under that denomination among us) and thoſe which were called the Servetians, or followers of Michael Servetus, among other of their whimſical opinions, denied the credit and authority of this Goſpel. Their principal arguments are, (1.) That the author of the Goſpel *has miſapplied*

---

[a] Auguſt. contr. Fauſt. Manich. lib. 17. c. 4.
[b] Gen. iv. 24. Num. xxiv. 3, 4. Jerem. xxviii. 5, 10, 15. Jonah i. 1. et per tot. Matt. viii. 20. xi. 19. xviii. 2. Luke xviii. 8. John v. 23, 25, &c. John xxi. 24. Vid. Auguſt. Tract. 61. in Joann. et Glaſſ. Gram. Sacr. lib. iv. Tract. 2. Obſerv. 17.

many prophecies of the *Old Testament* to prove the Divinity of *Christ.* (2.) That the *true Gospel of St. Matthew was wrote in Hebrew, whereas this which we now have under his name, seems originally to have been wrote in Greek*[a].

To the first of these my design does not oblige me to give any answer; because all I undertake to prove is, that the Gospel was received as St. Matthew's, and of as great authority in the primitive Church, without any respect to the several difficulties that may be in its contexture; though it were no difficult matter to shew the falsehood of their allegation.

To the second it will be sufficient to answer, that I have elsewhere proved[b] that St. Matthew's true Gospel was not originally written in Hebrew, and that it was a mistake in the Fathers to assert that it was wrote in that language, there never having been any other Hebrew Gospel of St. Matthew, but what was a translation out of his original Greek, and afterwards interpolated by the Nazarenes, was made use of by them as the true Gospel of this Evangelist.

CHAP. V.

Concerning the Time of St. Matthew's writing his Gospel. Irenæus and Eusebius differ in this Matter. The Opinion of the latter proved to be more probable than that of the former ; viz. that he wrote A. D. XLI. and not A. D. LIX. or LX.

IT remains now that I say somewhat *concerning the time*, in which it is most probable that St. Matthew's Gospel was written; and herein I find it difficult to come to any certainty, because of the disagreement there is between the antients themselves, as to the matter. I shall first lay down the different opinions, and then observe what appears more probable.

[a] Sixt. Senenf. Bibl. Sanct. l. 7. de Evang. Matt. Hæref. p. 581.
[b] Vindication of St. Matthew's Gospel, ch. xvii, xviii, xix. See also of this work, Vol. I. Part II. Ch. XXIX. p. 305, &c.

1. The

1. The firſt is that of Irenæus[a], who tells us, *that Matthew publiſhed his Goſpel among the Hebrews in their own language, while Peter and Paul were preaching at Rome, and laying the foundations of a church there.* Now as I have had occaſion to obſerve in another place, though it is not certain when Peter was at Rome, yet Paul was there in the third year of Nero; i. e. in or about the year of Chriſt LIX. or LX. as Euſebius relates in his *Chronicon*; and to this moſt Chronologers[b] and writers of church-hiſtory agree[c].

2. Euſebius in his *Chronicon* has placed the writing of St. Matthew's Goſpel in *the third of Caligula; i. e. eight years after Chriſt's aſcenſion,* or the year of Chriſt XLI.

Beſides theſe two, I know none of the writers of the firſt centuries who have aſſigned any time, in which they ſuppoſe St. Matthew to have wrote: Nicephorus[d] indeed has without any reaſon aſſerted, that *it was wrote fifteen years after Chriſt's aſcenſion*; but he being ſo late a writer (viz. of the ninth century), his teſtimony can deſerve no regard here. As to more modern writers, I find they generally credit and follow Euſebius in this matter; nor do I know any one beſides the famous Jeſuit Andradius[e], Chemnitius[f], and Dr. Mill[g], who have believed Irenæus in this matter. That which influenced the firſt of theſe to his opinion was, that he thereby was able the better to ſupport the Popiſh doctrine *of the neceſſity of traditions, and the inſufficiency of the Scripture.* For if the Chriſtians were without any authentick hiſtory of Chriſt, and St. Matthew did not write till the time which Irenæus mentions; i. e. till the year of Chriſt LIX. or LX. i. e. for the ſpace of twenty ſix or twenty ſeven years, it would ſeem ſomewhat fa-

---

[a] Adv. Hæreſ. lib. 3. cap. 1. Ὁ μὲν δὴ Ματθαῖος ἐν τοῖς Ἑβραίοις τῇ ἰδίᾳ αὐτῶν διαλέκτῳ καὶ γραφὴν ἐξήνεγκεν εὐαγγελίου, τοῦ Πέτρου καὶ τοῦ Παύλου ἐν Ῥώμῃ εὐαγγελιζομένων καὶ θεμελιούντων τὴν ἐκκλησίαν. See the Greek in Euſeb. Hiſt. Eccl. lib. 5. c. 8.
[b] Helvicus, Petavius, Dr. Lightfoot, Mr. Tallents, &c.

[c] Spanheim, Eachard, Le Clerc, &c.
[d] Lib. 2. c. 45. apud D. Cave Hiſt. Liter. in Matth. p. 8.
[e] Apud Chemnit. Exam. Concil. Trident. Pars I. p. 28.
[f] Lib. denuo cit. p. 31.
[g] Prolegom. in Nov. Teſt. §. 61, &c. I find Mr. Whiſton alſo fixes the time of St. Matthew's writing to this ſame period. Eſſay on Conſtit. p. 16.

vourable

vourable to the Popiſh ſcheme, viz. that religion might be propagated by mere tradition without any writing. Chemnitius, though he well refutes the Jeſuit's reaſonings, yet agrees with him, that Irenæus was in the right as to the time of St. Matthew's writing; becauſe, ſays he, it is fit we ſhould rather credit the more antient, than later Fathers. Dr. Mill alſo credits Irenæus, but without aſſigning the leaſt ſhadow of a reaſon, why that Father is to be credited rather. For my part, though I freely own it is difficult to come to any certainty in the point, yet I cannot but rather ſubſcribe to Eüſebius than Irenæus; i. e. I rather think St. Matthew's Goſpel was written in the third year of Caligula, eight years after Chriſt's aſcenſion, A. D. XLI. than in the third year of Nero, ſix or ſeven and twenty years after Chriſt's aſcenſion, A. D. LIX. or LX. And for this opinion I ſhall offer the following reaſons; viz.

1. Becauſe *it is altogether improbable that the Chriſtian churches ſhould* for ſo long a ſpace *as twenty ſix or twenty ſeven years after Chriſt's aſcenſion, be left deſtitute of any genuine and authentick hiſtory of the life and actions, of the miracles and doctrines of Jeſus Chriſt.* To ſuppoſe this, is plainly to ſuppoſe the Apoſtles either defective in their zeal for the intereſt of Chriſtianity, or elſe ignorant of one of the moſt likely means to promote it. But I find Mr. Le Clerc has prevented me on this head; I ſhall therefore omit ſaying any more on it, and give the reader a tranſlation of his words: " [a] They who think " that the Goſpels were written as late as Irenæus ſaith, and " ſuppoſe that for the ſpace of about thirty years after our " Lord's aſcenſion, there were many ſpurious Goſpels in the " hands of the Chriſtians, and not one that was genuine and " authentick, do unwarily caſt a very great reflection upon the " wiſdom of the Apoſtles; for what could have been more " imprudence in them, than tamely to have ſuffered the idle " ſtories concerning Chriſt to be read by the Chriſtians, and " not to contradict them by ſome authentick hiſtory wrote by " ſome credible perſons, which might reach the knowledge of

---

[a] Hiſt. Eccl. Secul. I. A. D. LXII. §. 9. p. 414.

" all men? For my part, I can never be perſuaded to entertain
" ſo mean an opinion of the prudence of men under the con-
" duct of the Holy Ghoſt. Beſides, Matthew has delivered to us
" not only the actions, but the diſcourſes of Chriſt ; and this he
" muſt needs be able to do with greater certainty, while they
" were freſh in his memory, than when through length of time
" he began to loſe the impreſſions of them. It is true, the
" Holy Ghoſt was with the Apoſtles, to bring all things to
" their remembrance, which they had received of Chriſt, ac-
" cording to the promiſe, John xiv. 26: but the Holy Ghoſt
" in this matter did not only inſpire, but deal with them ac-
" cording to their natural powers, as the variety of the ex-
" preſſions in the Goſpel ſhews." Thus far he ; from
whence it appears very improbable, that no Goſpel, which
, was authentick, was written before the time which Irenæus
mentions, viz. the year of Chriſt LIX. or LX.   I am ſenſible
this argument ſuppoſos, that St. Matthew's was the firſt true
Goſpel which was wrote ; and that it was ſo, is generally aſſerted by all the antients.

2. *Many of the moſt antient manuſcripts of this Goſpel do
agree with Euſebius, that St. Matthew's Goſpel was wrote in
the eighth year after our Saviour's aſcenſion.* Thus, for inſtance, Beza[a] tells us, it was in his famous Clermont manuſcript, which he gave to the Univerſity of Cambridge, and
which is generally eſteemed the oldeſt manuſcript of the Goſpels, which is now in the world. Thus alſo it is at the end of
ſeveral very antient Greek MSS. which Father Simon ſaw[b],
and more which are cited and referred to by Dr. Mill, among
the manuſcripts of the Goſpels in the Bodleian Library at
Oxford.   See Mill on Matt. xxviii. 20.

3. The old Arabick Verſion joins in the ſame account ;
viz. *that he, St. Matthew, wrote his Goſpel in Paleſtine, by the
influence of the Holy Spirit, in Hebrew, eight years after our
Lord Jeſus Chriſt aſcended in his fleſh to heaven,* and the firſt
year of the Roman Emperor Claudius[c]. This differs but very

[a] Annot. in Matt. xxviii. ult.   [c] Vid. Ludov. de Dieu ad Matt.
[b] Critic. Hiſt. of the New Teſt.   xxviii. ult.
part 1. c. 10.

little from Eufebius; for though he fays it was written in the third year of Caligula, and the Arabick Verfion in the firft year of Claudius, yet this will prove only half a year's difference; feeing Caligula reigned but three years and a few months, and Claudius immediately fucceeded him

4. Theophylaƈt and Euthymius *do alfo affert this Gofpel to have been written in the eighth year after Chrift's afcenfion;* the former in his *preface to his Expofition on Matthew;* the latter in his *Commentaries on the Gofpels,* which are in a manufcript in the Bodleian Library at Oxford[a]: and though thefe were late writers, yet their teftimony is for this reafon confiderable, as it coincides with the teftimonies of others; which cannot be faid of the opinion of Nicephorus above-mentioned.

5. It may not perhaps be foreign to the purpofe to obferve, *how diligent and careful Eufebius was in collecting his accounts of this fort;* and that though there are fome miftakes in his works (which in fo vaft undertakings could hardly be avoided) yet for the moft part he is very accurate and exaƈt, as a Chronologer and Hiftorian.

6. What gives force to all the preceding remarks is, *that Irenæus is moft certainly miftaken in the very next words to thefe;* viz. as to the time of St. Mark's writing his Gofpel: he faith, that St. Mark wrote his Gofpel μετὰ τὴν τύτων ἔξοδον: i. e. *after the death of Peter and Paul,* as thofe words undoubtedly mean, and are well expreffed by the old Latin Verfion, *poft horum exceffum.* But this, I fay, is falfe, and contrary to the exprefs affertions of many of the moft antient primitive writers, as will appear hereafter in my account of Mark. I know indeed that there have been fome, who have otherwife tranflated thefe words; but this has been obferved (by Valefius in Eufeb. lib. 5. c. 8. Father Simon's Crit. Hift. of the New Teft. Part I. c. x. p. 87, 88.) to be a miftake, made by them with defign to fave Irenæus from the charge of contradicting the other Fathers.

I will conclude the whole with adding, that whereas it was by fome made an objeƈtion againft this Gofpel, that ec-

---

[a] It is cited by Dr. Mill among the Greek teftimonies prefixed to St. Matthew's Gofpel, in his edition of the Greek Teftament.

clefiaftical

clefiaftical writers differed as to the time of its being wrote,
Eufebius fixing one time, and Irenæus another[a], it is anfwered
by Sixtus Senenfis in a method, which that learned man
thought would reconcile Irenæus and Eufebius together; viz.
*That St. Matthew firft publifhed his Gofpel in Judea for the
ufe of his countrymen, eight years after Chrift's afcenfion, in the
third year of Caligula*; and that this was what Eufebius
meant; but that *the fame Evangelift a long time after, when he
went among the Gentiles, publifhed it more univerfally for the
benefit of all Chriftians*; and that this was what Irenæus
meant[b].   But I leave this conjecture to the examination of
the learned in thefe things.

CHAP. VI.

*The Scripture Account of St. Mark. There is no other of this
Name mentioned in the New Teftament, but the Evangelift.
Objections to this anfwered. He was Affiftant to Peter and
Paul in the Miniftry of the Gofpel. The credible Relations,
which we have of St. Mark from the Antients, produced.
Peter ufed him as an Interpreter. Afterwards he preached
in Egypt, planted many Churches at Alexandria, and was
one of Chrift's feventy Difciples.*

CONCERNING St. Mark, the author of this Gofpel,
there is fcarce any thing left us in Ecclefiaftical Hiftory,
which can be depended upon with that certainty, which one
would wifh for, and have expected in fuch a matter.

In the writings of the New Teftament we have frequent
mention of one named Mark; and in the writings of the following ages there are alfo fome few things concerning him,

---

[a] Sixt. Senenf. Biblioth. Sanct.   Object. §. 3.
lib. 7. De Evang. Matth. Hæref.   [b] Ibid. Diffolut. Object. §. 3.

which

which may appear credible and material. I fhall confider each diftinctly.

I. *As to the accounts which the writings of the New Teftament give of Mark.* The name is mentioned four times in the *Acts of the Apoftles*, viz. xii. 12, 25. xv. 37, 39. thrice in St. Paul's Epiftles, viz. Coloff. iv. 10. 2 Tim. iv. 11. Philem. 24. once by St. Peter, 1 Epift. v. 13. Relating to which places I obferve;

1. *That it is generally agreed, that Mark the Evangelift is that Mark, which is mentioned* 1 Pet. v. 13. *The Church that is at Babylon elected together with you, faluteth you, and fo doth Marcus my fon.* So Origen [a], Eufebius [b], and Jerome [c] among the antients; Grotius [d], Maldonate [e], Dr. Lightfoot [f], Du Pin [g], and many other of the moderns. This is exceedingly probable for this reafon; viz. that it is the univerfal voice of antiquity, *that Mark was Peter's companion and affiftant* in preaching the Gofpel, and for that reafon called by him *his fon*, as Paul for the fame reafon calls Timothy *his fon* [h], and particularly fays of him [i], that *as a fon with a father he ferved with him in the Gofpel.*

2. It is very probable *that Mark, mentioned in the Acts and St. Paul's Epiftles* (fee the places above cited) *was the fame perfon as Mark the Evangelift, or author of this Gofpel.* The reafons I affign for this, are,

(1.) *That the office of Mark the Evangelift, and this Mark mentioned in the Acts of the Apoftles and St. Paul's Epiftles, was the very fame*, viz. to be an affiftant to the Apoftles (Paul and Peter) in the miniftry of the Word. Concerning the *former*, we find Barnabas and Paul made ufe of him for that purpofe, Acts xii. 25. And though Paul and Barnabas differed upon the point, yet the latter was for taking him to be

---

[a] Expofit. in Matth. apud Eufeb. Hift. Eccl. l. 6. c. 25.
[b] Hift. Ecclef. lib. 2. c. 15.
[c] Catalog. Vir. illuft. in Marco.
[d] Annot. in 1 Pet. v. 13.
[e] Prolegom. in Marc.

[f] Harmon. of the New Teft. at the year 65.
[g] Hiftory of the Canon of the New Teft. vol. 2. c. 2. §. 4.
[h] 1 Tim. i. 2. 2 Tim. i. 2. 1 Cor. iv. 17.
[i] Phil. ii. 22.

E 3   an

an 'affiftant and companion in vifiting the churches, and did
take him. In like manner Paul, who (as is generally agreed)
was foon reconciled again to Mark, defired Timothy to *bring
him to Rome to him, for* (fays he) *he is ufeful to me* (or affifting
to me) *in the work of the miniftry,* 2 Tim. iv. 11. And accordingly we find he was afterwards with Paul, Colof. iv. 10.
and is there called *fifter's fon* (or nephew) *to Barnabas*; which
is, by the way, no mean proof, that he was the fame perfon mentioned Acts xv. 37. it feeming probable, that Barnabas's affection to Mark, as a relation, was one reafon why he per-
fifted in his refolution to take him along with him. But to
fay no more of this, it is plain Mark, mentioned in the Acts
and St. Paul's Epiftles, was an affiftant to the Apoftles; and
the fame is certain as to Mark the Evangelift, viz. that he
was affiftant, companion, or interpreter of Peter, as will undeniably appear from the places, which will prefently be cited
from the Fathers. Unlefs therefore we will fuppofe, that St.
Paul's affiftant and St. Peter's were both of the fame name,
we muft conclude that the Mark, mentioned in the Acts and
St. Paul's Epiftles, was one and the fame perfon, who at different times was with Paul and Peter engaged in the fame work.

(2.) To fuppofe two Marks, one with Peter, and another
with Paul, *is to breed confufion where there needeth none, and
to conceive that for which the Scripture giveth not only no
ground, but is plain enough to the contrary.* It is eafily feen
how John Mark came into familiarity both with Paul and
Peter; and other Mark we can find none in the New Teftament, unlefs of our own invention. Thefe are the words of
Dr. Lightfoot [a], and feem to me to contain an argument fufficiently juft, till fome good proof be made that the contrary
opinion is true.

(3.) *The author of the Conftitutions of the Apoftles* (Lib. 2.
c. 57.) *makes Mark the Evangelift an affiftant of St. Paul*;
i. e. the fame who is mentioned in the Acts and St. Paul's
Epiftles; and the latter Fathers, as Œcumenius, Theophylact (Præf. in Marc.), tell us the Evangelift Mark was fur-

a Loc. jam cit.

named

named John, and the fifter's fon of Barnabas, and the companion of Paul.

I know indeed that Grotius [a], and after him Cotelerius [b],
Dr. Cave [c], Du Pin [d], Mr. Eachard [e], and others, are of the
contrary opinion, and fuppofe that Mark the Evangelift, and
Mark mentioned in the Acts and St. Paul's Epiftles, were two
different perfons. The two former of thefe have offered fome
reafons for their opinion, which I fhall briefly confider:

1.) They urge that they cannot be the fame, *becaufe the
antients never call the Evangelifts by the name of John, but always Mark; whereas, fay they, John was the proper name of
him who is mentioned in the Acts.*

Nothing is more common than the miftakes of learned perfons; but I have feldom obferved one more grofs than this; for,

(1. Though it is certain the furname of him mentioned in
the Acts was Mark, Acts xii. 12, 25. and xv. 37. yet even
the very fame chapter, two verfes afterwards, demonftrates (ver.
39.) that *the proper name of the perfon,* i e. *the name by which
he was commonly called, was Mark, and not John.* The words
are, *Barnabas took Mark, and failed to Cyprus.* It had been
ftrange therefore, if perfons in after ages fhould have called
him John.

(2. *It was the common practice among the Jews at that time,
to call perfons by that which was their furname, and not the other.*
So, for inftance, Simon, whofe furname was Peter (Matt. x. 2.
Mar. iii. 16. Acts x. 5, 18, 32.), was moft commonly called
Peter. Lebbeus, whofe furname was Thaddeus (Matt. x. 3.),
was always called Thaddeus. Jofes, who was furnamed Barnabas (Acts iv. 36.), was always called Barnabas. And fo I
have obferved above concerning St. Matthew, that he was
commonly called by his furname, viz. Levi, and fo is by
Mark and Luke.

(3. *In St. Paul's Epiftles* (where Grotius and I think Du
Pin acknowledge the fame perfon is fpoken of) *he is called al-*

---

[a] Prolegom. in Marc.   [d] Loc. jam cit.
[b] In Conftitut. Apoft. lib. 2. c.   [e] Ecclefiaft. Hift. b. ii, c. 3. §.
57. [c] Lives of the Apoftles, p. 214.   4.

ways Mark, and not John; though our tranflators aukwardly enough tranflate fometimes Marcus, and fometimes **Mark ;** which muft, as many other fuch things in our tranflation, confound a perfon unacquainted with the original.

2.) It is urged by Du Pin, *that Mark the Evangelift kept clofe to Peter, at the time when the other (Mark) was with Paul and Barnabas.* But this is not proving, but a plain begging of the queftion, or taking that for granted which is the thing to be proved.

I conclude therefore for the reafon above-mentioned, that Mark the Evangelift was the fame perfon, as he who is mentioned not only by Peter, but in the Acts and Epiftles of Paul ; and this then will be all we can collect out of Scripture concerning him ; viz. That he was an inhabitant of Jerufalem, and the fon of a pious convert, whofe houfe was employed in thofe perfecuting times for a place of the Chriftian affemblies for religious worfhip, Acts xii. 12. That he was a perfon of fo much vifible zeal for, and knowledge in Chriftianity, as to be efteemed proper by Paul and Barnabas to be taken along with them, to be an affiftant to them in executing their miniftry, Acts xii. 25. And though upon a difference between Barnabas and Paul, about taking him with them to vifit the churches, Paul declared againft taking him, yet Barnabas judged his affiftance neceffary, Acts xv. 37, 39. That notwithftanding this, the difpleafure of Paul did not continue long, for he appears to be with him at Rome, recommended him to the kind regards of the Coloffians, in a letter which he wrote to them from Rome, Col. iv. 10. wanted his company another time at Rome, as a perfon whom he judged and found of fervice and great help to him in the miniftry, 2 Tim. iv. 11. and accordingly honours him with the character of his *fellow-labourer*, Philem. 24. Befides all which, St. Peter ftiles him *his fon*; i. e. one who, as a *fon, ferved and helped him in the work of the Gofpel*, 1 Pet. v. 13.

II. I am next to confider *the accounts we have from the antients, relating to Mark the Evangelift.*

1. Thefe all agree, that Mark, the writer of the Gofpel, *was*

was a companion or interpreter of Peter. So Papias [a], Irenæus [b], the author of the Hypotoposes which went under the name of Clemens Alexandrinus, and was supposed to be his by Eusebius [c], Origen [d], Eusebius [e], Jerome [f], and many others of the Fathers. Several of these add, that he was with St. Peter at Rome.

2. Another account of the antients concerning Mark is, that he *afterwards went down to Egypt, where he preached the Gospel which he had written at Rome, and founded many churches in Alexandria, and made a vast number of converts to Christianity.* This is related by Eusebius [g], Epiphanius [h], Jerome [i], and many succeeding writers; such as Hippolytus [k], Dorotheus [l], Isidorus Hispalensis [m], Theophylact [n], &c. all which I shall pass over, only observing that the tradition of Mark's founding the church at Alexandria, which Du Pin [o] calls *an antient and certain tradition*, was always credited in Egypt, and that Eutychius, who was made patriarch of Alexandria, A. D. 933 [p], in his Arabick history of that church published by Mr. Selden, has not only asserted the same, but given us the particular method by which the Evangelist made his first convert at Alexandria, and in which he established the government of the Church there. But to return to Eusebius and Jerome, they tell us that Mark was not only successful in making numerous converts, but induced them to a more than common strictness in the profession and practice of their new religion; for which reason Philo Judæus wrote a peculiar treatise concerning them and their manner of living, viz. that intitled Περὶ βίου θεωρητικοῦ, i. e. *Concerning a contemplative Life,*

---

[a] Apud Euseb. Histor. Eccles. l. 2, c. 15, et l. 3. c. 39.

[b] Adv. Hæres. l. 3. c. 1.

[c] Euseb. Hist. Eccles. l. 6. c. 14.

[d] In Matth. apud Euseb. Hist. Eccles. l. 6. c. 25.

[e] Hist. Eccl. lib. 2. c. 15.

[f] Catalog. Viror. illustr. in Marco.

[g] Histor. Eccles. lib. 2. c. 16.

[h] Vid. Epiphan. Hær. 51. §. 6.

[i] Catalog. Viror. illustr. in Marco.

[k] MS. in Bibl. Bodleian. apud D. Mill in Testimon. Marco præfix.

[l] In Synopsi.

[m] De vit. et obitu Sanctorum, versus finem.

[n] Præfat. in Marc.

[o] Hist. of the Canon of the New Test. vol. 2. ch. 2. §. 4.

[p] He was also called *Said Ibn Batrick*. See Mr. Selden's Preface, and Account of the Author, and Prideaux's Life of Mahomet, p. 271, 272.

I shall

I ſhall not now enquire, how far theſe two Fathers and Epiphanius, who was of the ſame opinion, were in the right, in ſuppoſing that Philo's Eſſenes were Mark's Chriſtian converts; but would refer the reader to the authors which I have elſewhere cited upon this queſtion, and a conjecture of my own which I have in the ſame place propoſed[a], relating to this matter.

3. Another thing delivered by the antients to us concerning St. Mark is, *that he was one of the ſeventy Diſciples whom Chriſt ſent forth,* Luke x. 1, &c. *and that he left Chriſt an account of thoſe words of his,* Unleſs a man eat my fleſh, and drink my blood, he is not worthy of me, John vi. 53, &c. *but that he was afterwards reclaimed by Peter, filled with the Holy Ghoſt, and ſo wrote his Goſpel.*——This is related by ſeveral of the old Chriſtian writers; but it will be enough to mention the teſtimony of Epiphanius, who relates the ſtory with all the mentioned particulars[b]. Grotius[c] and Dr. Cave[d] queſtion the truth and genuineneſs of the tradition, becauſe[e] Papias affirms, that *he neither heard nor followed Chriſt.* But to ſay nothing of what is objected againſt Papias as a witneſs in theſe caſes, it is eaſy to anſwer to this argument; for Papias meant no more than that Mark was not ſuch a diſciple and follower of Chriſt, as to be able to form his Goſpel out of his own knowledge; and this is very conſiſtent with Epiphanius, whoſe account is, that Mark, though he was ſent out by Chriſt, yet left him on occaſion of his diſcourſe, John vi. 53. i. e. almoſt two years before our Lord's aſcenſion, and ſo could not be capable to write a hiſtory of Chriſt upon his own knowledge—I rather therefore incline to give credit to the tradition, and with the famous Jeſuit Petavius[f] obſerve, that there is nothing in the circumſtances of time, but what would incline a perſon to believe he might have ſeen Chriſt; and though Epiphanius ſhould think differently in this matter from other Fathers (viz. Papias, and thoſe who follow him),

---

[a] See above, Vol. I. Part II. Ch. XVI. p. 211, &c.
[b] Hæreſ. 51. §. 6.
[c] Proleg. in Marc.
[d] Life of S. Mark, §. 1. p. 214.
[e] Apud Euſeb. Hiſtor. Eccleſ. l. 3. c. 39.
[f] In loc. Epiphan. jam cit.

yet

yet his tradition is not to be rejected, in which he declares that Mark was of the number of the seventy-two Disciples [a].

Concerning the life of Mark in other instances, as also concerning his death, I know nothing that can be said with sufficient certainty. The later writers tell us, that he travelled westward to the most desert parts of Africa, and, upon his return to Alexandria, was by the idolaters there barbarously murdered. But I choose rather to refer to the authors of those relations, than to insert them. See Dorotheus [b], Eutychius Alexandrinus in his Arabick Annals [c], with Mr. Selden's translation and commentary [d], and Isidorus Hispalensis [e], who saith that Mark died, and was *placida quiete sepultus*; and among the moderns Dr. Cave [f], and Mr. Eachard [g], who has transcribed his words. I shall only add here, that there is a constant tradition received in the Roman Church, which is set down as fact by Dr. Cave, " That St. Mark's body, at least " the remains of it, were with great pomp removed from " Alexandria to Venice, where they are religiously honoured, " and he adopted as the tutelar saint and patron of that state, " and one of the richest and stateliest churches erected to his " memory, that the world can boast of at this day." He who would see a larger account of this fabulous translation, viz. when, and by what means, the Venetian merchants procured these reliques of Mark, may consult the learned Spanheim. Hist. Christ. Secul. ix. §. 5. and the authors cited by Mr. Selden, Comment. in Eutych. p. 169.

---

[a] So he read in his copies of Luke x. 1. as it is also in many others, viz. ἰβδομήκοντα δύο, though in the present Greek copies made use of, it is only ἰβδομήκοντα. Vid. Mill. in Luk. x. 1.

[b] In Synopsi.

[c] P. 38.

[d] P. 166—169.

[e] De vit. et obit. Prophet. &c. in fine.

[f] Life of S. Mark, p. 217.

[g] Eccles. Hist. b. 2. c. 6. §. 2.

C H A P. VII.

The Occafion of St. Mark's writing his Gofpel, viz. the Re-
queft of the Church at Rome. That it was wrote under the
Direction of St. Peter. The Places of the Antients pro-
duced, in which this is afferted. The Tradition fupported by
feveral Obfervations.

HITHERTO concerning St. Mark. I proceed now to
difcourfe concerning his Gofpel, and to produce the feveral accounts which we have from antiquity relating to it ;
which I fhall confider under the three following heads, viz.

I. The occafion of its being wrote.

II. The language in which it was wrote.

III. The time of its writing.

I. *As to the occafion or caufe, for which the Gofpel of St.*
Mark was written. This I have had occafion to obferve
largely elfewhere [a], but fhall neverthelefs particularly fet down
here what the antients have delivered to us upon this head.
Papias, Irenæus, Clemens Alexandrinus, Origen, Eufebius,
the author of the Synopfis under the name of Athanafius, and
Jerome, are the perfons whom I mean.

Eufebius out of Papias, and the book which went under the
name of *The Hypotopofes of Clemens Alexandrinus*, relates [b],
That when Peter, in the reign of Claudius, came to Rome, and
had defeated Simon Magus, the people were fo inflamed with
love for the Chriftian truths, as not to be fatisfied with the hear-
ing of them, unlefs they alfo had them written down. That ac-
cordingly they with earneft intreaties applied themfelves to Mark,

---

[a] Vindic. of St. Matth. Gofpel,   [b] Hift. Ecclef. lib. 2. c. 15.
Ch. VI. p. 47.

a companion

a companion of Peter's, and whose Gospel we now have, praying him that he would write down for them, and leave with them an account of the doctrines which had been preached to them: that they did not desist in their request, till they had prevailed upon him, and procured his writing of that which is now called The Gospel of MARK. *That when Peter came to know this, he was, by the direction of* [a] *the Holy Spirit, pleased with the request of the people, and confirmed the Gospel which was written for the use of the Churches.* This, says Eusebius, is related by Clemens Alexandrinus in the sixth book of his *Hypotoposes,* and confirmed by the testimony of Papias, Bishop of Hierapolis.

The same Eusebius, in two other places of his works, relates particularly what Papias and Clemens have wrote concerning Mark's Gospel; viz.

The former says to this purpose, *that Mark, who was Peter's interpreter, exactly wrote down whatsoever he remembered, though not in the same order of time, in which the several things were said or done by Christ; for he neither heard nor followed Christ, but was a companion of Peter, and composed his Gospel rather with the intent of the people's profit, than writing a regular history. So that he is in no fault, if he in some things wrote according to his memory, he designing no more than to omit nothing which he had heard, and to relate nothing false* [b].

The latter, viz. the *Hypotoposes* ascribed to Clemens Alexandrinus [c], relate, that, according to a tradition of the former presbyters, the Gospel of Mark was wrote on the following occasion, viz. *When Peter was publickly preaching the Gospel in Rome, by the influences of the Holy Spirit, many of the converts there desired Mark, as having been a long companion of Peter, and who well remembered what he preached, to write down his discourses; that upon this he composed his Gospel, and*

---

[a] This passage is very ill translated by Valesius, the words ἀποκαλύψαντος αὐτῷ τῦ πνεύματος, being to be referred, not to Peter's knowing the fact, which needed no divine revelation, but to his approving the book.

[b] Apud Euseb. Hist. Ecclef. lib. 3. c. 39.

[c] Apud ejusdem Hist. Ecclef. lib. 6. c. 14.

gave

gave it to thofe who made this requeſt, which when Peter knew, he neither obſtructed nor encouraged the work.

Irenæus[a] only ſays, *that after the death of Peter and Paul, who had been preaching at Rome, Mark, the diſciple and interpreter of Peter, wrote down what he had heard him preach.*

Origen[b] adds, *that Mark wrote his Goſpel according to the dictates or directions of Peter.*

The author of the *Synopſis* under the name of Athanaſius, ſaith the ſame as the laſt.

Jerome[c] tells us, that Mark, the diſciple and interpreter of Peter, *wrote a ſhort Goſpel from what he had heard of Peter, at the requeſt of the brethren at Rome, which when Peter knew, he approved and publiſhed it in the churches, commanding the reading of it by his own authority.*

Theſe are the relations of the antients, concerning the occaſion of St. Mark's writing his Goſpel; as to which I would offer the following remarks.

1. That they all agree, that St. Mark *wrote what he heard or learnt from St. Peter.*

2. *That Euſebius makes Clemens Alexandrinus directly to contradict himſelf in this matter:* for whereas he in one place (viz. lib. 2. c. 15.) ſaith, *that Clemens teſtifies Peter's approbation of the Church of Rome's requeſt to Mark to write, as alſo of the Goſpel written:* in another he ſaith, (viz. lib. 6. c. 14.) *that Peter neither obſtructed nor encouraged Mark in his undertaking.* This is ſo plain a contradiction, that I know not how it can be reconciled. Valeſius has indeed attempted a reconciliation[d], viz. *That Peter privately approved it, but not publickly;* but no one, who conſiders the words, can be ſatisfied with this. I doubt not but the former place is the true one, and that St. Peter did approve the writing of Mark, becauſe ſo many of the primitive writers aſſert it; and if we will ſuppoſe Jerome to have looked into this book of Clemens, which he cites, the matter will be paſt doubt; for he ſaith,

[a] Adv. Hæreſ. lib. 3. c. 1.
[b] Expoſit. in Matt. apud Euſeb. Hiſt. Eccleſ. lib. 6. c. 25.
[c] Catalog. Vir. Illuſtr. in Marco.
[d] Annot. in Euſeb. Hiſt. Eccleſ. lib. 6. c. 14. See Father Simon. Crit. Hiſt. New Teſt. part 1. c. 10.

that there it was faid, that *this Gospel was approved and deli-vered to the churches to be read by Peter.* Catalog. Vir. Il-luſtr. in Marco.

3. It feems more probable *that Mark wrote his Gospel from what he could remember of Peter's difcourfes concerning Chriſt,* than *from the immediate diſtatings of that Apoſtle*; for moſt of the accounts above fuppofe Peter ignorant of his writing, till after he had wrote. See Cotelerius's conjeſture to the fame purpofe; Not. in Conſtit. Apoſtolic. lib. 2. c. 57. and Va-lef. in Eufeb. Hiſt. Ecclef. lib. 3. c. 39.

4. That which is by all writers on this fubjeſt cited as the teſtimony of Papias, ought not to be looked upon fo much to be his, as the teſtimony of *John the Elder*; for it is not only declared by Papias, that *he had all traditions of this fort from Ariſtion and John the Elder*, but he introduces this very tef-timony thus, καὶ τὕτο ὁ πρεσϐύτερος ἔλεγε : i. e. *and this the Elder* (*John*) *faid*, viz. that Mark, the interpreter of Peter, &c.

5. St. Mark's charaſter, as interpreter of St. Peter, does not imply *that Apoſtle to have been deſtitute of the gift of tongues.* The word ἑρμηνευτὴς denotes an expofitor, not only of an un-known language, but of any thing elfe unknown; and in this fenfe, Mark was properly Peter's interpreter, as he was made ufe of particularly to explain to the people, what the Apoſtle had more largely preached. Dr. Cave has another way of ac-counting for the matter; viz. " That though the Apoſtles " were divinely infpired, and among other miraculous powers " had the gift of languages conferred upon them, yet was the " interpretation of tongues a gift more peculiar to fome than " others. This, fays he, might probably be St. Mark's talent " in expounding St. Peter's difcourfes, whether by word or " writing, to thofe who underſtood not the language wherein " they were delivered [a]."

6. *There are fome evidences in the Gospels now received, that St. Mark's Gospel was written according to the preaching or difcourfes of Peter, or that the accounts, which we have from the antients, are true.* This I gather from a remark, which I have

---

[a] Life of St. Mark, p. 214.

elfewhere

elſewhere made [a], and endeavoured to ſupport by proper arguments, viz. *That there are in the Goſpel hiſtory, ſeveral very
remarkable circumſtances relating to, and in favour of, St. Peter,
which are related by the other Evangeliſts, and not ſo much as
mentioned, or hinted at, by St. Mark.* The reaſon of which
ſeems to be, that as St. Peter's modeſty would not allow him
to publiſh and preach them, ſo neither would he ſuffer them to
be inſerted in a Goſpel, which was to go into the world with
his approbation, and even under his name. The paſſages in
the Goſpel, to which I refer, are ſeveral, that ſeem very much
to St. Peter's advantage, and tend to his ſuperiority or advancement above the reſt of the Apoſtles ; which as that Apoſtle
would decline from in preaching, ſo would he not encourage
to be written, and conſequently as they are in the other Goſpels, and not in St. Mark, ſeem clearly to intimate to us,
that St. Mark wrote from the preaching of Peter. I have in
the book laſt cited, collected ſeveral of theſe inſtances, which,
for the ſake of the curious in theſe ſtudies, I ſhall here ſet
down, viz.

*A Catalogue of ſeveral places in the Goſpel hiſtory, which relate
things tending to St. Peter's honour, which are not mentioned
by St. Mark in his Goſpel.*

I. *The account of Chriſt's pronouncing Peter bleſſed, when
he had confeſſed him ; his declaring that he had his faith and
knowledge from God ; his promiſe of the keys and of that large
power, which is made to him,* &c. are omitted by St. Mark,
though the former and ſucceeding parts of this diſcourſe are
both told by him. See Matt. xvi. 16—20. compared with
Mark viii. 29, 30.

II. *The relation of St. Peter's being commiſſioned by Chriſt to
work the miracle, by getting money out of the fiſh's mouth, to pay
the tribute money,* is told by St. Matthew, Ch. xvii. 24, &c.
but omitted by St. Mark, though the preceding and ſubſe-

---

[a] Vindication of St. Matthew's Goſpel, ch. vi. p. 48, &c.

quent ſtories are the very ſame as in St. Matthew. See
Mark ix. 30—33.

III. *Chriſt's particular expreſſions of love and favour to St.
Peter, in telling him of his danger, and that he prayed particu-
larly for him, that his faith might not fail,* is omitted by St.
Mark, but related Luke xxii. 31, 32.

IV. *St. Peter's remarkable humility above the reſt of the
Apoſtles, expreſſed in an unwillingneſs that Chriſt ſhould waſh
his feet, which none of the reſt did expreſs, with Chriſt's particular diſcourſe to him,* &c. John xiii. 6, &c. is omitted by
Mark.

V. *The inſtance of St. Peter's very great zeal for Chriſt,
when he was taken, in cutting off the High-Prieſt's ſervant's ear,*
John xviii. 10. is not mentioned by St. Mark in particular,
but only told in general of a certain perſon that ſtood by,
Mark xiv. 47.

VI. *St. Peter's faith, in leaping into the ſea to go to Chriſt,*
John xxi. 7. is not mentioned by St. Mark.

VII. *Chriſt's diſcourſe with Peter, concerning his love to
him, and his particular repeated charge to him to feed his ſheep,*
John xxi. 15. is omitted by St. Mark.

VIII. *Our Saviour's predicting to Peter his martyrdom, and
the manner of it,* John xxi. 18, 19. is not related by St.
Mark.

Theſe are ſome inſtances of things tending to St. Peter's
honour, recorded by the other Evangeliſts, none of which are
ſo much as hinted at by St. Mark. I add alſo, that there is
not any one ſingle inſtance in all his Goſpel, like to thoſe
mentioned, or which tends to advance the honour and prerogative of Peter above the reſt of the Apoſtles; all which cannot be accounted for by any way more probable, than ſuppoſing that the Apoſtle did not publiſh thoſe circumſtances
which were ſo much in his favour. In this remark I have the

pleasure to join with Eusebius, and the learned Doway pro-
fessor, Estius, whose words are to this purpose; " Why, says
" he, St. Mark should omit in his Gospel those great and ho-
" nourable promises made to St. Peter, which we read Matt.
" xvi. may be seen in Eusebius, Demonstr. Evang. lib. 3. c.
" 7. St. Peter's humility would not suffer him to tell these
" things to St. Mark, when he was writing his Gospel. It is
" remarkable that the three other Evangelists relate those
" things, which tend to advance the honour and prerogative
" of St. Peter : only St. Mark, who wrote his Gospel accord-
" ing to what he heard from St. Peter, hath omitted them ;
" which evidences the great modesty of the Apostle[a]."

Dr. Hammond has another argument, by which he endeavours to prove the truth of the account, given by the antients, of St. Mark's writing under the direction of Peter[b].
After he has produced the account, he adds ; " And of this
" there be some characters discernible in the writing itself ;
" as that, setting down the story of Peter's denying Christ
" with the same enumeration of circumstances, and aggrava-
" tions of the fault, that Matthew doth, when he comes to
" mention his repentance, and tears consequent to it, he doth
" it, as became the true penitent, *more coldly* than Matthew had
" done, only ἴκλαιι, *he wept* ; whereas Matthew hath ἴκλαιι πι-
" κρῶς, *he wept bitterly.*"

7. It is no small proof that the antients' account of St.
Mark's writing his Gospel under the direction of, or from,
Peter is true, that *the Gospel went under the name of Peter,*
and was styled *the Gospel of Peter,* being thought to be wrote
by him. This we are expresly told by Tertullian[c], and not
obscurely by Justin Martyr[d], as I shall shew hereafter.

8. *If the word Babylon,* 1 Pet. v. 13. *be put for Rome,* as
is generally thought by the antients[e], all the Popish writers,

---

[a] In Difficil. Script. loca, in Marc. viii. 29.
[b] Annot. on the title of Matthew.
[c] Evangelium, quod Marcus edidit, Petri affirmetur, cujus interpres Marcus. Adv. Marcion. l. 4.

[c.] 5.
[d] Dialog. cum Tryph. Jud. p. 333.
[e] Euseb. Hist. Eccl. lib. 2. c. 15. Hieron. Catalog. Vir. Illustr. in Marco, et alii passim.

and

and many Proteſtants; we have then hence a farther confirm-
ation of the truth of the antients' account of the occaſion of
St. Mark's writing, viz. his writing from Peter's direction at
Rome; viz. it will hence appear, that St. Mark was with Pe-
ter at Rome, and that he made uſe of him in the ſervice of the
Goſpel, becauſe he calls him his ſon—The words are, *The
Church which is at Babylon* [at Rome], *elected together with
you, ſaluteth you, and ſo doth Mark my ſon* (or aſſiſtant in the
Goſpel-work.)

C H A P. VIII.

*Concerning the Language in which St. Mark wrote his Goſpel.
The Arguments of Baronius and Bellarmine, to prove that he
wrote in Latin, refuted. Concerning the Time of St. Mark's
writing. Two different Opinions propoſed. St. Peter was
at Rome. When he came firſt thither; viz. not till the
ninth or tenth of Nero, or the Year of Chriſt, LXIII. or
LXIV.*

THUS I have given the beſt account I can of the original
of St. Mark's Goſpel, and added ſuch remarks, as appear
to me illuſtrating and confirming of it. I proceed now to
conſider,

II. *In what language this Goſpel of St. Mark was written.*

Beſides Baronius and Bellarmine, and a few zealous Pa-
piſts who have followed them, I know no one but ſubſcribes
to the common report of antiquity, that St. Mark wrote in
Greek. Theſe Cardinals pretend *he wrote in Latin;* but
nothing can be pretended upon more weak arguments: all
their reaſoning may be reduced to the three following heads,
which I ſhall briefly refute ;

1. They urge, *that St. Mark, writing his Goſpel at Rome,*

muſt

*muſt be ſuppoſed to write it in the language, which was moſt in
uſe there at that time;* i. e. in Latin.   But it is eaſy to reply;

(1.) That the *Greek language was very much known and in
uſe at Rome, when St. Mark wrote.* This was the univerſal
language, as Cicero, Seneca [a], and other writers of that time,
aſſure us; and even the very women at Rome ſpake in that
language [b].

(2.) The converts at Rome were, for the moſt part, of the
Jews (as they alſo were in other countries [c]), and theſe gene-
rally underſtood Greek, and made uſe of the Greek Bibles.
Grotius's words are as remarkable as true [d]; "The Jews,
"who dwelt at Rome, were for the moſt part ignorant of the
"Latin tongue, but by means of their long abode in Aſia and
"Greece, had learnt the Greek; and of which language
"there were ſcarce any of the Romans ignorant."

(3.) Hence St. Paul, writing an Epiſtle to the Romans,
wrote it in Greek, and not in Latin.

2. It is urged, that *there are ſeveral Latin words made
Greek in St. Mark's Goſpel,* and thence concluded, that the
whole Goſpel was wrote in Latin.

What can be more abſurd? The argument proves nothing, unleſs it be the directly contrary to what it is brought
for.   He who was tranſlating out of Latin into Greek, can
never be ſuppoſed to put Latin words for Latin words. Accordingly Dr. Mill has juſtly made this an argument to prove
St. Mark wrote firſt in Greek [e]; and there are Latin words in
each of the Evangeliſts, as well as Mark.

3. It is urged, that the Syriack, Arabick, and Perſick Verſions affirm St. Mark to have wrote in Latin.   To which I
anſwer,

---

[a] Orat. pro Arch. Poet. §. 23.
Senec. Conſolat. ad Helv. c. 6.

[b] See Du Pin's Canon of the
New Teſt. ch. 2. §. 4. p. 42.

[c] See above, Vol. I. Part I. Ch.
II. p. 26.

[d] Græce autem ſcripſit Marcus,
quanquam in gratiam præcipue Romanorum, ſicut et Paulus ad Ro-
manos epiſtolam Græca ſcripſit lin-

gua; quia Judæi qui Romæ age-
bant, plerique Latini ſermonis ig-
nari, longa per Græciam et Aſiam
habitatione Græcam linguam didi-
cerant, et Romanorum vix quiſquam
erat non Græce intelligens.   Annot. in Titul. Marci.

[e] Prolegom. in Nov. Teſt. §.
111.

(1.) That

(1.) That theſe epigraphs, or poſtſcripts, at the end of theſe Verſions, are of very uncertain authority.

(2.) That the Arabick and Perſick Verſions are generally agreed, by thoſe who have examined them, *to be made out of the Syriack Verſion*; and Lud. de Dieu has, by a very ingenious and ſolid criticiſm on the Epigraph at the end of the Arabick Verſion of Mark, proved that Verſion to be very late.

(3.) That the Epigraph of the Syriack Verſion, does not affirm Mark to have wrote in Latin, as is generally taken for granted, but only ſaith, that he *ſpoke and preached in Latin at Rome*; the words are, ܘܡܠܠ ܐܘܢܓܠܝܘܢ *He ſpake his Goſpel, and preached it.*

As to the teſtimony of Eutychius Alexandrinus, urged by Baronius, to prove St. Mark to have wrote in Latin, I think there is nothing needful to be ſaid, he being ſo late a writer ; and beſides, Mr. Selden [a] has largely ſhewn that the Arabick word روميـة, *Romana*, may be very well taken to denote the Greek language, and then Eutychius's teſtimony will be, that Mark wrote in Greek. Concerning this whole matter, ſee *Father Simon's Crit. Hiſt. of the New Teſt. Part I. ch. 11.*

III. It remains, that ſome enquiry *be made into the time* when St. Mark wrote his Goſpel. In this matter it is exceeding difficult to come to any clear determination. That which occaſions the difficulty, is the uncertainty we are under as to the time when St. Peter came to Rome. Some have abſolutely denied that he ever was there ; and as they endeavour from Scripture to ſhew, that during the reigns of Tiberius, Caligula, and Claudius, he was either at Jeruſalem, Samaria, or Antioch ; ſo from St. Paul's Epiſtles, which were written from Rome, and that which was written to Rome, all of them in the reign of Nero, they finding no ſalutations ſent to Peter, nor from Peter, they conclude, that he never was at Rome [b]. But theſe ſeem to be arguments too weak to counterbalance

---

[a] Comment. in Eutych. Orig. Alex. p. 152.

[b] See Bunting's Itinerar. tot. Script. in Engliſh, p. 496.

the

the univerfal teftimony of antiquity: there is fcarce any fact which is more generally attefted; fo that for my part, I know not how to deny St. Peter's having been at Rome, without af-ferting at the fame time, that the moft univerfal concurrence of the primitive Chriftians in relating a fact, is not to be de-pended upon. The queftion therefore before us now is, *When St. Peter was at Rome?* I fhall briefly lay down the differing opinions, and then, what appears more probable.

1. The Popifh writers generally affert, that St. Peter came to *Rome in the fecond year of Claudius, or the year of Chrift XLIV* [a]. This is well known: the foundation of their opinion is, that Eufebius in his Ecclefiaftical Hiftory [b] faith; *Peter, by the direction of Providence, came to Rome in the reign of Claudius, to contend with, and overcome Simon Magus*; and in his Chronicon, that *after he had been at Antioch, he went to Rome, in the fecond year of Claudius,* i. e. *the year of Chrift XLIV*. Thofe who are of this opinion, fuppofe the Gofpel of St. Mark to be written at this time, as Eufebius feems alfo to have thought; and fo it is afferted at the end of the Arabick Verfion [c], and of many antient manufcripts of this Gofpel, particularly one mentioned by Dr. Hammond [d], two referred to by Father Simon [e], and thirteen cited by Dr. Mill [f], as it is alfo by Theophylact [g], and others of the Greek Scholiafts.

2. Moft Proteftants, and fome learned writers among the Papifts, *fuppofe Peter's coming to Rome not to have been till many years after,* viz. not till Nero's reign, and the ninth or tenth year of that reign, i. e. about the year of Chrift 63, or 64. The foundations of this opinion are,

(1.) That St. Paul in his Epiftle to the Romans, *does not falute Peter,* though he fpends almoft a whole chapter in fa-luting particular perfons at Rome, and this Epiftle is fuppofed

---

[a] Vid. inter alios Dionyf. Petav. Rationar. Tempor. Par. I. lib. v. c. 3. & Achill. Primin. Gaffar. Epit. Hift. & Chronic. Mundi, p. 93.
[b] Lib. 2. c. 14.
[c] Vid. Lud. de Dieu in Marci cap. ult.
[d] Annot. in Titul. Matth.
[e] Crit. Hift. of the New Teft. Part I. c. 10.
[f] In Marc. cap. ult.
[g] Præfat. in Marc.

to

to be wrote about the year 53, or after, viz. in the end of Claudius's reign [a].

(2.) That upon St. Paul's coming to Rome firſt, which was about the year of Chriſt 58, or 59, viz. in the beginning of Nero, *he neither met with Peter there, nor any ſigns of his having been there*; but on the contrary, found the people there ignorant of, and much unacquainted with, Chriſtianity [b]. See Aɛts xxviii. 21, 22, &c. 28.

For my own part, I cannot but ſuſpeɛt the validity of this argument in part; for it is certain, that, before St. Paul's coming to Rome, there were many converts made there to the Chriſtian religion. The Epiſtle to the Roman converts, was wrote four or five years before Paul was at Rome; and when he came there, the brethren met him, ſome at Appii Forum, ſome at the Three Taverns; Aɛts xxviii. 15. yet, on the other hand, all this may be ſuppoſed, without any Apoſtle's having been there to preach to them; for the Goſpel having been now preached five or ſix and twenty years, it is no way unreaſonable to ſuppoſe it ſhould in this time reach Rome, where there was a general conflux of all ſorts of people. See Dr. Whitby on Aɛts xxviii. 15.

(3.) *That Paul makes no mention of Peter in any one of thoſe Epiſtles, which he wrote from Rome to the churches*; which in all probability he would have done, had Peter been there [c] any part of that time.

(4.) That on the contrary, in his Epiſtle from Rome to the Coloſſians, St. Paul tells them, *that (of the Jews) Mark, ſiſter's ſon to Barnabas, and Jeſus, called Juſtus, were the only fellow-labourers which he had in promoting the kingdom of God, Col.* iv. 10, 11. This evidently excludes Peter [d].

Theſe, with ſome other reaſons, make it evident to me, that St. Peter was not at Rome till the ninth or tenth year of Nero; i. e. till the year of Chriſt 63, or 64. and conſe-

---

[a] See Dr. Cave's Life of Peter, Seɛt. 11.

[b] Cleric. Hiſt. Eccleſ. Secul. I. ad Ann. 61. p. 412. and Dr. Cave loc. cit.

[c] Clerjc. Hiſt. Eccleſ. Secul. 1.

ad Ann. 62. p. 422. et ad Ann. 68. p. 447. Cave, ubi ſupra. Eachard's Eccleſ. Hiſt. b. 2. c. 6. §. 5.

[d] Cave & Cleric. loc. cit.

quently,

quently, that the Gospel of St. Mark was not written before this time, but between this and the martyrdom of this Apostle and St. Paul at Rome, i. e. the year of Christ 67, or 68, which happened at the same time. See the testimonies of Caius in his book against Proculus, and Dionysius, Bishop of Corinth, in his Epistle to the Romans to this purpose, both of whom lived in the second century [a]. I shall only add, that in the small tract of Lactantius, *concerning the death of perse-cutors,* we read, *that Peter came to Rome during Nero's reign, and made a great many converts there, and so formed a church in this place of the empire; which account* (says Bishop Burnet in the preface to his English translation of this tract [b]), *cuts off the fable of Peter's having been there for five and twenty years;* i. e. from the second year of Claudius, or the forty fourth year of Christ; and that in the Arabick Annals of Eutychius Alexandrinus, published by Mr. Selden, the time of writing this Gospel is said to have been in Nero's reign: his words are in English thus, *In the time of Nero Cæsar, Peter, the chief of the Apostles, wrote the Gospel of Mark together with Mark, in the Latin* (Greek) *tongue, in the city of Rome, but he gave the title of it to Mark.*

---

[a] Apud Euseb. Hist. Ecclesiast. lib. 2. c. 25.

[b] Pag. 4. Le Clerc, Secul. 1. ad Ann. 68. p. 448. (though I confess I know not upon what grounds) tells us this book was not wrote (as its editor Baluzius, and Translator Bishop Burnet supposed) by Lactantius, but L. Cæcilius.

CHAP.

CHAP. IX.

*St. Mark's Gospel proved to be Canonical. It is in all the an-
tient Catalogues of sacred Books. It is cited as Scripture by
the primitive Fathers. It was read in their Churches. It
is in the Syriack Collection, or Version. Objections against
its Authority answered. The last Chapter of this Gospel
proved to be genuine and authentick.*

I COME now to establish the Canonical authority of this
Gospel, which I shall endeavour by the following arguments.

Arg. I. The Gospel of St. Mark is of Canonical authority
by Prop. IV. because *it is in all the catalogues of Canonical
books, which we have among the writings of the primitive
Christians.* These catalogues I have collected and referred to
Vol. I. Part I. Ch. VIII. viz. the catalogue of Origen, Eusebius, Athanasius, Cyrill, the Council of Laodicea, Epiphanius, Gregory Nazianzen, Philastrius, Jerome, Ruffin, Austin, the third Council of Carthage, and the author of the
books under the name of *Dionysius the Areopagite.* To which
I add the general proof I have above made in this Part, that
the four Gospels only, which we now receive, were received
by the first Churches of Christians, and approved as Scripture, viz. the three first by St. John the Evangelist, and the
four together by Polycarp, Tatian, Irenæus, Tertullian, Clemens Alexandrinus, Origen, Eusebius, Athanasius, Ambrose,
Jerome, &c. See above in this Part the previous Dissertation.

Arg. II. The Gospel of St. Mark is of Canonical authority, because *it is cited as Scripture in the writings of the primitive Christians,* by Prop. V. How largely and frequently
St. Matthew's Gospel was appealed to by them, we have already seen; and if we do not find St. Mark as often cited, it
cannot be thought strange, because the far greatest part of St.
Mark's

Mark's Gospel, and what is related in it, is also related by St. Matthew. I shall however produce the several places which I have observed.

1. _In the writings_ (as they are called) _of the Apostolick Fathers, I have not observed any places of this Gospel referred to, which are not also in St. Matthew_, and accordingly set down above, as being taken out of that Gospel, though perhaps several of them were taken out of St. Mark. I shall therefore refer the reader to the collection or catalogue of the citations made by these Fathers out of St. Matthew.

2. _In Justin Martyr's works the case is the same as in the Apostolick Fathers_; only _one place_ I have observed, in which he cites something which is in St. Mark's Gospel, and not in St. Matthew's. The place I mean is (Dialog. cum Tryph. Jud. p. 333.) where he saith ; Καὶ τὸ εἰπεῖν μετωνομακέναι αὐτὸν τὸν Πέτρον ἕνα τῶν ἀποσόλων, καὶ γεγράφθαι ἐν τοῖς ἀπομνημονεύμασιν αὐτῦ γεγενημένον : i. e. _It is said that he changed the name of one of his Apostles into Peter_ ; _and the fact is related in his Commentaries or Gospel._ This is not in Matthew, but in Mark iii. 16. we read, Καὶ ἐπέθηκε τῷ Σίμωνι ὄνομα Πέτρον : i. e. _And Simon he surnamed Peter._ It is plain therefore that Justin had seen St. Mark's Gospel; and though indeed this be also related by Luke (vi. 14.), yet it is to me evident he cited Mark, and not Luke, because he says it was written ἐν ἀπομνημονεύμασιν αὐτῦ : i. e. in his Commentaries, viz. the _Commentaries or Gospel of Peter_, whom he had just named, and to whom the word αὐτῦ is undoubtedly to be referred, and not to Christ.

(1.) Because Justin Martyr, though he very _often mentions_ the ἀπομνημονεύματα, or Commentaries of the Apostles, _never once mentions_ the ἀπομνημονεύματα of Christ.

(2.) Because _it is certain the Gospel of Mark went at that time under the name of Peter._ This I have above proved out of Tertullian.

(3.) Because (if I mistake not) _it would not be very elegant Greek to write_ ἀπομνημονεύματα Χριςῦ ; this would be just the same as to call the Gospels in Latin, _Libri_ or _Commentarii Christi_, instead of _Libri_ or _Commentarii de Christo_.

III.

III. IRENÆUS.

St. MARK's *Gospel*.	The *Works of* IRENÆUS.
1 Ch. i. 1, &c.	1 Lib. 3. adv. Hæref. c. 11. 18.
2 —— 24.	2 Lib. 4. adv. Hæref. c. 14.
3 Ch. ix. 23.	3 —— c. 72.
4 —— 44, 46, 48.	4 Lib. 2. c. 56.
5 Ch. xiii. 32.	5 —— c. 48.
6 Ch. xvi. 17, 18. cited together with Luke x. 19.	6 —— c. 36.
7 —— 19.	7 Lib. 3. c. 11.

Note here;

1. That in the firſt and laſt of theſe places Mark *is cited by name*.

2. *That in every one elſe what is cited is in his Goſpel, and not in the others*, except one place which is in Luke.

3. That I have omitted all thoſe places *where there is the ſame in Matthew and Mark, though there is equal reaſon to ſuppoſe*, that Irenæus referred to Mark, as to Matthew.

IV. CLEMENS ALEXANDRINUS.

He has undoubtedly in ſeveral places of his Pædagogus and Stromata (viz. the works which are uſually bound together under his name), cited St. Mark's Goſpel; but inaſmuch as he has not, that I have found, cited it by name, nor produced any places but what are in St. Matthew's Goſpel too, I thought a collection of them would be needleſs; only I would obſerve, that in his little tract, intitled, *Quis Dives ſalvetur?* he has cited a long paragraph out of this Goſpel, viz. from ver. 17. of the tenth chapter to ver. 32. Ταῦτα μὶν ἰν τῷ κατὰ Μάρκον εὐαγſελίῳ γίγραπται; *Theſe things*, ſays he, *are written in the Goſpel according to Mark* (Vid. cap. 4, 5.)

V.

V. TERTULLIAN

Appears plainly to have made use of St. Mark's Gospel, and has many times cited out of it that which is not in any other, and sometimes that which is. I have collected the following instances.

St. MARK'S *Gospel.*	TERTULLIAN's *Works.*
1 Ch. i. 2.	1 Adv. Jud. c. 9. It is true Tertullian seems there to cite the Prophet Malachi iii. 1. but it is very evident he made use of Mark; for he has followed Mark's words, which are different both from the Hebrew and all the Greek copies of the LXX. In the Hebrew it is, I will send my messenger, and he shall prepare the way לפני i. e. *before me*; and so in the LXX. πρὸ προσώπου μου, i. e. *before me*, whereas Mark has it πρὸ προσώπου σου, and ὁδόν σου ἔμπροσθέν σου, i. e. *before thy face, and before thee*; and in this Tertullian follows him, *ante faciem tuam, qui præparabit viam tuam ante te*; i. e. *before thy face, who shall prepare thy way before thee*; which are the very words of Mark, not only differing St.

St. MARK's *Gospel.*	TERTULLIAN's *Works.*
1 Ch. i. 2.	from, but larger than either the Hebrew, or LXX.
2 Ch. i. 24.	2 Lib. adv. Prax. c. 26.
3 Ch. iii. 7.	3 Lib. de Pudicit. c. 21.
4 Ch. v. 9.	4 Lib. de Animâ, c. 25. et de Fugâ. in Perfecut. c. 2.
5 Ch. vii. 3.	5 Lib. de Baptifm. c. 15. Vid. Pamel. in Loc.
6 Ch. viii. 38.	6 Lib. de carne Chrifti, c. 5. et de Præfcript. adv. Gnoft. c. 9.
7 Ch. xiv. 13.	7 Lib. de Baptifm. c. 19.
8 Ch. xvi. 9.	8 Lib. de Animâ, c. 25.
9 ——— 19.	9 Lib. adv. Prax. c. 30.

Thefe are fome places in which Tertullian made ufe of St. Mark's Gofpel, none of which are to be found in St. Matthew; fo that it is as probable he cited this Gofpel in thofe places which are the fame in it and St. Matthew's, as that he cited St. Matthew's; and if fo, it would be eafy to produce almoft half a hundred inftances more.

It would be a fuperfluous tafk and endlefs labour to go, in like manner as above, through all the writers of the firft four centuries, and collect the citations which they have made of this Gofpel. Origen, Eufebius, Athanafius, Epiphanius, Jerome, Auftin, &c. have made too many references to this Gofpel to require a collection of them; befides, feveral of the Fathers of thefe times have wrote Commentaries or Homilies upon this Gofpel, as on the other parts of Scripture; which, with what is already faid, is enough to evince its Canonical authority by Prop. V.

Arg. III. The Gofpel of St. Mark is of Canonical authority (by Prop. VI.), becaufe *it was read as Scripture among the other books of facred Scripture in the Affemblies or Churches of the primitive Chriftians.* This will be evident to every one
who

who will confult Cyrill of Jerufalem, the fifty-ninth Canon of
the Council of Laodicea, as above referred to Part I. Ch. X.
and in this Part above, concerning St. Matthew, Chap. III.
where it is alfo fhewn, that in Juftin Martyr's time the Gofpels were wont to be read in the Churches; and as Juftin did
efteem St. Mark's Gofpel to be a true one, and cited it as
fuch, there can be no reafon to queftion but he includes this
among thofe other ἀπομνημονεύματα, or memoirs of the Apoftles,
which were read in the Churches.

Arg. IV. St. Mark's Gofpel is Canonical, becaufe *it was
efteemed fo by the Churches of Syria in or near the Apoftles' time,
and accordingly by them in thofe days tranflated, and inferted in
their collection of facred books*; Prop. XV. At the end of this
Gofpel in Syriack we accordingly read,

ܡܠܡ ܐܘܢܓܠܝܘܢ ܩܕܝܫܐ ܕܟܪܘܙܘܬܗ ܕܡܪܩܘܣ ܕܐܡܠܠ ܘܟܪܙ
ܪܗܘܡܐܝܬ ܒܪܗܘܡܝ;

i. e. *The end of the Holy Gofpel of the preaching of Mark,
which he fpake and preached in Latin at Rome.*

Having thus endeavoured to eftablifh the Canonical authority of this Gofpel of St. Mark, I fhall now briefly confider
that which has been or may be objected againft it.

1. It may feem a very confiderable objection againft this
Gofpel and its authority, *that it feems to be only an epitome, or
abridgment of St. Matthew's Gofpel.*

To this I anfwer, that were the fact certain, and it could be
made appear, that St. Mark did tranfcribe his Gofpel out of St.
Matthew's, it would very much weaken its authority, and
leffen the credit of its infpiration. This I have elfewhere
more largely obferved (viz. Vindicat. of St. Matthew's Gofpel, Ch. X.), and fhewn how abfurd it is to fuppofe a perfon
under the conduct of infpiration, tranfcribing or ftealing out
of another's labours. The little neceffity there is for infpiration in fuch a cafe, is no mean argument that there was none
at all. What need had a man of the guidance of the Holy
Ghoft, to read and write out here and there a piece of a hiftory,
where

where he had a mind? How odd is it to say, The Holy Spirit inspired one person to write a history, and then inspired another to abridge it! i. e. The Holy Spirit thought fit at first to have so much wrote, but then afterwards that it should not be quite so much, but the superfluities of his first work should be left out. Farther, as the supposing St. Mark an epitomiser of St. Matthew lessens the credit of inspiration, so it detracts from the honour and usefulness of St. Mark's work. It is little better than to say, this Gospel was stolen, and the author a plagiary; and accordingly Ruffin in the fourth century, and some bigotted Papists since, have called it *Religiosum Furtum*, a religious theft, or pious fraud [a]. Accordingly Spinoza [b] and Father Simon have by this very means attempted to ruin the credit of the books of the Old Testament, viz. by asserting them to be only extracts out of larger records now lost. All this and much more would follow, if we suppose St. Mark's Gospel an epitome of St. Matthew's; but the truth is, the world hath been mistaken entirely in the fact; and though some among the antients, and almost all later writers have asserted it, *it is utterly false*, and most evident, that St. Mark did not abridge St. Matthew, as I have in another book proved, by such arguments as appear to me undeniably conclusive; which I shall think it sufficient to refer the reader to [c], with what is above said in this work, Part I. Ch. XIII. Prop. XIV.

II. It is objected, *that Mark himself was not an Apostle and eye-witness of what he wrote, but only a companion of the Apostles, and consequently his Gospel is, and ought to be of no more authority, than the writings of Barnabas, Clemens, or any other companion of the Apostles.* This is urged by Mr. Toland, Amynt. p. 47, 48. His words are, " If they think them " (viz. the Epistle of Barnabas, Clemens, &c.) genuine, why " do they not receive them into the Canon of Scriptures, " since they were the companions and fellow-labourers of the

---

[a] See Chemnit. Exam. Concil. Trident. Pars. 1, p. 34.

[b] Tract. Theolog. Polit. c. 8.

and c. 9. in init.

[c] Vindicat. of St. Matthew, c. 6, &c.

" Apostles,

" Apoſtles, as well as St. Mark and St. Luke ? If this qua-
" lity was ſufficient to entitle the two laſt to inſpiration, why
" ſhould it not do as much for the two firſt ? And if this be
" not all the reaſon, pray let us know the true one, having
" never heard of any other."

. To all this I anſwer ;

1. That St. Mark is *not received as Canonical,* only becauſe
he was a companion of the Apoſtles, but becauſe *he wrote under
the direction of an inſpired Apoſtle St. Peter* ; *and who,* as Euſebius ſaith, *approved the book* ἀποκαλύψαντος αὐτῷ τοῦ πνεύματος,
i. e. *by the revelation of the Holy Ghoſt* [a].

2. That St. Mark's Goſpel *was approved by St. John,* as I
have above ſhewn ; ſee the Diſſertation prefixed to this
Part.

3. That *it was received by the primitive Churches as Canonical,* was read in their Aſſemblies, and cited in their writings as Scripture ; which cannot be proved of Clemens, Barnabas, &c.

4. That it contains nothing falſe or fabulous ; which I
have proved above, Part III. Ch. XLI. &c. that the Epiſtle
of Barnabas doth, and ſhall hereafter prove of Clemens.

It would ſcarce be juſtice to St. Mark, and the ſubject
which I have now in hand, if I ſhould finiſh it without obſerving, that whatever has been ſurmiſed to the contrary, *the
laſt chapter of this Goſpel is equally Canonical with any other
part.* The matter has been controverted, and there have been
thoſe who have thought it ſhould be excluded from the Canon ; I mean not the whole chapter (as many, Eraſmus,
Beza, Druſius, &c. *in loc.* have falſely underſtood the queſtion), but only that part of it which is after the words ἐφοβοῦντο
γὰρ, i. e. *after the end of the eighth verſe.* The reaſon of this
controverſy is, that Jerome in a letter to Hedibia, who deſired
him to reconcile the differences between the Evangeliſts Matthew and Mark, about our Saviour's reſurrection, anſwers,
" That there were two ways of ſolving the difficulty, viz.
" Either we muſt reject the teſtimony of Mark, *which is in*

[a] Hiſt. Eccleſ. lib. 2. c. 15.

" *few*

" *few copies of his Gospel, almost all the Greek copies wanting*
" *this section in the end of his Gospel, besides that it seems dif-*
" *ferent from, and contrary to, the accounts of the other Evan-*
" *gelists,* &c [a]." (The other answer I need not mention.)
And besides Jerome, Gregory Nyssene says, this last section
was wanting in several, *and those the most exact copies* [b]. Besides, Father Simon declares [c], that he saw two antient Greek
manuscripts in the French King's library, and one in Mon-
fieur Colbert's, in each of which was inserted a note in Greek
to this purpose, *that what followed after, ver. 8. in this last*
chapter of Mark, was only to be found in some copies. Dr. Mill
has mentioned some old Greek Scholiasts, viz. Euthymius,
Victor Antiochenus, and an anonymous writer, who says the
same [d].   But to all this I answer, and will endeavour to shew,
that this last part of the Gospel of St. Mark is equally authentick with the rest; for

1. Though Jerome says, this section was not in most of
the Greek copies of this Gospel, yet *he himself seems not to have*
rejected it, because he endeavours afterwards to reconcile Matthew and Mark together.

2. Because Irenæus (lib. 3. c. 11.) *has cited the nineteenth*
verse of this chapter, which is the last except one, and introduces it thus; *In fine autem Evangelii ait Marcus:* from
whence it is evident, that the whole chapter was in his copy
of Mark.

3. Athanasius [e] and Austin [f] have also cited this part of St.
Mark's Gospel.

---

[a] Hujus quæstionis duplex est so-
lutio: aut enim non recipimus Marci testimonium, quod in raris fertur
evangeliis, omnibus Græcis libris
pæne hoc capitulum in fine non ha-
bentibus; præsertim quum diversa
atque contraria evangelistis cæteris
narrare videatur: aut hoc respon-
dendum, quod uterque verum dixe-
rit, &c. Epist. ad Hedib. qu. 3.

[b] Apud Mill. Not. in Marc.
xvi. 8. et Fabric. Cod. Apocr.
Nov. Test. tom. 1. p. 326. *who has*

observed after Combefisius, who pub-
lished them, and Dr. Cave's Hist.
Liter. p. 443, *that those two ora-*
tions, de Resurrectione Christi, *under*
the name of Gregory Nyssene, were
made by Hesychius Hierosolymitanus.

[c] Crit. Hist. of the New Test.
Part 1. c. 11.

[d] Loc. jam cit.

[e] In Synops.

[f] De Consens. Evang. l. 3. c.
24.

4. *All the Greek manuſcripts which are in the world, have this part of St. Mark's Goſpel.* Eraſmus [a] and Beza [b] declare, it was in all the antient manuſcripts which they had ſeen.

5. *All the antient Verſions extant, Syriack, Latin, and* (as I find by De Dieu's Commentary) *Arabick, have it.*

6. Grotius [c] well argues, that *it, was very improbable St. Mark would omit the hiſtory of our Saviour's reſurrection, which is one of the moſt conſiderable parts of the Goſpel hiſtory.*

7. The ſame learned critick aſſigns this probable reaſon of this ſection being wanting in ſome Greek copies, viz. *It was left out with deſign, becauſe it ſeemed to contradict St. Matthew, that Porphyry, Julian, and ſuch others, might not take occaſion thence to ridicule the Goſpel,* as Mr. Fabricius [d], who follows Grotius, well obſerves, and adds, that it is a caſe like what happened to thoſe words (Mar. xiii. 32.) ἐδὲ ὁ υἱὸς, *neither the Son,* that they might the better evade the force of the Arian objections.

---

[a] Annot. in Mar. xvi. 14.
[b] Annot. in Mar. xvi. 9.
[c] Annot. in Mar. xvi. 1.

[d] Cod. Apocr. Nov. Teſtam. Par. 1. p. 337.

CHAP.

CHAP. X.

The Scripture Accounts of St. Luke. The Accounts of him from Antiquity, viz. that he was born at Antioch. Arguments to prove that he was not a Jew. He was a Physician. Of his painting. He was one of Christ's Seventy Disciples. An Objection to this answered. St. Luke was St. Paul's Companion and Assistant. Was acquainted with several of the Apostles. Concerning his Death.

IN treating of this Gospel, I shall endeavour to proceed in the same method as in the preceding Gospel ; viz. *first* to *give some account of the author, and then of his Gospel.*

As to St. Luke, the author of this Gospel, I shall distinctly consider,

I. What is said of him in the writings of the New Testament.

II. What is related concerning him in the antient writings of the Christians, which is credible.

I. *As to what is said of St. Luke the Evangelist in the writings of the New Testament.* The name is mentioned, Col. iv. 14. *Luke the beloved physician and Demas greet you.* 2 Tim. iv. 11. *Only Luke is with me.* Philem. 24. *Marcus, Aristarchus, Demas, Lucas, my fellow-labourers.* Concerning which places I observe, that it has been generally supposed by antient and modern writers, that Luke the Evangelist, or author of the Gospel, *is the person meant in each of those places.* Erasmus [a] indeed, and after him Calvin [b], suppose *another person meant, Col.* iv. 14. *by Luke the beloved physician.* The whole foundation of their opinion is, that it would have been needless for Paul to have given him the distinguishing character of a physician, he being a person more known than to need such a mark of distinction; and that it is much more reasonable to

---

[a] Annot. in Col. iv. 14.   [b] In eund. loc.

                 suppose

suppose St. Paul would have called him here, as he does elsewhere, his companion, or fellow-labourer. But to this it may be answered;

1. That there was no reason, why St. Paul should not give him this title, if it belonged to him.

2. That it is certain, Luke the Evangelist was now with St. Paul at Rome, when he wrote this Epistle from thence to the Colossians.

3. That he is named together with Demas in this place, as well as the others, about which there is no dispute.

4. That he is generally said to have been a physician in the antient writings.

Although there are no other places in the New Testament, in which we meet with the name of Luke, yet there are two places, in which it has been thought that St. Paul referred to him, viz.

(1.) That, Rom. xvi. 21. *Timotheus, my work-fellow, and Lucius, and Jason, and Sosipater, my kinsmen, salute you.* Some of the antients (as Origen [a] saith) *thought this Lucius to be Luke the Evangelist, who wrote the Gospel; and that his name received this little alteration according to the peculiar idiom of the country.* Sixtus Senensis seems to have been of the same opinion [b]; but this opinion seems evidently precarious, it being unaccountable that Paul should call the same person by two such different names.

(2.) The person intended by St. Paul, 2 Cor. viii. 18. in those words, *We have sent — the brother, whose praise is in the Gospel, throughout all the Churches,* is supposed by most of the antient and modern writers to have been Luke the Evangelist. So Origen [c], Jerome [d], and the interpolator of the Epistles of Ignatius [e], among the antients; Sixtus Senensis [f], Grotius [g],

---

[a] In Epist. ad Rom. xvi. 21. tom. 3. fol. 223. Sed et Lucium perhibent quidam esse Lucam, qui Evangelium scripsit, pro eo quod soleant nomina interdum secundum patriam declinationem, interdum etiam secundum Græcam Romanamque proferri.

[b] Bibl. Sanct. lib. 1. in Luc.

[c] Præfat. in Luc.

[d] Catalog. Vir. illustr. in Luc. Epist. ad Paulin. et Præf. in Com. in Matth.

[e] Epist. ad Ephes. §. 15.

[f] Loc. jam cit.

[g] Annot. in 2 Cor. viii. 18.

Dr.

Dr. Hammond [a], Dr. Cave [b], Dr. Whitby [c], and many others; although Chryfoftom, and fome of the antients, followed herein by Calvin [d], and others, fuppofe that Barnabas was the perfon meant; and Dr. Lightfoot endeavours largely to prove it was neither, but Mark the Evangelift [e].

II. *The credible accounts which we have from antiquity, concerning this Evangelift, are very fhort and imperfect.* I have collected what has fallen within my obfervation, under the following heads.

1. Many of the antients tell us, *that St. Luke was born at Antioch in Syria.* So Eufebius [f]; *He was of a family of Antioch.* Jerome [g]; *He was a phyfician of Antioch.* Dorotheus Tyrius [h], and Theophylact [i], &c. fay the fame. This tradition is fo much the more probable, as it is certain that St. Luke was not a Jew; and this appears to me certain:

(1.) Becaufe St. Luke, in his Hiftory of the *Acts of the Apoftles* (Ch. i. 19.), fpeaking of the field, which was purchafed with the money for which Judas fold our Saviour, fays, *it was called* Aceldama ἐν τῇ ἰδίᾳ διαλέκτῳ αὐτῶν: i. e. *in* THEIR *own language*; which plainly intimates, that the Syriack, or Syro-Chaldaick, i. e. the peculiar dialect of the Jews was not HIS language.

(2.) Becaufe St. Paul diftinguifhes him from thofe who were of the circumcifion, Col. iv. 10, 11. compared with 14. He faith, that Marcus, Ariftarchus, and Jefus called Juftus, were *the only fellow-labourers of the circumcifion who were with him*; yet it is plain that Epaphras, Demas, and Luke, were *fellow-labourers, that were then with him*; wherefore thefe were not of the circumcifion.

---

[a] Paraphr. ejufdem loci.
[b] Life of St. Luke, §. 2. p.223.
[c] In 2 Cor. viii. 18.
[d] In eund. loc.
[e] Harmon. of the New Teft. year 56.
[f] Λουκᾶς δὲ τὸ μὲν γένος ὢν τῶν ἀπ' Ἀντιοχείας. Hift. Eccl. lib. 3. c.4.
[g] Catalog. Viror. illuftr. in Luca, et Præfat. in Comment. ad Matth.
[h] In Synopf.
[i] Præfat. in Luc.

(3.) It was an obfervation among the antients, as it has been among many more modern writers, *that St. Luke's Gofpel and Acts are written in very pure and elegant Greek.* He was well acquainted *with the Greek language, as appears by his writings,* fays Jerome [a]; and in another place [b] he tells us, that *he was more fkilful in the Greek language than any of the Evangelifts, and would rather forbear tranflating a Hebrew word, than do it in Greek, which was not pure and elegant.* Ifidorus Hifpalenfis ftiles him *learned in the Greek tongue* [c]; and among the moderns, to omit all others, Dr. Cave [d] has expreffed the common opinion of learned men thus; " He " all along expreffes himfelf in a vein of purer Greek, than is " to be found in the other writers of the holy ftory. Indeed, " being born and bred at Antioch (than which no place more " famous for oratory and eloquence), he could not but carry " away a great fhare of the native genius of that place, though " his ftile is fometimes allayed with a tang of the Syriack and " Hebrew dialect." All this proves St. Luke not to have been a Jew; and accordingly it was a commonly received tradition in the fifth or fixth century, that he was a profelyte to the Jewifh religion, and ignorant of the Hebrew language, which (if we will credit Theophylact [e]) he afterwards went to Jerufalem to learn.

2. It is conftantly affirmed by the antients, that *St. Luke the Evangelift was a phyfician.* So we read in the places above-cited of Eufebius, Jerome, Dorotheus Tyrius, Ifidorus Hifpalenfis, and many others; and I have above obferved, that he feems to be the perfon whom Paul, Col. iv. 14. calls *the beloved Phyfician.* This (as Dr. Cave well obferves [f]) does by no means prove the dignity of his birth and fortune; this art being in thofe days generally managed by fervants. Upon which account, Grotius [g] fuppofes Luke to have been brought a fervant from Antioch to Rome, and there to have practifed phyfick. Concerning his fkill in painting, and the

[a] Catalog. Vir. illuftr. in Luca.
[b] Epift. ad Damaf.
[c] De vit. et obit. Sanctor. lib. 1. p. 599. Orthodoxogr. Vol. I.
[d] Life of St. Luke, §. 5.
[e] Præfat. in Luc.
[f] Life of St. Luke, §. 1.
[g] Annot. in Luc. 1.

feveral

feveral pictures which he drew of the Virgin Mary, fo much talked of by the Papifts, I fhall fay nothing, all this appearing to be the fiction of later ages. The firft time I find any mention of it, is in the beginning of the fixth century, when Theodore Lector tells us [a], that Eudocia, the wife of the Emperor Theodofius Junior, fent from her exile at Jerufalem (about the year of Chrift, 448) the image, or picture of the Virgin to Pulcheria, the Emperor's fifter, which was painted by Luke the Apoftle. The Papifts tell us of feveral of thefe at Kome and Conftantinople, and furprizing miracles wrought by them. See Monf. Durant de Ritibus Ecclef. Cathol. lib. 1. c. 5. p. 35.

3. It is probable, *St. Luke was one of thofe feventy difciples, which our Saviour fent forth*; Luke x. 1, &c. This is afferted by feveral of the primitive writers; fo Origen [b], Epiphanius [c], Hippolitus [d], &c. and fhould not, I think, without fome cogent reafons to the contrary, be rejected as falfe. I know indeed, that Dr. Cave [e], Du Pin [f], and others, have oppofed the tradition; becaufe, in the beginning of his Gofpel, he fays, he wrote not what he was an eye-witnefs of, and had feen, but that which he had learned from others. But to this I would reply;

That if we fuppofe St. Luke to have been one of the feventy difciples, it does not thence follow, that he muft needs be acquainted with, and have perfonally feen, all which he wrote concerning Chrift. But on the contrary, the very fuppofition excludes him from a great deal of perfonal knowledge of Chrift's actions, partly as the feventy were not chofen by Chrift till the laft year of his miniftry, and partly as their being fent abroad, neceffarily prevented their perfonal knowledge of what Chrift and his difciples did, during that fpace. St. Luke, therefore, might have been one of the feventy dif-

---

[a] Collectan. lib. 1. ipfo initio.
[b] Dialog. de recta fide. *That dialogue has been queftioned; and though Wetftenius contends for its genuinenefs, yet, I think, it is generally agreed not to belong to Origen.* Cave's Hift. Liter. Vol. 1. p. 84.

[c] Hæref. 51. §. 11.
[d] MS. in Bibl. Bodleian. apud Mill. Præf. in Luc.
[e] Life of Luke, §. 2.
[f] Hift. of Can. of New Teft. Ch. 2. §. 5.

　　　　　　　　　ciples

ciples of Chrift, though he was not fo long or fo much with Chrift, as to be able to write a hiftory of Chrift's life and actions from his own perfonal knowledge. This feems to me a much better folution of the difficulty, than that which Dr. Whitby has attempted, vainly endeavouring to prove, that *St. Luke's preface fhews him to have been an eye-witnefs of all that he wrote,* than which nothing can be more repugnant to the plain conftruction of the words [a].

4. *St. Luke was for a long time the conftant companion of St. Paul in his travels, and his affiftant in the work of the miniftry.* This is proved both from the New Teftament, and the Fathers. In the *Acts of the Apoftles,* (xvi. 10, &c.) which book, at prefent I fhall take for granted, was written by Luke, we find him accompanying St. Paul in his voyage from Troas to Macedonia; for he fpeaks there in the firft perfon plural, *Immediately we endeavoured to go into Macedonia;* and ver. 11. *Therefore loofing from Troas, we came with a ftrait courfe,* &c. and ver. 13. *On the fabbath we went out of the city, and we fat down, and we fpake to the women.* See ver. 16, 17, &c. The twentieth and twenty firft chapters tell us of Luke's accompanying Paul to Jerufalem, as the twenty feventh does of his going along with him to Rome; and accordingly St. Paul in feveral of his Epiftles, written from Rome, mentions St. Luke, as being with him there. See the places above. Nothing is more commonly affirmed by the antients; as Irenæus [b], Eufebius [c], Jerome [d], Ifidorus Hifpalenfis [e], &c. nor has it, that I know of, ever been queftioned.

5. *St. Luke was acquainted with feveral of the Apoftles.* This indeed feems neceffarily to follow, from his having been one of the feventy difciples, and the companion of St. Paul at Jerufalem, and fo many other places. Eufebius exprefsly tells us [f], *that he lived a long time with Paul, and was intimately acquainted with the reft of the Apoftles.* The fame we find alfo in Dorotheus Tyrius [g].

---

[a] Præf. on Luke.
[b] Adv. Hæref. lib. 3. c. 14.
[c] Hift. Eccl. lib. 3. c. 4.
[d] Catalog. Vir. Illuftr. in Luc.
[e] De vir. et obit. Sanctor. inter

Orthodoxograph. Vol. I. p. 599.
[f] Loc. jam cit. Τοῖς λοιποῖς δὲ ὁ παρέργως τῶν ἀποϛόλων ὡμιληκώς.
[g] In Synopf.

6. Epi-

6. Epiphanius says, that he preached the Gospel in Dalmatia, France, Italy and Macedonia[a].

7. Concerning his death there is scarce any thing certain. Jerome[b] tells us, *that he lived eighty four years, never married, was buried at Constantinople, being brought thither* (viz. his bones and reliques, together with those of the Apostle Andrew) *in the twentieth year of Constantius, from Achaia.* Dorotheus says[c], *he died and was buried at Ephesus, and that his reliques were brought, with those of Timothy and Andrew, to Constantinople, in the time of Constantius.* Isidorus Hispalensis[d] also relates the account of *his bones being translated to Constantinople,* but will have it to have been in the time of Constantine, not Constantius ; and that he died in the seventy fourth year of his age, and was buried in Bithynia. Aldhelmus[e], an abbot of Malmsbury, in the year 680, tells us likewise that he lived to the age of seventy four, and then died in an unmarried state, and that Constantine brought his bones to Constantinople. Concerning the manner of his death I have met with nothing, but that Nicephorus relates[f] his being hanged upon an olive-tree in Greece ; and Hippolitus[g], that according to some, he was burnt, according to others, was crucified upon an olive-tree. Some later disputes about St. Luke's body among the Papists, see in Spanheim. Histor. Christ. Secul. xv. p. 1336. Hitherto concerning St. Luke.

[a] Hæref. 51. §. 11.
[b] Catalog. Vir. Illustr. in Luca.
[c] In Synopf.
[d] De vit. et obit. Sanctor. inter Orthodoxograph. Vol. I. p. 599.
[e] De laudib. Virginit. inter Orthodoxograph. Vol. II. p. 1690.
[f] Lib. 2. c. 43. & D. Cave's Life of St. Luke, §. 3.
[g] MS. in Bibl. Bodleian. apud Mill. Procem. in Luc.

CHAP. XI.

Of St. Luke's Gospel. It was wrote from the information of the Apostles, and other Eye-witnesses of Christ's Actions. Also under the Direction and Approbation of St. Paul. The Design of it to confute the Apocryphal Gospels. An Enquiry into the Time of its being written.

I PROCEED now to give *some account of that Gospel* which we have under the name of St. Luke. Concerning which, I observe,

1. *That the Evangelist wrote it from the informations and relations of those, who were eye-witnesses of the things which it contains.* For though we cannot yet take his own testimony in the matter, (who ch. i. 2. saith, *he wrote the things, which were delivered unto him by those, who from the beginning were eye-witnesses and ministers of the word*) yet there is so much other evidence of the truth of the fact, that it cannot with any reason be disputed. Irenæus [a] saith, *that Luke has delivered to us, what the Apostles delivered to him.* This Tertullian calls *authenticam paraturam* [b]; i. e. *authentick intelligence, or sufficient and credible informations, out of which he compiled his Gospel.* Eusebius [c] testifies, *that he conversed intimately with the Apostles, and that he left the doctrines of curing souls, which he learned from them, in two divinely inspired volumes.* To the same purpose with all these, Jerome saith, *that Luke wrote not only what he learnt from Paul, but the other Apostles* [d]. This tradition receives no small confirmation from St. Luke's having been one of the seventy disciples, and so much with St. Paul at Jerusalem, and elsewhere, that it cannot without

---

[a] Adv. Hæref. lib. 3. c. 14. Ea quæ ab iis didicerat, tradidit nobis.
[b] Adv. Marcion. lib. 4. c. 2.
[c] Hist. Eccl. lib. 3. c. 4.

[d] Catalog. Vir. Illuftr. in Luca. Non folum a Paulo didiciffe Evangelium—fed a cæteris Apoftolis.

manifest

manifeſt abſurdity be ſuppoſed, that he knew none of the Apoſtles, or learnt nothing from them.

2. It is probable that *St. Luke's Goſpel was wrote under
the direction, and publiſhed with the approbation of St. Paul.*
Thus much at leaſt ſeems evident from the teſtimonies of
Irenæus[a], who carries the matter ſo far as to aſſert, *that Luke
compoſed his Goſpel out of what Paul preached*; of Tertullian,
who adds[b], *that St. Luke's Goſpel was aſcribed to Paul as its
author, for thoſe things may ſeem to be the maſter's, which the
diſciples have publiſhed.* How much this was the opinion of
the antients, will farther appear from this notion, which ſeems
to have been common among them, that when Paul in any of
his Epiſtles uſes the words, MY GOSPEL, (as he does Rom.
ii. 16. 2 Tim. ii. 8.) he particularly meant this Goſpel of
Luke. This was thought by ſeveral before Euſebius[c], and
Jerome[d]; and though Mr. Fabricius[e] will not believe it to
be ſo, yet it ſhews us clearly, that it was the common opinion
of thoſe times, that St. Paul was concerned in publiſhing this
Goſpel of St. Luke; to which I conceive alſo, that of Origen
is to be referred, where he ſaith, that the Goſpel of Luke was
ὑπὸ Παυλοῦ ἐπαινούμενον, i. e. *commended, or cited by Paul*[f]. But
how much ſoever St. Paul was concerned in approving or
directing the publication of this Goſpel, it is certainly a miſtake in Irenæus, and thoſe who have followed him, to ſuppoſe
St. Luke wrote only what he heard Paul preach, becauſe himſelf ſaith, and I have above proved, that he wrote what thoſe
who were eye-witneſſes delivered to him, of which number
St. Paul was not. I therefore choſe rather to lay it down in
my propoſition, that St. Paul approved or directed the publiſhing of this Goſpel, than that he dictated it.

3. *The particular view or deſign, which St. Luke had* in this
Goſpel, ſeems to have been, *to confute them any ſilly Apocryphal*

---

[a] Καὶ Λυκᾶς δὲ ὁ ἀκόλυθος
Παύλυ τὸ ὑπ' ἐκείνυ κηρυσσόμενον
εὐαγγέλιον ἐν βιβλίῳ κατέθετο.
Adv. Hæreſ. lib. 3. c. 1. Græc.
vid. ap. Euſ. H. E. lib. 5. c. 8.

[b] Nam et Lucæ digeſtum Paulo
adſcribere ſolent. Adv. Marcion.

lib. 4. c. 5.

[c] Loc. jam cit.

[d] Loc. jam cit.

[e] Cod. Apocr. Nov. Teſt. tom.
1. p. 372, &c.

[f] Apud Euſeb. Hiſt. Eccl. l. 6.
c. 25.

Gospels which were then extant, and to prevent the bad influence of them, and their heretical doctrines, upon the Christian converts. This is what is so manifest from the first words of the Gospel, and the universal voice of antiquity, that I need say no more, only shall refer the reader to the first Volume, Part I. Ch. II. p. 24. and the places there cited. Besides this, which is allowed by all as the principal occasion of St. Luke's writing his Gospel, there have been other more particular reasons guessed at by learned men. The two French criticks, Father Simon[a] and Du Pin[b], conjecture, that he wrote it *at the desire of Theophilus,* to whom he dedicates it; Dr. Grabe[c] and Dr. Mill[d] suppose, *that St. Luke wrote it in Egypt, and with a particular design to confute the Gospel of the Egyptians,* (of which above, Vol. I. Part II. Ch. XVI. &c.) but as the first of these seems but little to agree with the received notions of inspiration, so the latter seems very improbable, because we not only want any good evidence of St. Luke's having ever been in Egypt, but because we find none of those, which we know to have been the peculiar doctrines of the Egyptian Gospel, so much as once referred to in this of St. Luke.

4. *The time or period in which this Gospel was wrote, is very uncertain,* there being not (as far as I know) any monuments of antiquity, by which it can be fixed, or determined. The antients generally place the writing of this Gospel after those two of St. Matthew and St. Mark. In this order I find them ranged by Origen[e], Eusebius[f], Jerome[g], and many other writers of those times; from whence it is plain, they were bound together in their volumes in the order which they are now; this, I think, can be no better way accounted for, than by supposing, that they did imagine them written in the same order; and accordingly they are placed in all the old

---

[a] Critic. Hist. of the New Test. Part i. c. 12.
[b] Hist. of the Canon of the New Test. Vol. 2, c. 2. §. 5.
[c] Spicileg. Patr. Secul. I. p. 33, 34.

[d] Prolegom. in Nov. Test. §. 114.
[e] Apud Euseb. Hist. Eccl. l. 6. c. 25.
[f] Lib. 3. c. 24.
[g] Præf. in Comment. in Matth.

manu-

manuscripts, of which I have met with any account [a], except in that very antient manuscript of Beza, now called *The Cambridge Manuscript*, being given by Beza to that University. In this manuscript, the order stands thus [b]; Matthew is placed first, then John, after him Luke, then Mark. It is certain, this was not the order in which the Evangelists wrote; and it is very probable the writer of this manuscript intended to place first those of the Evangelists who were Apostles, viz. Matthew and John, and then those who were not, Luke and Mark; supposing perhaps, that as John wrote after Matthew, so Mark did after Luke. But according to the general opinion of the antients, Luke wrote after Mark; the particular time they have not determined. According to several old manuscripts, St. Luke wrote his Gospel fifteen years after the ascension of Christ [c], viz. about the year 49, but this must certainly be a mistake; for if he wrote after Mark, he must write after the year of Christ 63; i. e. above thirty years after our Saviour's ascension; for I have above proved, that Mark did not write till after that time. Jerome informs us, that St. Luke wrote in the regions of Achaia and Bithynia [d]; and as his words are commonly understood by Grotius [e], Dr. Cave [f], Father Simon [g], and others, that he wrote it when he accompanied St. Paul into those parts. If this be true, it was wrote about the year of Christ 52, or 53; but this is upon many accounts improbable; for, upon a close observation of Jerome's words, I find they have hitherto been quite misunderstood; and it is evident,

1. That Jerome does not say that Luke wrote his Gospel, while he was with Paul in Achaia and Bithynia; he only asserts, according to the common punctuation of the words, that he was a disciple of Paul, and composed his Gospel in Achaia and Bithynia; *Lucas—Discipulus Apostoli Pauli, in Achaiæ*

---

[a] See Father Simon's Critic. Hist. of the New Test. Part i. c. 10.

[b] Vid. Bez. in Titul. Marc.

[c] See Father Simon in the place now cited, and the same asserted, as to several other manuscripts, in Dr.

Mill on the last verse of Luke.

[d] Præf. in Comment. in Matth.

[e] Annot. in Titul. Luc.

[f] Life of St. Luke, §. 4.

[g] Critic. Hist. of the New Test. Part i. c. 12. p. 102.

Bithy-

Bithyniæque (other copies read *Bœotiæque*) *partibus volumen condidit.*

2. The prefent punctuation of Jerome's words feems not to be right; for the comma, or diftinction, ought rather to be put after the word *partibus*, than after the word *Pauli*; fo that the fenfe or conftruction feems rather to be, that Luke was the difciple of Paul in Achaia and Bithynia, and (afterwards) wrote his Gofpel; than that he was the difciple of Paul, and wrote his Gofpel in Achaia and Bithynia.

For any thing therefore which has been yet faid to the contrary, it feems moft probable, that St. Luke wrote his Gofpel after St. Mark's, i. e. after the year of Chrift 63: and as it is very likely that he wrote it not long before the *Acts of the Apoftles*, which muft needs be written after the year of Chrift 62, fo it is probable he wrote them both at Rome after Paul's departure thence; for that he continued at Rome after Paul, at leaft that he did not go away along with him is evident, becaufe his hiftory ends at that period. There is indeed a paffage, which I have obferved in the old book of *Hypotypofes*, under the name of Clemens Alexandrinus, cited by Eufebius (Hift. Eccl. lib. 6. c. 14.), wherein it is afferted that St. Luke's Gofpel was written before St. Mark's, viz. προγεγρά-φθαι ἔλεγεν τῶν εὐαγγελίων τὰ περιέχοντα τὰς γενεαλογίας: viz. *That thofe of the Gofpels were written firft, which contain our Saviour's genealogies*; but this book of the *Hypotypofes* not being wrote by Clemens, but the compofure of fome filly Heretick, (as I have proved, Vol. I. Part II. Ch. XXXVI. p. 373.) I think it needlefs to regard the teftimony.

CHAP. XII.

St. Luke's Gospel is Canonical. It is in the antient Catalogues, cited by the primitive Fathers, read in the Churches, and put in the Syriack Version.

Arg. I. ST. Luke's Gospel is to be efteemed of Canonical authority, by Prop. IV. becaufe *it is in all the Catalogues of Canonical books, which we have among the writings of the primitive Chriftians.* Thefe Catalogues I have collected, Vol. I. Part I. Ch. VIII. and referred to, in proving the authority of Matthew and Mark's Gofpels above, viz. the Catalogue of Origen, Eufebius, Athanafius, Cyril, that in the council of Laodicea, Epiphanius, Gregory Nazianzen, Philaftrius, Jerome, Ruffin, Auftin, that in the third council of Carthage, and in the books under the name of Dionyfius the Areopagite. To which I add, the general proof I have above made in this Part (Diflert. Præf.), that the four Gofpels which we now receive, were received by the primitive Chriftians.

Arg. II. The Gofpel of St. Luke is Canonical, becaufe *it is cited as Scripture in the writings of the primitive Chriftians,* Prop. V. I intend here, as in the former Gofpels, to fhew the feveral authors who have cited, and the places wherein they have cited this Gofpel, and fhall begin with,

I. St. PAUL.

It has been fuppofed by many of the antients (as I have obferved above, Ch. XI.), that as often as St. Paul ufes the words MY GOSPEL, he cites and refers to St. Luke (fee Rom. ii. 16. 2 Tim. ii. 8.). So many of the Chriftians before the time of Eufebius [a] and Jerome [b] thought, and Origen

---

[a] Hift. Eccl. lib. 3. c. 4.   [b] Catalog. Vir. Illuftr. in Luca.

exprefsly

expreſsly calls it the Goſpel ὑπὸ Παύλου ἐπαινούμενον, i. e. *commended or cited by Paul* [a]; but I confeſs, though I have mentioned this, it is not becauſe I believe St. Paul did cite this Goſpel (it being wrote, in my opinion, ſome years after the Epiſtle to the Romans, though perhaps not after that to Timothy), but becauſe it gives us clear intimation, how highly eſteemed this Goſpel was in the moſt antient times of Chriſtianity, being judged worthy by them to be cited by St. Paul, and called his own Goſpel.

II. CLEMENS ROMANUS.

St. Luke's Gospel.	The firſt Epiſtle of CLEMENS ROMANUS to the Corinthians.
1 Ch. vi. 36—39.	1 Chap. xiii. Several ſayings of our Lord are here referred to; ſome of which are in St. Matthew (as above ſaid), and ſome in St. Luke.
2 Ch. xvii. 1, 2.	2 Chap. xlvi. Cotelerius has obſerved upon this place, that Clemens not only cites Matthew, but Luke; and indeed the order of his words is more agreeable to this laſt.
	The ſecond Epiſtle of CLEMENS ROMANUS to the Corinthians.
3 Ch. xiii. 27.	3 Ch. iv. This ſeems to be rather taken out of Luke than Matthew, becauſe

---

[a] Apud Euſeb. Hiſt. Eccleſ. lib. 6. c. 25.

St.

St. LUKE's *Gospel.*	The *second Epistle of* CLEMENS ROMANUS *to the* Corinthians.
3 Ch. xiii. 27.	of the words ωόθεν ιρὶ, which are in Luke, and not in Matthew.
4 Ch. xvi. 26.	4 Ch. vi. It seems to be taken out of Luke, because the words are the same.
5 Ch. xvi. 10, 12.	5 Ch. viii. See the Appendix to Vol. I. p. 416.

III. IGNATIUS.

That he has cited Luke xxiv. 39. in his Epistle to the Smyrneans, Chap. III. I have proved above, Vol. I. Part II. Chap. XXVII. p. 294.

IV. JUSTIN MARTYR.

St. LUKE's *Gospel.*	JUSTIN MARTYR's *Works.*
1 Ch. i. 17.	1 Dialog. cum Tryph. Jud. p. 268.
2 —— 32.	2 Apolog. 2. pro Christ. p. 75.
3 —— 35, 38.	3 Dialog. cum Tryph. Jud. p. 327.
4 Ch. ii. 2. — ——	4 Apolog. 2. pro Christ. p. 75.
5 Ch. x. 19.	5 Dialog. cum Tryph. Jud. p. 301, 302.
6 —— 22.	6 —— p. 95, 96, 326.
7 Ch. xiii. 26, 27. }	7 Dialog. cum Tryph. Jud. p. 301.
8 Ch. xxii. 44.	8 —— p. 331.
9 Ch. xxiii. 46.	9 —— p. 333.

VOL. III.   H   V. IRE-

V. IRENÆUS.

St. Luke's Gospel is fo frequently cited by this Father, that it would be fuperfluous to collect the citations; befides Feuardentius has with fo much exactnefs collected them at the end of his edition of Irenæus, that it will be fufficient to refer the reader to his index. I fhall only obferve,

1. **That there are** *above a hundred citations* of this Gofpel made by Irenæus in his works.

2. That (Lib. 3. adv. Hæref. c. 14.) *he vindicates the authority and perfection of St. Luke's Gofpel,* and has made there a collection of many or moft of the hiftories which this Evangelift has recorded, which are not mentioned by either of the other, and fays, *the Hiftories of Chrift, which St. Luke alone has recorded, were received by all Chriftians* [a].

3. That he in very many places cites this Gofpel by the name of *Luke,* which the reader may fee in the following inftances.

St. LUKE's *Gofpel.*	IRENÆUS.
1 Luke iii. 23.	1 Lib. 2. c. 39.
2 —— iii. 4.	2 Lib. 3. c. 9.
3 —— i. 6, 8, 9, 15, 17, and a great part of that chapter.	3 —— c. 11.
4 Many places of this Gofpel.	4 —— c. 14.
5 —— iii. 24, &c.	5 —— c. 33.
6 —— iv. 5, 6.	6 Lib. 5. c. 21.

Many other fuch inftances might eafily be collected; but I fuppofe thefe, with what has been faid above *(Differt. præfix.)* may be fufficient to evidence to any one the fentiments, which Irenæus had of this Gofpel.

---

[a] Et plurimos Actus Domini per hunc (fc. Lucam) didicimus, qui- bus et omnes utuntur.

VI. CLEMENS ALEXANDRINUS.

St. LUKE's *Gospel.*	The *Works of* CLEMENS ALEXANDRINUS.
1 Ch. iii. 12, 13, 14.	1 Pædagog. Lib. 3. p. 261.
2 —— vi. 36.	2 Stromat. Lib. 2. p. 404.
3 —— 46.	3 —— Lib. 7. p. 766.
4 Ch. xii. 19.	4 Pædagog. Lib. 2. p. 210.
5 —— 20.	5 Stromat. Lib. 4. p. 487.
6 —— 36, 37.	6 Pædagog. Lib. 2. p. 185.
7 Ch. xiv. 8, 13, 16, &c.	7 —— p. 141.
8 —— 20.	8 Stromat. Lib. 3. p. 465.
9 —— 26.	9 —— p. 467.
10 Ch. xv. 1, &c.	10 Pædagog. Lib. 2. p. 144.
11 —— 7.	11 Stromat. Lib. 2. p. 390.
12 Ch. xvi. 19, &c. viz. the parable of the rich man and Lazarus.	12 This is referred to several times by Clemens, viz. Pædagog. Lib. 2. p. 199. Lib. 3. p. 234. et Stromat. Lib. 4. p. 486.
13 Ch. xviii. 8.	13 Stromat. Lib. 3. p. 447.
14 Ch. xix. 8.	14 —— Lib. 4. p. 488.
15 Ch. xxii. 31.	15 —— p. 503.
16 Ch. xxiv. 41.	16 Pædagog. Lib. 2. p. 148. In this laft place Clemens has cited Luke by name.

Befides thefe references to St. Luke, made by Clemens in his *Pædagogus* and *Stromata,* I have met with feveral others in that fmall tract of his, intitled, *Quis Dives falvetur?* Thefe are as follow.

St. LUKE's *Gospel.*	The *Treatife of* CLEMENS ALEXANDRINUS, *intitled,* Quis Dives falvetur ?
1 Ch. v. 29.	1 Cap. xiii. p. 34.
2 —— vi. 30	2 —— xxxi. p. 86.

St.

	St. Luke's Gospel.		The treatise of CLEMENS ALEXANDRINUS, intitled, Quis Dives falvetur ?
3	Ch. x. 29—37.	3	Cap. xxviii. p. 77.
4	—— xii. 32.	4	—— xxxi. p. 82.
5	—— xiv. 26.	5	—— xxii. p. 61.
6	—— xv. 9, 10.	6	—— xxxix. p. 102.
7	—— xvi. 9.	7	—— xiii. p. 34.
8	—— xix. 5.	8	Ibid.

The citations out of this Gospel in the works of Tertullian, Origen, Cyril, Cyprian, Ambrofe, Auftin, Jerome, &c. are fo very numerous, and fo eafy to be obferved every where in their writings, that I fhall omit making any collections out of them. Thefe, as the preceding Fathers, appeal always to this Gospel as Scripture; and no wonder they fhould, when they were affured it was, as Eufebius calls it, Θεόπνευσον Βιβλίον, an infpired book. Hift. Eccl. lib. 3. c. 4.

Arg. III. The Gospel of St. Luke is Canonical, becaufe *it was read as Scripture in the churches or affemblies of the primitive Chriftians,* by Prop. VI. For the proof of the fact I muft refer the reader to Part I. Ch. X. of this work, and what I have above faid, Ch. III. in this Part, concerning the reading of St. Matthew's Gospel.

Arg. IV. St. Luke's Gospel is Canonical, becaufe *it was efteemed as fuch by the Churches of Syria in or near the Apoftles' time;* and accordingly by them in thofe days tranflated, and inferted in their collection of facred books, Prop. XV.

Thus much concerning the Canonical authority of this Gospel; nor have I any farther to add, but that as Marcion and his heretical followers had a different Gospel of St. Luke, from that which we now receive, fo thefe differences were all owing to the impudence of Marcion, who inferted and left out what he thought convenient to ferve his own purpofes; which has largely been proved by Irenæus [a], Tertullian [b], and Epi-

[a] Adverf. Hæref. lib. 3. c. 11, 12.   [b] Adv. Marcion. lib. 4. c. 3, &c.

phanius,

phanius [a], to whom I muſt refer the reader ; and among later writers to Sixtus Senenſis [b], Father Simon [c], Du Pin [d], and Dr. Mill [e].

C H A P. XIII.

A Collection of all that is ſaid of St. John in the New Teſta-
ment. The Hiſtory of his Life from the Antients. He
ſettled in Aſia Minor. Suffered under Domitian. Was ba-
niſhed to Patmos. Returned to Epheſus. A ſtory of him
and Cerinthus. Another of him and a young Man. He
raiſed the dead, &c. When and how he died. Joh. xxi.
21. miſunderſtood by many of the Antients, who imagined
thence, that he never died.

FOR the clearer eſtabliſhment of the Canonical authority of this Goſpel, it will be requiſite that here, as in the former Goſpels, I ſhould firſt give ſome account of *the author*, and then of *his work.*

Concerning the author we have *ſome accounts in Scripture*, and ſome which are credible *in the primitive Chriſtian writ-*
ings. Each ſhall be diſtinctly conſidered.

I. The accounts which we have of St. John the Evangeliſt *in the writings of the New Teſtament*, are as follow ; viz.

1. His *father's name* was Zebedee, a fiſherman by trade, and his mother's Salome [f].

2. He was *born in Galilee*, as is probable, becauſe there Chriſt found him, and called him [g] with his brother James.

3. He was conſtituted one of Chriſt's *firſt Apoſtles*, and ſent out with the Twelve [h].

[a] Hæreſ. 42.
[b] Biblioth. Sanct. lib. 7. de Luc. Evang.
[c] Critic. Hiſt. of the New Teſt. Part I. c. 12.
[d] Hiſtor. of Canon, Vol. II. c. 2, §. 5.

[e] Prolegom. in Nov. Teſt. §. 306—328.
[f] Matt. iv. 21. xxvii. 56. compared with Mark xv. 40.
[g] Matt. iv. 21.
[h] Matt. x. 2.

4. He

4. He seems to have been of a *very warm and zealous tem-per.* This I gather; (1.) Because he is intitled by Christ, with his brother James, *Boanerges* [a], i. e. *Son of Thunder.* (2.) Because he was for *forbidding a certain person any more to cast out Devils in Christ's name*, because HE did not follow them [b]. (3.) Because he with his brother James *desired to call down fire* (i. e. thunder or lightning) *from heaven, to con-sume the Samaritans* [c]. (4.) Because after Christ's ascension, we find John with Peter was *the chief speaker and actor in the defence and propagation of the Gospel at Jerusalem* [d].

5. He received *several particular instances and marks of our Saviour's favour, above most or all the Apostles.* Hence he has often the character given him of *that Disciple whom Jesus loved* [e]; and particular evidences hereof seem to be, (1.) That he *was admitted* with Peter and James *to be present at our Sa-viour's transfiguration* [f]. (2.) That *he was sent* with Peter *to prepare the last passover* for our Saviour [g]. (3.) He was *placed in the most honourable seat at the supper*; he leaned on Jesus's bosom, or lay on his breast [h]; i. e. he sat in the next place to Christ; and as it was the custom of those countries then, to lie along on couches at meals, his head lay in the bo-som of Christ, who sat before him; (4.) *When Peter durst not himself, he desired John to ask Christ*, who should betray him; which he did, and received an answer [i]. (5.) *He alone, with his brother James and Peter, was admitted to the favour of our Lord's discourse and devotion in the Mount of Olives* [k]. (6.) *Christ upon the Cross appointed him the guardian of his mother, the Virgin Mary*, giving her instructions to own him as a son, and him to own her as a mother [l]: John accordingly took her to his home. (7.) *He was first favoured by Christ with the discovery of himself to him, at the sea of Tiberias,*

---

[a] Mar. iii. 17.
[b] Mar. ix. 38, and Luke ix. 49.
[c] Luke ix. 54.
[d] Acts iii. 1, &c.
[e] John xiii. 23. xix. 26. xx. 2. xxi. 20.

[f] Matt. xvii. 1, &c. Luke ix. 28.
[g] Luke xxii. 8.
[h] John xiii. 23, 25.
[i] John xiii. 23—26.
[k] Matt. xxvi. 36. and Luke xxii. 39.
[l] John xix. 16, 17.

after

after his reſurrection [a]. (8.) The anſwer which Chriſt gave to Peter, relating to John, ſeems not a little to his honour, *If I will that he tarry till I come, what is that to thee* [b] *?*

Beſides the above-mentioned, we have the following particulars concerning him; as (1.) That he with his brother James petitioned Chriſt to be advanced to high poſts in his (temporal) kingdom [c]: and though Matthew ſays, their mother preſented the petition for them [d]; yet ſeeing Mark ſo poſitively aſſerts their preſenting it themſelves, and both Matthew and Mark agree, that our Saviour directed his anſwer to the ſons, and not the mother, there can be no room to doubt but they were concerned therein. (2.) He was known to the High-Prieſt, attended our Saviour's trial, and procured introduction for Peter into the hall [e]. Though John be not named there, yet being ſpoke of as uſual in the third perſon, and it being certain that he afterwards attended Chriſt at his crucifixion [f], which we do not know that any other Apoſtle did, it is more than probable he was the perſon there intended. (3.) He ran with Peter to Chriſt's ſepulchre, on the firſt account of his reſurrection [g]. (4.) After Chriſt's aſcenſion he preached with Peter in the Temple, and healed the lame man, preached to the people [h], was apprehended of the Sadducees [i], impriſoned, and boldly pleaded in defence of Chriſtianity [k]. (5.) He was the deputy of the Apoſtles with Peter to go to Samaria, to confirm and enlarge the churches which were planted there [l]. And beſides this I find nothing related concerning him in the New Teſtament, except his being the author of three Epiſtles and the Revelation; of which in their proper places. There are indeed two other places of the Goſpel, in which John is ſuppoſed to be the perſon referred to, viz. that, John i. 35—40. where mention is made of two of John the Baptiſt's Diſciples who went to

[a] John xxi. 7.
[b] John xxi. 23.
[c] Mark x. 35.
[d] Matt. xx. 20.
[e] John xviii. 16.
[f] John xix. 26.

[g] John xx. 2, &c.
[h] Acts iii. 1, &c.
[i] Acts iv. 1, &c.
[k] Acts iv. per tot.
[l] Acts viii. 14, &c.

　　　　　　　　　　　Chriſt;

Chrift; the one is faid to be Andrew, the other not named is
fuppofed to be John our Evangelift, becaufe he particularly
relates all the circumftances of the hiftory, and conceals his
own name [a]; but this is by no means a fufficient reafon, efpecially confidering that John feems not to have known Chrift
till he was called, Matt. iv. 21. The other place is that,
Mark xiv. 51, 52. where we read of a young man that followed Chrift, when he was apprehended, having a linen cloth
caft about his naked body, which he left in the hands of thofe
who laid hold on him; this is fuppofed to be John by feveral
of the antients, Chryfoftom, Ambrofe, and Gregory [b], and Dr.
Cave among the moderns [c]; but as there is no evidence offered to fupport the conjecture, it cannot be unfair to reject
it.

II. *The accounts which we have from the antients concerning St. John, are large.* I fhall lay down what feems moft
remarkable.

It is generally agreed by the antients, that when the Apoftles determined to go abroad to propagate the Gofpel, *St.
John had Afia Minor for his province.* This is attefted by
Polycrates [d], Irenæus [e], Eufebius [f], Dorotheus [g], and many
others. I fhall only obferve, that *in the Life of this Apoftle* [h],
under the name of *Prochorus* (who was one of the feven dea-
cons appointed by the Apoftles, Acts vi. 5.), it is faid, that all
the Apoftles met at Gethfemane after Chrift's afcenfion, and
having their feveral provinces determined by lot, Afia fell to
John; which, though he received at firft with concern, he
afterwards complied with. It is however very probable, that

[a] Vid. Epiphan. Hæref. 51.
§. 14. Dr. Cave's Life of St.
John, §. 1. and Dr. Whitby on
John i. 40.
[b] Apud Whitby in Mar. xiv.
51.
[c] Lib. cit. §. 3.
[d] Epift. ad Victorem et Roma-
næ Urbis Ecclefiam de Pafchate,
cujus fragmentum extat apud Eufeb. Hift. Ecclef. l. 5. c. 24.
[e] Adverf. Hæref. lib. 3. c. 11.
[f] Hift. Ecclef. lib. 3. c. 1.

[g] In Synopf.
[h] This book is printed in Greek
and Latin among the Orthodoxographa, Vol. I. p. 85. but is juftly
rejected as fpurious by Bellarmine
(de Script. Ecclef. in Prochoro),
and many Papifts, as by all Pro-
teftant writers. Cocus Cenfur,
quorund. vet. Script. p. 13. Rivet. Critic. Sacr. lib. 1. c. 6.
Cave Hiftor. Liter. p. 23. Fabric.
Cod. Apocr. t. 1. p. 817.

St.

St. John did not till a long time after Chrift's afcenfion enter upon his charge; becaufe, as Dr. Cave [a] well obferves, had he been in Afia early, we muft needs have heard of him in the accounts which St. Luke gives of St. Paul's feveral journies into, and refidence in, thofe parts; it is therefore moft likely he ftaid for a long time after our Saviour's afcent at Jerufalem. The next thing we read of St. John, is his *being a fufferer in the fecond general perfecution under Domitian at Rome, where he was caft into a caldron of boiling oil, but miraculoufly pre-ferved, and the fire had no influence upon him.* This is re-lated by Tertullian [b], and by no one elfe except Jerome, who fays he tranfcribed it from him [c]; and, if it be true [d], hap-pened in the fourteenth year of Domitian, i. e. about the year of Chrift 96. So we read exprefsly in Eufebius's Chronicon and Jerome [e]. After this the *Apoftle was by the fame Empe-ror banifhed to a defolate ifland in the fouth-eaft part of the Egean Sea, called Patmos* [f]. So we are informed by Tertul-lian [g], Eufebius [h], Jerome [i], Severus Sulpitius [k], &c. though Dorotheus Tyrius feems to have believed that this banifhment was by Trajan, and not Domitian [l], which is certainly a mif-take. In this exile-ftate, it is faid St. John was fuitably com-forted and fupported with the *vifions and revelations from God*, which he afterwards publifhed; fee Irenæus [m], Eufebius [n], Je-rome [o], Severus Sulpitius [p], and Auftin [q]. The fecond gene-

---

[a] Life of St. John, §. 4.

[b] De Præfcript. adv. Hæretic. cap. 36. Apoftolus Joannes, poftea quam in oleum igneum demerfus nihil paffus eft, in infulam relega-tur.

[c] Lib. 1. contr. Jovin. c. 14. et in Matth. xx. apud Cleric. Hift. Ecclef. p. 508.

[d] However good Tertullian's cre-dit may be, yet the ftory cannot but appear dubious, when we confider that fo remarkable a fact fell only within the obfervation of one fingle writer.

[e] Catalog. Vir. Illuftr. in Jo-anne.

[f] According to fome it was reck-oned among the iflands called Cy-clades, according to others among thofe called Sporades. Vid. Plin. lib. 4. c. 12. Dionyf. Periegef. v. 530. et Gulielm. Hill Not. in loc. p. 134.

[g] De Præfcript. adv. Hæretic. c. 36.

[h] Hift. Ecclef. lib. 3. c. 18.

[i] Loc. jam cit.

[k] Hiftor. Sacr. lib. 2. p. 535. inter Orthodoxograph. Vol. I. Gry-næus, the editor, inftead of Severus Sulpitius, calls him by miftake Sul-pitius Severus. See Dr. Cave's Hift. Liter. tom. 1. p. 284.

[l] In Synopf.

[m] Adverf. Hæref. lib. 5. c. 30.

[n] Loc. jam cit.

[o] Loc. jam cit.

[p] Loc. jam cit.

[q] Quæft. ex Nov. Teft. §. 72.

ral perfecution ended with Domitian; and times more favourable to Chriftianity fucceeding, St. John had an opportunity to return to his former friends at Ephefus, which, as it was the place of his former abode in Afia, fo became now his fettlement for life. Here he acted the part of a Chriftian Bifhop or Minifter, and together with feven other Bifhops prefided over that diocefe, if we may credit the author of the book intitled Μαςτύριον Τιμοθέκ; i. e. *The Martyrdom of Timothy*[a].

The other accounts which I have met with concerning St. John, cannot be reduced to any certain order of time: Dr. Cave and Du Pin have collected them already; for which reafon I fhall but juft name them, in the order in which the feveral authors lived, who have mentioned them.

IRENÆUS[b] informs us, there were fome in his time who had the following account from Polycarp, who was one of John's difciples, viz. " That St. John going to a certain " bath at Ephefus, and perceiving that Cerinthus, that noted " arch-heretick, was in the bath, immediately leaped out " without bathing himfelf, and faid, *Let us go hence, left the* " *bath fhould fall down upon us, having in it fuch an heretick* " *as Cerinthus, that enemy of truth.*" What the herefy of Cerinthus was, may be largely feen in Irenæus[c], Epiphanius[d], and many of the antients. Some account of his principles is given above, Vol. I. Part II. Ch. XII.

CLEMENS ALEXANDRINUS concludes his treatife, intitled, *Quis Dives falvetur*[e]? with a remarkable hiftory, which moft of our Ecclefiaftical writers have taken notice of. I fhall recite it therefore briefly, viz. " That when St. John was re- " turned from his exile in Patmos to Ephefus, he vifited the " neighbouring churches, and obferving in one of the cities a

---

[a] Apud Phot. Cod. 254. This book goes under the name of Polycrates of Ephefus, a writer of the fecond century, but is rejected as fpurious by Dr. Cave, Hift. Liter. p. 60. and Fabricius Cod. Apocr. Nov. Teft. p. 812.

[b] Adverf. Hæref. lib. 3. c. 3. et in Eufeb. lib. 4. c. 14.
[c] Lib. 3. paffim.
[d] Hæref. 28.
[e] It was publifhed 1683, at Oxford, by Bifhop Fell.

" young

" young man of an uncommon genius and handsome body, he
" commended him in the presence of the Church to the care
" of the Bishop [a] of the place, who, taking the charge of him,
" instructed and baptized him; at length giving him his li-
" berty, he fell into the worst of company, and entered into a
" strict alliance with some persons, who were not only in
" other respects debauched in their morals, but notorious
" robbers, of whom he became the captain, and led them in
" all their acts of murder, robbery, &c. Some time after St.
" John's occasions calling him to this city, he enquired after
" the young man. The Bishop with concern replied, he was
" dead, meaning he was dead to God, and joined to a band of
" villains and robbers. Upon which St. John took a horse
" and guide, came to the place where the robbers were, and
" being seized by their centinels, he desired to be brought to
" their captain, who, when he saw him, fled through shame;
" but St. John pursued him, desiring him not to fly, and pro-
" mising him pardon from Christ, by whom he said he was
" sent; upon this he staid, and in the greatest distress threw
" down his arms, and embracing the Apostle, he groaned,
" and floods of tears poured down from his eyes. Upon
" which St. John, assuring him of pardon, prayed for him,
" and brought him back to the Church."

APOLLONIUS, a writer in the second century against the
Montanists, tells us [b], that *he raised a dead person to life.*
This I find no where else related, unless that should be
thought to be the same, which I observe in Isidore Hispalensis [c],
concerning *his raising a widow from the dead* by the command
of the people, or *his restoring and bringing a young man's soul
into his body again,* related in the same place.

---

[a] I cannot but observe here, that
when Clemens delivers the young
man to his charge, he calls him
Ἐπίσκοπος, and a few lines after,
when he speaks of the care which
he took of him, he calls him Πρεσ-
βύτερος an undeniable demonstra-
tion, that *Presbyter* and *Bishop* were
two names of one person in the
time of Clemens Alexandrinus.
   [b] Lib. contr. Cataphryg. apud
Euseb. Hist. Ecclef. lib. 5. c. 18.
   [c] Loc. supr. cit.

POLYCRATES,

POLYCRATES, a writer of the fame time, makes *St. John to be a prieſt, and as ſuch to have worn a* Πέταλον, *or plate* [a]. Jerome, citing this of Polycrates, paraphraſes it thus [b]; *Pontifex ejus (ſcil. Chriſti) fuit, auream laminam in fronte portans;* i. e. " He was High-prieſt of Chriſt, and wore a golden plate " on his forehead." This is ſaid alſo of James, Biſhop of Jeruſalem, by Epiphanius [c], who cites Clemens and Euſebius for the truth of it; and, if it be true, is well accounted for by Valeſius [d], who ſuppoſes thoſe firſt Chriſtians to have done it in imitation of the Jewiſh High-prieſts.

TERTULLIAN informs us, that St. John convicted an Aſiatick preſbyter of forging and publiſhing *the Acts of Paul and Thecla*, under the name of Paul [e]. See the place at large above, Part III. Ch. XXXIV. p. 387.

The time, place, and manner of St. John's death, are very differently related by the antients. Irenæus affirms [f], that *he continued till the reign of the Emperor Trajan*; and elſewhere [g], that *he preſided over the Church of Epheſus till that time.* Irenæus was followed in this opinion by moſt of the antients. Euſebius makes St. John's exit to have been in the third year of Trajan [h]; and agreeably thereto, Jerome [i] places it in the ſixty-eighth year after Chriſt's death, which coincides with the third year of Trajan, and the hundred and firſt, or hundred and ſecond year after our Saviour's nativity. That St. John did live till this reign, I find alſo aſſerted in the antient book, of which we have an abſtract in Photius [k], which is intitled, *The Martyrdom of Timothy*, in Iſidore Hiſpalenſis's *Treatiſe of the Lives and Deaths of the Prophets and Apoſtles* [l], and in the *Synopſis* of Dorotheus [m], though he make St. John to have

[a] Epiſt. ad Victor. et Eccleſ. Roman. apud Euſeb. lib. 5. c. 24.
[b] Catalog. Vir. Illuſtr. in Polycrat.
[c] Hæreſ. 29. §. 4. et Hæreſ. 78. §. 14.
[d] Annot. in Loc. Euſeb. denuo cit.
[e] Lib. de Baptiſm. c. 17.

[f] Adv. Hæreſ. lib. 2. c. 39.
[g] Lib. 3. c. 3.
[h] In Chronic. ad Ann. CIII.
[i] Catal. Vir. Illuſtr. in Joanne.
[k] Cod. CCLIV.
[l] Inter Orthodoxogr. Vol. I. p. 598.
[m] Edit. Latin.

lived

lived to the age of an hundred and twenty; which, if it were certain, would prove that he died not in the beginning, but in the end of Trajan's reign, if not rather in the reign of A-drian [a]. He that would read more of the time of St. John's death, may consult Mr. Dodwell [b].

It is impossible to say any thing certain concerning the manner of St. John's death. Polycrates [c] says, he *died a martyr at Ephesus*, as do some other of the antients, viz. Chrysostom [d], and Theophylact [e], his constant follower. Whether the later writers, who have asserted St. John's martyrdom, were induced to that opinion, only by supposing that those words of Christ, Matt. xx. 23. to John and James, implied their violent death, viz. *Ye shall drink indeed of my cup, and be baptized with the baptism that I am baptized with*, &c. I shall not determine. To me the fact seems probable, not only from the testimony of Polycrates, but because all the rest of the Apostles did suffer martyrdom, and the text seems not obscurely to imply it.

The mistaken judgment of the Apostles, that John should never die, founded upon those words of our Saviour, John xxi. 21, &c. *If I will that he tarry till I come, what is that to thee?* led many of the antients also into a persuasion, that St. John did never die. St. Austin [f] has largely discussed the question, and tells us of an opinion of some, founded upon some Apocryphal Scriptures, viz. That St. John in perfect health ordered his grave to be made, and then laid himself down in it, as in a bed, and died. Others say, he did not then die, but only lay down asleep like a person dead; and in this state of sleep, not death, he will continue till Christ come: that he is not dead, says he, they prove by the motion of the grave-dust, which is continually occasioned to boil and bubble by the motion of his breast. This opinion, says St. Austin, I

---

[a] It being reasonable to suppose John, when he was called to the work of the ministry, was not under the age of Christ, i. e. not under his thirtieth year, none undertaking that office earlier.

[b] Addit. ad Pearson. Dissert. 2.

de Success. Rom. Episc. c. 5.

[c] Epist. ad Victor. apud Euseb. Hist. Eccl. l. 5. c. 24.

[d] Homil. 66. in Matth.

[e] In Matth. xx. 23.

[f] Tract. 124. in Joann.

will

will not oppofe; for I have been informed of the fact from grave and credible witneffes. Ifidore Hifpalenfis [a] relates the fame ftory, with feveral other particular circumftances, too trifling to be mentioned. Ephraim Theopolitanus, Bifhop of Antioch, about the year of Chrift, 510 [b], endeavours to prove, that St. John never died, but was tranflated, as Enoch and Elijah. I will add no more, but that the fame opinion feems to have been received in the feveral fucceeding ages of Chriftianity. Georgius Trapezuntius, a learned writer, though late, has wrote five whole treatifes, which he dedicates to the Pope, with defign to prove that St. John never did die. I fhall think it fufficient to refer the reader to the ingenious tract [c]. Hence it came to pafs, that feveral impoftors have profeffed themfelves to be this Apoftle; one particularly in the time of Martinus, about the year 400 [d], and another in Queen Elizabeth's time, who was afterwards burnt at Thouloufe in France, as we are told by Beza [e].

C H A P. XIV.

St. John's Gofpel wrote againft the Hereticks, viz. the Cerinthians and Ebionites, who denied our Saviour's Divinity; as alfo to enlarge the Gofpel Hiftory. It was wrote after the year of Chrift XCVII. An Objection to this anfwered. Other mifcellaneous Remarks.

CONCERNING St. John's Gofpel, whatever appears to me confiderable, I fhall lay down in the following obfervations.

[a] De vit. et obit. Prophet. et Sanctor. inter Orthodox. Vol. I. p. 598.
[b] Refponf. ad Anatol. Scholaft. Quæft. apud Phot. Cod. 229.
[c] Inter Orthodoxogr. Vol. II.
p. 1231.
[d] Vid. Sever. Sulpit. de vita Martin. inter Orthodoxogr. Vol. I. p. 556.
[e] Annot. in Joann. xxi. 21.

I. St.

I. St. John seems to have had two particular designs in the writing of his Gospel, viz. *the confuting of certain Hereticks, and supplying the defects of the history of Christ in the other Gospels.*

1. St. John wrote his Gospel with *the intent, or design, of confuting certain Hereticks of that early age, who denied the divinity of our Saviour.* This is largely attested by the antients. Irenæus tells us, " [a] That the Evangelist designed by
" his Gospel to confute the errors, which Cerinthus had in-
" fused into the minds of the people, and had been infused by
" those who were called Nicolaitans ; and to convince them,
" that there was one God, who made all things by his WORD,
" and not, as they imagined, ONE who was the Creator, and
" ANOTHER who was the Father of the Lord (Jesus) ; ONE
" who was the Son of the Creator, and ANOTHER who was
" the Christ, who continued impassible, and descended upon
" Jesus the Son of the Creator, &c." Epiphanius proves,
St. John's Gospel could not be written by Cerinthus, because
it was wrote against him [b]. Jerome is most particular, and
informs us [c], " That when St. John was in Asia, where then
" arose the Heresies of Ebion and Cerinthus, and others, who
" denied that Christ was come in the flesh, i. e. denied his di-
" vine nature, whom he in his Epistle calls Antichrists, and
" St. Paul frequently condemns in his Epistles, he was forced
" by almost all the Bishops of Asia, and the deputations of
" many other churches, to write more plainly concerning the
" divinity of our Saviour, and to soar aloft in a discourse on
" the WORD, not more bold than happy." Whence we are
told in Ecclesiastical History, that when he was solicited by
the brethren to write, he answered, he would not do it, unless
a publick day of fasting and prayer was appointed to implore
God's assistance ; which being done, and the solemnity being
honoured with a satisfactory revelation from God, he broke
forth into those words, *In the beginning was the Word, and
the Word was God,* &c. To the same purpose Austin [d] saith,

---

[a] Adv. Hæref. lib. 3. c. 11.   See the same. Catal. Vir. Illustr.
[b] Hæref. 51. §. 4. & 12.   in Joann.
[c] Præfat. in Comment. in Matt. [d] Præf. in Tract. in Joann.

This

this Evangelist *wrote concerning the co-eternal divinity of Christ against the Hereticks*; and the same Father has in several places observed, that he above the rest of the Apostles has asserted Christ's equality with the Father; and while they are content to give an account of Christ's miracles and moral precepts, he rather chose to relate those things which pertained to our Saviour's divinity [a].

2. St. John wrote his Gospel with intent to *supply the defects of our Saviour's history in the other three Gospels*; for whereas they say little of that part of our Saviour's life, which preceded the imprisonment of *John the Baptist*, he has inserted it in his Gospel. This is related by Eusebius [b], Jerome [c], &c. though the author of the antient book of *Hypotyposes*, under the name of Clemens Alexandrinus [d], assigns this reason somewhat differently, viz. John observing that in the other Gospels τὰ σωματικὰ—διδήλωται, i. e. *The things pertaining to our Lord's human nature were wrote*; he, *inspired by the Holy Ghost*, at the request of his friends, composed πνυματικὸν εὐαγγέλιον, i. e. *a spiritual Gospel*, or *an account of our Saviour's divinity*. To the same purpose we read in Epiphanius [e], that the other Gospels had so fully related the affair of Christ's incarnation, and the things which he did as incarnate, that he judged it needless to write the same, and therefore wrote his Gospel against Ebion, Cerinthus, Marcion, &c. who affirmed, that Christ had no being before he was born of Mary.

II. St. John's Gospel seems to have been written about the year of Christ, XCVIII.

---

[a] Loc. cit. & de Consens. Evang. l. 1. c. 4.

[b] Hist. Eccl. lib. 3. c. 24. *See the place at large above in this Part, in the previous Dissertation.*

[c] Aliam causam hujus scripturæ ferunt, quod quum legisset Matthæi, Marci, et Lucæ volumina, probaverit quidem textum historiæ, et vera eos dixisse firmaverit, sed unius tantum anni *(This was a common, but unaccountable mistake of the antients, that the three other*

Evangelists relate only the history of Christ for one year), in quo et passus est, post carcerem Joannis historiam texuisse. Prætermisso itaque anno, cujus acta a tribus exposita fuerant, superioris temporis, antequam Joannes clauderetur in carcerem, gesta narravit. Catal. Vir. Illustr. in Joann.

[d] Apud Eusb. Hist. Eccl. l. 6. c. 14.

[e] Hæres. 51. §. 12.

The

The moſt antient Chriſtians have fixed no time of its writing. Irenæus only ſaith, *that it was wrote at Epheſus, during his abode there*[a]; but whether it was before his baniſh-
ment from thence by Domitian to Patmos, or after, he ſaith
not. It is upon many accounts moſt probable, that it was
written after his return. Epiphanius expreſsly aſſerts, *that he
wrote it in his ninetieth year, after his return from Patmos to
Epheſus*[b]; though I know not by what ſtrange ſort of miſtake,
he makes it to have been in the reign of the Emperor Claudius, inſtead of the reign of Nerva, or Trajan; between the
firſt of which and Claudius there intervened the reigns of
ſeven ſeveral Emperors, viz. Nero, Galba, Otho, Vitellius,
Veſpaſian, Titus, and Domitian. It is plain therefore, St.
John did not write his Goſpel before the reign of Nerva, i. e.
not before the year of Chriſt, XCVII. for ſooner he could not
return from Patmos; but whether he wrote it in that year
immediately after his return, or ſome time later, I ſhall not
enquire. This is, I think, the moſt received opinion about
the time of St. John's writing his Goſpel; nor is there any
conſiderable difference between the later Fathers and Epiphanius on this head. The author of the Martyrdom of Timothy (if I underſtand his words right), aſſerts the ſame as
Epiphanius, viz. that he wrote it after his return from Patmos to Epheſus[c]; and ſo does Iſidore Hiſpalenſis[d]. Dorotheus differs only, in ſaying, that he wrote it during his exile-
ſtate in Patmos, and publiſhed it afterwards by Gaius at
Epheſus[e]; and this is only one year's difference. There are
indeed ſome manuſcripts[f], and later writers, as Theophylact[g],
&c. who *will have this Goſpel written much ſooner*, viz. about
the year of Chriſt, LXV. viz. thirty two years after our Saviour's aſcenſion; but the authority of theſe is ſo ſmall in
reſpect of thoſe above-mentioned, that I need ſay no more,
had not Mr. Whiſton fallen in with their opinion[h]. He of-

[a] Joannes diſcipulus Domini e-
didit Evangelium Epheſi Aſiæ com-
morans. Adv. Hæreſ. lib. 3. c. 1.
[b] Loc. jam cit.
[c] Apud Phot. Cod. CCLIV.
[d] Inter Orthodoxogr. Vol. I.
p. 598.
[e] In Synopſ.

[f] Vid. Mill. in Calc. Joan.
[g] Præf. in Joan.
[h] Eſſay on the Conſtit. p. 19.
See concerning the time of St.
John's writing his Goſpel, Dallæum
de Script. Dionyſ. Areopag. &c.
l. 1. c. 16.—p. 102, &c.

fers indeed feveral reafons for it, in which I cannot fee the leaft fhew of evidence: the bare propofing them would be a fufficient confutation of them. The moft confiderable of them is the fourth, viz. that John, c. v. ver. 2. *fpeaks of the pool of Bethefda in the prefent tenfe*, there is at Jerufalem, and not there was, which better agrees to the time he affigns (as he imagines) *before the deftruction of Jerufalem, when that pool and porch were certainly in being, than to the time afterward, when probably both were deftroyed.* Dr. Whitby[a], feveral years before Mr. Whifton, obferved and fubmitted (though at the expence of a contradiction to what he[b] feemed elfe-where to affert) to the force of this argument; " If, fays he, " ἐν δὲ, THERE IS, be the true reading, as the confent of almoft " all the Greek copies argues; it feems to intimate that Jeru-" falem and this pool were then ftanding, when St. John " wrote this Gofpel; and therefore, that it was written, as " Theophylact and others fay, before the deftruction of Jeru-" falem, and not, as the more antient Fathers thought, long " after."

To this I anfwer;

(1.) That unlefs *John* had *certainly known* the deftruction of this particular place at Jerufalem, *it was more proper for* him to fpeak *in the prefent time*, as fuppofing it ftill ftanding, than in the paft time, afferting what he knew not. And indeed, who can fuppofe that John, at the diftance which Ephefus was from Jerufalem, fhould be particularly informed of the deftruction of every particular place in the city?

(2.) That in all probability *the pool was not filled up, but ftill in the fame ftate after the deftruction of Jerufalem, as before.* Pools were of great fervice, and as it probably could anfwer no end for the conquerors to deftroy it, fo it would be a prodigious work to fill it up, efpecially if the accounts, which we have of the feveral ftreams that fed it, may be depended upon[c]. Add to this, that Tertullian[d] fays, this pool loft its virtue after Chrift's time, undoubtedly referring to times after

[a] Annot. in loc.
[b] Pref. to John.
[c] See Dr. Lightfoot, Chorogr.
Enquiry prefixed to his Exercitations on John, ch. 5.
[d] Adv. Jud. cap. 13.

the

the deſtruction of the city, which ſuppoſes the pool ſtill ſtanding.

(3.) Suppoſe the pool was deſtroyed, and John to have known it, *there is no impropriety in uſing the verb* ἰρὶ, nothing being more common among writers, than to uſe verbs in the preſent tenſe to denote the preterperfect tenſe. This is eſpecially remarkable in, and obſerved by all the criticks on, the New Teſtament. See inſtances in Glaſſius, Gram. Sacr. l. 3. Tract. 3. Can. 48.

(4.) Several of the antient manuſcripts and verſions read the verb in the paſt time. (See Dr. Mill Annot. in loc.) and ſo Nonnus paraphraſes the place,

Ἡν δέ τις εὐποίητος ἰν εὐύδρῳ προϐατικῇ
Εὐρυτενὴς ἀσάμινθος———

III. St. John's Goſpel *was tranſlated into Hebrew.* The credit of this depends upon what we read in Epiphanius, in the three ſeveral places referred to at the bottom of the page[a].

IV. St. John's Goſpel *was admired by the Platoniſts.* A-melius[b] *ſwore, the Barbarian* (ſo the Grecians called all but themſelves) *was in the right in his account of the* Word, *&c.* and Auſtin tells us, *he was informed by Simplicianus, Biſhop of Milan, that a certain Platoniſt ſaid,* the beginning of St. John's Goſpel deſerved to be written in letters of gold, and to be read in all publick aſſemblies[c].

V. *The ſtyle* of St. John's Goſpel was judged by Dionyſius Alexandrinus[d], *to be elegant and pure in reſpect of the Greek, and the whole compoſure to be beautiful in words and thoughts, without any barbariſms, ſoleciſms, or idiotiſms in it, the author being endowed both with the advantage of learning, and words, or eloquence.* Some of the moderns have very poſitively determined otherwiſe ; Grotius[e] and Dr. Cave[f] have

---

[a] Hæreſ. 30. §. 3, 6, 12.
[b] Apud Euſeb. Præp. Evang. lib. 11. p. 540. See Dr. Cave's Life of St. John, §. 15.
[c] De Civit. Dei, lib. 10. c. 29.
[d] Apud Euſeb. Hiſt. Eccl. l. 7. c. 25.
[e] Annot. in Joan. Titul.
[f] Lib. cit. §. 16.

told

told us, one after the other, *That his Greek generally abounds with Syriacifms, his difcourfes many times abrupt, fet off with frequent antithefes, connected with copulatives, paffages often repeated, things at firft more obfcurely propounded, and which he is forced to enlighten with fubfequent explications, words peculiar to himfelf, and phrafes ufed in an uncommon fenfe.* How juft this is, I fhall leave to the reader to determine, only adding a remark of Sixtus Senenfis [s], That St. John had this peculiarity in his ftyle, to make *the laft word of the former fentence, to be the firft of the next* [b].

C H A P. XV.

St. John's Gofpel proved by feveral Arguments to be Canonical. An Objection againft it refuted. It was not wrote by Cerinthus.

THAT which remains farther, is to evidence the Canonical authority of St. John's Gofpel, by the Propofitions which are laid down in the firft Part, viz.

Arg. I. St. John's Gofpel is to be efteemed Canonical by Prop. IV. becaufe *it is found in all the Catalogues of Sacred books, which we have among the writings of the primitive Chriftians.* See what is faid under this argument in treating of the preceding Gofpels, and how it is in the Catalogue of Origen, Eufebius, Athanafius, Cyril, that of the council of Laodicea, Epiphanius, Gregory Nazianzen, Philaftrius, Jerome, Ruffin, Auftin, that in the third council of Carthage, and in the books under the name of Dionyfius the Areopagite. Vol. I. Part I. Ch. VIII.

---

[a] Bibl. Sanct. lib. 6. Annot. 173.   [b] See Vol. I. of this work, Part I. Ch. XII. p. 80.

Arg.

Arg. II. The Gospel of St. John is Canonical, because *it is cited and appealed to as Scripture, in the writings of the primitive Christians*, by Prop. V.

I shall here, as in treating of the former books, shew the several places of those antient authors, who have cited this Gospel. It is cited;

I. By CLEMENS ROMANUS.

I find but one place in his Epistles, wherein he appears to have cited St. John, viz. Epist. I. §. 49. he manifestly uses those words of this Gospel, Ch. x. 15.

II. By BARNABAS.

The author of this Epistle seems plainly to have made use of this Gospel, Ch. VII. for he there not only mentions the circumstance of our Saviour's *being pierced at his crucifixion,* which is related only by St. John, (xix. 34.) but manifestly applies that prophecy, Zech. xii. 10. *And they shall look upon me whom they have pierced,* to this circumstance of Christ's passion; as St. John also does, ver. 37. What strengthens and seems to render this evidence undeniable is, that the author cannot be supposed to have thus applied the prophecy from his own reading of it in the prophet; for he, not being a Jew, understood not the Hebrew, but must be supposed to have cited (as he usually does) out of the LXX. Version. Now the LXX. have rendered this place very different from the Hebrew, and that through a blunder or mistake in their reading, confounding ד with ר and ר with ד in one and the same word, reading, viz. רקדו instead of דקרו, and so translating καταωρχήσαντο, *they insulted,* instead of ἐξεκέντησαν, *they pierced*; as St. John following the Hebrew does rightly translate. This observation of the LXX.'s mistake, was first made by Jerome [a], and after him by Erasmus, Beza, Lightfoot, Hammond,

mond,

---

[a] Ad Pammach. de optimo Genere Interpret. c. 3. An instance of a like mistake committed by the LXX. the learned may observe, Amos ix. 12. where instead of the Hebrew words, ירשו שארית אדום i. e. that *they may possess the remnant of Edom,* the

m'ond, and other critics on John xix. 37. Hence it is plain, that the author of this Epiſtle did certainly uſe St. John's Goſpel ; and what is farther remarkable to my purpoſe, uſes the very ſame verb'. I am ſenſible indeed, that ſome of the old Greek copies have theſe words, as St. John; but it is plain from Jerome, that it was not ſo in the old LXX. and if it was ſo in the Verſions of Aquila, Symmachus, or Theodotion, theſe were made after the time, in which the author of this Epiſtle is ſuppoſed to have wrote.

III. By Ignatius.

St. John's *Goſpel.*	*The leſſer Epiſtles of* Ignatius.
1 Ch. v. 19, 30. and viii. 28.	1 Epiſt. ad Magneſ. ch. vii.
2 Ch. i. 1, &c.	2 ——— ch. viii.
3 Ch. xii. 31. xiv. 30. xvi. 11. viz. the title given Satan, *The prince of this world.*	3 ——— ad Roman. ch. vii. Ἀρχῶν τῆ αἰῶνος τότε.

IV. By Justin Martyr.

St. John's *Goſpel.*	Justin Martyr's *Works.*
1 Ch. i. 1, &c.	1 Dialog. cum Tryph. Jud. p. 284, 285.
2 ——— 14.	2 Apolog. 2. pro Chriſt. p. 74.
3 Ch. iii. 3.	3 Apolog. p. 94.
4 ——— 14.	4 Dialog. cum Tryph. Jud. p. 322.
5 Ch. xix. 9.	5 Dialog. p. 329.

the LXX. read אָדָם for אֱדוֹם and ידרשו for יירשו i. e. *that the reſidue of men might ſeek the Lord.* This is the more conſiderable, be- cauſe the LXX. are followed in this tranſlation by St. James, in his inſpired diſcourſe, Acts xv. 17.

' St. John's word is ἐξεκέντησαν, and Barnabas's κατακεντήσαντες.

V. By

V. By Theophilus Antiochenus.

In his second book to *Autolycus*, he cites John i. 1, 2, &c. and introduces it thus, Διδάσκουσιν ἡμᾶς αἱ ἅγιαι γραφαὶ, καὶ πάντες οἱ πνυματοφόροι, ἐξ ὧν 'Ιωάννης λέγει, &c. i. e. *So the holy Scriptures teach, and all the* inspired writers, *among whom is John,* who saith, *In the beginning was the word,* &c.

VI. By Irenæus.

I have observed above, treating of St. Matthew's Gospel, that Feuardentius, at the end of his edition of this Father, has made with great exactness an index of most of the citations, made by Irenæus from St. Matthew. The same is to be said of his index of St. John, in which though he has not collected all, yet he has most of, the references made to it. I have examined all those, and observed several others, and dare affirm, that Irenæus has appealed to, or cited this Gospel, in above one hundred and twenty several places. It would be needless to transcribe them. I shall select only those places, where St. John's Gospel is referred to by name, viz.

1 John i. 1, &c. Adv. Hæref. lib. 1. c. 1. lib. 2. c. 2. lib. 3. c. 11. &c. lib. 5. c. 18. lib. 3. c. 8. lib. 3. c. 18, &c.
2 John iv. 6. lib. 3. c. 32.
3 ——— v. 39. lib. 4. c. 23.
4 ——— 46. lib. 4. c. 3.
5 ——— xiii. 25. lib. 3. c. 1.
6 ——— xx. 31. lib. 3. c. 18.

I will only observe farther from this antient Father, that he several times cites this Gospel under the express and distinguishing name of Scripture, or the Scripture; so for instance, citing John i. 3. (lib. i. cap. 19.) he introduces it thus, *Quemadmodum Scriptura dicit,* i. e. As the Scripture saith. *Again, citing John xiv. 6. (lib. 3. c. 5.)

---

* Though the words do indeed introduce another text, yet it is evident they are also to be referred to this.

I 4

he

he fays, he takes his proof *ex Scripturis*, i. e. *from the Scrip-tures.*

VII. By CLEMENS ALEXANDRINUS.

The editor of the Paris edition of this Father's works, has prefixed a collection of above thirty places, which are cited, as he fays, by Clemens out of St. John's Gofpel; but, as I have above obferved on St. Matthew, his collection is in fo many refpects inaccurate, falfe, and defective, that as I could not depend upon it myfelf, fo neither could I refer the reader to it. I have therefore made the following collection, which is juft, and may be fafely depended upon.

A Collection of the places of St. John's Gofpel, cited by Clemens Alexandrinus.

St. JOHN's *Gofpel.*	The *Works of* CLEMENS ALEXANDRINUS.
1 Chap. I. 1.	1 Admonit. ad Gentes p. 5. et Pædagog. lib. 1. c. viii. p. 113.
2 ——— 3.	2 Pædagog. lib. 3. c. 5. p. 233. Stromat. lib. 1. p. 292. et lib. 6. p. 662.
3 ——— 12.	3 Stromat. lib. 4. p. 484.
4 ——— 14.	4 Pædagog. lib. 1. c. 3. p. 83. et Stromat. lib. 5. p. 553.
5 ——— 16.	5 Stromat. lib. 1. p. 312.
6 ——— 17.	6 Pædagog. lib. 1. c. 7. p. 112.
7 ——— 18.	7 Stromat. lib. 5. p. 587.
8 ——— 27.	8 ——— p. 573
9 ——— 29.	9 Pædagog. lib. 1. c. 5. p. 91, 92.
10 Ch. ii. 7.	10 Pædagog. lib. 2. c. 2. p. 156.
11 Ch. iii. 6.	11 Stromat. lib. 3. p. 462.

12 Chap.

St. JOHN's *Gospel.*	The *Works of* CLEMENS ALEXANDRINUS.
12 Chap. iii. 16.	12 Pædagog. lib. 1. c. 6. p. 94. et Strom. lib. 5. p. 591.
13 ———— 19.	13 Admonit. ad Gentes, p. 63.
14 Ch. iv. 6.	14 Pædagog. lib. 1. c. 9. p. 126.
15 ———— 7.	15 Pædagog. lib. 2. c. 3. p. 161.
16 ———— 32.	16 Pædagog. lib. 1. c. 6. p. 104.
17 Ch. v. 24.	17 Pædagog. c. 6. p. 93.
18 Ch. vi. 27.	18 Stromat. lib. 1. p. 272. Stromat. lib. 3. p. 463.
19 ———— 32.	19 Pædagog. lib. 1. c. 6. p. 104.
20 ———— 36.	20 Stromat. lib. 4. p. 542.
21 ———— 39.	21 Pædagog. lib. 1. c. 6. p. 94.
22 ———— 51.	22 Pædagog. c. 6. p. 100—102.
23 Ch. vii. 16.	23 Stromat. lib. 1. p. 312.
24 ———— 18.	24 Ibid.
25 ———— 33.	25 Stromat. lib. 4. p. 468. Stromat. lib. 6. p. 666.
26 Ch. viii. 24.	26 Stromat. lib. 5. p. 591.
27 ———— 34, 35.	27 ———— lib. 2. p. 368.
28 ———— 44.	28 ———— lib. 1. p. 311.
29 Ch. x. 1.	29 ———— lib. 5. p. 590.
30 ———— 7, 9.	30 Admonit. ad Gentes, p. 8.
31 ———— 8.	31 Stromat. lib. 1. p. 309.
32 ———— 11.	32 Pædagog. lib. 1. c. 7. p. 108. Pædagog. c. 9. p. 126. Pædagog. c. 11. p. 133.

33 Chap.

St. JOHN's *Gospel.*	*The Works of* CLEMENS ALEXANDRINUS.
33 Chap. xi. 43.	33 Pædagog. lib. 1. c. 2. p. 81.
34 Ch. xiii. 5, &c.	34 Pædagog. lib. 2. c. 3. p. 161.
35 Ch. xiv. 6.	35 Stromat. lib. 1. p. 285. Stromat. lib. 5. p. 553.
36 Ch. xv. 1.	36 Pædagog. lib. 1. c. 8. p. 115. Stromat. lib. 1. p. 291.
37 —— 11, 12.	37 Stromat. lib. 2. p. 391.
38 Ch. xvi. 27.	38 Pædagog. lib. 1. cap. 3. p. 82.
39 Ch. xvii. 23.	39 Ibid.
40 —— 21—27.	40 Pædagog. lib. 1. c. 8. p. 117, 118.
41 Ch. xx. 29.	41 Stromat. lib. 2. p. 362.
42 Ch. xxi. 9, &c.	42 Pædagog. lib. 2. cap. 1. p. 147.

By all that is above said, it is undeniably evident, that this Gospel of St. John was appealed to as Scripture, in the writings of the first and most early Christians. The matter is so clear, and the citations so numerous in the writings of Tertullian, Origen, Jerome, Austin, &c. that I thought it needless to collect them.

Arg. III. The Gospel of St. John is of Canonical authority by Prop. VI. because *it was read as Scripture in the assemblies or the churches of the primitive Christians.* Not to repeat what I have above said, for the proof of this I must refer the reader to Vol. I. Part I. Ch. X. of this work, and what is said above, concerning the reading of St. Matthew's Gospel, in this Part, Chap. III.

Arg. IV. The Gospel of St. John is of Canonical authority, by Prop. XV. because *it was esteemed as such by the*

churches

churches of Syria in or near the Apostles' time, and accordingly placed by them among their collection of sacred books.

All the objection, which has been made against the authority of this Gospel, is, *that it was not written by St. John, but a noted Heretick, Cerinthus,* who was cotemporary with St. John. This was first asserted by the Hereticks, whom Epiphanius calls Ἄλογοι, *Alogians,* because they did not believe the λόγος, or *word,* spoken of in the first chapter of the Gospel; (see Epiphan. Hæres. 51. §. 1, 2, 3.) Nor do I know, that any of the antient Hereticks besides these were of this opinion. Sixtus Senensis [a] and Father Simon [b] tell us, the Theodotians, or followers of Theodotus Byzantius, followed the Alogians herein; but I believe these two learned writers were led into this mistake by a too hasty reading of the words of Epiphanius, (Hæres. 51. §. 1.) where this is not asserted of the Theodotians. Mr. Toland indeed, has insinuated this objection against the credit of St. John's Gospel [c]; but it is easy to answer him and his brethren the *Alogi.*

1. *That the Gospel is directly contrary to the doctrines of Cerinthus.* He taught, that Christ *was in all respects a mere man,* ψιλὸς ἄνθρωπος, born as other men. This Gospel evidently *asserts the contrary. How can it be* (says Epiphanius, §. 4.) *that those things should be wrote by Cerinthus, which are directly contrary to Cerinthus?* See this argument farther pursued, and well managed, by that Father in the place cited.

2. The antient writers assure us, that *this Gospel was written by St. John, with the particular intention of confuting the heresy of Cerinthus.* So Irenæus [d], Epiphanius [e], Jerome [f], &c. See this proved above, Ch. XIV. in the beginning.

3. Besides these silly and late Hereticks, the Alogians, *all the Christians do unanimously ascribe it to St. John.* I call them late, because, according to Epiphanius, (Hær. 51. §. 1.) they did not arise till after the Montanists, i. e. not till

[a] Biblioth. Sanct. l. 7. de Evang. Joan. Hæres.

[b] Critic. Hist. of the New Test. Part 1. ch. 13. p. 117.

[c] Amyntor, p. 65.

[d] Adv. Hæres. lib. 3. c. 11.

[e] Hæres. 51. §. 4. & 12.

[f] Præfat. in Comment. in Matt. & Catal. Vir. Illustr. in Joan.

after

after the latter end of the second century. The fathers who have ascribed this Gospel to St. John, as its author, are above cited in the preceding Chapter; to which I add, that in the *Hypotyposes*, under the name of Clemens Alexandrinus [a], the author stiles him πνύματι θεοφορηθέντα: i. e. *inspired by the Holy Ghost in writing his Gospel*; and Origen [b] says, this Gospel was received as his, among the ἀναντιῤῥητα ἐν τῇ ὑπὸ τὸν οὐρανὸν ἐκκλησία τῦ Θῦ: i. e. *the books which were admitted by all the churches in the world.* He who has a mind, may see more in answer to the opinion of Cerinthus being the author of St. John's Gospel, in Epiphanius, Sixtus Senensis, and Father Simon, in the places already cited; and besides these, in the two answers of Mr. Nye [c], and Mr. Richardson [d], to Amyntor, and Dr. Whitby's preface to his Annotations upon this Gospel.

As to the portions of this Gospel, which are supposed not to be written by John, viz. the history of the adulterous woman, ch. viii. and the whole last chapter of the Gospel; I have no more to say, than that concerning the former I have said somewhat, Vol. I. Part I. Ch. XVIII. p. 111. and the latter is only a conjecture of Grotius [e], without any solid foundation; as is well judged by the French critics, Father Simon [f] and Du Pin [g]; and after them, by Dr. Mill, Prolegom. in Nov. Test. §. 249.

---

[a] Apud Euseb. Hist. Eccl. l. 6, c. 14.
[b] Exposit. in Matt. lib. 1. apud Euseb. Hist. Ecclef. lib. 6. c. 25.
[c] Defence of the Canon, p. 81.

[d] Canon Vindicated, p. 73.
[e] Annot. in Joan. xx. 30.
[f] Crit. Hist. New Test. loc. cit.
[g] Hist. of the Canon of the New Test. Vol. ii. c. 2. §. 6.

CHAP.

CHAP. XVI.

*St. Luke was the Author of the Acts of the Apostles. This
proved from many Testimonies of the antient Fathers. An
Objection from the Synopsis, under the Name of Athanasius,
refuted. The Acts contain the History of the Christian
Church for the Space of twenty-eight Years. The Time of
St. Luke's writing the Acts discovered. Whether he went
to Alexandria? The Acts were soon translated into Hebrew.*

I. ST. Luke, the author of the Gospel under that name,
was also the author of the book intitled, THE ACTS OF
THE APOSTLES. This is apparent from the constant testimony of all antiquity, the matter being never once questioned
by any of the Catholick Church.   I shall mention only those
which are most antient.

1. Irenæus has in several places *ascribed this History to
St. Luke, as its author*; for instance, citing the History, Acts
viii. 9. he introduces it thus: *Luke, the disciple and follower
of the Apostles,* says thus, *A certain man, named Simon*[a]; in
another place[b], citing Acts xv. 39, &c. he saith, *Luke was the
inseparable companion and fellow-labourer of Paul, and wrote
thus,* viz. concerning the contention of Paul and Barnabas;
and then proceeds largely to prove, that St. Luke was the
constant companion of St. Paul, because in the Acts, Chap.
xvi. 10, 11, 12, 16, 17, and Chap. xx. xxi. and xxvii. he
speaks in the *first person plural,* " WE endeavoured, WE came,
" WE went, WE sate down, and WE spake, &c." all which
proves, that Irenæus looked upon Luke as the undoubted author of this book.   The same he proves from several places of
St. Paul's Epistles (viz. 2 Tim. iv. 11. Col. iv. 14.) and
concludes from the whole *St. Luke's fitness for writing a just*

---

[a] Discipulus et sectator Aposto-   *mon,* &c. adv. Hæref. lib. i. c. 20.
lorum ait; *Vir quidam, nomine Si-*   [b] Adv. Hæref. lib. 3. c. 14.

and

and true history. In another place [a] he shews, that St. Luke's
Acts of the Apostles *ought to be equally received with his Gospel; for that in them he has carefully delivered to us the truth, and given us a sure rule for salvation,* &c. Again, lib. 3.
c. 13. he observes, that *St. Paul's account,* Gal. ii. 1. of the
time when he went to Jerusalem, *exactly agrees with Luke's
account in the Acts.* Lastly, this Father, citing part of Stephen's speech, Acts vii. introduces it thus, *So Luke writes,*
&c [b].

2. Clemens Alexandrinus [c], citing *Paul's speech at Athens,*
Acts xvii. 22, &c. introduces it, *So Luke in the Acts of the
Apostles relates that Paul said,* &c.

3. The Author of the Hypotyposes, under the name of
Clemens Alexandrinus [d], speaking of the *Epistle to the Hebrews,* says it was translated out of its original Hebrew, in
which it was written by Paul, into Greek by Luke; whence,
says he, we may observe, that there is a *great likeness in the
style of that Epistle, and the Acts of the Apostles*; from whence
it is manifest, this author esteemed Luke the author of *the Acts
of the Apostles.*

4. Tertullian cites several places out of *the Acts of the Apostles,* which he calls *Commentarius Lucæ,* i. e. the Commentary
of Luke [e].

5. Origen ascribes *the Acts of the Apostles* to Luke [f].

6. Eusebius saith, *Luke has left us two inspired volumes,* viz.
the Gospel and *the Acts* [g].

---

[a] Adv. Hæref. lib. 3. c. 15.
[b] Lucas Stephanum fic dixiffe
fcripfit. Adv. Hæref. lib. 4. c. 29.
[c] Καὶ ὁ Λουκᾶς ἐν ταῖς Πράξε-
σι τῶν ἀποτόλων ἀπομνημονεύει τὸν
Παῦλον λέγοντα.   Strom. lib. 5.
p. 588.
[d] Ὅθεν τὸν αὐτὸν χρῶτα ἐυρίσ-
κεσθαι κατὰ τὴν ἑρμηνείαν ταύτης τι
τῆς ἐπιστολῆς καὶ τῶν Πράξεων.

Apud Eufeb. Hift. Eccl. lib. 6.
c. 14.
[e] Lib. de jejun. adverf. Pfych.
cap. 10.
[f] Λουκᾶς ὁ γράψας τὸ Εὐαγγέλιον, καὶ τὰς Πράξεις. Apud Eufeb.
Hift. Ecclef. lib. 6. c. 25. It may
indeed be queftioned, whether thefe
are the words of Origen, or Eufebius himfelf.
[g] Hift. Ecclef. lib. 3. c. 4.

7. Jerome

7. Jerome also expressly asserts *the Acts* to be *the compo-sure of Luke* [a].

8. *Several antient manuscript Greek copies have the name of St. Luke prefixed to this History* (Simon. Crit. Hist. of the New Test. Part I. c. 14.); as also hath the old Syriack Ver-sion, which seems in this case to have some weight, as agreeing with all antiquity.

From all this testimony my proposition is abundantly evi-dent; nor have I met with any thing which can be objected hereto, unless that it be made an objection, which we read in the author of the *Synopsis Scripturarum*, under the name of Athanasius, viz. that *Peter dictated the Acts of the Apostles, but Luke wrote them* [b]; but it is easy to reply;

1. *That one single testimony is not to be credited against the universal concurrence of antiquity.*

2. It is very evident, that *Luke wrote the greatest part of this book of his own knowledge*, and so had no need of any one to dictate to him. And hence Eusebius says, *he wrote the Acts not from tradition, or hearsay, but as what he saw and heard* [c]; and Jerome expressly [d], *he wrote the Acts from what himself saw.* Besides, as Luke was the constant companion of Paul, he was more capable of writing his history, which is the greatest part of the book, than Peter could be.

II. *The Acts of the Apostles*, written by St. Luke, *contain the history of the infant state of the Christian Church, for the space of about twenty-eight years.* He begins this History where his Gospel-history ended, viz. with an account of our Saviour's ascension, and what followed in the Church after-wards. He ends his History with the relation of Paul's being brought to Rome, and his abode there for the space of two years (xxviii. 30, 31.) Hence the truth of the proposition will be clearly evinced; for, whereas our Saviour ascended in

[a] Catalog. viror. illustr. in Jo-an.
[b] Τὰς Πράξεις τῶν ἀποστόλων, ὑπηγόρευσι μὲν Πέτρ۞ ὁ ἀπόστολος,
συνεγράψατο δὲ ὁ αὐτὸς Λουκᾶς. Vid. Synops.
[c] Loc. cit.
[d] Acta apostolorum, sicut vide-rat, composuit. Loc. cit.

the year from his birth 33, and St. Paul went to Rome in the fourth or fifth year of Nero's reign, i. e. in the year of Chrift 58, or rather 59; if we add to this number the two years of his abode there, with which account the hiftory of the Acts is concluded, it will produce the year 61, which from the year 33, makes juft twenty-eight years.

: There is indeed the difference of *two years* between the above account, and that of Bifhop Pearfon [a], Spanheim [b], Dr. Mill [c], and fome others; but as the difference is fo fmall, and my account is conformable to the common chronology of Chriftianity, I fhall fay no more.

COROLL. *Hence we fee* near to what time *this Hiflory of the Acts was written*, viz. *either in the year of Chrift* 62, *or not long after*. It being altogether probable, that St. Luke would not defer his writing long after his departure from St. Paul; which feems to have been now, when the Apoftle was fet at liberty from his confinement at Rome. I have above obferved (Chap. XI.), treating of St. Luke's Gofpel, that St. Luke continued at Rome after St. Paul went thence; and there it is probable, he wrote very foon both his *Gofpel* and *Acts*. That he wrote them both in the fame year feems very probable, as it is certain that one of them is only to be looked upon as the fecond part, or continuation of the other. Dr. Grabe [d], to ferve a particular defign, and after him Dr. Mill [e], fuppofe St. Luke to have gone, immediately upon his parting from St. Paul, into Egypt, and there at Alexandria to have publifhed both his Gofpel and Acts of the Apoftles, A. D. 64. The foundation of this opinion is partly the affertion of it in the title of the Syriack Verfion, and partly the credit of the Conftitutions of the Apoftles, in which it is faid, that Luke ordained Avilius, fecond Bifhop of Alexandria (lib. 7. c. 46.); but neither of thefe are of any weight, the titles and epigraphs of

[a] Annal. Paulin. p. 18.
[b] Hiftor. Chrift. Sæcul. I. §. 6.
[c] Prolegom. in Nov. Teft. §. 121.

[d] Spicileg. Patr. tom. 1. p. 32, 33.
[e] Prolegom. in Nov. Teft. §. 114, et 121.

this

this Version not being of very certain authority, and the Constitutions of the Apostles of much less, or none at all.

III. *The Acts of the Apostles* seem to have been very early translated out of Greek into Hebrew. This, Epiphanius tells us [a], he had by information from several Jews, and afterwards [b], that one Josephus found a copy of the Acts in Hebrew in the Jewish archives at Tiberias.

CHAP. XVII.

The Acts of the Apostles proved to be Canonical by various Arguments. A Mistake of some learned Men corrected; viz. that the Acts were not so much known or regarded, as the other Books of the New Testament. A Passage of a Book under the Name of Chrysostom to this Purpose, largely considered. Who among the antient Hereticks rejected the Acts.

Arg. I. THE *Acts of the Apostles* are of Canonical authority by Prop. IV. because it is found in all the catalogues of sacred books, which we have in the writings of the primitive Christians. See Vol. I. Part I. Ch. VIII.

Arg. II. *The Acts of the Apostles* are of Canonical authority, because they are cited and appealed to as Scripture, in the writings of the primitive Christians, by Prop. V. as will appear from the following instances.

The Acts of the Apostles are cited,

I. By CLEMENS ROMANUS, Epist. I. *ad Corinth.*
Ch. II. He cites the words, which are Acts xx. 35.
Ch. XVIII. *He certainly made use of, and appears to have read,* Acts xiii. 22. For, whereas Paul in that place manifestly

---

[a] Hæref. 30. Ebionit. §. 3.   [b] Ibid. §. 6. et §. 12.

VOL. III.   K   cites

cites Pſalm lxxxix. 26. and makes an addition or paraphraſe in the citation, inſerting thoſe words κατα την καρδιαν μυ, which are not in the Pſalm, Clemens citing the ſame Pſalm has inſertcd Paul's addition. Nor is there any room to objeĉt, *that perhaps they both cited according to the Septuagint* ; for there are no ſuch words in any of the copies of the Septuagint, nor any various reading like it to be found.

II. By POLYCARP, *Epiſt. ad Philipp.*

Ch. I. He cites thoſe words of Peter's ſpeech, which are recorded, Aĉts ii. 24.

III. By JUSTIN MARTYR.

Cohort. ad Græc. p. 11. he cites Aĉts vii. 22. viz. *that Moſes was learned in all the wiſdom of the Egyptians.* And as Juſtin could not gather this out of the book of Exodus, ſo among other reaſons it is certain he did not, becauſe he cites thoſe whom he calls σοφωτατοι των ισοριογεαφων, thoſe excellent hiſtorians, who wrote Moſes's life and aĉtions ; which cannot refer to the Pentateuch.

In the book under Juſtin's name, undoubtedly antient, the Aĉts are often referred to ; e. g. Expoſit. Fidei de reĉt. Conſeſ. p. 375. reference is made to Aĉts ix. 15. and Quæſt. et Reſponſ. ad Orthodox. which perhaps is partly Juſtin's, it is often cited, viz. Aĉts i. 7. Quæſt. 112. iv. 18. Reſponſ. ad Quæſt. 24. et Reſponſ. ad Quæſt. 108. vii. 22. Quæſt. 25. x. per tot. Quæſt. 89. xxiii. 3. Quæſt. 125. and many other places.

IV. By IRENÆUS.

This Father has often appealed to theſe Aĉts of St. Luke: I have made the following collection.

The Aĉts of the Apoſtles.	*The Works of* IRENÆUS.
1 Chap. i. 7.	1 Lib. 1. adv. Hæreſ. c. 33.
2 ——— 8.	2 Ib. 3. c. 1.
3 ——— 16, 17.	3 ——— 12.
4 ——— 20.	4 ——— 12. et Lib. 1. c. 36.

The

The Acts of the Apostles.	*The Works of* IRENÆUS.
5 Ch. ii. 15, 16, 17, 22, 29.	5 Lib. 3. c. 12.
6 ——— 41.	6 Ib. 4. c. 40.
7 Ch. iii. 6, 7, 8, 12.	7 Ib. 3. c. 12.
8 Ch. iv. 8, 9, 24, 31, 33.	8 Ib. p. 264.
9 ——— 32.	9 Ib. 1. c. 3.
10 Ch. v. 30, 42.	10 Ib. 3. c. 12.
11 Ch. vii. 2—7.	11 Ib.
	N. B. *Here he calls this book Scripture several times.*
12 Ch. vii. 38, 39, 40.	12 Lib. 29.
	Here Luke is named.
13 ——— 56, &c.	13 Ib. 3. c. 12.
14 Ch. viii. 9.	14 Ib. 1. c. 20.
	Here Luke is named also, and called a Disciple and companion of the Apostles.
15 ——— 17.	15 Ib. 4. c. 75.
16 ——— 20, &c.	16 Ib. 1. c. 20.
17 ——— 30, &c.	17 Ib. 4. c. 40. et Lib. 3. c. 12.
18 ——— 33, 37.	18 Ib.
19 Ch. ix. 4, 5, &c.	19 Ib.
20 ——— 4, 5, 15, 16.	20 Ib. 3. c. 15.
	Here Irenæus argues for the credit of Luke and his Acts.
21 ——— 20.	21 Ib. 3. c. 12.
22 Ch. x. 1, &c. 25.	22 Ib.
23 ——— 28.	23 Ib.
24 ——— 35, 37.	24 Ib.
25 Ch. xiv. 15.	25 Ib.
26 Ch. xv. 7, &c.	26 Ib.
27 ——— 23, &c.	27 Ib.
28 Ch. xvi. 9, &c.	28 Ib. 3. c. 14.
	This whole chapter is taken

up

The Acts of the Apostles.	*The Works of* IRENÆUS.
	up in afferting the credit of St. Luke, and the ufefulnefs of his writings.
29 Ch. xvii. 24—31.	29 ——— 12.
30 Ch. xx. 6.	30 ——— 14.

V. By CLEMENS ALEXANDRINUS.

The Acts of the Apostles.	*The Works of* CLEMENS ALEXANDRINUS.
1 Ch. vi. 2.	1 Pædagog. lib. 2. c. 7. p. 172.
2 Ch. x. 11—16.	2 ——— lib. 2. c. 1. p. 149.
3 ——— 34, 35.	3 Stromat. lib. 6. p. 646.
4 Ch. xv. 28, &c.	4 Pædagog. lib. 2. c. 7. p. 172. et Strom. lib. 4. p. 512.
5 Ch. xvii. 22, &c.	5 Stromat. lib. 5. p. 588. *Here Luke is cited by name as the author of the Acts.*
6 ——— 24, &c.	6 ——— p. 584. *See this speech of Paul, also Strom. lib. 1. p. 314, 315.*
7 Ch. xxvi. 17, &c.	7 Ib.

VI. By TERTULLIAN.

He makes very numerous appeals to, and citations from, thefe Acts; it would be tedious to collect them all; I choofe rather to obferve, that this Father cites it under the exprefs name of *Scripture: which part of Scripture,* fays he, *they who do not receive, muft deny the defcent of the Holy Ghoft, and be ignorant of the infant ftate of the Chriftian Church* [a]. In like

---

[a] Quam Scripturam qui non recipiunt, nec Spiritum Sanctum poffunt agnofcere, difcentibus miffum, &c. De Præfcript. adv. Hæretic. cap. 22.

manner

manner he calls it *Scripture* in another place [a], *disputes* against the Marcionites, and *condemns* them for rejecting the Acts, proving *their truth and genuineness by* the testimonies of St. Paul in his Epistles, and in another place [b] expresly calls it the *composure of Luke.* I will not tire the reader with any more collections of the Fathers' appeals to these Acts. The later Fathers cite them continually, as the only authentick history they had, of the primitive state of the church. I proceed:

Arg. III. The Acts of the Apostles are Canonical, *because they were read as Scripture in the churches or assemblies of the Christians in the first ages, by Prop. VI.* For the evidence of this, it will be sufficient to consult Vol. I. Part I. Ch. X. and what is above said, concerning the reading of St. Matthew's Gospel, in this Part, Ch. III.

Coroll. I. From this and the preceding arguments, it is evident, that several learned men are *very grosly mistaken,* who conclude, that the Acts of the Apostles *were less known, less read, and less regarded in the first centuries, than the other books of the New Testament.* The foundation of their opinion is a passage in the *Prolegomena* upon the *Acts,* under the name of *Chrysostom* [c], which begins thus: *This book is not so much as known to many; they know neither the book, nor by whom it was written.* Hence those, who always labour to lessen the credit of the Canon, have drawn fine conclusions.

1. Father Simon [d] concludes hence, that *the Gospels and the Epistles of St. Paul were then* (viz. in Chrysostom's time, i. e. in the fifth century) *only accounted to belong to the New Testament:* perhaps, says he, *none but these two works, were read in the churches in those primitive ages.*

---

[a] Scripturam Actorum Apostolorum confirmat. Adv. Marcion. l. 5. c. 2.

[b] Commentarium Lucæ. Lib. de Jejun. adv. Psych. cap. 10.

[c] Πολλοῖς τατὸ τὸ βιβλίον ὅο

ὅτι γνώριμόν ἐςιν, ὅτι αὐτὸ, ὅτι ὁ γράψας αἰτὸ καὶ συνθείς. Vid. Mill. Præf. in Act. p. 254.

[d] Critic. Hist. of the N. T. Par. 1. ch. 14.

2. Dr.

2. Dr. Mill[a], after having faid the Gofpels were foon fpread into every one's hands, adds, " The cafe was not fo " with the other books of the New Teftament; for the books " of the Acts being of fomewhat lefs ufefulnefs, than the Gof- " pel of Luke, as containing the hiftory, not of Chrift, but " of his Apoftles, or rather indeed only of Paul, was neither " read in the churches, nor wrote out but by very few;" then he cites the paffage of Chryfoftom above produced.

Thus did thefe two learned men endeavour, without any arguments, to leffen the credit of this facred book: for if my preceding arguments are good, and the Acts of the Apoftles be in all the catalogues of the facred books among the antients; if it was cited by all the firft Chriftians in their writings, and was read in their churches (all which I have undeniably proved); with what face could thefe gentlemen tell the world, that it was not read nor known among the Chriftians? The book appears, by all the writings of antiquity, to have been almoft as much known as the Gofpels themfelves, and as conftantly ufed: but their refuge is the paffage of Chryfoftom: he fays, *It was not known to many.* To which I reply,

1. *That this does not appear to be the work of Chryfoftom,* and Dr. Mill himfelf[b] fufpected it: *Chryfoftomus,* fays he, *vel alius quifpiam fub ejus nomine,* &c. Bellarmine indeed contends for its genuinenefs[c]. Erafmus[d] feems to have thought that it was not his; and fo it is moft probable.

2. It does not follow, that, *becaufe feveral perfons, or moft, in the country, where this author wrote, were ignorant of the Acts; that therefore it was not known to the greateft part of the Chriftian church.* Erafmus fuppofes[e], that the author means only, that *it was unknown to the rabble; but the learned know it.* It is much better explained by the learned Fabricius[f].

---

[a] Proleg. in N. T. §. 242, 243.
[b] Ibid.
[c] De Script. Ecclef. in Chryfoftom.
[d] Annot. in Act. i. 1.
[e] Ibid.

[f] Sed apparet hifce verbis potius fupinam quorundam inícitiam et torporem, quam publicam Ecclefiæ fuorum temporum negligentiam, a viro difertiffimo reprehendi et increpari. Ced. Apoc. N. T. t. 2. p. 751.

Thefe

These words, fays he, *rather fhew, that the wretched ignorance and lazinefs of fome particular perfons was condemned by Chryfoftom, than the negligence of the univerfal church in his time.*

3. If Chryfoftom himfelf had pofitively afferted, that the Acts of the Apoftles were not known and read in his time, he ought not to be believed, becaufe the evidence is fo plain to the contrary from fo many authors.

4. Add to this, that Chryfoftom himfelf in another place faith, that the Acts of the Apoftles was wont to be read in their churches after Eafter, and before Whitfuntide; for this he affigns this reafon, that nothing can more convictively evidence the refurrection of Chrift, which is the bafis of all our religion, than the pouring forth of the Holy Ghoft, and the propagation of the Gofpel by their miniftry over the world; all which is recorded in the Acts. Vid. Fabric. Cod. Apoc. N. T. Præfat. in tom. 2. And this, by the way, feems to me no fmall evidence of what I have above faid, viz. that the book upon the Acts, from whence the paffage under debate was taken, was not made by Chryfoftom; if it was, Chryfoftom muft contradict himfelf in a plain matter of fact, viz. In one place he afferts the book not to be known; and in another, that it was publickly read in the churches.

Erafmus, though he feems not to give any credit to the paffage under the name of Chryfoftom, yet, for another reafon, concludes the Acts were not fo much known in the Greek church, as the Gofpels and Paul's Epiftles, viz. *becaufe,* as he fays, *major erat lectionis varietas, he found more various lections in the MSS. of this, than any other of the facred books.* What this learned critic means, I know not; if his argument will prove any thing, it is the direct contrary; for the more various lections there are of any book, the more often it has been tranfcribed, and confequently the more it appears to have been in ufe.

Arg. IV. The Acts of the Apoftles are Canonical, becaufe the book is found among thofe which were received by the churches of Syria as fuch, and which they collected together as Scripture, and tranflated; Prop. XV.

From

From what is said it appears, that the Acts have as much evidence of their genuineness and Canonical authority, as they need to have, or can be supposed to have, at this distance of time from their writing. I know nothing that has been objected against the authority of this sacred volume ; nor indeed that can be, unless it should be said, that *some of the first and most early Hereticks of the church did not receive it as Scripture.* The fact is indeed certain. The Acts appear to have been rejected by several of them. Tertullian tells us, that Cerdo (whose disciple Marcion was) rejected the Acts as false [a] ; and in the same book [b] disputes against some whom he does not name, who denied this part of Scripture ; and in his dispute against Marcion [c], confutes him and his disciples for their absurd opinion of rejecting the Acts. Philastrius informs us, that the Cerinthians also did not receive it [d] : as Austin likewise [e], that the Manichees did not, because they looked upon Manes or Manichæus *to be the Paraclete foretold, John* xvi. *whereas the Acts of the Apostles expressly declare it* to have been the Holy Ghost, who descended upon the Apostles. I have carefully examined the several places, where these Hereticks are said to have rejected the Acts, but find not any one reason assigned for their doing so. But to end in Father Simon's words [f] ; " Let us leave these enthusiasts, who had no " other reason to refuse the books that were approved by the " whole Church, than this, that they did not suit with the idea, " which they had formed of the Christian religion."

---

[a] Lib. de Præscript. adv. Hæretic. c. 51. Acta Apostolorum quasi falsa rejicit. Vid. Pamel. Annot. in loc.

[b] Cap. 22. Quam Scripturam qui non recipiunt, nec Spiritum Sanctum possunt agnoscere, &c.

[c] Adv. Marcion. lib. 5. c. 2.

[d] Hæref. 26.

[e] De Utilitate credendi, ad Honorat. cap. 3.

[f] Critic. Hist. of New Test. Par. I. c. 14. in fine.

A

VINDICATION

OF

THE FORMER PART

OF

Sᴛ. MATTHEW's GOSPEL,

FROM

Mʀ. WHISTON's CHARGE ᴏꜰ DISLOCATIONS.

ᴏʀ

An Attempt to prove, that our prefent Gʀᴇᴇᴋ Cᴏᴘɪᴇs of that Gᴏsᴘᴇʟ aɽe in the fame Order, wherein they were originally written by that Eᴠᴀɴɢᴇʟɪsᴛ.

ɪɴ ᴡʜɪᴄʜ ᴀʀᴇ ᴄᴏɴᴛᴀɪɴᴇᴅ,

Many Things relating to the Harmony and Hiftory of the Fᴏᴜʀ Gᴏsᴘᴇʟs.

———

By JEREMIAH JONES.

Mr. SAMUEL JONES.

Sir,

OF all thofe various ftudies in which mankind are employed, there are none in which the
Chriftian fhould more heartily engage, than
thofe which have a tendency to advance the
honour, and promote the knowledge, of the
facred Scriptures.

The underftanding the two original languages, in which the Bible was written, an acquaintance with the dialects of the Hebrew,
the antient Verfions of the Old and New Teftament, the cuftoms of the Jews, and other
neighbouring nations, are means very neceffary
for obtaining thefe ends.   By thefe and fome
other fuch means, very great advances were
made towards the knowledge of the Scriptures,
in the beginning of the laft century.   Difficulties, which before feemed infuperable, were
folved, and feeming contradictions, which gave
occafion to the enemies of Chriftianity, to *blaf-
pheme the good word of God,* were by thefe
means happily and fully reconciled.   Grotius,
Scaliger,

Scaliger, Cafaubon, Drufius, Spanheim, Hammond, Lightfoot, &c. to the great advantage of Chriftianity, employed their endeavours in thefe ftudies; and nothing is more to be lamented, than that fo few fince their time have followed their example, and endeavoured to promote the fame fort of knowledge.

How unwearied and fuccefsful your endeavours, Sir, have been, to revive this fort of learning among us, there are many who will gratefully acknowledge, and future generations will have juft occafion to own. It is owing to you, Sir, and your inftructions, that a great number of youth are now employed in endeavours, by the ufe of the forementioned means, to underftand, and make others underftand, the facred Scripture. I defign not to fill an Epiftle with any of the trite naufeous flattering expreffions, of which dedications ordinarily confift. Flattery is what, I know, you neceffarily hate, and, to fpeak your praife, I need not. All I defign is to improve the opportunity I now have, publickly to acknowledge myfelf obliged to you for all the proficiency I have made, either in the forementioned, or any other ftudies, and withal to exprefs my defire of your future greater fuccefs in your ufeful work.

Go on then, Sir, and may heaven ftill blefs you with the continuance of your health, and defired fuccefs; may you ftill be the happy in-
ftrument

ftrument of making many fit for publick ufefulnefs, and eminent fervice to the Church of
Chrift, and the intereft of true Religion.

This, Sir, is the very earneft defire of

Your moft Obliged

Humble Servant,

JEREMIAH JONES.

THE

... and eminent service to the Church of Christ, and the interest of true Religion.

Your most Obliged

Humble Servant,

JEREMIAH JONES.

THE PREFACE.

EVERY one, who makes a profeſſion of Chriſtianity, does thereby oblige himſelf to uſe his utmoſt
endeavours, in all poſſible inſtances, for the ſupport, defence, and advancement of that excellent
Religion ; and if, in this matter, our zeal and diligence ought to be proportionable to the induſtry
and numbers of thoſe, who would ſubvert our Religion, perhaps there never was a time, in which
our zeal and diligence ſhould be greater. Irreligion
indeed, *in its practice,* has been the reproach of all
ages, but its open and publick defence ſeems to be
peculiar to ours. It is but of late, that men have
learnt to ſecure the undiſturbed poſſeſſion of their
vices and immoralities, by a profeſſed diſbelief of
the grand maxims of piety and virtue. It is but of
late, that it has been reckoned *a perfection,* boldly
to beat down, and level, the eternal *differences of
good and evil.* In many companies he now makes
the beſt figure, who gives the largeſt proofs of his
profaneneſs; and he is a man of the greateſt fire and
wit, that dares to ſpeak moſt contemptibly of God,
and his providence. It is now become a faſhion-

able accomplifhment, wittily to deride, and droll upon, facred things, and boldly to doubt and dif-believe every thing in the facred Scriptures, *only becaufe it is there.*

How it comes to pafs, that profanenefs and fcep-ticifm fhould fo much abound in the prefent age, may very well deferve a ferious enquiry. Among other unhappy caufes, I cannot but believe the growing difbelief and contempt of Revealed Re-ligion, and that growth of profanenefs, which ne-ceffarily follows fuch difbelief, are very much owing to the imprudent treatment, the facred Scrip-tures have met with from many of thofe, who pró-fefs to believe their infpiration. The many me-thods that have been taken (even by feveral of the Chriftian Clergy) *to render the Canon of Scripture uncertain*; the preferring fome *forry Verfions before the Originals*, and confequently correcting and al-tering the Originals by thefe Verfions; *the great freedoms that have been taken with the facred text,* by a groundlefs fuppofition of corruptions and contradictions therein, have been the unhappy means of making many reject the Revelation it-felf. The unguarded difcourfes of divers learned and ingenious men on thofe heads, have fupplied the enemies of Chriftianity with arguments againft it, and been many ways improved by evil minds to its difhonour. Thefe are the weapons, with which Hobbes, Spinozá[a], Toland[b], and the *club of De-*

---

[a] Tractat. Theolog. Politic. c. 8, 9.　　[b] In his Amyntor.

ifts,

ifts, or *free-thinkers*[a] (as they love to be called), have fought againft all Revealed Religion; and it is but too well known, how eafily weak and degenerate minds have been influenced, and impofed upon, by their fophiftry.

Among the various methods that have been taken to weaken the credit of the holy Scriptures, I cannot but reckon that which Mr. Whifton has taken, to reconcile the difference which there is between St. Matthew and the other Evangelifts, *in point of time*, to be one. The third propofition of his Harmony is, that *the former part of St. Matthew's Gofpel, in our prefent copies, is very much mifplaced, contrary to the method and order, originally intended by the Evangelift.* He accounts for this by fuppofing, *that the feveral parts or periods of this former part of St. Matthew's Gofpel, were written at firft feparately, and upon feveral diftinct papers; which papers, or whatever they were written upon, were put together into their prefent order, by thofe who did not perfectly know the true feries of the hiftory.* Thefe diftinct pieces of paper muft have been (according to this fuppofition) about twenty in number, of very unequal fizes, fome containing feveral chapters, others but a few verfes, and others not above one or two lines. Such a propofition, and fuch confequences, muft needs tend to leffen the value and authority of this Gofpel, and make it lefs to be depended upon than any common profane hiftory.

[a] Difcourfe of Free-Thinking, p. 85, 86, &c.

Hence Spinoza and Father Simon (who have la-
boured above all men, to prove the uncertainty of
the facred text) fuppofe feveral parts of the writings of the Old Teftament tranfpofed and difordered. The former tells us, " that if we will ob-
" ferve how little regard is had to the order of
" time, in the five books of Mofes, we fhall eafily
" perceive, that the feveral parts of it were con-
" fufedly fet together²." The latter tells us, " that
" we are not to attribute to Mofes, the little order
" which is to be found in fome places of the Pen-
" tateuch : it is (fays he) more probable, that, as
" in thofe times the books were written on little
" fcrolls or feparate fheets, that were fewed to-
" gether, the order of thefe fheets might be
" changedᵇ." Mr. Whifton in another book, (viz.
His Accomplifhment of Scripture Prophecies) is of the
fame opinion concerning the books of the Old Teftament. " I muft (fays he) be fo free and fair to
" confefs, I cannot every where look upon the pre-
" fent order, either of the hiftories or prophecies
" of the Old Teftament, to have been the original
" one, or that which was intended by the penmen
" of themᶜ." How direct a tendency fuch an opinion as this has, to weaken the authority, and leffen the value, of thefe facred books, is but too evident. Mr. Whifton does himfelf call his propofition, *a new and ftrange one,* and is very careful to
guard himfelf againft thofe cenfures and imputa-

Tractat. Theolog. Polit. c. 9.
ᵇ Critic. Hiftor. of the Old. Teft. B. 1. c. 5. p. 40.
ᶜ Pag. 67.

tions,

tions, to which fo bold an affertion did expófe him. He eafily forefaw, that fo fevere an attack made upon one, and by confequence upon all the facred writers, muft needs meet with the warmeft refent-ment from every mind, that had juft value for the infpired volume. After a clofe and impartial con-fideration of Mr. Whifton's propofition, I not only concluded it falfe, but very injurious to the honour of this Gofpel, and therefore refolved (according to my ability) to vindicate this part of the Gofpel hiftory from fo great an injury. This is the defign of the following difcourfe. It were to be wifhed fome more able perfon had undertaken this work fooner, when Mr. Whifton's book firft came out. But if his affertion be proved falfe, it is better now than not at all; *Sat cito, fi fat bene.*

I fhould do Mr. Whifton injuftice, if I did not here mention, that he has changed his opinion in refpect of St. Matthew's Gofpel being originally written in Hebrew; but I muft defire the reader alfo to obferve, that the information Mr. Whifton was pleafed to give me of this, was after I had wrote all I defigned on that head.

The reader will obferve that the Greek words in the following difcourfe are all printed without their ufual accents[a]. I do not think it needful to make any long apology for this; only would ob-ferve, that they are but a late appendage to the language, and not found in any manufcripts, which

[a In this Edition the accents are preferved.]

are

are a thoufand years old. The original defign of them was, to affift and direct in the pronunciation of the language ; but it not being at all needful for us to pronounce it as the Grecians did, the accents are to us ufelefs, and no more neceffary in Greek than Latin.

THE

THE

CONTENTS.

CHAP. I.

CHAP. II.

CHAP III.

CHAP.

counts are generally larger, and contain many more particular circumſtances, than St. Matthew's do. *This evidenced by ſeveral inſtances.*

CHAP. VIII.

The third argument, by which it appears, that St. Mark's Goſpel is not an epitome of St. Matthew's, viz. the remarkable diſagreement there ſeems to be, between theſe two Evangeliſts, in ſeveral parts of their Goſpels. It is firſt premiſed, that all theſe are reconcileable. Then the particular inſtances of their diſagreement produced.

CHAP. IX.

The fourth argument, to prove St. Mark's Goſpel is not an epitome of St. Matthew's, viz. becauſe it has a great many hiſtories, which are not in St. Matthew. A catalogue of them. The fifth argument, viz. that it wants ſeveral remarkable hiſtories.

CHAP. X.

The ſixth argument, to prove St. Mark's Goſpel is not an epitome of St. Matthew's, viz. becauſe that ſuppoſition makes its inſpiration more dubious and uncertain; it makes the author look like a plagiary. *Two objections againſt this argument anſwered. The ſeventh argument, the ſuppoſing this Goſpel an epitome,* detracts from its honour and uſefulneſs. *Spinoza and Father Simon for this reaſon aſſert moſt of the books of the Old Teſtament, to be only epitomes, made out of records that are loſt. Laſtly, ſuppoſing this Goſpel an epitome, invalidates*

L 4

in

ſhewn from the antient way of writing. The moſt antient methods conſidered.

CHAP. XV.

That St. Matthew did not write his Goſpel on ſmall pieces of paper, proved by a large diſſertation on the manner, in which the antients wrote their books. The ordinary method was to write upon large ſkins, which were faſtened together, and rolled up. This the practice of the Jews long before, and in our Saviour's time. The words opened *and* cloſed the book, Luke iv. 17, 20, *diſcuſſed. The words,* bring the parchments, 2 Tim. iv. 13. *conſidered. It does not appear that the Jews made uſe of paper, or any other material beſides that mentioned, to write their books upon.*

CHAP. XVI.

Mr. Whiſton's ſtrange ſuppoſition, of St. Matthew's writing this part of his Goſpel on ſmall pieces of paper, confuted from the conſideration of their number and unequal ſize. A table of them, by which it appears, that they were at leaſt twenty in number, of very different ſizes. Some contained ſeveral chapters, others but a few verſes, others but one verſe. The improbability of St. Matthew's writing thus. The ſize of the parchment rolls, on which the Jews wrote.

CHAP. XVII.

Mr. Whiſton's obſervation, that our preſent Greek copies of this Goſpel, are a tranſlation out of Hebrew, and for that reaſon more liable to the diſ-

order

A VIN-

A

VINDICATION

OF

THE FORMER PART

OF

St. MATTHEW's GOSPEL, &c.

———————

CHAP. I.

The Design and principal Authors of Gospel Harmonies. The Design of the following Discourse.

THE difference which there is between the Evangelists, in relating several circumstances of the Gospel-history, and particularly their disagreement as to *the order of time*, in which the things they relate were done, has in all ages of Christianity been objected as an argument against the truth of the history itself. Porphyry, Celsus, and many others, have for this reason reviled both the Gospels, and the religion which they contain. Hence it has been judged necessary by many pious and learned men, to employ themselves in endeavours to reconcile the seeming contradictions of these sacred writers, and to reduce the Gospels to a perfect Harmony. Among the antients, Tatian, the scholar of Justin Martyr, composed a Harmony in some part of the second century [a], and after him Ammonius, of Alexandria, in the beginning of the third com-

———————

[a] Euseb. Hist. Eccl. l. 4. c. 29.

posed

pofed another, and after him Eufebius, in the beginning of thē fourth [a]. In the laft age great pains was taken in this work, by Chemnitius, Gerhard, Calvin, Dr. Lightfoot, and many others. Mr. Le Clerc, Mr. Whifton, and Mr. Toinard, are (I think) the only perfons, who have done any thing confiderable in this matter of late years. To fay nothing of the others, the world is exceedingly obliged to Mr. Whifton, for the many curious and ufeful difcoveries he has made in his performance on this fubject; the propofitions he has advanced, are certainly, for the moft part, very ingenious and happy expedients, to folve the difficulties they are defigned for. There are however fome of them, that do not feem to be fo very evident and fo fully proved, as others; and in this number is that which I have now undertaken to difcufs, viz. [b] *That the former part of St. Matthew's Gofpel, in our prefent copies, is very much mifplaced, contrary to the method and order originally intended by the Evangelift.*

That part of this Gofpel, which Mr. Whifton fuppofes difordered and mifplaced, is from the middle of the *fourth*, to the end of the *thirteenth* chapter; in which fmall portion of the hiftory there muft have been, according to his fuppofition, at leaft twenty feveral diforders and mifplacings.

However good Mr. Whifton's defign might be in advancing fo ftrange a propofition, I cannot but think he has failed in his proof of it. My bufinefs therefore in the following difcourfe will be, firft, To fhew the invalidity of Mr. Whifton's arguments, and then offer fome reafons, by which it will appear, that no fuch diforder can, without the greateft abfurdity, be fuppofed to have happened to this, or any other part of this Gofpel.

---

[a] A fpecimen of which is to be feen in Sixt. Senenf. Bib. Sanct. l. 3.

[b] P. 100.

CHAP. II.

Mr. Whiston's Proof considered. The Question thereupon stated. Mr. Whiston's first Argument, viz. That St. Matthew designed to observe the Order of Time, answered. St. Luke's Words, Chap. i. 1. do not prove, that either of the Gospels we now receive, were intended according to the Order of Time.

IN order to establish this *new* and *strange* proposition (as Mr. Whiston himself calls it) he undertakes to prove,

1. That St. Matthew appears originally to have observed the *order of the time, through his whole Gospel, as well as the rest of the Evangelists.* 2. *That from the fourth to the fourteenth chapter, the several branches of St. Matthew's history are not according to the order of time.*

These two things, could they be sufficiently proved, do evidently demonstrate the truth of the proposition; for if St. Matthew wrote his Gospel according to the order of time, and it is not now according to that order, it is plain it is misplaced since it was first wrote. The latter of these two, viz. whether these branches of St. Matthew's Gospel are according to the order of time in our present copies, or not, I will not now dispute. It seems it was believed in the first ages, that St. Mark, and consequently St. Luke (for it is certain that, for the most part, they observed the same order, and Mr. Whiston's Harmony evidently shews it), did not follow that order. So we are informed by that very antient account of Papias [a], viz. " That St. Mark, being the interpreter of St. " Peter, very carefully wrote down all the things he could re- " member, but not in that order, in which the several things " were said or done by Christ." To the same purpose St. Jerome [b]. " That St. Mark, the interpreter of St. Peter, who " himself did not see our Lord, but wrote the things which he " had

[a] Μάρκος μὲν ἑρμηνευτὴς Πέτρου γενόμενος, ὅσα ἐμνημόνευσεν, ἀκριβῶς ἔγραψεν, ὦ μέντοι τάξει τὰ ὑπὸ τῦ Χριςῦ ἢ λεχθέντα ἢ πραχθέντα, &c. Apud Euseb. Hist. Eccl. l. 3. c. 39.
[b] Marcus interpres Apostoli Petri—qui Dominum quidem salvatorem

" had heard St. Peter preach, was more concerned to be true
" in his account of things, than to obferve the order, in which
" the things were done." I might add here, that feveral more
modern writers have been of the fame opinion ; and that St.
Matthew's Gofpel is more according to the order of time, than
either St. Mark's or St. Luke's. But (as I faid before) I will
not difpute this head ; and then the queftion between us will
be only this, Whether St. Matthew appears originally to have
obferved the order of time through his whole Gofpel.

Mr. Whifton, for the following reafons, afferts it, viz.

1. *Becaufe all the other writers of the Gofpel-hiftory in-*
tended to obferve this order.

2. *St. Matthew, in the greateft part of his Gofpel, does ob-*
ferve the order of time in his narrations.

3. The notes *of the* order of time *are as many, and the*
fame in that part which is now difordered, as in that which is
regular, and in its proper order.

1. *Mr. Whifton fuppofes, that all the other accounts of our*
Saviour's Acts were intended according to this order. For the
proof of this he refers us to the firft and third propofitions
(which, by the way, feem to be very near the fame, only differently expreffed). The principal proof in both places is
taken from thofe words of St. Luke, chap. i. 1, 2, 3, viz.
Forafmuch as many have taken in hand, to fet forth in order a
declaration of thofe things, which are moft furely believed among
us ; it feemed good to me alfo, having had perfect underftanding
of all things, to write unto thee in order, moft excellent Theophi-
lus. " St. Luke (fays Mr. Whifton) [b] affures us, not only
" that himfelf had obferved the *order of time,* but that the fame
" was intended by thofe many others, who had written the
" Evangelical Hiftory before him." This indeed feems plaufible, but will by no means prove that for which Mr. Whifton
contends. For

I. It is very probable, that St. Luke in thefe words had no
reference to either of thofe Gofpels, which we now receive ;

---

rem ipfe non vidit, fed ea, quæ audierat magiftrum prædicantem, juxta fidem magis geftorum narravit,

quam ordinem. Hieron. Præfat .in
Comment. in Matth.
[b] P. 97.

but

but to fome other accounts of our Saviour's life and acts,
which were at that time wrote. As to St. John's Gofpel, it
is very certain he could not refer to that, becaufe it was undoubtedly wrote a long time afterwards. Nor is it at all likely,
he had any refpect to either of the other two Gofpels which
we now have, as will be apparent from a fhort confideration
of St. Luke's word. The defign of them evidently, is to give
us an account of the *reafons* or *motives*, which induced him to
write his Gofpel, viz. as he fays, becaufe many others had undertaken the like work before him. Now how the writing of
others fhould be the *reafon* or *occafion* of his writing, is very
hard to conceive, unlefs we fuppofe fome inaccuracies and defects in their writing. If the other accounts or hiftories he
is fuppofed to refer to, were wrote as they ought to have been,
this fhould have been fo far from inclining him to write, that
it fhould rather have prevented him, if he had had any fuch defign. And therefore the hiftories or accounts, which St. Luke
here refers to, were inaccurate and falfe. This is fo very evident, that Mr. Whifton himfelf, in another place [a], has afferted the very fame thing, where he thus paraphrafes thefe
words of St. Luke, viz. *That feveral of the hiftories of our
Saviour, which he (St. Luke) had perufed, though they attempted it, were not able to arrive at a fufficient accuracy in
the order of time.* St. Luke therefore, in thefe words (even
according to Mr. Whifton), cannot refpect either St. Matthew or St. Mark, becaufe they both wrote very accurately,
and, according to him, obferved the order of time. I conclude,
therefore, that not the Gofpels we now receive, but the other
falfe Gofpels, which were then wrote, were intended by St.
Luke in thefe words: this opinion will appear yet much more
probable, if we confider that there were, even at this time, a
great number of *falfe* and *fpurious* Gofpels fpread abroad in
the world. Irenæus [b] tells us, that, before his time, the hereticks had an *infinite number of fpurious and Apocryphal
Scriptures,* which contained (as is plain from what he fays

---

[a] P. 114.

[b] Ἀμύθητον πλῆθος ἀποκρύφων κ᾽ νόθων γραφῶν. Adv. Hæref. lib.
1. c. 17.

afterwards) 'an account of our Saviour's life and acts. Men immediately upon the publishing of Christianity, formed themselves into various parties of different denominations; and many or most of these had their own Gospel, which was different from that of others. It would be endless, as well as needless, for me to mention the several Gospels of the Ebionites, Marcionites, Nazarenes, the Gospel of St. Peter, Andrew, James, Bartholomew, &c. Every one, who has in the least made Christian antiquity his study, is acquainted with these things; those that are not, may be fully satisfied in the matter, by a bare casting their eyes upon the authors cited at the bottom of the page [a], who have, especially some of them, made a very full collection of the *false* Gospels, which were spread abroad in the world, in the very infancy of Christianity. These were the Οἱ πολλοὶ, *the many*, whom St. Luke referred to. I would only add here, that this hath been the opinion of many, if not most, antient and modern writers. "St. Luke (says "Austin [b]) gives us this reason for his writing in order, be- "cause many others had attempted it; but we are to under- "stand him of such, who had no authority nor esteem in the "Church, having undertaken what they were by no means "able to perform." To the same purpose says Eusebius. " [c] St. Luke, in the beginning of his Gospel, tells us what "was the occasion of his writing; intimating, that because "many others had rashly and inconsiderately undertaken to "write of those things, of which he had a full and certain "knowledge, he also would write to prevent the mischief of "those uncertain accounts." So Theophylact, in explain-

---

[a] Dr. Grabe's Spicileg. Patr. Fabric. Codex Apocryph. N. T. Sixt. Senenf. Biblioth. Sanct. l. 2. Father Simon's Critic. Hist. of the New Test. Part 1. c. 3. Du Pin's Hist. of the Canon, Vol. II. c. 6. Toland's Catalogue in his Amyntor. Suicer. Thesaur. Ecclef. ad voc. Εὐαγγέλιον. Spanheim, Histor. Eccles. Christ. p. 582, &c.

[b] Ideo autem dicit sibi visum esse ex ordine diligenter scribere, quoniam multi conati sunt; sed eos de-

bemus accipere, quorum in Ecclesia nulla extat auctoritas, quia id, quod conati sunt, minime potuerunt implere. August. de consens. Evangel. l. 4. c. 8.

[c] Ὁ δὲ Λουκᾶς ἀρχόμενος καὶ αὐτὸς τοῦ κατ' αὐτὸν συγγράμματος, τὴν αἰτίαν προύθηκι, δι' ἣν πεποίηται τὴν σύνταξιν δηλῶν, ὡς ἄρα πολλῶν καὶ ἄλλων προπετέστερον ἐπιτετηδευκότων διήγησιν ποιήσασθαι, &c. Euseb. Hist. Eccl. l. 3. c. 24.

ing

ing thefe words [a], puts the queftion, *Who were thofe men, intended by St. Luke, that took in hand to write,* &c. and anfwers, *They were falfe Apoftles; for many fuch had wrote Gofpels.* In the fame opinion are the learned Erafmus [b], Grotius [c], Father Simon [d], Bellarmin [e], Calvin [f], all afferting St. Luke here had no regard to St. Matthew or St. Mark, but to fome other writers, who had not wrote as they ought to do. The learned Mr. Dodwell carries the matter further, and (if I miftake not) does by a good argument conclude from thefe words of St. Luke, not only that he had no reference to either of thefe two Gofpels, but that he never faw them. What he faith is to this purpofe, viz. [g] " St. " Luke, in the Preface to his hiftory, giving this reafon for " his writing, that he had received his accounts from thofe " who were eye-witneffes, plainly intimates, that the writers of " thofe other Gofpels, which he had feen, were not furnifhed " with that help ; fo that neither being eye-witneffes them- " felves, nor duly confulting fuch as were, their credit muft " be doubtful : and thence it muft neceffarily follow, that the " Gofpels, which St. Luke had feen, were not any of thofe we " now receive." Upon the whole, therefore, I hope I may juftly fay, that Mr. Whifton has here failed in his proof; becaufe thefe words of St. Luke, having no reference to either of the Gofpels we now receive, cannot prove what Mr. Whifton brings them for : that St. Matthew, or any of the Gofpel-writers, defigned to obferve the order of time in their hiftories. But,

II. If it fhould be allowed and taken for granted, that St. Luke in thefe words had refpect to the Gofpels we now receive, yet there is nothing in his words, which will prove,

---

[a] Vid. eum ad Luc. i. 1.
[b] Annot. in N. T. ad Luc. i. 1.
[c] Annot. ad eund. loc.
[d] Critic. Hift. of the New Teft. par. 1. c. 3.
[e] De Matrimon. Sacram. l. 1. c. 6.
[f] Harmon. Evangel. in init.
[g] Et cum novæ fcriptionis edit in Præfatione caufam, quod ipfe αὐτόπτων narrationibus adjutus fuerit aggreffus, id plane innuit defti-

tutos hoc fubfidio fuiffe viforum a fe Evangeliorum auctores, ita nimirum non fuiffe αὐτόπτας, ut ne quidem αὐτόπτας cum cura aliqua et fedulitate confuluerint, vacillare proinde meritoque dubiam fuiffe eorum fidem. Ut plane alios fuiffe neceffe eft Evangelicæ Hiftoriæ fcriptores a Luca vifos, a noftris, quos habemus, Evangeliftis. Differt. 1. in Iren. p. 68, 69.

they

they were intended and wrote according to the order of time. Indeed, according to our Englifh Tranflation, one would be apt to think fo; *Forafmuch as many have taken in hand, to fet forth in order a declaration, &c.* From the words *to fet forth in order*, Mr. Whifton concludes, that thefe Gofpels, and particularly St. Matthew's, were wrote according to the order of time; but the original word ἀναταξαϛθαι implies no fuch thing, but only in general to *compile*, or *compofe*, or *fet together*, without any particular regard to the order of time, or any other order whatfoever. This is the fenfe Suidas and Hefychius give of the word ἀναταξαϛθαι [a]; and fo it is taken by the old Syriack interpreter, and the beft modern tranflators. So Beza [b], *componere narrationem*, and Caftalio, *contexere narrationem*; De Dieu, *apparare feu concinnare*; fo that the whole meaning is, *Forafmuch as many have undertaken to write the hiflory, &c.* and confequently nothing can hence be concluded, concerning the Evangelifts defigning to obferve the *order of time* in their hiftories.

The three other arguments which Mr. Whifton offers, to prove the Gofpels were wrote according to the order of time, p. 97, 98, 99. are fo much the fame, with thofe which are brought to prove this concerning St. Matthew in particular, that they need not be diftinctly confidered.

---

[a] Ἀναταξαϛθαι, Εὐτρεπίϛαϛθαι, i. e. apparare, inftruere, componere, Εὐτρεπιϛμὸς, ἡ Ἐτοιμαϛία, Suid.

[b] Mihi vero τὸ ϛυνταϛθϛθαι idem videtur generaliter declarare, atque confcribere, et conficere. Bez. ad loc.

CHAP.

CHAP. III.

The Writers of the Gospel-History did not intend or observe the Order of Time in their Writings. This proved particularly of St. Luke by several Instances. The Phrase, write in order, Luc. i. 3. *discussed.*

WHETHER the writers of the Gospel-history did design to relate the several acts and circumstances of our Saviour's life, according to that order of time, in which each of them came to pass, is a question of very considerable importance. Mr. Whiston very earnestly contends for the affirmative [a]; which indeed if it be true, it is very certain, that not only that part of St. Matthew's Gospel, which he supposes, but also several parts of the other Gospels, are in our present copies very much misplaced, confused, and disordered. I rather think, the Evangelists had not any such regard to that order, but were principally concerned in relating the several matters of fact truly and faithfully. This has been the opinion of, I think, almost all those who have considered this matter, both antient and later writers. *The truth is,* (says a learned writer [b]) *that the Apostles* (he means all the Evangelists) *had not properly any design in writing, but to inform us, of the doctrine and miracles of our Lord; not much regarding those things, which may be thought requisite to an exact and methodical history.* I do not suppose, that the Evangelists had no regard at all to the order of time, in composing their Gospels. The contrary is very certain; and a bare view of Mr. Whiston's Harmony, will sufficiently convince any one, that, for the most part, each of these sacred writers, not only intended to observe, but do exactly agree in observing, this order. All

---

[a] Prop. 1.

[b] La vérité est, que les Apôtres n'ont eu proprement dessein, que de nous apprendre la doctrine et les miracles de notre Seigneur, sans se mettre en peine de ce que l'on demande dans une histoire méthodique. Le Clerc Biblioth. choisie, tom. 15. art. 5. p. 251.

    that

that I contend for, is, that they do not *always* confine themselves to this method, but very often for juft and good reafons infert feveral particular tranfactions, not in that order in which they were done. This might be proved, beyond doubt, of every one of the Evangelifts. But it will be fufficient to prove it, only concerning St. Luke; becaufe his Gofpel is by Mr. Whifton fuppofed to be perfectly in this order of time, and therefore he corrects St. Matthew's by it. The following inftances will abundantly evidence the truth of what I fay.

St. Luke, ch. iii. ver. 19, 20. relates the hiftory of *John's imprifonment by Herod*, before the account of *our Saviour's baptifm*, ver. 21, &c. which certainly is contrary to the order of time; Chrift being no doubt baptized long before *John's imprifonment*; fee Matt. iii. 13, &c. and iv. 12. Hence Mr. Whifton himfelf has taken the liberty here to tranfpofe thefe verfes in his Harmony, although he tells us, (pag. 100.) that he had ventured but in one inftance (viz. that of our Lord's mother and brethren coming to him), to change the order of St. Luke.

Ch. iv. 33, &c. St. Luke relates the *hiftory of the unclean fpirit being caft out of the man, in the fynagogue at Capernaum*, and v. 38, &c. *the account of Peter's mother in law being cured of a fever*, and after thefe, ch. v. 1. *The calling of Peter and the other Apoftles by the fea fide*; whereas it is very certain, that thefe Apoftles were called before thefe miracles. And fo this hiftory ought, if the order of time had been obferved, to have been placed fooner, as both the other Evangelifts have placed it, Matt. iv. 18, &c. compared with ch. viii. 2, &c. and 14, &c. and Mark i. 16, 30. This is fo undeniable a proof of St. Luke's fometimes leaving the order of time, that nothing can reafonably be urged or objected againft it. Indeed Mr. Whifton, finding this fo directly overthrowing his fcheme, which he had before formed, was refolved to fay fomething againft it, and therefore he fuppofes ª, that *the hiftory here recorded by St. Luke, is quite different from that recorded by St. Matthew*,

----

ª P. 123, & 125.

and.

and St. Mark. But I cannot think any one, who confiders the matter without prejudice, can be of that opinion. The circumftances are fo very like, that I believe every one that reads thofe two hiftories, concludes them to be the fame. I own indeed, there are fome different circumftances in the hiftories, and fo there are in almoft every one of the ftories, which are related by two Evangelifts. But thofe here are very inconfiderable, and very eafily to be reconciled. Mr. Whifton however has made them fo many arguments to prove the ftory in St. Matthew and St. Mark, and that in St. Luke to be different. I need not be at the pains diftinctly to confider them; Dr. Whitby[a] has in a few words fufficiently fhewed, that they do not prove the two different *callings* of thefe Apoftles, which Mr. Whifton contends for. The four firft reafons, by which Mr. Whifton endeavours to prove thefe two ftories different, are only *additional circumftances*, mentioned by St. Luke, and not by St. Matthew nor St. Mark. The other two are really not different at all. A bare cafting the eye upon them will evidently fhew it:

St. MATTHEW and St. MARK.	St. LUKE.
Follow me, and I will make you fifhers of men.	*From henceforth thou fhalt catch men.*
They left their nets, and followed him.	*They left all, and followed him.*

Are thefe fuch *differences*, as to prove the hiftories to be different? One would rather think thefe very circumftances to be the fame; and if fo, it is plain, that St. Luke did not always defign to obferve the order of time in his hiftory.

Another inftance to the fame purpofe, (viz. of St. Luke's not obferving the order of time in the ftories which he relates) we have, ch. viii. 19, 20, 21. where he places the hiftory *of our Lord's mother and brethren, after the parable of the fower,* which begins at ver. 4. of that chapter, but according to the

---

[a] Annot. on Matt. iv. 18. vid. & Spanheim. Dub. Evang. tom. 3. Dub. 72.

other

other Evangelifts, viz. St. Matthew and St. Mark, it is evident this account fhould have been before this parable, if the order of time had been obferved; fee Matt. xii. 46, &c. and xiii. 1, &c. and Mark iii. 31, &c. and iv. 1, &c. Hence Mr. Whifton has in this inftance alfo, receded from St. Luke's order in his Harmony [a].

Thefe, were there no other, feem to be fufficient arguments to prove, that St. Luke did not confine himfelf always ftrictly, to relate the acts and circumftances of our Saviour's life, in the fame order, in which they came to pafs. That which induced Mr. Whifton [b]; as well as many others, to the contrary opinion, are thofe words in St. Luke's preface, c. i. ver. 3. where he fays, he defigned, καθιξῆς γραψαι, *to write in order*. But to this it may be anfwered, that it is not at all neceffary this word fhould be thus tranflated; it may be as well rendered *particularly, ferie perpetua*; fo it is certain the word commonly fignifies, and the beft criticks have taken it in this fenfe. " They are miftaken (fays Grotius [c]), who con-" clude from this word, that St. Luke defigned more clofely " to obferve the order of time, than the others had done be-" fore him; for on the contrary it is evident, that he more " than once relates things of the fame nature together, though " they were done at different times. Καθιξῆς means nothing " more than *particularly*, as is plain from the ufe of the word " Acts xi. 4. and xviii. 23. So that St. Luke's meaning here is no more than this, *My defign is to write to thee a* particular *account of the things done by Chrift*. But if after all καθιξῆς γραψαι fhould be tranflated to *write in order*, why muft it needs regard the order of time more than any other order? Are there not feveral other orders and methods of writing made ufe of by hiftorians, befides this? viz. fuch as placing actions and difcourfes of a like nature together, or things which were done at the *fame place*, though not at the

[a] P. 287, & 289.
[b] P. 97. & 114.
[c] Falluntur, qui hinc colligunt propofitum Lucæ *temporum ordinem* preffius fequi, quam alii ante ipfum feciffent; nam contra apparet, illum non femel ob rerum cohærentiam connexuiffe, quæ temporibus erant difcreta. Sed καθιξῆς nil aliud eft quam *figillatim*, ut videre eft Act. xi. 4. & xviii. 23. Grot. ad Luc. i. 3.

fame

same time. An hiſtorian may be very properly ſaid to write in order, who does not exactly obſerve the order of time.

But if we ſuppoſe further, that St. Luke by the word καθεξῆς did intend the order of time; why muſt he be ſuppoſed to limit and confine himſelf to it in every particular branch of his hiſtory, ſo that he could not, when he ſaw a juſt occaſion, recede from it? He may be well ſaid to write in the order of time, who doth ſo for the moſt part. And hence it is excellently obſerved by our late Engliſh critick[a]; that, " It being " certain, that St. Luke in his Goſpel doth not give us " Chriſt's miracles, ſermons, and journeys, in that order of " time, in which they were done and ſpoken: it remains, " that, when he promiſed to write καθεξῆς *in order*, we under- " ſtand this of Chriſt's conception, birth, circumciſion, bap- " tiſm, preaching, death, reſurrection, and aſcenſion, of which " he truly writes in order." Upon the whole, then, I conclude, that St. Luke in writing his Goſpel did not deſign exactly to obſerve the order of time, and conſequently alſo, that St. Mark did not; becauſe, according to Mr. Whiſton[b], he every where agrees with St. Luke: and ſo Mr. Whiſton's argument, to prove St. Matthew originally obſerved the order of time, viz. *becauſe other Goſpel writers did ſo,* is plainly inſufficient.

---

[a] Dr. Whitby, Annot. on Luc. i. 3.   [b] P. 114.

C H A P. IV.

The Practice of other Historians, as well as the Evangelists, to neglect the Order of Time. Several Instances out of the Old Testament History. Instances out of Profane Authors. Several Reasons, why the Evangelists neglect the Order of Time.

HOWEVER strange it may seem to some, that these sacred writers should thus disregard the order of time, and consequently differ so much from each other; yet this will not at all derogate from their honour and authority, if the matter be duly and impartially considered. For as this is very often, upon many accounts, undoubtedly the best way of writing history, so it has been the practice of the best historians, both sacred and profane, in all ages and countries. Mr. Whiston indeed tells us, that those who do not take his method, and suppose St. Matthew's Gospel in our present copies misplaced, *are forced on another method, which plainly implies the frequent inaccuracy, if not falsehood, of the inspired writers themselves*[a]. This is a very hard charge indeed, which at once falls upon all the harmonizers and commentators of the Gospels, that ever wrote before Mr. Whiston. It is strange that all these good men, who had so great a veneration for inspired writers, should thus charge the Evangelists with *inaccuracies*, if not *falsehood*; Mr. Whiston will agree with me, they had none of them this design, and then I am not afraid to assert, that no such thing follows from *the method they took, to reconcile the Evangelists.*

The substance of their charge amounts to no more than this, viz. That they suppose the Evangelists, not to have *always*, and *in every particular instance*, observed the order of time; but this is so far from supposing an *inaccuracy* or *falsehood* in the Evangelists, that it is only supposing them to have

[a] P. 112.

taken

taken the beſt method, and the method the beſt hiſtorians have taken, before and ſince their time.

For the clearing of this matter, I will endeavour to ſhew :

I. *That this is a thing very common in the hiſtory of the Old Teſtament.*

II. *That it has been the practice of the beſt profane hiſtorians.*

III. *Offer ſome reaſons, why the Evangeliſts neglected the* order of time.

I. *The writers of the hiſtory of the Old Teſtament very frequently deviate from the order of time, in relating ſeveral branches of their hiſtory; ſometimes placing them much* ſooner, *ſometimes much* later, *than the time, in which they really came to paſs.* This was very remarkably the practice of that beſt and moſt accurate of all hiſtorians, Moſes. For inſtance,

Gen. xxv. 7, 8, 9. He places the *death of Abraham* before the birth of Iſaac's two ſons, Eſau and Jacob, ver. 24, 25, &c. whereas it is very certain, that Abraham was alive when they were born, aud lived at leaſt *fifteen years* afterwards, as will appear by the following account.

Abraham was a *hundred years* old, when his ſon Iſaac was born, Gen. xxi. 5. Iſaac was *threeſcore years* old, when his ſons Eſau and Jacob were born, ch. xxv. 26. therefore Abraham was but a *hundred and threeſcore* at their birth. But Abraham lived till he was a hundred and ſeventy five, ch. xxv. 7. and therefore it is evident, that the death of Abraham is placed at leaſt fifteen years too ſoon, being placed before the birth of Eſau and Jacob; whereas if the order of time had been obſerved, it muſt have been placed at leaſt fifteen years afterwards.

The ſame may be obſerved alſo, concerning the hiſtorian's placing his account of the death of Iſaac, Gen. xxxv. 28, 29. It is placed *before the ſelling of Joſeph into Egypt by his brethren,* ch. xxxvii. whereas, if the order of time had been obſerved, it ought to have been placed *after* ; it being certain,

that

that Ifaac lived at leaft *twelve years* after that time, as will appear by the following account.

Jofeph was *thirty years* old, when he was advanced by Pharaoh in Egypt, Gen. xli. 46. After this there came *feven years of plenty,* ver. 47, 53. and *two years of famine,* before Jacob came down to Egypt, ch. xlv. 6. So that Jofeph was at leaft *thirty nine years* old, when Jacob his father came down to Egypt; Jacob, when he came down to Egypt, was a *hundred and thirty years* old, ch. xlvii. 9. Now from the time of Jofeph's being fold by his brethren, till this time, (viz. till his 39th year) were *twenty two* years, becaufe he was fold in his *feventeenth* year, ch. xxxvii. 2. If then we take the *twenty two* years, which Jofeph was in Egypt, from the *hundred and thirty* of Jacob; it is plain that Jacob was a *hundred and eight,* when Jofeph was *feventeen,* and confequently, when Jofeph was fold to Egypt, Ifaac was no more than *a hundred and fixty eight;* for Jacob (who was at this time but *a hundred and eight*) was born, when Ifaac was *fixty years* old, ch. xxv. 26. Now Ifaac lived till he was *a hundred and eighty years old,* ch. xxxv. 28. and confequently *twelve years* after Jofeph was fold into Egypt. So that it is evident, the account of Ifaac's death is not placed according to the order of time, but at leaft twelve years fooner, than that order required.

Another very remarkable inftance to the fame purpofe, viz. of the author of the book of Genefis not obferving the order of time in his hiftory, we have ch. xxxviii. The feveral matters there related, are placed between the account of *Jofeph's being fold into Egypt,* and *his advancement before Pharaoh.* This interval, or fpace of time, confifts of no more than thirteen years; for Jofeph was fold in his feventeenth, and advanced in his thirtieth year. Now upon a clofe confideration of the circumftances of the hiftory, it will appear morally impoffible, that all the feveral matters, related in that chapter, fhould have come to pafs in that time, as will be evident by juft naming them.

Firft, Judah leaves his father's family, and marries, and fucceffively begat three fons, Er, Onan, and Shelah. When the eldeft came to age, he married Tamar; fome time after

the

the Lord flew him, and Onan the fecond brother married his widow; after his death fhe continued a confiderable time a widow, expecting the time, when the third fon would be grown up and marry her. He grows up, but refufes to marry her; therefore fhe plays the harlot with her father in law Judah, and by him fhe hath two fons. And all this muft have been in lefs than the fpace of thirteen years, unlefs we fuppofe the hiftorian not to have obferved the order of time; which certainly he did not, a great part of what is here related, having undoubtedly come to pafs, a confiderable time before Jofeph was fold into Egypt [a].

Thefe are inftances fufficient to prove, that though the Evangelifts did not always confine themfelves to obferve the order of time, yet they had the example of the beft hiftorian in the world, to juftify their practice in neglecting it.

Nor was this only the practice of Mofes, but of moft, if not all, the writers of the facred hiftory of the Old Teftament. There is a noted example of this in the book of Judges, *the laft five chapters* of which hiftory ought, if the order of time had been obferved, to have been placed near the beginning of it. The ftory of *Micah's idolatry,* and *the expedition of the tribe of Dan,* ch. xvii. and xviii. *of the Levite's concubine, and the war on her account,* ch. xix. xx. and xxi. are each of them placed above 200 years too late, which is eafy enough to be proved. Hence Jofephus has placed the *hiftory of the three laft chapters,* before *the hiftory of the Judges [b],* and the Old Hebrew Chronologer [c] has placed *the ftory of Micah,* and *the tribe of Dan's idolatry,* and *the ftory of the Levite's concubine* in the time of Othniel, the firft of the Judges; and, as far as I can find, moft chronologers and commentators are of the fame mind [d].

[a] Quomodo ergo hæc omnia intra tam paucos annos fieri potuerint, merito movet; nifi, ut forte folet, fcriptura per recapitulationem, aliquot annos ante venditum Jofeph, hoc fieri cæpiffe intelligi velit, &c. Auguft. Quæft. Sup. Gen. l. 1. c. 128.

[b] Antiq. Jud. lib. 5. c. 2.

[c] Seder Olam Rabba, c. 20. p. 50.

[d] Dr. Lightfoot Chronic. and Harmon. of the Old Teft. on Judges, &c. Ufher Chronol. Sacr. p. 199. Petav. Rationar. Temp. l. 1. c. 6. Junius ad Jud. 17. 1. Spanheim. Hift. Eccl. V. T. Epoch. 4. c. 10.

The

The story of *Shimei's death*, 1 Kings ii. 39. &c. is evidently placed three years too soon in the history.

Abundance of other such instances might be collected out of the historical books, were it necessary. Those that have a mind to see them, may consult Dr. Lightfoot[a] and Usher[b], &c. I would only add, that this has been a very antient and common observation; and that for this purpose the famous sixth rule of Ticonius[c], called *Recapitulatio*, was invented. But,

II. This is not a practice peculiar to the sacred writers, *but made use of by all historians*. The most accurate and exact among those, who are called profane writers, have taken this liberty in composing their histories. Livy, Plutarch, Tacitus, Suetonius, Florus, &c. have all upon particular occasions neglected the exact order of time. Suetonius, for instance, is very frequent in this practice; continually laying matters of a like nature together, without regard to the order of time, in which they were done. In the Life of Augustus he expressly tells us, it was his design to do so[d]: " not to confine himself to " strict chronology, or the order of time, in which the several " things were done; but instead of being punctual to the " time, join actions of a like nature together, that so they " might be more clearly perceived and known." This any one, who reads his memoirs of Augustus's life, will perceive he has done, just as St. Matthew and the other Evangelists, in writing the memoirs of our Saviour's life.

To the same purpose Lucius Florus[e] intimates, " That he " would not observe the strict order of time; but that the

---

[a] Lib. jam cit:

[b] Chronol. Sacr.

[c] Apud August. de Doct. Christ. l. 3. c. 36.

[d] Proposita vitæ ejus velut summa, putes sigillatim, neque per tempora, sed per species, exsequar; quo distinctius demonstrari cognoscique possint. Suetonius in August. c. 9.

Sic solent scriptores—*per species exsequi*, i. e. secundum actiones et genera, narrare statum et condi-

tionem vitæ. Sic cum narramus, quæ quis publice, quæ privatim, quæ fortiter, quæ moderate, quæ serio, quæ jocose egerit, non observato annorum ordine. Pitisc. ad Loc.

[e] Quæ etsi involuta inter se sunt omnia atque confusa, tamen, quo melius appareant, simul et ne scelera virtutibus obstrepant, separatim proferentur, &c. L. Flor. lib. 2. c. 19.

" things

" things he fhould relate might the better appear, he would
" relate them diftinctly and feparately, &c." If then other
writers, facred and profane, have fo very frequently neglected
this order, we need not be furprized, that St. Matthew and
the other Evangelifts have done fo too; efpecially when we
confider, that it is only in a few inftances, that they have done
it, and then *for the moft part*, if not *always*, fome good reafon
may be affigned, why they have done fo. This leads me,

III. To confider, *Why, and for what reafons, the Evangelifts receded from the order of time, in their hiftories.*

I fhall not be at the pains to confider all the feveral
branches of their hiftories, in which this order is neglected,
and fhew the *particular occafions* why they are placed as they
are; all that I defign, is to mention fome general *caufes or
occafions* of their relating things in a different order, from that
in which they were done, and particularly,

1. *Sometimes the Evangelifts relate thofe facts together,
which were done at a different time, becaufe they were done in
the fame place.* It feemed a very good expedient to affift the
memory, fometimes to relate the feveral miracles our Saviour
wrought at one place together, though they were done at different times. So, *the healing of the leprous perfon; the cure of
the centurion's fervant; the recovering of Peter's mother-in-
law*, are placed immediately one after another by St. Matthew, ch. viii. from ver. 2, to the 16th, becaufe each of thefe
miracles was wrought at Capernaum, though at different
times. " Hence (fays Dr. Lightfoot) the mention of a place
" doth oftentimes occafion thefe holy penmen to fpeak of ftories
" out of their proper time, becaufe they would take up the whole
" ftory of that place all at once, or together [a]." For this reafon
it is, that St. Luke places the hiftory of *the unclean fpirit being
caft out of the man in the fynagogue at Capernaum*, ch. iv. 33,
&c. and the account of *Peter's mother-in-law being cured of a
fever*, ver. 39, &c. before *the call of the Apoftles by the fea-fide*,
ch. v. 1. (which has been proved [b] to be contrary to the order of

---

[a] Lightfoot, Harmon. of the New Teft. §. 20.
[b] P. 30.

time);

time); viz. becaufe having mentioned our Lord's being and preaching at Capernaum (ver. 31.) he had a mind to record together the miracles our Lord did there, though done at another time.

2. Another reafon, why the Evangelifts fometimes place a fact out of its proper order of time, is, *becaufe they having been fpeaking of the perfon concerned in it before, had a mind there to finifh all they defigned to fay of him.* So, for inftance, the ftory of John the Baptift's being imprifoned by Herod, Luke iii. 19, 20. (which has been proved not to be in the order of time) was placed where it is, becaufe the Evangelift, having before been giving an account of John's miniftry, and not defigning to fay much more of him, had a mind here to finifh his whole ftory together. This is fo far from being any fault in a hiftory, that it is really oftentimes the beft and moft accurate way of writing it; becaufe by a ftrict and conftant adherence to the order of time, there muft neceffarily be *continual breaches* and *frequent interruptions* in the hiftory. Stories muft be often brought in without any connection or coherence, and confequently are not fo like to be remembered [a]. It may therefore be fometimes much better that the whole ftory of a perfon or thing be told together, though fome other things intervene, which are told afterwards. For this reafon, we may obferve, the infpired penman of the book of Genefis has placed the death of Ifaac (ch. xxxv. 28, 29.) fo much too foon, as it has been above proved to be [b], viz. becaufe having, ver. 27. given an account of his fon *Jacob's* coming to him to Hebron, and defigning to fay no more concerning his life, but to proceed to the hiftory of his pofterity; it feemed very proper there to mention his death, that he might not be forced elfewhere to bring it in, by any breach or interruption in his hiftory [c]. For

the

---

[a] Facilius cujufque rei in unum contracta fpecies, quam divifa temporibus, oculis animifque inhæret. Vellei. Paterc. 1. 14.

[b] P. 36.

[c] Conftat ante mortem Ifaaci venditum fuiffe Jofephum, cum tamen

hanc hiftoriam (fc. Jofephi) Mofes poft obitum et fepulturam recitet: ut neceffario concedenda fit hyfterologia, cujus ratio hæc fuit; quia poft adventum Jacobi in Hebron, nihil amplius de vita Ifaaci vellet narrare Mofes, et ad ea, quæ de Jacobo Patriarcha

the fame reafon alfo is the ftory of Shimei's death placed too foon, 1 Kings ii. 39. that the whole ftory of him might be finifhed at once, and not brought in without any connection, as it muft neceffarily have been, if it had been placed afterwards.

3. It is not at all abfurd or unreafonable to fuppofe, *that divine Wifdom ordered it to be thus, to prevent all fufpicion of the Evangelifts' writing in concert, or by combination, with defign to impofe upon the world.* Chriftianity was looked upon at firft, by many, as a delufion, and the authors of thefe facred books as cheats and impoftors. Againft this the Chriftians commonly argued, that, if the writers of the Gofpel-hiftory had had any fuch defigns, they would not have fo many things, which feem contrary to each other. The reafoning of Chryfoftom on this head is fo very juft, that it well deferves tranfcribing [a]. He brings in a perfon making this objection, that the *Evangelifts do not agree in their accounts.* To this he anfwers; " Their not agreeing in every particular, is a full " demonftration of their truth; for if they had in all things " agreed with a perfect exactnefs, both as to time, and place, " and words, none of our adverfaries but would have believed " that they met together, and wrote by compact and confent " to deceive: but now that difference there feems to be be- " tween them in thefe fmaller matters, defends them from all " fuch fufpicion, &c." Such arguing feems to be very juft; and if it be, what is there abfurd in fuppofing, that divine Wifdom ordered thefe little differences, thofe in refpect of time among others, for this good end? " The Holy Spirit," fays a learned man, "influenced the Evangelifts to write many

---

triarcha notanda acciderent, pergere deliberaffet, hiftoriam Ifaaci operæ pretium judicavit concludere per mortem ipfius, &c. Rivet. Exercit. 144. Gen.

[a] Πολλαχῆ γὰρ διαφωνοῦντες ἐλέγχονται. Αὐτὸ μὲν οὖν τοῦτο μέγιςον δεῖγμα τῆς ἀληθείας ἐςίν. Εἰ γὰρ πάντα συνεφώνησαν μετὰ ἀκριβείας, καὶ μέχρι καιροῦ, καὶ μέχρι τόπου, καὶ μέχρι ῥημάτων αὐτῶν, οὐδεὶς ἂν ἐπίςευσε τῶν ἐχθρῶν, ὅτι μὴ συνελθόντες ἀπὸ συνθήκης τινὸς ἀνθρωπίνης ἔγραψαν——Νυνὶ δὲ καὶ ἡ δοκοῦσα ἐν μικροῖς εἶναι διαφωνία πάσης ἀπαλλάττει αὐτοὺς ὑποψίας, &c. Chryfoftom. Homil. in Matth. i. Idem vid. apud Theophylact. Præfat. in Matth.

" things in a different order, that they might not feem to have
" wrote by compact, or to have borrowed one from another [a]."

4. Mr. Whifton has furnifhed me with another reafon, why
the Evangelifts are thus different from one another, and do
not obferve the fame order in relating the feveral acts of our
Saviour's life. " It ought not (fays he) [b] to feem ftrange, if
" that book, which contains the revealed will of God, be fo
" framed, as to have divers feeming contradictions in it, for
" the perplexing the ungodly, and the exercife of the pious."
This obfervation of Mr. Whifton's, is what feveral other
learned men have upon this and other occafions made [c], and
is, if true, a very good reafon, why the Evangelifts were not fo
very exact, in obferving the order of time in their hiftories.

Thus I have endeavoured to juftify the practice of the
Evangelifts, in relating things in a different order from that
in which they came to pafs, both by fhewing it was the practice of the beft hiftorians, and by feveral other reafons. I only
add, that, as it has been already proved concerning St. Luke [d],
that he did not tell us he defigned to obferve the exact order of
time, fo it is certain *no one of the Evangelifts has told us fo* ;
and if they did not engage and promife to obferve this order,
certainly they are not to be accufed of falfehood in not obferving it. Hence the learned Dr. Hammond [e] well obferved,
" That all thefe, and (if there were) many more [*differences*]
" do nothing derogate from the fidelity of the writers ; who,
" undertaking to make fome relations of what was done by
" Chrift, do no where undertake, nor oblige themfelves, to ob-
" ferve the order wherein every thing fucceeded, that being
" generally extrinfical, and of no importance to the rela-
" tions."

---

[a] Voluit vero Spiritus Sanctus
diverfo ordine multa ab Evangeliftis
narrari ;—ne vel ex compacto, vel
collatis capitibus, fcripfiffe, vel fua
a fe invicem defcripfiffe viderentur,
&c. Spanheim. Dub. Evang. tom.
iii. Dub. 69.
[b] Chronolog. of the Old Teft.
p. 3.

[c] Multa diverfo ordine ab Evangeliftis narrari voluit Spiritus Sanctus, exercendæ et fubigendæ fidei
noftræ, &c. caufa. Spanheim. Dub.
Evang. tom. iii. Dub. 69.
[d] P. 24, &c.
[e] Annot. on Mark v. 2.

And

And to the same purpose, it is well remarked by the author just now cited[a], " That no one can charge that writer with " a falsehood or contradiction, for relating things in a different " order from that in which they came to pass, if he did not " before-hand engage to observe that order." The principal thing these sacred writers were concerned about, was *truth*, to be faithful and just in the accounts they gave us ; and this indeed is the most necessary requisite, and best character of an historian. Hence Lucian, in his excellent directions for writing history, tells us [b], " The one thing most peculiarly re- " quisite to history, is *truth*. If any go about to write a his- " tory, he must principally regard truth, not concerning him- " self about any thing else."

CHAP. V.

Mr. Whiston's second Argument considered. It does not follow, that because St. Matthew for the most part observed the Order of Time, therefore he did in every Particular. The third Argument discussed The Notes of Time Mr. Whiston mentions, do not prove the Order of Time.

THE second argument, which Mr. Whiston makes use of to prove, that St. Matthew originally observed the order of time through his whole Gospel, is, *because he does so in the greatest part of his Gospel.* After what hath been said in the two former chapters, there seems very little necessary to be said in answer to this. I agree with Mr. Whiston, that St.

[a] Immo nemo mendacii vel contradictionis insimulaverit illum, qui eadem diverso ordine recitat, modo non præfertur se ordinem relaturum, æque ac res ipsas. Spanheim. Dub. Evang. tom. iii. Dub. 56.

[b] Ἐν γὰρ τῦτο (scil. ἀλήθεια) ἴδιον ἱσορίας, καὶ μόνη θυτέον τῇ ἀλη-

θία, εἴ τις ἱσορίαν γράψων ἴοι, τῶν δ' ἄλλων ἁπάντων ἀμελητέον αὐτῷ, &c. Lucian. de Conscrib. Histor. §. 39. Historicus itaque, si ad verum et fidem de re proposita retulerit, officio suo satisfecisse existimabitur. Isaac. Pontan. Orat. Isagog. ad L. Flor. p. 1.

Matthew

Matthew (and so indeed each of the other Evangelists) does for the most part exactly observe the order of time; yet it will by no means follow, that that inspired writer was always so confined to a strict observance of this order, that he could upon no occasions whatsoever depart from it. Several reasons have been assigned, upon the account of which an historian may sometimes deviate from this order, though for the most part he strictly observe it. And it has been proved, that St. Luke sometimes relates things in a different order from that in which they came to pass, though for the most part he exactly observes the order of time. Mr. Whiston's argument therefore, that because St. Matthew for the most part writes in this order, therefore he does never recede from it, will not hold.

Mr. Whiston's last argument, by which he endeavours to prove, that St. Matthew originally observed the order of time through his whole Gospel, is, that *the notes of the order of time, and coherence of parts, are as many in that part which is now disordered and misplaced, as in that which is regular and in its proper order.* It is true indeed, those which Mr. Whiston has here collected, and calls *notes of the order of time,* are as frequent in this as any other part of the Gospel; but then these are such which are only (if they may be so called) *notes of transition,* generally inserted by the historian *only for the sake of connecting the several stories together, and not to denote the regular succession of the facts related.* They are most of them such as can only relate to the story that follows them, and do not at all connect it with that foregoing. This will appear by a very slight consideration of them: they are such as these : Ἰδὼν δέ· καὶ ἀνοίξας τὸ ϛόμα αὐτȣ̑· καταϐάντι δὲ αὐτῷ ἀπὸ τοῦ ὄρȣς· καὶ ἰδȣ́· εἰσελθόντι δέ· καὶ ἐλθών· καὶ προσελθȣ́ν· &c. *and seeing* ; *and opening his mouth* ; *and coming down from the mountain* ; *and behold* ; *and as he was entering* ; *and coming,* &c. Is it not evident that these, and such as these, are designed only for the better transition from one story to another ? Is it not very plain that they regard only the subsequent story ? For instance, Ἰδὼν δέ· καὶ ἰδȣ́· *and when Jesus saw* ; *and behold* ; have these phrases any reference at all to what goes before ? Do they intimate that the next fact related, was immediately in

order

order of time after that which was before related? Let us suppose the ſtory, to which one of theſe notes is prefixed, a conſiderable time after that which immediately precedes it in the hiſtory, might not the hiſtorian very properly prefix one of theſe notes to it? Might he not ſay, καὶ ἰδὼν, or καὶ ἐλθὼν ὁ Ἰησοῦς, *and Jeſus ſeeing*, or *coming*, did ſuch or ſuch a thing, only regarding what he was about to tell, without the leaſt reſpect to what he had ſaid before? Nay, let us go further, and ſuppoſe one of thoſe notes prefixed to a ſtory, which in the order of time was before that which it immediately ſucceeds, yet would the prefixing of ſuch a note be very proper. For inſtance, to the ſermon on the Mount (Mat v. 2.) is prefixed καὶ ἀνοίξας τὸ ςόμα αὑτοῦ (which is one of Mr. Whiſton's notes of the order of time) *and he opened his mouth*. Might not this note be very well prefixed to our Saviour's preaching, although the ſermon, in the order of time, were really before that which immediately precedes it in the hiſtory? The ſame may be proved of almoſt every one of theſe notes, which Mr. Whiſton has here mentioned, if it were neceſſary.

The truth is, it is a common thing in all hiſtories to make uſe of ſuch *tranſitory* or *introductory* phraſes as theſe; nay even of thoſe which ſeem moſt to imply an immediate and orderly ſucceſſion of events, *in a very great latitude*. So for inſtance, Gen. xxxviii. 1. immediately after the account of Joſeph's being ſold into Egypt, it follows, *at that time Judah went down from his brethren*, &c. when as it is certain this happened a *conſiderable time before Joſeph's being ſold into Egypt* [a]. Hence, ſays Dr. Lightfoot [b], " The words *at that time* are not to be refer-
" red to the next words going before in the preceding chap-
" ter, concerning Joſeph's ſale to Potiphar, but are of *a more*
" *large extent*; as that phraſe, and the phraſe *in thoſe days*, are
" oft in Scripture." It is a trite obſervation among the writers of ſacred chronology, that theſe phraſes in Scripture are frequently uſed with a great deal of latitude. It has been obſerved, that this phraſe, *In that day or time*, is uſed *ſixteen* times in the Old and New Teſtament in a lax ſenſe, and not im-

---

[a] See above, p. 36.   [b] Harmon. and Chronic. of the
                                 Old Teſt. Gen. c. xxxviii.

plying a regular fucceffion of events [a]. So the words 'Εν δὲ ταῖς ἡμέραις ἐκείναις, Matt. iii. 1. are put to introduce the hiftory, which is next to Chrift's fixing at Nazareth; which was about thirty years after. Upon the whole then, if this be the ufe of moft of thefe notes, only to introduce the following ftory, if thofe which feem moft to be notes of time regard principally what follows, and are ufed in fuch a lax fenfe; then they do not prove, that this part of St. Matthew's Gofpel was originally wrote according to the order of time.

Thus I have confidered Mr. Whifton's firft affertion, viz. *That St. Matthew defigned originally to obferve the order of time through his whole Gofpel,* and have endeavoured to fhew that the feveral arguments he brings to fupport it, are not conclufive.

[a] Locutionem autem illam *(in tempore illo)* eodem modo in Deuter. x. 8. ufurpari notat Aben-Ezra; quomodo et ab aliis eft obfervatum, *in die illo*, fine determinata aliqua temporis notatione, fedecies in Veteri et Novo Teftamento effe pofitum; hocque ipfo in loco, *in tempore illo,* non ad illud, quo in Egyptum venditus eft Jofephus, fed quo ipfe Judas in Cananæam cum Patre advenit, referendum effe defendimus. Uffer. Chronol. Sacr. c. 10. Vid. Spanheim. Dub. Evang. tom. ii. Dub. 10, et 95.

CHAP.

CHAP. VI.

Mr. Whiston's Proof of the main Proposition considered. It suppofes St. Mark's Gospel an Epitome of St. Matthew's. This the Opinion of most learned Men, but certainly false. That St. Mark is not an Epitome of St. Matthew, proved, First, from the Account given in Antiquity of the Manner and Occasion of his Writing, viz. that he wrote at Rome from St. Peter's Mouth. The Testimonies out of Antiquity produced. Two Observations from Scripture to support these Testimonies.

MR. Whiston having attempted to prove, that St. Matthew, in this part of his Gospel, defigned to obferve the order of time, proceeds to fhew, *that the feveral branches of the hiftory in this part, are not according to the order of time.* But before he comes to a particular proof of this, he fays, *He will in general prove the main propofition by the moft authentick evidence,* viz. *the teftimony of St. Mark* [a]. This indeed, if it be any evidence at all, will be moft authentick and indifputable. Let us a little confider it.

" St. Mark (fays Mr. Whifton) was the epitomizer of St.
" Matthew—gives us fuch an account of our Saviour's Acts,
" as demonftrates that St. Matthew's Gofpel lay then before
" him, and was the almoft only guide he followed in his hif-
" tory. Now fuppofing this (fays he), it will follow, that
" either that copy of St. Matthew, which St. Mark made ufe
" of, was in a different order from that which we now have
" (in the chapters under confideration), or elfe that he knew
" the order of his copy to be wrong, and contrary to the ori-
" ginal one, and fo reduced it in his epitome to the true and
" regular feries of events, which he learned from St. Peter.
" Now either of thefe is fufficient for my prefent purpofe ; for
" it is evident, that St. Mark does not obferve the order of the
" prefent copies of St. Matthew (whom he epitomizes), in that
" part we are fpeaking of, &c." This now is St. Mark's tefti-

[a] P. 102.

mony, and Mr. Whiston's *most convincing argument*, of the truth of the propofition, viz. *that the former part of St. Matthew's Gofpel, in our prefent copies, is not now in its true and firft intended order.*

However fpecious and plaufible this argument may at firft appear, I doubt not but every unbiaffed mind, after a more clofe examination, will be very far from thinking it conclufive and convincing. The two following confiderations will fufficiently invalidate the force of this reafoning, viz.

I. *St. Mark did not epitomize or abridge St. Matthew's Gofpel, nor had he it lying before him, when he wrote.*

II. *Suppofe St. Mark did abridge, and make ufe of St. Matthew's Gofpel in compofing his, yet it will not follow either that the copies he then ufed were, or our prefent copies now, are mifplaced, and out of the order originally intended by St. Matthew.*

I. *St. Mark did not epitomize or abridge St. Matthew's Gofpel, nor had he it lying before him, when he wrote.* In undertaking to prove this, I am very well aware, that I oppofe the fentiments of learned men in all ages of the church : antient and modern writers have almoft all, with one common confent, voted and agreed St. Mark's Gofpel to be an epitome of St. Matthew's.

Auftin [a], among the antients, and among later writers Erafmus [b], Sixtus Senenfis [c], Alfted [d], Grotius [e], Spanheim [f], Toinard [g], and many others, affert it. Nay, Erafmus [h] in another place has carried the matter fomewhat further, and by a certain likenefs, which he imagined he obferved in the ftyle and idiom of thefe two Gofpels (contrary to all antiquity, and even to himfelf in the place firft cited), is induced to believe *they both were wrote by the fame perfon.*

---

[a] Marcus Matthæum fubfecutus tanquam pediffequus et breviator eius videtur. Aug. de Confenf. Evang. l. 1. c. 2.

[b] Annot. in Nov. Teft. ad Marc. i. 1.

[c] Biblioth. Sanct. l. 1. ad voc. Marc.

[d] Præcognit. Theolog. l. 2. p. 263.

[e] Annot. ad Marc. i. 1.

[f] Hiftor. Ecclef. Secul. I. c. 6.

[g] Prolegom. in Harm. Evang. p. 4.

[h] Erafmus, in Apolog. contra Albertum Carporum Principem, fcribit, eundem fuiffe utriufque Evangelii fcriptorem. Vid. Sixt. Senenf. l. 7. de Marci Evangelio.

But

But notwithstanding this so universal agreement of learned men in this matter, I am not afraid to undertake the defence of the contrary opinion. It is no new or uncommon thing for the bulk of criticks and commentators to agree in an error. An opinion that is plausible, and has some appearance of probability, first started by a person of reputation, and ushered into the world under some great name, is very often universally received, and for a long time entertained as an unquestionable truth, though all the while it be really false : but if in process of time it has the good fortune to be espoused by more men of reputation and character, for sense and learning, it then acquires a sort of sanctity, and, through I know not what sort of fearfulness, men dare not so much as suspect or call in question the truth of a proposition, which has been believed by almost all learned men. This I verily believe was the case, in respect of the point we are now upon. Austin, and some others of reputation, first started it : to others, who would not be at the pains of examining into the truth of it, it seemed plausible, and so they received it. And by this means many learned men suffered themselves to be imposed upon, taking that for truth, which they certainly had rejected as false, had they but ventured strictly and closely to examine it. But numbers are no evidence of truth, and (as Mr. Whiston well observes in another place [a]) *a common opinion without a solid foundation, is of no great value.* He that heartily and in good earnest seeks after truth, must not suffer himself to be impressed either with the *number*, or *reputation* of those, who think otherwise than he does. It was a noble resolution of Seneca's [b], " That he " would obstinately persist in the search of truth ; not making " his understanding a slave to any man's, nor giving in to " any opinion, only because it was published under a great " name."

I shall therefore endeavour to prove this *common opinion* (viz. that St. Mark epitomized St. Matthew) *false* ; and I shall take the more pains in the matter, not only because I shall

---

[a] Chronol. of the Old Testam. p. 16.
[b] Verum—contumaciter quæram;

non en'm me cuiquam mancipavi, nullius nomen fero, &c. Sen. Epist. 45.

thereby

thereby invalidate Mr. Whifton's *moſt authentick evidence,* but ſet a matter in a clear light, which (as far as I can find) no one yet has attempted to do, and ſo withal recover the honour of this Goſpel (viz. St. Mark's), which has ſo long lain under this hard and injurious charge, *of being extracted, and compiled out of St. Matthew.*   And,

1. It is very evident, that St. Mark's Goſpel is not an epitome of St. Matthew's, *from the accounts we have in eccle-fiaſtical hiſtory, of the manner and occaſion of St. Mark's writ-ing his Goſpel.*   The ſubſtance of all thoſe accounts which we have, is this, viz. *That St. Mark, (who was the companion and interpreter of St. Peter) being at Rome with him, was deſired by the brethren there, to give them an account in writing, of what he had learnt from St. Peter, of the doctrines and life of Chriſt ; that they did not deſiſt in their intreaties, till they had prevailed, and this was the cauſe or reaſon of the Goſpel, we now call St. Mark's, being firſt wrote.*   This in ſhort is the account, and it ſeems to be as largely atteſted by the antients, as almoſt any matter of fact whatſoever, at that diſtance from us.   Papias, Irenæus, Origen, Clemens Alexandrinus, Je-rome, and many others, all agree as to the main of this fact.

The moſt full and antient relation of this matter, is that of Clemens Alexandrinus, cited by Euſebius in two ſeveral places[a], and confirmed in the firſt of thoſe places, by the moſt antient teſtimony of Papias.   To the ſame purpoſe (though not quite ſo full) is the account of Irenæus, viz. *That St. Mark committed to writing the things which he heard St. Peter preach*[h].   So Origen[c], *That St. Mark made or wrote his*

---

[a] Παρακλήσισι δὲ παντοίαις (ſcil. οἱ Ῥωμαῖοι) Μάρκον, ὖ τὸ Εὐαγγέλιον φέρεται, ἀκόλεθον ὄντα Πίτρῳ λιπαρῆσαι, ὡς ἂν καὶ διὰ γραφῆς ὑπόμνημα τῆς διὰ λόγε παραδωθείσης αὐτοῖς καταλείψοι διδασκαλίας· μὴ πρότερόν τε ἀνεῖναι ἢ κατεργάσασθαι τὸν ἄνδρα, καὶ ταύτη αἰτίως γενέσθαι τῆς τῷ λεγομένε κατὰ Μάρκον Εὐαγγελίε γραφῆς—Συνεπιμαρτυρεῖ δ' αὐτῷ καὶ ὁ Ἱεραπολίτης ἐπίσκοπος ὀνόματι Παπίας.   Euſeb. Hiſt. Eccl. l. 2. c. 15. Idem vid. lib. 6. c. 14. vid. et lib. 3. c. 39.

[b] Μάρκος ὁ μαθητὴς καὶ ἑρμηνευτὴς Πίτρε, καὶ αὐτὸς τὰ ὑπὸ Πίτρε κηρυσσόμενα ἐγγράφως ἡμῖν παραδίδωκε. Iren. Adv. Hæreſ. lib. 3. c. 1.

[c] Apud Euſeb. Hiſt. Eccl. lib. 6. c. 25.

Goſpel,

Gospel, ὡς Πέτρος ὑφηγήσατο αὐτῷ, *as St. Peter directed or taught him.* The same account we have from Jerome [a] several times, Theophylact [b], and several others of the antients. It was so far believed in the first ages, that St. Mark wrote his Gospel under the conduct and direction of St. Peter, that this Gospel was by a great many called *The Gospel of St. Peter,* and not St. Mark; so Tertullian [c] tells us, that " the Gospel " which St. Mark published, was affirmed to be wrote by " St. Peter." Such is the account, which we have from antiquity, of the writing of this Gospel. There is one remark which I have made in reading this Gospel, which (though it may seem to some to be too nice a speculation) yet perhaps, considering the very many testimonies of the antients, *that St. Mark wrote what he heard from St. Peter,* may have some weight in it, and be some confirmation of the preceding relation. The remark I mean is this, viz. *That there are in the Gospel history, several very remarkable circumstances, relating to St. Peter, which are told by the other Evangelists, and not so much as mentioned or hinted at by St. Mark.* The reason of which seems to be, that St. Peter's modesty would not permit them to be inserted, being generally such as were to his advantage, and would tend to advance his honour above the rest of the Apostles, a thing which no doubt the good Apostle would endeavour to prevent. For the manifesting of this, I will select a few out of the other instances, which might be produced, viz.

1. The account of *Christ's pronouncing St. Peter blessed,* when he had confessed him, *the promise of the keys, and of that large power,* &c. made to him, are omitted by St. Mark, though the former and succeeding parts of the story, are both told by him. See Mark viii. 29, 30. and compare it with Matt. xvi. 16—20.

2. The relation of St. Peter's working the miracle, *by get-*

---

[a] Marcus—juxta quod Petrum referentem audierat, rogatus Romæ a fratribus, breve scripsit Evangelium. Catalog. Script. Eccl. in voce Marcus. Vid. Præfat. in Comment. in Matt.

[b] Præfat. in Comment. in Marc.

[c] Evangelium, quod Marcus edidit, Petri affirmetur, cujus interpres Marcus. Tertull. Adv. Marcion. lib. 4. c. 5.

ting money out of the fish's mouth, to pay the tribute-money, told by St. Matt. ch. xvii. 24, &c. is omitted by St. Mark, though the preceding and subsequent stories are the same as in St. Matthew. See Mark ix. 30—33.

3. Chrift's particular love and favour expreffed to St. Peter, *in telling him of his danger, and that he had prayed for him in particular, that his faith might not fail,* Luke xxii. 31, 32. is omitted by St. Mark.

4. *St. Peter's remarkable humility* above the reft of the Apoftles, *about Chrift's wafhing his feet, &c.* John xiii. 6—9. omitted by St. Mark.

5. The inftance of St. Peter's very great zeal for Chrift, when he was taken, *in cutting of the High-Prieft's fervant's ear.* John xviii. 10. is not mentioned by St. Mark concerning St. Peter in particular, but only told in general of a certain perfon that ftood by; Mark xiv. 47.

6. St. Peter's faith *in leaping into the fea,* to go to Chrift, John xxi. 7. not mentioned by St. Mark.

7. Chrift's difcourfe with St. Peter concerning *his love to him,* and his particular, repeated charge to him *to feed his fheep,* John xxi. 15. &c. omitted by St. Mark.

Thefe are fome inftances of things tending to St. Peter's honour, recorded by the other Evangelifts, none of which are fo much as hinted at by St. Mark. I add, that there is not any one fingle inftance in all that Gofpel, like unto any of thofe which have been mentioned. There is nothing in that Gofpel, which does in the leaft tend to advance the honour and prerogative of St. Peter, above the reft of the Apoftles. Now, why thefe and fome other particulars of a like nature fhould be omitted by St. Mark, is fomewhat ftrange, unlefs we account for it thus; that St. Peter, who dictated this Gofpel to St. Mark, through modefty and for fear of fome bad confequences, caufed him to leave out thofe things, which fo particularly concerned himfelf. Had not St. Mark had his Gofpel from St. Peter, I cannot conceive, why he fhould fo ftudioufly avoid the mention of all thofe remarkable things, which tended fo much to his honour. Much to the fame purpofe, is the arguing

guing of a learned Popifh divine on this head[a], out of Eufebius. " Why (fays he) St. Mark fhould leave out thofe great
" and honourable promifes made to St. Peter, which we read
" in St. Matthew (ch. xvi.), may be feen in Eufebius (De-
" monftr. Evang. l. 3. c. 7.) St. Peter's humility would not
" fuffer him to tell thefe things to St. Mark, when he was
" writing his Gofpel. We may obferve the three other Evan-
" gelifts relating thofe things, which tend to advance the ho-
" nour and prerogative of St. Peter. Only St. Mark, who
" wrote his Gofpel from St. Peter's dictating to him, has
" omitted them; which evidences the great modefty of St.
" Peter." This reafoning is abundantly confirmed by a very
common and well-known obfervation, that authors of modefty are feldom forward to mention thofe things, that tend to
their own praife; fo that we have at leaft a probable argument from the Gofpel itfelf, to prove the account we have
from antiquity, of the writing of it, true. The learned Dr.
Hammond has another argument taken out of the Gofpel itfelf, by which he endeavours to prove the account, that has
been given of its being dictated by St. Peter, to be true. After
having cited the account, he adds[b]; " Of this there be fome
" characters difcernible in the writing itfelf; as that, fetting
" down the ftory of Peter's denying of Chrift, with the fame
" enumeration of circumftances, and aggravations of the
" fault, that Matthew doth; when he comes to mention his
" repentance and tears confequent to it, he doth it (as became
" the true penitent) *more coldly* than Matthew had done, only
" ἴκλαιι *he wept*; whereas Matthew hath ἴκλαυσι πικρῶς, *he wept*
" *bitterly*." How far this argument is conclufive, I fhall not

---

[a] Cur Marcus omittit illa mag-
nifica promiffa Petro facta a Chrifto,
quæ leguntur apud Matth. vid.
apud Eufeb. lib. 3. Demonftr. E-
vang. c. 7. Petrus ex humilitate
noluit hoc referre Marco fcripturo
Evangelium; ubi nota reliquos tres
Evangeliftas ea commemoraffe, quæ
ad Petri excellentiam et præroga-
tivam pertinent. Matt. ch. 16.
Beatus es, Simon Bar-Jona, &c.

Luc. c. 22. *Ego rogavi pro te*, &c.
Et apud Joan. 21. *Pafce oves
meas.* Solum Marcum, qui Evangelium fcripfit, ficut Petro referente
audierat, de his tacuiffe. Quæ res
infignem B. Petri modeftiam nobis
infinuat et commendat. Eftius in
Difficilior. Script. loc. ad Marc. 8.
29.

[b] Introduc. to Matt.

now enquire; if this be not, perhaps there may be several of
the like nature, that are. I would only add, that St. Peter
himself in his 1st Epistle [a] makes mention of St. Mark, as
being along with him, and calls him *his son: The Church
which is at Babylon, elected together with you, saluteth you, and
so doth Marcus my son.* There can be no just reason to question,
whether the same Mark is here intended, who wrote the Gospel; and if the word Babylon be here taken for Rome, as the
Fathers, the papists in general, and many other among the
Protestants [b] do take it, then the foregoing account receives a
very great confirmation, from St. Peter and St. Mark's having been at Rome together. So Jerome [c] and Eusebius [d]
make use of this argument for this very purpose. The words
of the latter are these; " But Peter makes mention of Mark in
" his first Epistle, which they say was wrote at Rome, and it
" was that which Peter himself meant, when by a strong fi-
" gure he makes use of the word Babylon to denote that
" city, viz. Rome, in these words, The Church which is at
" Babylon, chosen together with you, saluteth you, and Mark
" my son."

If then upon the whole it be reasonable to conclude, that
St. Mark wrote his Gospel at Rome, at the request of the
brethren there, from the things which he had heard of St. Peter; we have, I think, an undeniable argument, that this
Gospel is not an abstract, or epitome of St. Matthew's. If
his Gospel be a collection of what St. Peter had told him, then
it is not a bare transcript of St. Matthew: for to say, he took
his Gospel from St. Peter's mouth, and transcribed it from St.
Matthew's writing, is somewhat like a contradiction. But
besides this, if St. Mark had had St. Matthew's Gospel along

[a] 1 Pet. v. 13.
[b] See Dr. Hammond on 1 Pet. v. 13. and on Rev. xviii. 2.
[c] Petrus in Epistola prima sub nomine Babylonis figuraliter Romam significans. Hieron. De Vir. Illustr. in voc. Marc.
[d] Τῦ δὶ Μάρκε μνημονεύειν τὸν Πέτρον ἐν τῇ προτέρᾳ Ἐπιστολῇ, ἣν καὶ συντάξαι φασὶν ἐπ' αὐτῆς Ῥώμης· σημαίνειν τε τῦτ' αὐτὸν τὴν πόλιν τροπικώτερον Βαβυλῶνα προσειπόντα, διὰ τύτων· Ἀσπάζεται ὑμᾶς ἡ ἐν Βαβυλῶνι συνεκλεκτὴ, καὶ Μάρκος ὁ υἱός μυ. Hist. Eccl. lib. 2. c. 15. Vid. etiam Valet. ad h. loc.

with

with him at Rome, why should the Romans have pressed him so very earnestly to make an epitome of it? Was it too long, and did it contain any things that were tedious or superfluous? The truth is, if St. Mark, or any one else, had had St. Matthew's Gospel at Rome, there would have been no need of St. Mark's writing. " If (says the famous Cardinal Bellarmine[a]) " the Gospel of St. Matthew had been then at Rome in the " hands of any of the Christians, when St. Mark wrote there, " he would not have wrote." And one would think they should rather have desired St. Matthew's Gospel, being wrote by one that was an eye and ear-witness of what he said. Besides, those for whom he wrote, wanted much of the zeal of the primitive Christians; nay, and of that zeal, which Eusebius says they had for the Gospel history, if they did not desire an account of all that our Lord said, and did. They would hardly desire, and be contented with a less full, when they could have a more full and perfect account. I conclude therefore, that St. Matthew's Gospel was not then at Rome, and consequently that St. Mark did not epitomize, or make any use of it, when he composed his Gospel.

---

[a] Immo si tunc (scil. quando Marcus Romæ scripsit) Evangelium Matthæi in manibus fidelium Romæ fuisset, credibile est Marcum scripturum non fuisse. Bellarm. de Matrimon. Sacr. lib. 1. c. 16.

C H A P. VII.

The Second Argument, to prove St. Mark's Gospel not to be an Epitome of St. Matthew's, because his Accounts are generally larger, and contain many more particular Circumstances, than St. Matthew's do. This evidenced by several Instances.

Arg. II. ST. *Mark's Gospel is not an abridgement or epitome of St. Matthew's, because for the most part his accounts are much more large and full, and related with many more particular circumstances, than the same accounts are by St. Matthew.* There is scarce any one story related by both these Evangelists, in which St. Mark does not add some considerable circumstances, which St. Matthew has not ; and if this be so, I think there can be no more convincing evidence, that St. Mark did not design to epitomize St. Matthew : but if we were to conclude any thing of this nature from comparing them together, the conclusion must be, that St. Matthew in all these parts did design to abridge St. Mark.

The matter of fact, which I have here asserted, will easily appear to be true to any one, who reads these two Gospels with this view, and compares them together. To save the reader the pains, I have collected some instances, and set them down in such a manner, that by a bare casting the eye upon them, the truth of that which I contend for, will sufficiently appear, viz. that St. Mark is generally larger in his accounts than St. Matthew.

A Table

A Table of several instances, in which St. Mark relates his stories more fully and with more particular circumstances, than St. Matthew.

The story of the devils cast into the swine.

St. MATTHEW.	St. MARK.
Chap. VIII.	Chap. V.

Ver. 28. And when he was come to the other side, into the country of the Gergesenes, there met him two possessed with devils, coming out of the tombs, exceeding fierce, so that no man might pass by that way.

Ver. 1. And they came over unto the other side of the sea, into the country of the Gadarenes.

2. And when he was come out of the ship, immediately there met him out of the tombs, a man with an unclean spirit;

3. Who had his dwelling among the tombs, and no man could bind him, no not with chains.

4. Because that he had been often bound with fetters and chains, and the chains had been plucked asunder by him, and the fetters broken in pieces; neither could any man tame him.

5. And always night and day he was in the mountains, and in the tombs, crying and cutting himself with stones.

6. But when he saw Jesus afar off, he ran and worshipped him;

29. And behold they cried out, saying, What have we to do with thee, Jesus, thou

7. And cried with a loud voice, and said, What have I to do with thee, Jesus, thou

St. MATTHEW.

Chap. VIII.

Son of God? Art thou come hither to torment us, before the time?

St. MARK.

Chap. V.

Son of the moft high God? I adjure thee by God, that thou torment me not.

8. (For he faid unto him, Come out of the man, thou unclean fpirit.)

9. And he afked him, what is thy name? And he anfwered, faying, My name is Legion; for we are many.

10. And he befought him much, that he would not fend them away out of the country.

11. Now there was there nigh unto the mountains, a great herd of fwine feeding.

30. And there was a good way off from them, an herd of many fwine feeding.

31. So the devils befought him, faying, If thou caft us out, fuffer us to go away into the herd of fwine.

32. And he faid unto them, Go; and when they were come out, they went into the herd of fwine, and behold the whole herd of fwine ran violently down a fteep place into the fea, and perifhed in the waters.

33. And they that kept them fled, and went their ways into the city, and told every thing, and what was befallen to the poffeffed of the devils.

12. And all the devils befought him, faying, Send us into the fwine, that we may enter into them.

13. And forthwith Jefus gave them leave, and the unclean fpirits went out, and entered into the fwine, and the herd ran violently down a fteep place into the fea, (they were about two thoufand) and were choaked in the fea.

14. And they that fed the fwine fled, and told it in the city and in the country. And they went out to fee what it was that was done.

15. And they come to Jefus,

St. MATTHEW.

Chap. VIII.

St. MARK.

Chap. V.

fus, and fee him that was poffeffed with the devil, and had the Legion fitting, and clothed, and in his right mind, and they were afraid.

16. And they that faw it told them, how it befel to him, that was poffeffed with the devil, and alfo concerning the fwine.

34. And behold the whole city came out to meet Jefus; and when they faw him, they befought him, that he would depart out of their coafts.

17. And they began to pray him to depart out of their coafts.

18. And when he was come into the fhip, he that had been poffeffed with the devil, prayed him, that he might be with him.

19. Howbeit Jefus fuffered him not, but faith unto him, Go home to thy friends, and tell them how great things the Lord hath done for thee, and hath had compaffion on thee.

20. And he departed, and began to publifh in Decapolis, how great things Jefus had done for him; and all men did marvel.

The

The story of the paralytick healed.

St. MATTHEW.	St. MARK.
CHAP. IX.	Chap. II.
1. And he entered into a ſhip, and paſſed over, and came into his own city.	1. And again he entered into Capernaum, after ſome days, and it was noiſed that he was in the houſe.
	2. And ſtraightway many were gathered together, inſomuch that there was no room to receive them, no not ſo much as about the door ; and he preached the word unto them.
2. And behold they brought to him a man ſick of the palſy, lying on a bed.	3. And they come unto him, bringing one ſick of the palſy, which was borne of four.
	4. And when they could not come nigh unto him for the preſs, they uncovered the roof where he was ; and when they had broken it up, they let down the bed wherein the ſick of the palſy lay.
2. —— And Jeſus ſeeing their faith, &c.	5. When Jeſus ſaw their faith, &c.

The story of Jairus the Ruler of the Synagogue's daughter reſtored to life.

Chap. IX.	Chap. V.
Ver. 18. While he ſpake theſe things unto them, behold there came a certain ruler and worſhipped him, ſaying, My daughter is even	Ver. 22. And behold there cometh one of the rulers of the ſynagogue, Jairus by name; and when he ſaw him, he fell at his feet,
	23. And

St. MATTHEW.

Chap. IX.

now dead; but come and lay thy hand upon her, and she shall live.

19. And Jesus arose and followed him; and so did his disciples.

23. And when Jesus came into the ruler's house, and saw the people, and the minstrels making a noise,

24. He said unto them, Give place, for the maid is not dead, but sleepeth. And they laughed him to scorn.

St. MARK.

Chap. V.

23. And besought him greatly, saying, My little daughter lieth at the point of death: I pray thee come and lay thy hands on her, that she may be healed, and she shall live.

24. And Jesus went with him, and much people followed him, and thronged him.

35. While he yet spake, there came from the ruler of the synagogue's house certain, which said, Thy daughter is dead: why troublest thou the master any further?

36. As soon as Jesus heard the word that was spoken, he saith unto the ruler of the synagogue, Be not afraid, only believe.

37. And he suffered no man to follow him, save Peter, and James, and John, the brother of James.

38. And he cometh to the house of the ruler of the synagogue, and seeth the tumult, and them that wept and wailed greatly.

39. And when he was come in, he saith unto them, Why make ye this ado, and weep? The damsel is not dead, but sleepeth.

40. And

St. MATTHEW.   St. MARK.

Chap. IX.   Chap. V.

25. But when the people were put forth, he went in, and took her by the hand, and the maid arofe.

26. And the fame hereof went abroad into all that land.

40. And they laughed him to fcorn; but when he had put them all out, he taketh the father and the mother of the damfel, and them that were with him, and entereth in where the damfel was lying.

41. He took the damfel by the hand, and faid, Talitha Cumi, which is, being interpreted, damfel (I fay unto thee) arife.

42. And ftraightway the damfel arofe, and walked, for fhe was of the age of twelve years; and they were aftonifhed with a great aftonifhment.

43. And he charged them ftraitly, that no man fhould know of it, and he commanded that fomething fhould be given her to eat.

The ftory of the woman healed of the bloody iffue.

20. And behold, a woman, which was difeafed with an iffue of blood twelve years—

25. And a certain woman which had an iffue of blood twelve years;

26. And had fuffered many things of many phyficians, and had fpent all that fhe had, and was nothing bettered, but rather grew worfe;

27. When

St. MATTHEW.

Chap. IX.

—came behind him, and touched the hem of his garment.

21. For she said within herself, If I may but touch his garment, I shall be whole.

22. But Jesus turned him about, and when he saw her, he said, Daughter, be of good comfort; thy faith hath made thee whole: and the woman was made whole from that hour.

St. MARK.

Chap. V.

27. When she had heard of Jesus, came in the press behind, and touched his garment.

28. For she said, If I may but touch his clothes, I shall be whole.

29. And straightway the fountain of her blood was dried up, and she felt in her body that she was healed of that plague.

30. And Jesus immediately knowing in himself, that virtue had gone out of him, turned him about in the press, and said, Who touched my clothes?

31. And his disciples said unto him, Thou seest the multitude thronging thee, and sayest thou, Who touched me?

32. And he looked round about, to see her that had done this thing.

33. But the woman fearing and trembling, knowing what was done in her, came and fell down before him, and told him all the truth.

34. And he said unto her, Daughter, thy faith hath made thee whole; go in peace, and be whole of thy plague.

The

The story of a boy dispossessed of a dumb spirit.

St. MATTHEW. Chap. XVII.	St. MARK. Chap. IX.
14. And when they were come to the multitude, there came to him a certain man, kneeling down to him, and saying,	17. And one of the multitude anfwered, and faid, Mafter, I have brought unto thee my fon, which hath a dumb fpirit:
15. Lord, have mercy on my fon, for he is a lunatick, and fore vexed; for ofttimes he falleth into the fire, and oft into the water:	18. And wherefoever he taketh him, he teareth him; and he foameth, and gnafheth with his teeth, and pineth away: and I fpake to thy difciples, that they fhould caft him out, and they could not.
16. And I brought him to thy difciples, and they could not cure him.	19. He anfwered him, and faith, O faithlefs and perverfe generation, how long fhall I be with you? How long fhall I fuffer you? Bring him unto me.
17. Then Jefus anfwered, and faid, Oh faithlefs and perverfe generation, how long fhall I be with you? How long fhall I fuffer you? Bring him hither to me.	20. And they brought him unto him, and when he faw him, ftraightway the fpirit tare him, and he fell on the ground, and wallowed foaming.
	21. And he afked his father, How long is it ago, fince this came unto him? And he faid, Of a child.
	22. And ofttimes it hath caft him into the fire, and into the water, to deftroy him; but if thou canft do any thing, have

St. MATTHEW.	St. MARK.
Chap. XVII.	Chap. IX.

St. MARK.

Chap. IX.

have compaſſion on us, and help us.

23. Jeſus ſaid unto him, If thou canſt believe, all things are poſſible to him that be-lieveth.

24. And ſtraightway the father of the child cried out, and ſaid with tears, Lord, I believe, help thou mine unbe-lief.

25. When Jeſus ſaw that the people came running to-

St. MATTHEW.

18. And Jeſus rebuked the devil, and he departed out of him; and the child was cured from that very hour.

gether, he rebuked the foul ſpirit, ſaying, Thou dumb and deaf ſpirit, I charge thee come out of him, and enter no more into him.

26. And the ſpirit cried, and rent him ſore, and came out of him; and he was as one dead, inſomuch that many ſaid, he is dead.

27. But Jeſus took him by the hand, and lifted him up, and he aroſe.

The ſtory of the fig-tree curſed by Chriſt.

Chap. XXI.	Chap. XI.

Chap. XXI.

18. Now in the morning, as he returned into the city, he hungered.

19. And when he ſaw a fig-tree in the way, he came

Chap. XI.

12. And on the morrow, when they were come from Bethany, he was hungry.

13. And ſeeing a fig-tree afar off, having leaves, he came,

St. Matthew.

Chap. XXI.

to it, and found nothing thereon, but leaves only, and faid, Let no fruit grow on thee henceforward for ever; and prefently the fig-tree withered away.

20. And when the difciples faw it, they marvelled, faying, How foon is the fig-tree withered away!

St. Mark.

Chap. XI.

came, if haply he might find any thing thereon; and when he came to it, he found nothing but leaves, for the time of figs was not yet.

14. And Jefus anfwered, and faid unto it, No man eat fruit of thee hereafter for ever. And his difciples heard it.

20. And in the morning, as they paffed by, they faw the fig-tree dried up from the roots.

21. And Peter calling to remembrance, faith unto him, Mafter, behold, the fig-tree, which thou curfedft, is withered away.

The ftory of our Saviour's Difciples preparing a place for celebrating the paffover.

Chap. XXVI.

17. Now the firft day of the feaft of unleavened bread, the difciples came to Jefus, faying unto him, Where wilt thou that we prepare for thee, to eat the paffover?

18. And he faid, Go into the city to fuch a man, and fay unto him, The mafter faith, my time is at hand, I will

Chap. XIV.

12. And the firft day of unleavened bread, when they killed the paffover, his difciples faid unto him, Where wilt thou that we go and prepare, that thou mayeft eat the paffover?

13. And he fendeth forth two of his difciples, and faith unto them, Go ye into the city, and there fhall meet you

a man

St. MATTHEW.

Chap. XXVI.

keep the paſſover at thy houſe with my diſciples.

19. And the diſciples did, as Jeſus had appointed them ; and they made ready the paſſover.

St. MARK.

Chap. XIV.

a man bearing a pitcher of water ; follow him.

14. And whereſoever he ſhall go in, ſay ye to the good man of the houſe, The maſter ſaith, Where is the gueſt-chamber, where I ſhall eat the paſſover with my diſciples ?

15. And he will ſhew you a large upper room, furniſh-ed and prepared ; there make ready for us.

16. And his diſciples went forth, and came into the city, and found as he had ſaid unto them ; and they made ready the paſſover.

By a very curſory and tranſient view of the preceding in-ſtances, every one, who is unprejudiced, will conclude, that St. Mark could not poſſibly deſign to abridge St. Matthew, unleſs abridging and enlarging do ſignify the ſame thing. His ac-counts are ſo much fuller, and contain ſo many more particular circumſtances, than St. Matthew's do, that to ſuppoſe his Goſ-pel to be an epitome of St. Matthew's, is ſomewhat like ſup-poſing the whole to be leſs than a part. Nor is it only in the inſtances which have been produced, that St. Mark's relations are larger than thoſe of St. Matthew, but alſo in abundance of others. It would be tedious to mention all the particular in-ſtances of this nature, eſpecially to write them down at length, as I have done the former ; I ſhall therefore only mention a few, and briefly hint what they are.

A Catalogue of some other instances, in which St. Mark adds more circumstances to his relations, than St. Matthew.

Chap. i. 45. The leper's publishing what Christ had done for him, after his cure.

III. 20, 21. The multitudes following Christ, his friends laying hold on him, and charging him with distraction.

IV. 10. The disciples asking our Saviour the meaning of the parable of the sower, *when he was alone.*

Ver. 36. *Several ships* accompanying our Saviour in his voyage.

VI. 2. Our Lord's preaching *on the Sabbath-day in his own country.*

Ver. 5. The particular work our Saviour did in his own country, viz. healing some sick.

Ver. 6. His wondering at their unbelief.

Ver. 7. The manner of sending forth the Apostles, viz. *by two and two.*

Ver. 37. The disciples' unwillingness to go to buy bread for the multitude, and the sum it would cost.

Ver. 40. The manner of the multitudes sitting down to be fed by Christ.

VII. 24. Our Saviour's desire to be concealed, but could not.

VIII. 3. Some of our Lord's disciples came from far.

Ver. 6, 7. The blessing the seven loaves, and blessing the fishes, mentioned as done distinctly and separately; St. Matthew joins the blessing the loaves and fishes both together.

Ver. 14. The disciples had but one loaf.

IX. 10. The three disciples questioning one with another, what our Lord meant *by rising from the dead.*

Ver. 32. The rest of the disciples at a loss in the same particular, and afraid to ask Christ.

Chap. vi. 14—30. There are several particular circumstances in the history of John's death, which are not mentioned by St. Matthew.

Ver.

Ver. 44, 48. A further defcription of the torments and mifery of hell.

X. 15. Chrift's declaring, that they who did not receive the kingdom of heaven as little children, fhould not enter into it.

Ver. 32. The difciples afraid, when they were going up to Jerufalem.

Ver. 49, 50. Chrift's ordering the blind man to be called, comforting him, his cafting away his garment, and coming to Chrift.

XI. 4, 5. A defcription of the place where the colt was found, and the owners demanding the reafon of the two difciples, why they took it away.

XII. 32, 33, 34. The Scribe approves what our Lord had faid, repeats it, makes a juft and ufeful remark upon it: our Saviour approves him, &c.

Ver. 37. The common people take pleafure in hearing Chrift.

XIII. 3. The names of the Apoftles, who made the enquiry concerning the deftruction of the Temple.

XIV. 3, &c. Several particulars in the ftory of the woman's anointing our Saviour; fuch as the quality of the ointment, the breaking of the box, the value of the ointment in money, &c.

Ver. 12. The paffover was to be killed on the firft day of unleavened bread.

Ver. 54, 67. Peter fat warming himfelf at the fire.

Ver. 70. Peter faid to be a Galilean.

XV. 7. The crime for which Barabbas was imprifoned.

Ver. 8. The Jews plead their privilege of having a criminal releafed at the paffover.

Ver. 25. The precife hour, in which our Saviour was crucified.

Ver. 42. The reafon why Jofeph of Arimathea came on that day to beg the body of Jefus, viz. becaufe *it was the preparation,* i. e. *the day before the Sabbath.*

Ver. 43. The character and office of Jofeph of Arimathea.

Ver.

Ver. 44. Pilate wonders Chrift was fo foon dead. His enquiring about it.

XVI. 1. The defign of Mary Magdalen, and the other Mary, to embalm the body of Jefus, with ointments they had bought for that purpofe.

Thefe are fome inftances of circumftances, related by St. Mark in his hiftories, and not by St. Matthew: a perfon, that will be at the pains carefully to compare thefe Gofpels, with this view, will find many more. But thefe feem to be fufficient for my prefent purpofe, fufficient to evidence, that St. Mark did not defign to abridge or epitomize St. Matthew's Gofpel.

C H A P. VIII.

The third Argument, by which it appears, that St. Mark's Gofpel is not an Epitome of St. Matthew's, viz. the remarkable Difagreement there feems to be between thefe two Evangelifts, in feveral Parts of their Gofpels. It is firft premifed, that all thefe are reconcileable. Then the particular Inftances of their Difagreement produced.

Arg. III. *T*HE difagreement which there feems to be between thefe two Evangelifts, viz. St. Matthew and St. Mark, in relating feveral circumftances of their hiftory, is a clear and demonftrative evidence, that St Mark did not abridge St. Matthew, nor had his Gofpel lying before him, when he wrote his. To go about to collect the difference of thefe facred writers, to make them appear *as many* and *as great* as poffible, may feem very ftrange and unneceffary work in one, who profeffes a value and refpect for them. I think it needful therefore to premife, that however *great* and *many* the differences may feem to be between thefe two (or indeed between any of the Evangelifts), yet they have all been happily reconciled,

ciled, by the labours of ingenious and learned men. Of the many that have undertaken this matter, there are none who feem to have been more fuccefsful therein, than Auſtin[a] among the antients, and the learned Frederick Spanheim[b] among the more late writers. Surprifing difcoveries have been made in the laſt age in this matter, by a further acquaint- ance with the cuſtoms and manners of the Jews, among whom our Saviour and his Apoſtles converfed; difficulties, which feemed to be infuperable, have been fometimes eaſily folved by the difcovery of fome particular cuſtom, that was among the Jews at that time; and thefe difcoveries have been fo many, and our helps of all forts in this matter fo great, that I will not be afraid to aſſert; that whatever difagreement may feem to be between thefe two Evangeliſts, or either of the other, it is capable of a very fatisfying and reaſonable folu- tion.

This premifed, I fay the difference between St. Matthew and St. Mark *is fo great, and in fo many inſtances,* as evidences almoſt to a demonſtration, that St. Mark did not collect his Goſpel out of St. Matthew: I do not now regard the differ- ence, that is between them, in refpect of the *order of time,* but in other circumſtances.

I fhall not be at the pains to obferve every fmall difference, which there is between thefe two Evangeliſts in their hiſto- ries. Thofe which are in the following catalogue, will be fufficient to my prefent purpofe.

A Catalogue of fome inſtances, in which the accounts of St. Mat- thew and St. Mark do feem to difagree.

The firſt remarkable inſtance we find of any difference be- tween them, is in the ſtory of the miracle, which our Saviour wrought, in caſting the devils into the herd of fwine, in the country of the Gadarenes or Gergefenes. The accounts we

---

[a] In his book intitled, *De Con- fenfu Evangeliſtarum.*

[b] In his excellent Diſſertations, which he calls *Dubia Evangelica.*

have,

have, Matth. viii. 28, &c. and Mark v. 1. in which accounts we may obſerve a diſagreement in two particulars.

I. As to the place where the miracle was wrought.

II. As to the number of perſons diſpoſſeſſed.

1. As to the *place or country* where the miracle was wrought, according to St. Matthew, it was when our Saviour was landed εἰς τὴν χώραν τῶν Γεργεσηνῶν, *in the country of the Gergeſenes*; ſee ch. viii. 28. According to St. Mark, v. 1. and ſo St. Luke, viii. 26. it was when our Saviour was come εἰς τὴν χώραν τῶν Γαδαρηνῶν, *into the country of the Gadarenes.* Now theſe were certainly the names of the inhabitants of two different places, as is very plain from Joſephus, who ſeveral times mentions them as ſuch. So when he is reckoning up [a] ſome of thoſe cities, which the Jews had deſtroyed in Syria, he firſt mentions their coming to Γέρασα, *the city of the Gergeſenes*, and after that Γαδάροις, *to the city of the Gadarenes.* And in the ſame chapter [b], mentioning the ſeveral cities, that fell upon the Jews, who dwelt in them, he names the Γαδαρεῖς *the Gadarenes*; and immediately after [c], reckoning up the cities, that were kind to the Jews, who dwelt among them, and did not deſtroy them, he mentions the Γερασηνοὶ *the Gergeſenes*; for there can be no doubt but Γερασηνοὶ and Γεργισηνοὶ were the ſame perſons. The old Syriack interpreter, who was perhaps a native of this, or ſome country near it, perceiving this difference between the Evangeliſts, thought it too great a one to be admitted into his Verſion, and therefore in St. Matthew, as well as in St. Mark, tranſlates it by the ſame word, *the country of the Gadarenes.*

2. *They differ, as to the number of perſons diſpoſſeſſed.* St. Matthew tells us, they were *two*, St. Mark mentions only *one*. Theſe, though they are not circumſtances contrary to each other, yet are ſo different, that they undeniably prove, that neither of theſe ſacred writers could make uſe of the other's Goſpel, in compoſing his.

[a] De Bell. Judaic. lib. 2. c. 18. §. 1.
[b] Ibid. c. 18. §. 5.
[c] Ibid. Vid. Suid. ad Γάδαρα et Γέρασα, et Lud. Dieu ad Matth. viii. 28.

Another

Another inftance to the fame purpofe, is the ftory of the daughter of Jairus, the ruler of the fynagogue, being reftored to life again by our Saviour, told by St. Mark, chap. v. 22, &c. with circumftances very different from thofe, with which it is told by St. Matthew, chap. ix. 18. For inftance, according to St. Matthew's account, the ruler told our Saviour, that his daughter ἄρτι ἐτελεύτησιν, *was already dead,* and defired, that he would reftore her to life again : but according to St. Mark, the young woman was not dead, when the ruler came to our Saviour ; for he only fays, Θυγάτριόν μου ἐχάτως ἔχει, *my little daughter lieth at the point of death*; and afterwards, when our Saviour was going along with him, fome of the family came, and tell him, his daughter was actually dead, and therefore it would be needlefs to give our Saviour any further trouble.

St. Mark, chap. viii. 10. tells us, that, after the miracle of multiplying the loaves and the fifhes, our Saviour immediately took fhip, and failed into the parts of Dalmanutha ; St. Matthew, chap. xv. 39. tells us, that in this voyage he went to the coafts of Magdala.

St. Mark, chap. x. 35, &c. tells us, that the two fons of Zebedee, James and John, came *themfelves* with a petition to our Saviour, that they might be advanced to the higheft places of dignity in his kingdom ; that our Lord fpoke to *them,* and reproved them for their ambition : according to St. Matthew, chap. xx. 20. not *they,* but *their mother,* came with this petition to Chrift, and he fpake to *her.*

St. Mark, chap. x. 46. relates the account of our Lord's reftoring a blind perfon to his fight, when he was coming out of Jericho ; St. Matthew, chap. xx. 30, &c. tells the very fame ftory, with moft of the fame circumftances, concerning two blind perfons.

St. Mark, chap. xii. 9. in the parable concerning the letting out of the vineyard, mentions a queftion of our Lord's, viz. *What therefore fhall the Lord of the vineyard do?* and makes him to anfwer it himfelf; on the contrary St. Matthew, chap. xxi. 40. intimates, that our Lord put this queftion to the Jews, and tells us, ver. 41. that they made him the anfwer ;

and fo thofe words are a confeffion extorted from the Jews, and not the words of Chrift, according to St. Mark.

St. Mark, chap. xiv. 30, and 68, 72. recites our Saviour's predixction concerning Peter's denial of him, and his axctual denying of him, in a very different manner from St. Matthew. Our Lord tells him, ver. 30. *Before the cock crow twice, thou fhalt deny me thrice*; and accordingly St. Mark tells us, ver. 68, &c. that he denied him once, and then the cock crowed; denied twice afterwards, and the cock crowed again: on the other hand, according to St. Matthew, our Saviour told him (chap. xxvi. 34.) that he fhould deny him three feveral times, before the cock fhould crow at all; and accordingly, he makes him axctually to deny Chrift three times, before the cock crew. See ver. 69—74.

St. Mark, chap. xv. 23. tells us, that when our Saviour was upon the crofs, *they gave him to drink, wine mingled with myrrh*; according to St. Matthew (chap. xxvii. 34.), that which they gave him to drink, was *vinegar mingled with gall.*

St. Mark faith, the fuperfcription on the crofs was this, THE KING OF THE JEWS; chap. xv. 26. According to St. Matthew it was thus, THIS IS JESUS THE KING OF THE JEWS; chap. xxvii. 37.

St. Mark, chap. xv. 34. gives us our Saviour's dying words upon the crofs, all in Syriack or Syro-Chaldaick, viz. *Eloi, Eloi, lama Sabaxcthani*; which was the language of the country, and that in which our Saviour fpake [a]. On the other hand St. Matthew puts down thefe words, partly in pure Hebrew, and partly in Syriack, *Eli, Eli, lama Sabaxcthani*; chap. xxvii. 46.

Thefe are fome of thofe inftances, in which thefe two Evangelifts differ; there are feveral other fuch to be found. But as there is not any one, which will not admit a very reafonable reconciliation; fo I think there is fcarce any one of them,

---

[a] See the Syriack tranflation of Mark xv. 34. Inftead of *Eli, Eli*, he renders it *Eloi, Eloi*, as it is in St. Mark. And though he ufe the word *Lemono* inftead of *Lama*, yet there is no doubt but *Lama* or *Lomo* was a very proper Chaldaick word.

but

but is of itſelf ſufficient to prove, that neither of theſe Goſpels was tranſcribed from the other.   How can St. Mark be ſuppoſed to have had St. Matthew's Goſpel lying before him, and to *have made that* (as Mr. Whiſton would have it) *his almoſt only guide,* when he differs in ſo many particulars from him? I deſire Mr. Whiſton, and thoſe who are of the ſame opinion with him in this matter, to conſider this argument impartially; and to tell us, if it be poſſible, what thoſe reaſons were, which made St. Mark differ ſo much from St. Matthew in his accounts, when he had his Goſpel lying before him at the time of his writing.   Were not St. Matthew's accounts juſt and true, and expreſſed as they ought to have been?   This cannot be ſuppoſed.   One inſpired writer certainly never entertained ſuch thoughts of another.   Or did St. Mark make theſe differences with deſign to prevent any ſuſpicions men might have, that his Goſpel was not his own, but borrowed, and made out of another?   Indeed if this had been the caſe, he could not have taken a better method to have accompliſhed his end.   One would have thought, that ſuch and ſo many differences, would have effectually ſcreened and protected his Goſpel from ſuch a charge.   But far be it from us, to have any ſuch thoughts of an inſpired writer.   Until therefore it be ſhewn, how it could come to paſs, that there ſhould be ſo many different circumſtances in the accounts of St. Matthew and St. Mark, when the latter is ſuppoſed to have made uſe of the Goſpel of the former in compoſing his, I muſt conclude he did not make uſe of it at all.   I own indeed there is one method ſuppoſeable, by which we may account for theſe differences between St. Matthew and St. Mark, though the latter did make uſe of the former's Goſpel.   The method I mean, is that which Mr. Whiſton has taken to reconcile their diſagreement as to the order of time, viz. *Suppoſing our preſent copies corrupted in all theſe places, where they differ in other circumſtances; as Mr. Whiſton does ſuppoſe them to be in all theſe places, where they diſagree as to time.*   But it being certain, that no ſuch corruption ever happened to the ſacred text of either St. Matthew or St. Mark, it ſtill remains unaccountable, how theſe differences ſhould have happened between

them,

them, suppofing the one to have made ufe of the other's Gofpel. Hence it was juftly argued by Mr. Dodwell [a]; " That
" the later Evangelifts did not fee the writings of the former;
" for if they had, it is impoffible there fhould have been fo
" many feeming contradictions, which have exercifed the
" minds of learned men almoft ever fince the firft conftitu-
" tion of the Canon." To the fame purpofe fays Mr. Le
Clerc [b]; " It is not credible that Mark or Luke had feen the
" Gofpel according to St. Matthew, who otherwife would
" have avoided—all feeming clafhings."

CHAP. IX.

*The fourth Argument, to prove St. Mark's Gofpel is not an
Epitome of St. Matthew's, viz. becaufe it has a great many
Hiftories, which are not in St. Matthew. A Catalogue of
them. The fifth Argument, viz. that it wants feveral remarkable Hiftories.*

Arg. IV. ST. Mark's Gofpel is not an epitome of St.
Matthew's, *becaufe he hath related feveral very
confiderable hiftories, of which there is not the leaft mention made
by St. Matthew.* I have already proved [b], that he does, for
the moft part, add many more particular circumftances to his
ftories, than St. Matthew. I fhall now fhew, that he relates
feveral entire hiftories, which St. Matthew does not; not only
a few additions which St. Peter informed him of (as Mr. Whifton [d] fuppofes), but many remarkable and ufeful ftories. This

---

[a] — Ut ne quidem refciverint
recentiores Evangeliftæ, quid fcrip-
fiffent de iifdem rebus antiquiores;
aliter foret, ne tot effent ἐναντιοφανῆ,
quæ fere a prima ufque Canonis
conftitutione eruditorum hominum
ingenia exercuerint. Differt. 1. in
Iren. §. 39.
[b] In his third Differtation, concerning the Four Gofpels, annexed
to his Harmony.
[c] Ch. 7.
[d] P. 102.

observation

obfervation will be fufficiently fupported by the following in-ftances.

A Catalogue of fome hiftories in St. Mark's Gofpel, which are not in St. Matthew.

Chap. I. 21, &c. The hiftory of our Saviour's cafting the unclean fpirit out of the man, in the fynagogue at Capernaum.

Ver. 35, &c. The account of our Lord's retiring to a folitary place to pray, and Peter and many others following him.

Ch. III. 13, &c. Our Saviour's going up to a mountain to pray, there firft choofing his twelve difciples; their names, commiffion, office, &c.

Ch. IV. 26, &c. The parable of the kingdom of heaven coming without obfervation.

Ch. VI. 12, 13. The Difciples going out to preach, cafting out devils, recovering many that were fick, by anointing with oil.

Ver. 30, &c. The Apoftles' report of their fuccefs, &c.

Ch. VII. 2, &c. The Pharifees obferve our Lord's Difciples eating with unwafhen hands, and the cuftom of the Jews in this matter, ver. 3, 4.

Ver. 32, &c. The miracle of the deaf and dumb perfon being reftored to his hearing and fpeech.

Ch. VIII. 22, &c. The hiftory of a blind perfon reftored to his fight at Bethfaida.

Ch. IX. 14, 15. The Difciples' difpute with the Scribes, and Chrift's enquiry into it.

Ver. 33, &c. The Difciples' difpute among themfelves by the way, who fhould be the greateft.

Ver. 38, &c. The ftory of John's forbidding a perfon to caft out devils in the name of Chrift, with Chrift's difcourfe to John thereupon.

Ch. X. 10, &c. The Difciples' enquiry about the bufinefs of divorce.

Ch. XII. 41, &c. Our Saviour's obferving the money caft into the treafury, the widow's mite, &c.

Ch.

Ch. XIV. 51, 52. The account of the young man, that appeared naked with a linen cloth about his body, at the time when our Saviour was taken.

Ch. XVI. 9, &c. Chrift's firft appearance, after his refurrection, to Mary Magdalen.

Ver. 12. His appearing to the two Difciples, on the road.

Thefe feveral hiftories (befides a great many particular circumftances already mentioned) are in St. Mark, and not in St. Matthew; which certainly never would have been, if he had defigned his Gofpel only for an abridgment of St. Matthew's. It is a thing unufual; nay, I believe I may venture to fay, it is a thing which never has been known, for an epitomizer to make fuch large additions to the hiftory, which he abridges. St. Mark's Gofpel therefore is not an epitome of St. Matthew's.

Arg. V. Perhaps, on the other hand, it may add to the improbability of St. Mark's Gofpel being an epitome of St. Matthew's, *that there are feveral things wanting in it, and not fo much as hinted at, which are in St. Matthew.* He that undertakes to epitomize a hiftory, ought not to omit any confiderable part of it. Now it is evident, that St. Mark has not the leaft remote regard to many of the parts of St. Matthew's Gofpel. As near as I can guefs, St. Matthew is about one fourth part larger than St. Mark, and thofe things in which he is larger are fome fermons and difcourfes of our Lord, efpe-'cially the Sermon on the Mount; befides, St. Mark entirely omitteth the genealogy, and the birth of Chrift with all its circumftances. There are alfo two or three miracles, mentioned by St. Matthew, and not by St. Mark. Now if St. Mark had St. Matthew's Gofpel lying before him, and defigned to make an abridgment of it, it is ftrange he fhould entirely omit, and not fo much as flightly mention thefe things. He could not think that, which an infpired writer had penned, not worthy his notice; if therefore he had had St. Matthew by him when he wrote, it is reafonable to fuppofe he would have mentioned thefe things, though he had omitted fome circumftances, and done it more briefly. If any perfon were now to make an epitome of St. Matthew, and were in this

refpeCt

respect to make it like St. Mark's, I am sure every one would blame it, as not duly done. Mr. Whiston has made an epitome of the Gospel history; and it is no compliment at all, nor a character so great, as that ingenious performance deserves, to say, it is a much better epitome of the Gospels (not only in this respect, but many others) than St. Mark's Gospel is of St. Matthew's. A just epitomizer should have at least the general heads of the history, which he abridges, in his epitome; St. Mark has not so much as this, and therefore Father Simon hath reasoned very justly on this matter [a]; " It is, " says he, worth observing, that St. Mark cannot pass for a " simple abbreviator of St. Matthew, because he insists more " at large, than he doth in some places; besides, if he had only " a design to publish an epitome of St. Matthew's Gospel, " he would not have taken away the entire genealogy of Je- " sus Christ, which makes one of the most principal parts of " it : it is not the custom of those that epitomize the works " of others, to retrench the most considerable part of them."

[a] Critic. Histor. of the New Test. Par, 1. c. 10. p. 89.

CHAP. X.

The sixth Argument, to prove St. Mark's Gospel is not an Epitome of St. Matthew's, viz. because that Supposition makes its Inspiration more dubious and uncertain; it makes the Author look like a Plagiary. Two Objections against this Argument answered. The seventh Argument, the supposing this Gospel an Epitome detracts from its Honour and Usefulness. Spinoza and Father Simon for this reason assert most of the Books of the Old Testament, to be only Epitomes, made out of Records that are lost. Lastly, the supposing this Gospel an Epitome, invalidates in a great Measure its Testimony to the Truth of Christianity. The Evangelists did not see one another's Gospels.

Arg. VI. ST. Mark's Gospel is not an epitome or abridgment of St. Matthew's; because the supposing it to be so, *makes its inspiration more dubious and uncertain.* That this Gospel (as well as the other historical books, which are received into the Canon of the Old and New Testament) was wrote under the conduct and immediate influences of the divine Spirit, is what I must at present take for granted. Mr. Whiston, when he wrote the proposition, which I am now endeavouring to disprove, believed the writers of the Gospel history to be *inspired* [a]; and therefore it is not at all necessary I should now undertake the proof of this matter. There is only one thing I would offer to Mr. Whiston's consideration on this head, and that is, that many of the most antient and genuine writers of the Christian Church (such as Mr. Whiston himself reckons most valuable) give us abundant evidence that they believed, nay, and sometimes expreslly make mention of, the inspiration of the Gospel history [b].

[a] P. 112.
[b] In this number are Clemens Romanus, Irenæus, Justin Martyr, and many others, who lived not much later than them.

Taking

Taking it then for granted, that St. Mark's Gospel was wrote under the conduct of the divine Spirit, it is not reasonable to suppose it to be an epitome of St. Matthew; to be an epitomizer, and to be under the immediate influence of the Holy Spirit, seems to be a little inconsistent. For if, as Mr. Whiston says, *St. Matthew's Gospel, lying before him, was his guide in writing his history,* what need was there of the inspiration and guidance of the Spirit? If he had St. Matthew's Gospel lying before him, why could he not, without any immediate influences from Heaven, transcribe out of it, here a piece, and there a piece, of the history, where he had a mind? a person endowed with the common and ordinary powers of nature, if he were but able to read, might have made as good, nay I may venture to say a much better epitome of St. Matthew's Gospel, than this of St. Mark's is supposed to be. For my part, I freely own, that if it could be proved, that St. Mark made St. Matthew's Gospel, lying before him, his main guide in writing his history, I should very much question whether he were inspired at all or no. The little necessity there was for inspiration, or the influences of the Spirit, to assist a person in transcribing another man's book, is a sufficient argument, there was no inspiration at all. I conclude therefore, upon the supposition of St. Mark's Gospel being inspired, that it was not transcribed or extracted out of St. Matthew's.

Besides, to argue further upon the same supposition, how odd does it found to hear a Christian say; " the Holy Spirit " inspired one person to write a history, and then inspired an- " other person to abridge it? The Holy Spirit thought fit at " first to have so much wrote, but then afterwards, that it " should not be quite so much." This is to make the Holy Spirit to cut off the superfluities of his own works. But this is an absurdity so great, that no one sure will be willing to defend; and yet defended it must be, and certainly true it is, if St. Mark be an epitome of St. Matthew.

It may indeed be objected here, that the same difficulty attends the account I have given out of the antients, of the original manner of St. Mark's writing, as does attend the supposition

fition of his being an epitomizer.   It may be faid, infpiration
was as little neceffary to St. Mark writing from St. Peter's
mouth, as tranfcribing out of St. Matthew's Gofpel.

To this, I think, it is fufficient to anfwer, that, if the account that has been given be true, viz. that St. Mark wrote
what he heard St. Peter preach, the infpiration muft be rather
fuppofed in St. Peter, than in St. Mark, who was only as his
fcribe or amanuehfis; and fo no more was required of him,
than faithfully to write down, what St. Peter told him.   Hence
Eufebius tells out of Clemens Alexandrinus, that, when St.
Mark had wrote down, what he had heard St. Peter preach,
St. Peter, *ἀποκαλύψαντος αὐτῷ τᾶ πνίματο*, *by the inftigation of
the Holy Spirit, approved and confirmed this Gofpel, for the ufe
of the Churches* [a].

Arg. VII. St. Mark's Gofpel is not an epitome of St.
Matthew's, becaufe the fuppofing it to be fo, *detracts from its
honour, and ufefulnefs.*   The enemies of revealed religion may
many ways improve fuch a conceffion, to the leffening the
juft efteem we ought to have for this facred Book.   To fay
this Gofpel is only an abridgment of another, makes it liable
to the opprobrious charge of being ftolen, and its author to
the black name of being a plagiary.   An epitome indeed of
another perfon's work, known and owned to be fuch, is not
in the leaft liable to this charge; but for a perfon to tranfcribe the greateft part of another's book, to publifh it in the
world under his own name, without the leaft hint or intimation, that he did make ufe of that other perfon's book, though
he have the beft ends and defigns in his work, will be looked
upon as a fort of pious fraud.   This is not only, what might
be reafonably imagined and fuppofed, but has been really matter of fact.   For as long fince as *the latter end of the fourth
century* (in Jerome's time), Ruffinus plainly called it *religiofum
furtum, a religious theft*; and Pighius, a great advocate for

[a] Hift. Eccl. lib. 2. c. 15. I
own indeed, Eufebius, citing this
account of Clemens in another
place, feems to make it contrary to
this, as though St. Peter *did neither
encourage nor difcourage this under-*
taking of St. Mark. Vid. lib. 6.
c. 14.   For the reconciliation of
which difference, I fhall only refer
the reader to Valefius's notes on
the place laft cited.

Popery

Popery in the beginning of the Reformation, mightily pleafed himfelf with thefe words of Ruffinus, defigning, fays my au- thor Chemnitius [a], *thereby to leffen the authority of the Scrip- ture.* Hence Spinoza and Father Simon (who were two as true enemies, as ever the facred volume met with) have en- deavoured to perfuade us, that the feveral books of the Old Teftament, are only *extracts and abridgments of fome larger records.* The former (Spinoza), after he had largely endea- voured to prove, that the five books of the law were not wrote by Mofes, but a long time afterwards, and alfo that the fuc- ceeding hiftories of Jofhua, Judges, Ruth, Samuel I. and II. the books of Kings I. and II. were wrote a great many ages after the perfons, who are mentioned in them, were dead, concludes they were *all wrote by Ezra, and that they are only epitomes or abridgments of fome larger records, which he made ufe of* [b]. The fame alfo is his opinion concerning the books of the Prophets; " When, fays he, I clofely confider the " books of the Prophets, I perceive the prophecies, which are " contained in them, were collected out of other books; and " that they are not in the fame order, in which they were faid " or wrote by the Prophets, &c. Wherefore thefe books are " only fcraps and fragments of the Prophets [c]." Father Si- mon's opinion, and his conjectures to fupport it, are fo very like thofe of Spinoza, that there can be no doubt but he bor- rowed his hints (however, the greateft part of them) from him; he tells us exprefsly [d], " That it evidently appears, that " the moft part of the Holy Scriptures, that are come to us, " are but abridgments and fummaries of antient acts, which " were kept in the regiftries of the Hebrews." It is very eafy

---

[a] Pighius delectatur Ruffini ver- bis, qui Evangelium Marci vocat *religiofum furtum*; ut, fcilicet, eo facilius Scripturæ auctoritatem pof- fet extenuare. Chemnit. Exam. Con- cil. Trident. Par. 1. De Script. Evangelift.

[b] Tractat. Theolog. Polit. c. 8. & c. 9. Hefdras (eum pro prædic- torum librorum fcriptore habebo)— non aliud fecit, quam hiftorias ex diverfis fcriptoribus colligere.

[c] Cum ad hos (fcil. Prophetas) attendo, video Prophetias, quæ in iis continentur, ex aliis libris col- lectas fuiffe; neque in hifce eodem ordine femper defcribi, quo ab ipfis Prophetis dictæ vel fcriptæ fuerunt. —Quare hi libri non nifi fragmenta Prophetarum funt. c. 10.

[d] Critic. Hift. of the Old Teft. B. I. c. 2.

to perceive, the defign of thefe gentlemen in this their opinion, was to leffen the value and authority of the facred Scriptures; the former, that he might banifh at once all revealed religion out of the world; the latter, that he might advance the honour of the Church and priefthood, to which he belonged. And indeed the method now mentioned, feems to have a very natural and direct tendency to the end they aimed at. It is impoffible to have the fame value for the facred Books, which we ought to have, if we believe them to be only extracts out of fome records and regiftries, that we know nothing of. There is indeed this difference between the opinion of Spinoza and Father Simon, concerning the books of the Old Teftament, and the common one of St. Mark's being an epitome of St. Matthew, that they fuppofe the original records, out of which the books of the Old Teftament were taken, are all loft, but the book, out of which St. Mark was taken, we have ftill; this indeed is true, but let it be confidered, that this difference makes them more neceffary and ufeful, and St. Mark lefs fo. As there could not be any very good reafon, which could induce St. Mark, to make an abftract of St. Matthew's Gofpel (as has been in part argued already[a]), fo it could not be (if a mere abridgment) of any great ufe, when it was made. Upon what grounds could St. Mark believe his epitome would be more ufeful than St. Matthew's original? An epitome of a hiftory, every particular part whereof is abfolutely neceffary to be known by all thofe, who could know them, would be but of very little ufe to them, that either had or could procure the original.

Laftly, The fuppofing St. Mark's Gofpel to be an epitome of St. Matthew, *does in a great meafure invalidate, and fet afide his teftimony to the truth of the Gofpel hiftory.* If his Gofpel be taken out of St. Matthew's, then it is evident, that his teftimony depends upon, and confequently amounts to no more, than the fingle teftimony of St. Matthew. It is true indeed, that an account of a matter of fact, attefted by one credible and duly qualified witnefs, is fufficient to fatisfy any

---

[a] Pag. 54.

reafonable

reafonable and unprejudiced mind, and confequently one of the Gofpels would have been enough, to have rendered thofe, who rejected Chriftianity, inexcufable; yet fince men's minds are naturally fo corrupt, the more evidence and teftimonies we have, the more ftrong and confirmed our faith is like to be, and we have greater probability of convincing unbelievers. Now, as has been faid, if St. Mark's Gofpel be taken out of St. Matthew's, it is of no ufe nor fervice in this refpect. But on the other hand, if we receive the account we have from all antiquity, that he wrote his Gofpel from the mouth of St. Peter; we have another very good evidence for the truth of Chriftianity, even the teftimony of one, who was continually with our Saviour, from the beginning of his publick miniftry till his afcenfion.

Now from all that has been faid, I hope it is very reafonable to conclude, that St. Mark's Gofpel is not an epitome of St. Matthew's. If the accounts we have from antiquity be of any value, that he wrote it at Rome from St. Peter's mouth; if he relates the fame ftories much larger than St. Matthew does; if he relates the fame accounts with very different, and feemingly contrary circumftances to thofe of St. Matthew's; if he gives us an account of feveral very confiderable things, which St. Matthew does not fo much as hint at; if he omits feveral confiderable hiftories; if the fuppofing this Gofpel an epitome, makes its infpiration more dubious and uncertain, and invalidates its teftimony to the truth of Chriftianity; if all thefe things are fo, then there can be nothing more reafonable, than to conclude, *that St. Mark's Gofpel is not an epitome of St. Matthew's.*

I might, if it were neceffary, carry this matter fomewhat further, and make it at leaft probable, that neither of the three Evangelifts (St. Matthew, St. Mark, or St. Luke) had fo much as feen the Gofpel of the other, when he himfelf wrote. For had either of them feen the Gofpel of the other, it is very probable they would not have gone about to write the fame things, which were wrote before: and hence it is very obfervable that St. John, who (as will appear hereafter) faw the Gofpels of the other three, does not relate the fame facts, which

he

he faw the other three had done before him. I am partly be-
holden to Mr. Le Clerc[a] for this obfervation, and partly to
the learned Mr. Dodwell[b], who endeavours alfo by feveral
other arguments, to prove the point I am now contending for.
Upon the whole, that which is moft probable, is, that the
Evangelifts, who were fcattered up and down the earth, into
very diftant countries, to preach the Gofpel ; by the folicita-
tion and importunity of thofe whom they converted, were prevailed upon to write down the fubftance of what they had
preached to them ; in which good undertaking, God by his
Spirit was pleafed to affift them, keeping them from all error,
leading them (according to his promife, John xvi. 13.) *into all
truth,* and *bringing* (as our Saviour had foretold he fhould do,
John xiv. 26.) *all things to their remembrance, whatfoever he
had faid unto them.*

C H A P. XI.

*If it be allowed that St. Mark did epitomize St. Matthew ; it
will not from thence follow, that our prefent Copies of St.
Matthew are mifplaced, and contrary to the Order, originally
intended by the Evangelift.*

SINCE then St. Mark did not make ufe of St. Matthew's
Gofpel in compiling of his, it is very evident, that Mr.
Whifton hath failed in his *main proof,* in what he calls his

[a] Quoi qu'ils n'aient pas vû les
écrits les uns des autres : car ils
n'auroient pas redit ce qu'ils auroient vû avoir été publié avant
eux, furtout par des Apôtres. Auffi
remarque-t-on que St. Jean, qui a
vû fans doute les autres Evangiles,
a évité de redire les mêmes chofes.
See his French Teft. at Luk. i. 1.
[b] Sed et reliquos ab invicem non

fuiffe vifos Evangeliftas vel exinde
fufpicio eft, quod primo illi prædi-
cationis anno res geftas duntaxat e-
narrent ; reliquorum annorum Paf-
chatumque memoriam folus confer-
vavit S. Joannes Evangelifta : unde
poffet quis fortaffe colligere, vifa
effe ab eo et probata, fuppletaque
decefforum Evangelia. Differtat.
1. in Iren. §. 39.

moft

most authentick evidence, and *most convincing argument,* to prove, that *the former part of St. Matthew's Gospel in our present copies is very much misplaced, contrary to the method originally intended by the Evangelist.* But

II. If it were to be granted that St. Mark did abridge St. Matthew, yet it would by no means follow, that our *present copies of St. Matthew's Gospel are not in their true and first intended order.* Let us then suppose St. Mark's Gospel to be an epitome, and consider how Mr. Whiston* does argue upon that supposition. " If, says he, St. Mark was the epitomizer " of St. Matthew, and had his history before him, when he " wrote his own ; it will follow, that either that copy of St. "Matthew, which he made use of, was in a different order, " from that which we now have (in the chapters under confi- " deration); or else that he knew the order of his copy to be " wrong, and contrary to the original one, and so reduced it in " his epitome to the true and regular series of events, which " he learned from St. Peter. Now either of these is sufficient " for my present purpose ; for it is evident that St. Mark does " not observe the order of the present copies of St. Matthew " (whom he epitomizes), in that part we are speaking of. &c."

This is Mr. Whiston's arguing; but, with submission to so great a judgment, I think it is very far from being conclusive, as will very evidently appear by the following consideration; viz. St. Mark making use of a copy of St. Matthew's Gospel, which was exactly the same with our present copies of that Gospel, might deviate and recede from St. Matthew's order, and yet not believe that order to be wrong, and contrary to the original one intended by St. Matthew. Mr. Whiston has here very artificially joined two things together, as the same, which are certainly different. *To be wrong in respect of the order of time, and to be contrary to the original copy,* are certainly two things very distinct. St. Mark's being supposed an epitome of St. Matthew's, proves indeed the former, viz. that he believed St. Matthew not to have observed the order of time in every particular, but not the latter. Why might he

* P. 102.

not, even having St. Matthew's Gospel lying before him, sometimes relate his histories in a different order from that of St. Matthew ? He might easily perceive it was not St. Matthew's design (as indeed it was not his own in every particular instance), to relate all things exactly in the order, in which they came to pass ; and therefore might, if at any time he saw just occasion, recede from his order. Certainly this is a much more reasonable supposition, than that our present copies of St. Matthew are so much confused and disordered. For making the matter more clear, I would illustrate my argument by the following example.

Let us suppose, that, when Lucius Florus made his abridgment of Livy's History, there were several branches of it, which were not placed by Livy exactly according to the order of time, in which they came to pass, but interspersed up and down in the history, as the circumstances required. Let us suppose further, that Florus in his epitome had taken every one of these particulars, and placed them according to the most exact order of time, in which they came to pass. Are we under any necessity of concluding, either that Florus knew his copy of Livy to be wrong, and contrary to the original one, or that the copies of Livy are since corrupted and disordered ? By no means. Now this is exactly the case here, and therefore I conclude, that although St. Mark did make use of St. Matthew's Gospel in writing his, yet it does not follow, that our present copies of St. Matthew are confused and misplaced.

CHAP.

CHAP. XII.

The particular Branches of St. Matthew's Gospel, which Mr. Whiston supposes misplaced. Four Propositions for the discovering the true Order of Time in the Gospel History. Several of those Branches which Mr. Whiston supposes misplaced, are so far from that, that they are in the exact Order of Time, in which they came to pass. Instances of this produced.

IN the following pages [a] Mr. Whiston proceeds to shew, which those several branches or periods of St. Matthew's Gospel are, which he supposes misplaced in our present copies; and contrary to the order, originally intended by the Evangelist. They are contained in that part of the history, which is *from the twenty-third verse of the fourth, to the end of the thirteenth chapter.*

For the use of those, who may not have Mr. Whiston's book, I thought it proper particularly to set them down ; that the reader himself may, from the rules hereafter laid down, judge concerning those, which I do not particularly consider.

The periods of St Matthew's Gospel, which, according to Mr. Whiston, are misplaced in our present copies.

1. The Sermon near the mount, in the fifth, sixth, and seventh chapters; together with some verses at the end of the fourth, and part of the eighth chapter belonging thereto.

2. The voyage to the Gergesenes, towards the end of the eighth chapter.

3. The healing of the paralytick, the calling of Levi, his feast, and the discourse at it, in the former part of the ninth chapter.

4. The healing Jairus's daughter, with the woman that

---

[a] P. 103, 104, &c.

had the flux of blood in the way thither, of two blind men as he went thence, and of a dumb demoniac juſt afterwards ; towards the concluſion of the ninth chapter.

5. The miſſion and inſtruction of the twelve Apoſtles, in the tenth chapter.

6. The meſſage from John in priſon, with our Saviour's anſwer, and the following diſcourſes, in the eleventh chapter.

7. The vindication of the diſciples plucking the ears of corn, with the healing the withered hand on the Sabbath, and Chriſt's avoiding the deſigns againſt him, in the beginning of the twelfth chapter.

8. The healing a blind and dumb man, and Chriſt's vindication of himſelf from the imputation of caſting out devils by Beelzebub, with many diſcourſes and parables following, in the reſt of the twelfth, and almoſt the whole thirteenth chapter.

9. The cure of the leper, juſt after the Sermon on the mount.

10. The cure of Peter's wife's mother, towards the middle of the eighth chapter.

11. Chriſt's anſwer to two, that were ready to follow him, ſucceeding the former.

12. His coming the ſecond time to Nazareth, in the end of the thirteenth chapter.

Theſe are the twelve branches of St. Matthew's Goſpel, every one of which Mr. Whiſton ſuppoſes to be miſplaced, and put, in our preſent copies, out of their true and originally intended order. Any one that conſiders theſe ſeveral branches, their number, ſize, &c. will be ſurprized to find ſuch diſorders here, and not ſo much as one ſingle diſorder in all the other part of this, or either of the other Goſpels. But of this I ſhall ſay more hereafter. My buſineſs now ſhall be to conſider the matter of fact, viz. whether theſe ſeveral periods are miſplaced, or not. In order to the more clear diſcuſſing of which queſtion, I ſhall lay down the following propoſitions.

Prop.

Prop. I. *Sometimes each of the three Evangelists, St. Matthew, St. Mark, and St. Luke, have related matters in a different order of time, from that in which they came to pass.*

That several portions of St. Matthew's Gospel are not now according to the order of time, in which the things came to pass, is, I think, agreed by all, except the whimsical Osiander, and after him Molineus, and Codomannus. That St. Luke did not design in all things to observe the order of time, has been already proved[a]. That St. Mark did not is also evident, because he in several particular instances agrees with the order of St. Luke, which is not the order of time, as has been already hinted, and will more fully appear hereafter.

II. *The principal and almost only methods of discovering, whether any particular matter be in its proper order of time, or not, in the Gospel History, are these two, viz.*

1. *By considering the phrases of transition or connexion, by which it is joined, either to that which precedes, or that which follows it, or both.*

2. *By comparing it with the same history, in one or more of the other Gospels.*

This is sufficiently evident to any one, who has in the least considered the harmony of the Gospels. Sometimes there are indeed some circumstances in the story itself, which infallibly direct us, where it is to be placed; but this is what happens but very rarely in the Gospel history.

III. *The phrases, by which the Evangelists do connect one story or discourse to another, are very often such, as do not at all imply an immediate succession, in point of time, to that which precedes it in the history.*

For the proof of this, I need only refer the reader, to what has been already said above, Ch. V. and desire him withal to consider, that the phrases or notes I mean, are such as these; καὶ ἐγένετο· ἰδὼν δὲ· καὶ ἐλθών· ἐμπατῶν δὲ· καὶ ἀνοίξας τὸ στόμα· &c. *and it came to pass; and Jesus seeing; and Jesus coming; as he walked; and opening his mouth; &c.* These are evidently such, as can be no way notes of the order of time. I would

---

[a] P. 30, &c.

Q 2

only

only obferve here further, that fuch as thefe are generally the phrafes, that conneƈt the parts of the Gofpel hiftory.

IV. On the other hand, *fometimes two ftories or difcourfes are connected by fuch a phrafe, as does neceffarily imply the immediate fucceffion of one to the other, in point of time.*

This will be evident by mentioning a few of them : they are fuch as thefe; καταϐάντι δὶ αὐτῷ ἀπὸ τῦ ὄρυς· καὶ ἰδὺ· ταῦτα αὐτῦ λαλῦντος αὐτοῖς· ἰν ἰκιϐη τῇ ὥϱạ· &c. *And when he was come down from the mountain; and behold; while he fpake thefe things unto them; behold there came; in that hour or inftant &c.*

Coroll. Hence it follows, that, if any two of the Evangelifts appear to relate a faƈt in a different order from the third, and do not make ufe of fuch a note, as neceffarily joins it with the preceding or fubfequent part of the hiftory; the other Evangelift, who does ufe fuch a note, muft be fuppofed to have obferved the order of time.

This obfervation is not only very juft and reafonable, but neceffary; the want of which has apparently produced many miftakes in the compilers of Gofpel harmonies, who have too often made the agreement of two Evangelifts (commonly St. Mark and St. Luke) the rule of placing a ftory, without regarding the manner of its conneƈtion with the preceding or following ftory.

Thefe things premifed, I will endeavour to prove the two following particulars, which will be a fufficient confutation of Mr. Whifton's propofition.

I. Several of thofe branches, which Mr. Whifton fuppofes mifplaced, and contrary to the order originally intended by St. Matthew, are fo far from that, that they are not out of the proper order of time, in which they came to pafs.

II. It does not appear, that any of thofe, which are in our prefent copies placed contrary to the order of time, are contrary to the order originally intended by St. Matthew.

1. Several of thofe branches, which Mr. Whifton fuppofes mifplaced, and contrary to the order originally intended by St. Matthew, are fo far from that, that they are not out of the
proper

proper order of time, in which they came to pass. This will appear by the two following instances.

1. The history of the person whom our Lord cured of his leprosy, Matt. viii. 2—5. is not misplaced, but in the proper order of time in which it came to pass. It is placed by St. Matthew (supposing our present copies of that Gospel to be right) as what happened immediately upon our Saviour's descent from the mountain, where he had been preaching; *whereas*, says Mr. Whiston, *that miracle was some months before that sermon.* I own indeed, several of the Gospel harmonizers are of the same opinion, and the reason why they are so is, because they found St. Luke (and perhaps St. Mark) to have placed this story a considerable time *before* the Sermon on the mount. This indeed is true; but then it must be observed, that these two Evangelists have related this miracle without any express notation of the time[a], when it was wrought. There is no circumstance, nor phrase, which connects it, either to the foregoing or the following part of the history: see Mark i. 40. and ii. 1. and Luke v. 12, 17. On the other hand, as it stands in our present copies of St. Matthew (as Mr. Whiston rightly observes), *it is immediately subjoined to the Sermon on the mount, in such a manner, as implies it to have happened just upon Christ's descent from the mount.* I appeal then to any unprejudiced person, whether it be not more reasonable to suppose, the other two Evangelists have placed this story out of the order of time, as sometimes they are wont to do; than that it is transposed in our present copies of St. Matthew. This (viz. the present order of St. Matthew) will be abundantly confirmed, if we consider, that there is a very good reason to be assigned, why the two other Evangelists have related this story out of its proper order; viz. *because it was wrought in a place, where the other miracles, which they had just before given an account of, were done.* They had before been giving an account of two miracles, which our Lord had

---

[a] Hæc autem eadem leprosi miraculose sanati historia narratur a Marco c. i. 40. et a Luca c. v. 12. sed solus Matthæus hujus miraculi tempus atque ordinem significat his verbis, *Cum descendisset de monte*, &c. *Et ecce*, &c. Car. Mar. de Veil. ad loc.

wrought

wrought at Capernaum, viz. the casting out the unclean
spirit in the synagogue there : and after that, the recovery of
Peter's mother in law from a fever (Mark i. 23--29, &c. and
Luke iv. 33—38, &c.) in the same town. Now this miracle
of the leper's cure being done at this place, they mention it
here together with those other miracles, though it was really
done at another time. Indeed it is true, St. Luke relates,
ch. v. 1, &c. the call of the four Apostles between these two
miracles, and that of the leper ; but this is a very great confirmation of the foregoing observation, because this call of the
Apostles hath been already proved, not to be in the order of
time [a], and so is for the same reason placed here, because it
was in the city or suburbs of Capernaum. If what has been
said be duly considered, I cannot but think it will prove this
branch of St. Matthew's history to be in the proper order of
time. And indeed, if it be not proved, I must do Mr. Whifton's hypothesis that justice to own, that it is, as to this instance, most certainly true : if the story of the leper be not in
the proper order of time, either there must be a transposition
in the history, or St. Matthew was mistaken, which no body
will suppose. Hence I cannot but wonder that Dr. Lightfoot, Mr. Le Clerc, and others, have in their Harmonies, left
St. Matthew's order, and followed that of St. Mark and St.
Luke. I cannot see how they could join the first and fifth
verse of this chapter, without supposing a transposition, which
yet they certainly never thought of. Chemnitius [b], Osiander,
and some few more, are much more consistent with themselves; who imagine this in St. Matthew, and that in St.
Mark and St. Luke, to be different miracles ; though there
seems to be no foundation for this supposition, but only the
difference in time.

What Mr. Whiston offers in defence of his opinion (viz.
that this miracle was not wrought at this time), certainly very
well deserves to be considered. " St. Matthew," says he, " as
" well as the other Evangelists, relates our Saviour's caution

[a] P. 30.   [b] Harmon. Evang. c. 42.

[c] "to

" to the leper, to keep the miracle fecret; *See no man know it* ;
" which certainly fhews, it was not done fo publickly as his
" prefent order implies, viz. when the multitude was pre-
" fent."

To this I anfwer, that our Lord may very well be fuppofed
to give this charge of fecrecy to the leper, when the multitudes were prefent ; becaufe we have an inftance of his doing
the fame, at another time, where a tranfpofition cannot poffibly
be fuppofed. The place I refer to, is Matt. xii. 15, 16. *And*
great multitudes followed him, and he healed them all, and
charged them, that they fhould not make him known. Befides,
there may be very good reafons affigned, why our Lord fhould
give this charge in the prefence of a multitude, viz.

1. That it might appear to the multitude, *that he was not*
at all fond or ambitious of human applaufe, and fo withal fet his
difciples a lively pattern of modefty and humility. Our bleffed
Saviour himfelf tells us, that he *fought not to advance his own*
glory; John viii. 50. This was a character, which our Lord
not only deferved, but which he feemed peculiarly careful to
eftablifh. To do this he had now (when he was come down
from the mountain) a very fair opportunity. He could at
once give a whole multitude to underftand, that he did not
affect or covet popular applaufe ; *See thou tell no man*; i. e.
do not publifh and blaze abroad the cure that is wrought for
thee ; *I defire not the honour, that men will be apt to give me on*
fuch an account. What could the people who were prefent
conclude, but that he was a perfon of the utmoft modefty?
Befides, our Saviour was not only careful to be thought humble himfelf, but was concerned that his difciples fhould *learn*
of him, and imitate his example in this refpect : hence he tells
them, Matt. xi. 29. *to learn of him* ; *for*, fays he, *I am meek and*
lowly in heart. Now here, in the prefence of the multitude,
he had a very fit feafon to recommend the practice of this virtue to them by his own example. " Hence" fays Theophylact [a], " our Lord, by this caution, teaches us, that we are not

---

[a] Vid. eum ad Marc. i.

" to

" to make oftentation of our virtues." And to the fame
purpofe, Cornelius à Lapide, Zegerus, and many other learned
men [a].

2. It is not at all abfurd, that our Saviour fhould give the
leper this charge of fecrecy, in the prefence of the multitude;
becaufe *hereby he gave them a very plain intimation, that he
did not defign to fet up a temporal kingdom in the world; and fo
ufed a very likely means to prevent the ill confequences of their
entertaining fuch an opinion of him.* Every body knows the
Jewifh nation had this expectation from the Meffiah, that,
when he came, he would deliver them from their fubjection
to the Roman power, and reftore their kingdom to its antient
grandeur. This is evident from abundance of paffages in the
New Teftament [b]. Now it is very evident, our Lord took
all poffible methods to prevent the Jews from entertaining this
opinion of him. As foon as he perceived their defign to pro-
claim him a king, he retired, and went from them all into a
mountain alone, John vi. 15. Nay it is obfervable, that our
Lord fo much declined this character, that, for this very reafon, he forbad his difciples to publifh him as the Chrift:
Matt. xvi. 20. *Then charged he his difciples, that they fhould tell*

---

[a] Id juffit ad vitandam oftenta-
tionem, et ut nos doceret, virtutes
dotefque noftras non jactare. Ita
Chryfoftomus. Cornel. a Lapid. ad
loc.

Noverat quidem Dominus illos
non tacituros (he is fpeaking of a
like inftance); verum hoc ita præ-
cipiens, nobis voluit humilitatis
contemnendæque gloriæ præbere ex-
emplum. Zeger. ad Mat. ix. 30.

[b] Hence it was, that the mother
of Zebedee's fons came with her petition, that her fons might have the
higheft pofts in his kingdom. Il
paroît par cette demande, que la
femme de Zebedée, et fes fils (à qui
St. Marc attribue cette demande
ch. x. 35.) s'attendoient toujours
à un regne temporel, quoique Jefus
Chrift leur eût pu dire au contraire,
tant les préjugés de la nation Juda-

ique étoient violens. It appears by
this petition, that the wife of Zebedee, and her fons (to whom St.
Mark attributes this petition), were
always in expectation of a temporal
kingdom, notwithftanding all that
Jefus Chrift was able to fay to the
contrary, fo very great were the pre-
judices of the Jewifh nation. Le
Clerc on Matt. xx. 22. This is
confirmed alfo by the difcourfe of
the two difciples, after our Lord's
refurrection, Luke xxiv. 21. *We
trufted that it had been he, which
fhould have redeemed Ifrael.* And
St. John tells us (ch. vi. 14, 15.),
that when they were convinced by
a miracle, which our Lord had
wrought, that he was the true Meffiah, they immediately were for pro-
claiming and making him a king.

:   *no*

no man that he was Jesus the Christ. He knew that the idea of the Messiah, and that of a temporal prince, were almost the same in the minds of the Jews, at least that the idea of the one implied, and was inseparable from, the other; and therefore, that he might avoid the suspicion of the latter, he would not, till after his resurrection, be publickly owned as the former. He knew, if he had indulged them in this their opinion of him, seditions, tumults, and insurrections, must necessarily have ensued. By this he had too soon drawn upon him the suspicion of the Roman governor, and so had been hindered to go through the time of his publick ministry, which he designed. And now by this it appears, that a caution given to the leper, not to publish what was done for him, was not unreasonable, though in the presence of the multitude. Hereby they could not but perceive, that our Saviour had no design to draw great multitudes after him; which was the most likely method to advance him to a temporal kingdom. They could not but conclude, he was against being popular, and consequently against being made a king. This undoubtedly was that, which, among other reasons, influenced our Saviour to give the leper this caution; for we find that, the leper disobeying our Lord's commands, and publishing his cure, he was for that reason obliged to retire, and could no more enter into the city, Mark i. 45. Hence it is well observed by Mr. Le Clerc, in an instance like this, that our Saviour commanded secrecy, that " he might not draw a great multitude of people " after him, for fear of a suspicion, which might be enter- " tained, that he had no design but to raise a rebellion [a]."

3. It was not absurd for our Saviour, at this time, to give the leper a caution of secrecy; because his case and circumstances, notwithstanding the presence of the multitude, seemed necessarily to require such a caution. Under the Jewish dispensation, a person, that had been leprous, and now supposed himself cured, was, by divine appointment, obliged to submit

---

[a] *Leur defendit d'en parler,* pour ne pas s'attirer plus de foule, de peur du soupçon, que l'on pouvoit former, qu'il ne cherchât qu'à ex- citer quelque sedition. Le Clerc on Matth. ix. 30. See also Dr. Hammond on Matth. viii. 4.

himself

himfelf to the examination of the Prieft, whether it were fo or not; Levit. xiii.   Now had this miraculous cure of his been fpread abroad, and reached the Prieft's ears, before this was done, there feems to have been danger of the two following ill confequences.

1. Very probably the malice of the Priefts would have carried them fo far, that when they found he was cured by a perfon, whom they fo mortally hated, they would not have pronounced him clean.   This is the opinion of Grotius, Le Clerc, Dr. Whitby, &c.   For the confirmation of it, Grotius urges, that the miracle was wrought in Galilee, a great diftance from Jerufalem, where the Priefts were; and that our Saviour (according to St. Mark's account, ch. i. 43.) fent him away in hafte, left the fame of the miracle fhould reach the Priefts' ears, before he could get there.   •

2. Had this ftory been told to the Priefts, it is very likely it would have raifed their malice againft our Saviour, and incited them to perfecute him, under the fpecious pretence of his having taken upon him, to do that which belonged to the office, and was the fole prerogative, of the Priefts ª, viz. pronouncing a leprous perfon clean.

From all that has been faid, I think it is very reafonable to conclude, that our Saviour might give the leper a charge, not to publifh what was done for him, till he had been with the Prieft, though there were feveral people prefent when the cure was wrought; and then there feems not to be any reafon, but we may conclude this hiftory is in its proper order of time.

2. Another inftance of a hiftory, which in our prefent copies is in its due and proper order of time, and yet fuppofed by Mr. Whifton to be mifplaced, is that of the two perfons, who came to our Saviour, profeffing their readinefs to follow him, Matth. viii. 19, &c.   It is placed in St. Matthew, between our Saviour's ordering a fhip to be got ready, and his entering

---

ª Il femble que notre Seigneur ne vouloit pas s'attirer la haine des facrificateurs, à qui la Loi donnoit le droit de juger, fi un homme étoit gueri de fa lépre, ou non. It is probable, our Saviour had not a mind to draw upon himfelf the hatred of the Priefts, to whom the Law had given the power of judging, whether a perfon was cured of his leprofy, or not. Le Clerc ad loc.

into

into it. And there cannot be any probable reafon affigned, why it fhould be placed any where elfe; for

1. *It is a hiftory not mentioned by either of the other Evan-gelifts.* St. Luke indeed (ch. ix. 57, &c.) has an account ex-ceedingly like this; but Mr. Whifton himfelf (as well as fe-veral other harmonizers) fuppofes thefe to be two different hiftories; and confequently the order of time, in this inftance, is not to be proved from either of the other Evangelifts.

2. *The circumftances of the hiftory are all fuch as agree very exactly with that part of St. Matthew's hiftory, in which it is placed in our prefent copies.* At what time is it more likely to fuppofe, that perfons fhould come to Chrift, and declare their willingnefs to go along with him, than juft then, when they had heard him give orders to get a fhip ready, to go to ano-ther country? And when could our Saviour more properly make the anfwer, which he here does (viz. *The foxes have holes, and the birds of the air have nefts, but the fon of man hath not where to lay his head*), than at this time, when he was leaving his own habitation and city, and going to travel in a ftrange country? There cannot be any place in the whole Gofpel hiftory, where it will be more agreeable to the con-text, than here. Mr. Whifton has however placed it after this voyage to the Gergefenes, which as, I think, no one be-fides him has done, fo no good reafon can be affigned for his doing fo. The reafons which he offers for his placing it thus, are,

1. *That thefe accounts are, in our prefent copies, interpofed between two verfes, which are perfectly coherent, and have a manifeft connection without them.* This is indeed true, but does not imply the leaft abfurdity in St. Matthew's prefent or-der. This branch is only a relation of fomething, which came to pafs between our Saviour's ordering his difciples to get a fhip ready, and his going into it. It is true, if it had been entirely omitted, and St. Matthew had told us of our Sa-viour's entering into the fhip, immediately after he had given orders to prepare it, the connection had been very good and juft: but if a ftory be told of fomewhat, which happened in the mean time, it does not at all fpoil the connection, as evi-dently

dently appears by confidering it. Ver. 18. our Saviour gives commandment to fome of his difciples, to go down out of the city to the fea-fide, to prepare a veffel to carry them over to the other fide : when they were gone, and *while the ſhip was getting ready* (as Dr. Wells rightly paraphrafes the place), or *preparing for their departure* (as Dr. Whitby), thefe perfons came to our Saviour; he gave them their anfwers; and then went on board [a].

2. Mr. Whifton further argues, " that the nature of our " Saviour's anfwer to the Scribe, ver. 20. *(The foxes have* " *holes, and the birds of the air have nefts*; *but the fon of man* " *hath not where to lay his head)* plainly fhews, that thefe ac- " counts ought to follow the voyage to the Gergefenes. For " fuch an anfwer (fays he) there could be no occafion before " this voyage; but after it, when he had been juft expelled " by the Gergefenes, there was the fitteft opportunity ima- " ginable for fuch a complaint." Mr. Whifton will excufe me that I am forced to obferve, that he has not been fo cautious, as he is wont to be, in this matter. The place, which he affigns to this branch of the hiftory in his Harmony, does moft evidently overthrow his own argument for placing it as he does. This will undeniably appear, if we confider, that the place (according to our prefent copies of St. Matthew) where our Saviour had this conference with the Scribe, was Capernaum, which is called Chrift's own city, and lay clofe by the fea-fide. This is manifeft by the context. Now, fays Mr. Whifton, at the place, where it is faid to be in our prefent copies of St. Matthew, i. e. at Capernaum, there could be no occafion for that anfwer, *The foxes have holes, the birds* &c. (the reafon of which muft be, becaufe our Saviour was then in his own city, where his habitation was); and yet in his Harmony he has himfelf placed this very fame hiftory at Capernaum, when our Saviour was returned home [b]. A plain

---

[a] Dumque alii ex difcipulis artis nauticæ periti præeunt, ut navem parent, atque Dominum venientem fufcipiant, in viâ ipfum fcriba, et unus ex difcipulis adeunt, animi fui voluntatem ipfi proponentes, et quifque eorum feorfim fuum refponfum a Domino accipit. Chemn. Harm. Evang. cap. 63.
[b] P. 301.

.inftance, how far the minds of the moft learned men are biaffed by their favourite and preconceived opinions. I conclude therefore, that this branch alfo of St. Matthew's hiftory is fo far from being mifplaced, that it is in its proper order of time. It would be tedious to prove this of all the other inftances. A due application of the rules laid down in the beginning of this chapter, will fhew us, that there are feveral of the other branches, that are in the order of time in which they came to pafs, which are not only by Mr. Whifton, but fome others, fuppofed not to be fo.

C H A P. XIII.

None of thofe Branches, which are not according to the Order of Time, in this Part of St. Matthew's Gofpel, are mifplaced. This evidenced by confidering feveral of them.

II. $\underset{\text{L}}{A}$LTHOUGH there are feveral paragraphs or periods in this part of St. Matthew's hiftory, which are not according to the order of time ; *yet it does not appear, that any of them are mifplaced, or put into an order, different from that originally intended by the Evangelift.* It having been already proved, that thefe facred writers did not always intend ftrictly to obferve that order, in which the facts they relate came to pafs ; it follows, that we are not haftily to conclude, that a hiftory is mifplaced, becaufe it is not in that order. This is for the moft part Mr. Whifton's argument, there being in feveral of the particulars, which he afferts to be mifplaced, not fo much as an attempt to prove any more, than that they are not in the true order of time ; though, in other inftances, there feems at the firft fight to be fomething more.

For the clear difcuffing of this matter, I muft obferve, that *the almoft only method, by which it is poffible to difcover whether a ftory be mifplaced or not, is by confidering the notes of its cohe-rence with the context.* If it be apparent, by comparing any

period

period of the hiftory with the other Evangelifts, that it is not in its proper order of time, and if it have fuch a note of cohe-rence, as neceffarily joins it with the foregoing or following ftory (as it ftands in our prefent copies); we muft conclude, either that the Evangelift was miftaken in writing, or that our copies are corrupted and altered, fince he wrote. The queftion then in this matter lies principally in this, viz. *whe-ther in this part of St. Matthew's Gofpel, there are any periods of the hiftory, which are not in the order of time; and yet, as they ftand in our prefent copies, are neceffarily connected, either with the foregoing or following part of the hiftory.* Of this fort there is not one; but, on the other hand, all thofe that are really out of the order of time, are laid by the Evangelift in his hiftory, in fuch a manner, as plainly evidences that he had no defign that we fhould believe, that he intended to place them in that order.

I do not think it neceffary, diftinctly to confider all thefe particular branches, becaufe, in fo doing, I fhall be obliged to a dull repetition of the fame things again and again; I fhall only mention fome, and, among them, thofe which feem moft confiderable.

The cure of Peter's mother-in-law, ch. viii. 14, &c. is placed by St. Matthew after the Sermon on the Mount; whereas it is plain, from the other Evangelifts, that this mi-racle was wrought a confiderable time before. But then it is introduced by St. Matthew, and laid in his hiftory in fuch a manner, as makes it plain, that he had no defign we fhould think it was in the order of time. He begins it thus, Καὶ ἐλθὼν ὁ Ἰησοῦς εἰς τὴν οἰκίαν Πέτρου, &c. *and when Jefus was come into Peter's houfe,* &c. But on the other hand, St. Mark and St. Luke have fo connected this ftory with the former, that it is impoffible to feparate the one from the other. They both agree that our Saviour went from the fynagogue immediately to St. Peter's houfe, and there wrought this miracle: fee Mark i. 29, &c. and Luke iv. 38, &c. [a]

The

---

[a] Marcus certiorem notationem temporis et ordinis fervat.—Mani-feftum eft Matthæum—non fervaffe ordinem—unde et tali ufus eft locu-tione,

The fame may be argued in refpect of the other branches, viz. *the miffion, and infruction of the twelve Apoftles,* chap. x. 1, &c. and *the fending of John's difciples to Chrift,* chap. xi. 2, &c. which, being out of the order of time, are not connected to the context, by any notations of that order.

Of the other feven branches, there are two, or perhaps more, that feem to be in the fame order, in which they came to pafs; though I muft own, there are alfo two, which feem not to be in the order of time; and yet have fuch notes of time prefixed to them, as feem to imply immediate fucceffion. It is neceffary that both thefe inftances be particularly confidered.

1. The firft is the cure of Jairus's daughter, ch. ix. 18, &c. " This (fays Mr. Whifton) fo immediately follows the
" difcourfe at Levi's feaft, and with fuch an exprefs notation
" of the very moment of time, as is peculiarly remarkable,
" Ταῦτα αὐτῷ λαλοῦντος αὐτοῖς, &c. *as he was speaking, or while*
" *he spake, thefe things unto them, behold a ruler,* &c. So that
" no unbiaffed reader could imagine the leaft fpace poffible
" interpofed between them; whereas above a half a year was
" gone, after the feaft of Levi, before the healing of Jairus's
" daughter. An undeniable inftance of the diflocations be-
" fore-mentioned in this Gofpel; and I think I may well
" call it an undeniable one, fince truly it was fo to me. For
" though, at the firft, I durft not fo far depend upon the other
" notes of time, as to believe the prefent order of this part of
" St. Matthew to be different from the original one; yet
" when I came to this, after a little attempt, I found it impof-
" fible to be got over, &c." This inftance therefore is plainly the main fupport of Mr. Whifton's hypothefis; and I own indeed it feems very much to his purpofe, though, upon a clofe examination, I find it will not prove what he defigns it fhould. There are feveral more probable methods of accounting for the difficulty, than by fuppofing a diflocation; but

tione, quæ non neceffario exigit ordinem confequentiæ eorum, quæ narrantur; dicit enim, *Et cum venissent in domum Petri,* &c. Chemnit. Harmon. Evang. cap. 38.

before

before I come particularly to confider any, I think it neceffary a little more clearly to ftate the cafe.

St. Matthew, ch. ix. 9. gives us an account of his call by our Saviour to follow him; ver. 10. he tells us of a feaft at his houfe, where many publicans and finners were alfo prefent; ver. 11. he informs us of a queftion, put by the Pharifees to our Saviour's difciples, concerning his eating with finners; and ver. 12, 13, our Saviour's anfwer; after this, ver. 14. we have an account of John's difciples coming to Chrift, and afking him, why his difciples did not faft? and ver. 15, 16, 17. our Saviour's anfwer to their queftion, *which whilft he was giv-ing, Jairus came*, ver. 18.   But, fays Mr. Whifton, there was half a year's fpace between the feaft of Levi, and Jairus's com-ing to Chrift.   This is indeed eafily afferted; but not the leaft reafon offered for the affertion.   It were to be wifhed, that in this, as well as other inftances, he had told us, for what reafons he fuppofes them to be out of the order of time.   A bare afferting that a ftory is fo much too foon, or fo much too late, or a referring us to his Harmony, where he has fo placed it, cannot be thought fufficient; and indeed, this is all that Mr. Whifton has done in this, and feveral other inftances. But this is too confiderable a point to be given up fo eafily. For the fake of ftating the cafe more fully, let us confider the reafon of this affertion.   It is in fhort only this, that St. Mark and St. Luke place a great many of our Lord's dif-courfes and miracles, between this feaft of St. Matthew and the difcourfes which follow it, and the coming of Jairus to our Saviour.   The former is placed by St. Mark, ch. ii. 14, &c. and by St. Luke, ch. v. 27, &c.   The latter by St. Mark, ch. v. 22, &c. and St. Luke, ch. viii. 41, &c.   This is the difficulty, for the folution of which there may be two or three expedients, but I fhall only make ufe of one, which is, that *of fuppofing there was fome time interpofed between St. Matthew's being called to be an Apoftle, and his entertaining our Saviour at his houfe.*   This fuppofed, will reconcile the Evan-gelifts, and make St. Matthew's notation of the time, when Jairus came, to be very juft and proper.   Let us then fup-

pofe,

pofe, that St. Matthew was called at the time, where St. Mark and St. Luke place it, viz. before the fermon on the Mount, and the voyage to the Gergefenes (and this indeed is probable), and that thofe Evangelifts, having a mind to finifh *at once and together*, all they defigned to fay concerning St. Matthew in particular, mentioned there alfo his feaft, and the difcourfe at it, though they were fome time after his call. On the other hand, let us fuppofe, that St. Matthew being about to mention his feaft, and the difcourfe at it, in its proper order of time (viz. foon after the return from the country of the Gergefenes), premifed there the account of his call, which yet was fome time before. If this be allowed, then there is no abfurdity in fuppofing Jairus's coming to Chrift, while he was talking to John's difciples at Levi's feaft. I own indeed the preceding hypothefis is not entirely my own; I received the firft hints of it from Chemnitius and Dr. Lightfoot, and thereupon examined into the matter with the utmoft diligence and impartiality; and after having weighed all the feveral circumftances of the ftories under confideration, I made the following obfervations, which feem to fupport the account that has been given.

1. *There are many inftances of a like nature with this, both among the writers of the Gofpel hiftory, and other hiftorians.* It is a very common thing with all writers, when they defign to fay but little of a perfon in their hiftory, to join it all together, although what they relate came to pafs at very diftant times. This has been already fhewn [a], and is very evident in the cafe of Shimei, 1 Kings ii. 36, &c. His building a houfe at Jerufalem, and his being put to death, are connected together (like St. Matthew's call and feaft), though they were plainly three years diftant in point of time. But this is an obfervation, too common and obvious to need any inftances to be produced to fupport it.

2. The fuppofing St. Matthew's call and feaft to have been at two different times, *does not make the hiftory of either of the Evangelifts at all the more inaccurate.* It is fo far from giving

[a] P. 40.

colour to any such charge, that it is really the best method of writing a history, as has been proved above [a].

3. It is very observable, *that neither of the three Evangelists do join the account of Levi's call, and his feast together, by any such notes of time or phrases, as imply the immediate succession of one to the other.* St. Matthew and St. Mark, after having related the call, subjoin the story of the feast, introduced thus, Καὶ ἐγένετο, *and it came to pass.* St. Luke only tells us, that *Matthew made him a feast,* not at all specifying the time, when it was made.

4. It is also remarkable, that St. Mark and St. Luke, when they had finished the account of Levi's feast, and the discourse at it, *do not join the following history to this with any note of time, so as to imply that it immediately followed it.* But on the other hand, both of them begin the next story thus, Καὶ ἐγένετο, *and it came to pass,* Mark ii. 22, 23. and Luke v. ult. and vi. 1. Now hence it follows, according to the corollary above, p. 92. that St. Matthew, who has prefixed a plain note of time to this history, is to be supposed to have observed the right order of time.

5. *The story of Jairus's coming to our Saviour, cannot be placed any where else in St. Matthew's Gospel, but where it is in our present copies.* This will appear from the phrase, by which it is introduced, Ταῦτα αὐτοῦ λαλοῦντος αὐτοῖς, *while he was speaking these things unto them.* It is plain, that, when St. Matthew wrote this, it immediately followed some discourse of our Lord's to *several persons.* But I assert, upon a close review of all the branches of this part of the history, there is not any one of them, after which St. Matthew can possibly be supposed to have wrote it, but after the discourse, to which it is now subjoined in our present copies. Hence it is very ridiculous in Mr. Le Clerc, and some other harmonizers, to place this period of the history after that which is not a discourse of our Saviour's, but the words of the historian, viz. those, Matt. viii. 33. Mr. Whiston indeed has placed it after a discourse of our Saviour's to one of his disciples, Matt.

---

[a] Ibid.

viii.

viii. 22. but it is certain it was not wrote by St. Matthew, immediately after that branch, becaufe that has been proved to be in its proper order of time *. Befdes, the words immediately preceding, according to Mr. Whifton's Harmony, are, Ὁ δὲ Ἰησοῦς εἶπεν αὐτῷ, Ἀκολούθει μοι, καὶ ἄφες, &c. *But Jefus faid unto* him, *Follow* thou *me, and do* thou *fuffer the dead,* &c. Our Saviour is fpeaking to one perfon in the fingular number; and is it then likely, that St. Matthew's next words fhould be, Ταῦτα αὐτῷ λαλῦντο· αὐτοῖς, *While he was fpeaking to* them, &c. in the plural number? But now as it ftands in our prefent copies, *fpeaking to them* (αὐτοῖς) very well follows the difcourfe with John's difciples. All this confidered, makes it, I think, exceeding probable, that Jairus's coming to our Saviour was immediately after the difcourfe, that immediately precedes it in our prefent copies; and confequently, if that difcourfe was at Levi's feaft, that feaft is now in its proper order: and fo, if the call of Matthew was at that other time, where St. Mark and St. Luke do place it, the call and the feaft were at two different times.

6. This will be yet further confirmed, if we confider the place where St. Mark and St. Luke relate this account of Jairus's coming to Chrift. They place it immediately after the hiftory of our Saviour's return from the country of the Gergefenes, and not after any difcourfe of our Lord's immediately preceding it. Now it is certain by St. Matthew's account, that it was at a time when our Lord was difcourfing with feveral people; it is plain therefore, that, in St. Mark and St. Luke's account, this ftory does not in point of time immediately follow that which it follows in the hiftory, but fome difcourfe of our Lord intervened in the mean time. Now either this intervening difcourfe is fomewhere related in thefe Gofpels of St. Mark and St. Luke, or it is not. If we fay it is, there can be no doubt, but that it is the difcourfe, which now immediately precedes it in our prefent copies of St. Matthew, and fo the difpute is ended. On the other hand, to fay it is not, feems very unreafonable, when we confider that

---

* P. 99, &c.

R 2

the difcourfe, which immediately precedes it in St. Matthew, is in thefe Gofpels; and that a very good reafon has been affigned, why they put it in another place, viz. becaufe they had a mind to relate St. Matthew's call and feaft, and the dif-. courfe at it, all together.

7. It may not be improper to obferve, that in the antient Harmonies of Tatian and Ammonius (one of which was made in the fecond, and the other in the beginning of the third century), St. Matthew's call and feaft were placed at two very diftant times, and many hiftories interpofed between them [a]. Auftin, in his excellent treatife of the Harmony of the Gofpels, by a very good argument, proved that St. Matthew's call is not in his Gofpel in the right order of time, but was before the fermon in the Mount; becaufe, fays he, *St. Luke mentions St. Matthew among the reft of the Apoftles, that were with our Saviour in the Mount* (ch. vi. 15.). He feems indeed to have been inclined to believe, that the feaft was fome time after the call; and hence Gerfon, Chemnitius, and many others, have imagined this Father of that opinion; but it is very plain to any one, who will confider his words clofely, they have miftaken his meaning [b].

Thus I have endeavoured, by feveral arguments, to confirm the fuppofition of Levi's call and feaft, being at two different times, and by a great deal of pains have endeavoured to get over a difficulty, which Mr. Whifton, *after a little attempt, concluded impoffible to be got over.* There is indeed another way of folving this difficulty, propofed by Dr. Wells, in his late paraphrafe on this place. That I may not mifrepre-

---

[a] Atque hoc modo vetuftiffimæ etiam Harmoniæ Tatiani et Ammonii diftinéte ponunt, primo vocationem Matthæi, et poftea convivium Matthæi in alio loco Harmoniæ, ut alio tempore poft factum, collocant. Chemnit. Harm. Evang. cap. 43. in princ.

[b] Hinc autem probabilius videtur, quod hæc prætermiffa recordando Matthæus commemorat; quia utique ante illum fermonem in monte habitum, credendum eft vocatum

effe Matthæum: in eo quippe monte, tunc Lucas commemorat omnes duodecim ex pluribus Difcipulis, electos, quos et Apoftolos nominavit. *Afterwards fpeaking of his feaft he adds*; Poffet videri, non hoc ex ordine fubjunxiffe, fed quod alio tempore factum eft, recordatus interpofuiffe, nifi Marcus et Lucas, qui hoc omnino fimiliter narrant, manifeftarent in domo Levi difcubuiffe Jefum. &c. de Confenf. Evang. l. 2. c. 26, 27.

fent him, I shall set it down in his own words. " A confi-
" derable time after what is related in the foregoing para-
" graph, namely, when Jesus was just come back from the
" country of the Gergesenes (as was related chap. viii. 28.
" and ix. 1.), some others seem to have come to Jesus about
" the same subject ; whereupon he gave them the same rea-
" sons, why it was not proper for his disciples to fast yet.
" *And* now it was, that while he spoke these things unto them,
" behold there came a certain ruler, &c." In his annotations
on the place, he tells us ; " This seems the best, because the
" most natural and easy, way to reconcile this, ταῦτα αὐτῦ λα-
" λοῦντος αὐτοῖς, ἰδοὺ ἄρχων, &c. of St. Matthew, with Mark v. 22.
" and Luke viii. 41." This opinion supposes the call of
Levi, his feast, and the discourse that followed it, to be in our
present copies of St. Matthew out of its proper order of time;
and also that our present copies are exactly in this place, as St.
Matthew wrote at first, viz. that after the discourse with
John's disciples, St. Matthew immediately wrote, ταῦτα αἰτῦ
λαλῦντος αὐτοῖς, *while he spake these things to them.* Now according to the Doctor, this αὐτοῖς, *them,* must not refer to
those to whom our Saviour was talking at Levi's feast, but to
some others that he had discoursed with about half a year before. Is it credible that St. Matthew would write thus ?
Christ spake such and such things to John's disciples; and
while he was speaking *to them,* i. e. according to the Doctor,
while he spake to *some other persons.* This is far from being
natural and *easy*; it makes the Evangelist write not only in-
accurately, but to a high degree absurdly [b]. But this is no
new thing with Dr. Wells.

2. The other instance which seems to be out of its due order of time, and yet to have a note of immediate succession
prefixed to it, is *that of the disciples plucking the ears of corn
on the Sabbath-day,* chap. xii. 1, &c. As it lies in our pre-

---

[a] Matt. ix. 18.

[b] Le Clerc, in his Paraphrase upon the Harmony of the Gospels, is the only person that I know of (besides the Doctor), who has taken this method of reconciling the Evan- gelists; and I cannot but think, when the Doctor comes to consider this matter again, he will not be ashamed to own, that he borrowed his opinion from Le Clerc.

fent

fent copies, it follows the meſſage of John the Baptiſt out of priſon to Chriſt, with this notation of ſucceſſion, Ἐν ἐκείνῳ τῷ καιρῷ, *At that time, Jeſus went out on the Sabbath-day through the corn*, &c. whereas, ſays Mr. Whiſton, this plucking of the ears of corn, was ſome months before the meſſage of John the Baptiſt. For the proof of this, Mr. Whiſton thinks it enough here, as well as in moſt of the other inſtances, to refer us to his Harmony; *As*, ſays he, *will be evident in the Harmony.* He attempts no other proof than this; and this really amounts to no more than if he had ſaid, *I have placed it ſo in my Harmony, and therefore St. Matthew wrote ſo.* It is true St. Mark and St. Luke have placed this matter a great deal ſooner in their hiſtory, *viz.* before the ſermon on the Mount; but then it does not appear, that they deſigned to con-nect it to the preceding hiſtory by any expreſs notation of the time. But though we take this for granted, and ſuppoſe that in our preſent copies of St. Matthew, this ſtory of *the diſciples plucking the ears of corn on the Sabbath-day*, is not in its pro-per order of time; yet it does not appear to be miſplaced ſince it was firſt wrote, becauſe it is not connected to the preceding part of the hiſtory by a phraſe, that neceſſarily implies imme-diate ſucceſſion in point of time. The phraſe here made uſe of by St. Matthew is, ἐν ἐκείνῳ τῷ καιρῷ, *at that time,* or *about that time*; which phraſe is undoubtedly made uſe of in Scrip-ture chronology in a very large ſenſe. So in the inſtance above-mentioned [a] out of the Old Teſtament, *viz.* that of Ju-dah's going down to his brethren, Gen. xxxviii. 1. the ſtory is introduced with the very ſame phraſe, בעת ההוא *At that time*; whereas that hiſtory, to which it is prefixed, happened a con-ſiderable time before that, which it immediately ſucceeds. This phraſe therefore is not, as Mr. Whiſton calls it, *a notation of ſucceſſion,* and conſequently does not prove a diſlocation in this part of the Goſpel hiſtory. Mr. Whiſton does indeed in an-other book (*viz.* his Accompliſhment of Scripture Prophe-cies, p. 71.) make uſe of this ſame note for the ſame end, *viz.* to prove the tranſpoſition of the ſixth and ſeventh verſes of the

[a] P. 45.

tenth

tenth chapter of Deuteronomy. But I need take no more
pains to fhew, that this phrafe does not imply immediate fucceffion; Mr. Whifton himfelf, in his Chronology of the Old
Teftament, p. 73, in direct contradiction to himfelf in thefe
two places, has very well proved it, by the fame inftance
which I juft now mentioned out of Gen. xxxviii. 1. His
words are; " But then we muft remember, that although the
" words, *at that time*, feem to refer us to the foregoing hif-
" tory of Jofeph, yet the expreffion is of a much larger ex-
" tent in the language of Scripture, and includes a great fpace
" of time, as will appear by a view of the inftances in the
" margin [a], of that and the like ways of fpeaking, both in the
" Old and New Teftament. Nay indeed, it feems to be little
" more than a particle of tranfition, or common way of intro-
" ducing and beginning a new branch of an hiftory ; juft like
" the Englifh particle, *Now*, as it is ufed at this day; which
" though at firft it might infer a connection, in point of time,
" with what went before, yet now it is plain it is frequently
" no more than a particle of tranfition, to introduce a new
" period, after we have made a full end of that which went
" before." It is well obferved by Mr. Whifton here, that
this phrafe is often ufed thus in Scripture. Dr. Wells has
obferved [b], that this phrafe is ufed *three times* in St. Matthew, in this lax fenfe. " The Greek expreffion aforemen-
" tioned (viz. Ἐι τῷ καιρῷ ἰκίνῳ) is not to be underftood in a
" ftrict fenfe, or fo as to denote, that the particulars which
" they ufher in, were done or fell out in that point of time,
" which followed next in order to the time wherein came to
" pafs the particulars next afore related by St. Matthew ; but
" the faid Greek phrafe is to be underftood in a large fenfe, fo
" as to denote a confiderable interval or fpace of time, in, or
" during, which the feveral particulars, which are ufhered in
" by the faid Greek phrafe, did come to pafs, &c." Thus
rightly has the Doctor explained this phrafe. The obferva-

---

[a] Deut. x. 8. 2 Kings xx. 1.   [b] See his Paraphrafe on Matt. ii.
2 Chron. xxxii. 24. Ifai. xxxviii. 1.   25.
Matt. iii. 1.

                                tion

tion is indeed very trite and common ; Uſher, Spanheim, Dr. Lightfoot, Chemnitius, and many others, have made the ſame remark. I rather choſe to cite the Doctor's words on this head, becauſe he ſeems in them to have had a direct deſign to con-. fute Mr. Whiſton's hypotheſis ; for he adds, " Hereby are " eaſily ſolved all objections urged againſt St. Matthew's " Goſpel, as being faulty as to wrong dating of ſeveral par- " ticulars of our Saviour's hiſtory, without having recourſe " to ſuch notions, as that St. Matthew writ on looſe papers, " which have not been put together in their due order." I was the more willing to mention this, becauſe I know not that any one beſides has taken the leaſt publick notice of this pro- poſition of Mr. Whiſton's, which ſeems ſo injurious to the honour of this part of the ſacred volume.

C H A P. XIV.

Mr. Whiſton's Method of accounting for the Diſorder he ſup- poſes in this Part of St. Matthew's Goſpel, viz. that St. Matthew wrote it on ſmall Pieces of Paper ; that theſe were confuſedly put together by thoſe, who did not perfectly under- ſtand the true Series of the Hiſtory. Mr. Toinard of the ſame Opinion. The Improbability of it, propoſed to be ſhewn from the antient Way of writing. The moſt antient Methods conſidered.

HAVING conſidered thus far Mr. Whiſton's proof, that the ſeveral periods of the hiſtory in this part of St. Matthew's Goſpel are miſplaced, I proceed now to conſider the following ſection. ª The deſign of the ſection is, to *ob- ſerve what might be the probable occaſions of the preſent miſtaken places of theſe ſeveral branches.* Now in order to this, Mr.

ª P. 108.

Whiſton

Whifton is forced to a very odd and ftrange fuppofition, fuch
as I am very much inclined to believe he never would have
efpoufed, had he fufficiently weighed, and been aware of, its
confequences. " I muft," fays he, " here take it for granted,
" that the feveral parts or periods of this former part of St.
" Matthew's Gofpel, were written at firft feparately, and upon
" feveral diftinct papers; which papers (or whatever they were
" written upon) were put together into their prefent order by
" thofe, who did not perfectly know the true feries of the
" hiftory."

I have more largely obferved in the Preface, that Spinoza
and Father Simon have taken this method to depreciate and
vilify the facred volume, fuppofing that feveral parts of it were
confufedly put together, by thofe who did not know the right
and true order of the hiftory. It is indeed a very eafy way of
accounting for many of the difficulties of Chronology in the
Old Teftament, as well as in the Gofpels, if the matter of
fact could be made certain. If there are indeed feveral parts
of the hiftory tranfpofed and mifplaced, I cannot conceive any
other way fo probable, by which the fuppofed diforders can
be accounted for, as this; I muft therefore do Mr. Whifton
that juftice to own, to his honour, that he has hit upon the
only poffible method of accounting for the diflocations he fuppofes to have happened to this part of St. Matthew's Gofpel.
In the next fection he tells us indeed [a], " that he once de-
" figned to have attempted to offer fome conjectures, how
" fo many of thefe fections came to be fo ftrangely tranf-
" pofed;" but this, I confefs, is what I am not able to underftand. He fays here, " that he fuppofes the feveral difordered
" parts or periods were wrote at firft feparately, and upon
" diftinct pieces of paper, and placed in this wrong order by
" thofe, who did not know the true feries of the hiftory;"
and then adds, " that he will obferve, what were the probable
" occafions of their prefent miftaken places." And is not
this offering conjectures, how they came to be tranfpofed? I
afk Mr. Whifton's pardon, if it appear that I am miftaken in

[a] Pag. 110.

faying,

saying; that he had before offered all the conjecture, that either he, or any man could offer. Mr. Toinard[a], a French gentleman (who was reputed in his country one of the greatest scholars of the age), composed a *Harmony of the Gospels in Greek*, which was published about a year after his death, (A. D. 1707.) in which he seems to be of the very same opinion with Mr. Whiston in this matter. I have not been able to procure the book itself; and so could not compare his and Mr. Whiston's Harmony together. A general account of his opinion I learnt from the abstract of his book, which Mr. Le Clerc hath given us in his *Bibliothéque Choisie*[b], and from a short paragraph out of his Prolegomena, which Mr. Whiston did me the honour to send me. His words are to this purpose[c]; " St. Matthew's text was the only one of the four " Evangelists, which I could not always place in my Har- " mony in that same order, in which it is in our common co- " pies; because from the twenty-second verse of the fourth " chapter, to the thirteenth verse of the fourteenth chapter, he " differs very much from the order of the other Evangelists. " This indeed seems very strange, when we consider, that the " Evangelist St. Mark, who seems to be a sort of an epi- " tomizer of him, does exactly agree with St. Luke and St. " John, in relating all those particulars, which are now so " much transposed in St. Matthew. This seems very hard to

---

[a] See his character in the supplement to the last edition of Mr. Moreri's French Dictionary.

[b] Toutes les Evangelistes sont dans l'ordre, auquel ils ont écrit, excepté St. Matthieu, depuis le chap. iv. 22. jusqu'au chap. xiv. 13. parce qu'en cela cet Evangeliste s'est éloigné de l'ordre des autres. Mr. Toinard ne sait, d'où ce désordre peut être arrivé, à moins que depuis le commencement, les papiers de l'Evangeliste n'aient été transposés par quelque accident. Biblioth. Choisie, tom. 15. Art. 5. p. 251.

[c] Matthæi solius ex quatuor Evangeliis textum, eodem quo in vulgatis legitur ordine, a principio ad finem exhibere non licuit, propterea quod ab aliorum Evangelistarum ordine, a capitis quarti Evangelii sui versu vicesimo secundo, ad ejusdem Evangelii capitis decimi quarti versum decimum tertium, plurimum discedit. Quod sane mirari subit; cum Evangelista Marcus, ejus veluti epitomator, cum Luca et Joanne æquo pede in iis omnibus narrandis decurrat, quæ apud Matthæum varie transposita leguntur. Quod unde evenerit, nisi ex perturbatione aliqua eaque antiquissima Schedarum Evangelistæ hujus, difficile est perspicere. Proleg. p. 5.

" be

" be accounted for, unlefs we fuppofe it done by fome very
" antient confufion, or diforder, of the fheets (or papers) on
" which this Gofpel was wrote."

This is the hypothefis of thefe two learned men: it is
ftrange a propofition, which feems fo much to need proof;
fhould by them be taken for granted. This is fuch a poftu-
latum, as one very feldom meets with; and it will be fo far
from being granted to Mr. Whifton to be a truth, that needs
not to be proved, (viz. that St. Matthew wrote his Gofpel on
loofe fcraps of paper) that it will appear to every impartial
examiner to be a moft unreafonable fuppofition. For the
manifefting of this, I fhall offer the beft proof I can; and if it
fhould be thought by any, that I have been at more pains in
confuting this hypothefis, than was neceffary; I defire it may
be confidered, that my arguing tends not only to overthrow
this propofition, about St. Matthew's Gofpel being difordered,
but may be made ufe of (at leaft a good part of it) againft
Spinoza, Father Simon, and Mr. Whifton's opinion of feveral
books of the Old Teftament, which has been mentioned in
the Preface.

The method I defign to proceed in fhall be; firft, to fhew,
what the manner of writing among the antients was, and particularly, *after what manner the Jews wrote in our Saviour's
time;* and from thence fhew, how highly abfurd it is to imagine, that St. Matthew wrote after that manner, which Mr.
Whifton fuppofes.

The accounts we have from antiquity of their manner of
writing, are very defective and imperfect; and it is with no
fmall difficulty and pains, that we are able to fay any thing
clear on this head. The firft and moft antient account that
we have of any writing, is that which Jofephus tells us of the
fons of Seth, before the flood; viz. that they " having made
" fome obfervations about the heavenly bodies, that they might
" not be loft, made two pillars, the one of brick, the other of
" ftone, on both of which they wrote the difcoveries they had
" made; &c. [a]" It was after this manner the Decalogue was
wrote,

---

[a] Σοφ'αντι την περι τα ερανια, και την τουτων διακ'σμησιν επινοησαν·
υπερ

wrote, viz. *on tables of stone*[a]. In succeeding ages they were wont to write, in several countries, upon leaves of some certain trees, which they found most convenient to their purpose. Pliny tells us, these were made use of for writing *before the invention of paper, and particularly the leaves of palm-trees*[b]; *and that afterwards they wrote upon the inner bark of some trees.* What these trees were, we are informed by that learned antiquary Alexander ab Alexandro[c]. *Afterwards, they wrote their publick records in volumes or rolls of lead, and their private matters on fine linen and wax*, as the same authors tell us[d]; hence Suidas also tells us of writing upon plates or leaves of lead[e]. And this (if I may be allowed to guess) seems to be a method of writing, which was in use in the time of Job, as is intimated in these words, ch. xix. 23, 24. *Oh that my words were now written; oh that they were printed in a book; that they were graven with an iron pen and* lead, *in the rock for ever.* Hence we read in Suetonius, that Nero made use of a *plumbea charta, a plate of lead*, called *charta*, not only because it was like it in form, but because they used to write not only on paper, but on plates of lead[f].

Afterwards, viz. about the time when Alexander the Great was in Egypt, the *use of paper* was first found out; I do not mean such sort of paper as we now use, but the inner coat or skin of the great Ægyptian rush, which they called *papyrus*, from whence comes our present English word *paper*. The coats or thin skins of this rush, when duly dried and prepared

---

ὑπὲρ δὲ τοῦ μὴ διαφυγεῖν τὰς ἀνθρώπους τὰ εὑρημένα—τήλας δύο ποιησάμενοι, τὴν μὲν ἐκ πλίνθε, τὴν δ' ἑτέραν ἐκ λίθων, ἀμφοτέραις ἐνέγραψαν τὰ εὑρημένα, &c. Antiq. Jud. l. 1. c. 2. §. 3.

[a] Exod. xxxi. 18. and xxxii. 16.

[b] Antea ncn fuisse chartarum usum; palmarum foliis primo scriptitatum, deinde quarundam arborum libris. Plin. Nat. Hist. l. 13. c. 11.

[c] Hæ fuere a principio ex cortice platani, fraxini, aceris, populi albæ, item fagi et ulni; aut, sicut Ulpianus censuit, ex tilia, philyra,

et papyro. Liber enim interior pars est corticis, quæ ligno cohæret. Alex. ab Alexand. Gen. Dier. l. 2. c. 30.

[d] Pliny, and Alexand. ab Alexand. ibid.

[e] Εἰς ἱλασμὲς μολύβδωι γράφοντες. Suid. ad voc. μόλυβδος.

[f] In Ner. c. 20. Quid autem similius, quam plumbi lamina et chartæ expansæ pagina? quin etiam in plumbi laminis interdum ita scribebant, ut in chartæ paginis. Casaub. ad loc. Vid. Tacit. Annal. l. 2. c. 69.

for

for ufe, they called *chartæ*. A larger account of the nature of this material for writing, the reader may fee in the place of Pliny laft referred to[a], and concerning the time of its invention, Polydore Vergil[b]. Now if indeed any of thofe forementioned had been the method of writing in ufe among the Jews, when St. Matthew wrote his Gofpel, there had then been a much better foundation for the conjecture of Mr. Whifton and Mr. Toinard, than there really is. Had it been then the cuftom to write upon the leaves of palm-trees, or the little fkin or inner bark of any other trees, the leaves of their books muft have been very fmall, and confequently muft confift of a great number of feparate pieces and fcraps; and fo perhaps, by reafon of the difficulty of faftening them together, would be more liable to confufion and mifplacing. But it is very certain none of thefe methods were then in ufe amongft the Jews. If ever they were in ufe among them, they had now for a long time been difufed, and another more expedient, and far more commodious invented, as will appear in the following chapter.

[a] Priufquam digrediamur ab Ægypto, et papyri natura dicetur, cum chartæ ufu maxime humanitas vitæ conftet et memoria. Et hanc Alexandri magni victoria repertam auctor eft M. Varro, condita in Ægypto Alexandria, &c. Plin. ubi fup.

[b] De inventor. Rerum, l. 2. c. 8.

C H A P. XV.

*That St. Matthew did not write his Gospel on small Pieces of
Paper, proved by a large Dissertation on the Manner, in
which the Antients wrote their Books. The ordinary Method
was to write on large Skins, which were fastened together,
and rolled up. This the Practice of the Jews long before,
and in our Saviour's Time. The Words opened and closed
the Book, Luke iv. 17, 20. discussed. The Words, Bring
the Parchments, 2 Tim. iv. 13. considered. It does not appear that the Jews made use of Paper, or any other Material
besides that mentioned, to write their Books upon.*

HAVING, in the foregoing Chapter, premised some short
account of the various methods of writing in use among
the antients, I come now to consider, that which was of all
the most common, viz. *the writing on large skins of parchment, which they rolled up.* This was the way, in which the
Jews, Greeks, and Romans, wrote their books, both before,
and in our Saviour's time; and therefore it is very probable,
this was the way St. Matthew wrote his Gospel, and not on
small scraps or scrolls of paper. For the manifesting of this
matter, I will endeavour to shew,

　1. That the antients did very much make use of *parchment,*
or large skins, to write upon.

　2. That when they had wrote on these, *they were wont to*
fasten them together, and roll them up.

　3. That the Jews *long before our Saviour's time* did write
their books *after this manner.*

　4. That the Jews usually wrote thus *about the time, when*
St. *Matthew wrote his Gospel.*

　These things fully shewn, will make the supposition of St.
Matthew's writing his book upon small pieces, or scraps of
paper (some of which would not contain above a line or two),
very absurd and unreasonable.

　1. *The antients did very much use parchment, or large skins,*

to

to write upon. This is a matter of fact so very well known, that there needs not be much said to prove it. Herodotus, who lived above four hundred years before our Saviour's time, mentions it as a very antient custom among the Ionians; " The " Ionians," says he " have for a long time called their books, " skins, because in the scarcity of (Egyptian) paper, they " made use of goat-skins, and sheep-skins; nay, and even in " our time, many foreign nations write upon such skins [a]." Suidas cites out of some antient author an account, probably older than the time of Herodotus, in these words [b]; " Hermion, " writing down their determinations upon skins, sent them to " the enemy." Pliny indeed, out of Varro, gives us an account of the original of this sort of writing on parchment a long time afterwards, viz. in the time of Eumenes; which I think was near three hundred years before our Saviour's time. The account is this [c]; that there being an emulation or strife between Eumenes and Ptolemy concerning their libraries (viz. whose should be the largest), the latter being the King of Egypt, forbad the exportation of the Egyptian paper; whereupon Eumenes, King of Pergamus, first invented the use of parchment, and so from Pergamus that material for writing was called Pergamena. The same account, a little more full, is given us by Alexander ab Alexandro, in the place before cited [d]. I shall not now dispute concerning the time and antiquity of this invention: if it was even so late as Varro's account, it is sufficient for my present purpose; for as soon as

---

[a] Καὶ τὰς βίβλυς διφθέρας καλέυσι ἀπὸ τῦ παλαιῦ οἱ Ἴωνες, ὅτι κοτὲ ἐν σπάνει βίβλων ἐχρέωντο διφθέρησι αἰγέησί τε καὶ οἰέησι· ἔτι δὲ ἢ τὸ κατ᾽ ἐμὶ πολλοὶ τῶν βαρβάρων ἐς τοιαύτας διφθέρας γράφυσι. l. 5. c. 58. I translate ἐν σπάνει βίβλων, *in the scarcity of Egyptian paper;* because the word commonly signifies so, and nothing else can be meant. So the Latin translator paraphrases it: Βίβλων, i. e. Scirporum; per Biblum videtur potius intelligenda papyrus Ægypti;

though this overthrows Varro's account, that this material for writing was found out, when Alexander was in Egypt.

[b] Εἰς διφθέρας γὰρ τὰς διανοίας αὐτῶν γράψας ὁ Ἑρμίων ἔπεμπε τοῖς πολεμίοις. Suid. ad Διφθέρα.

[c] Mox æmulatione circâ bibliothecas regum Ptolemæi et Eumenis, supprimente chartas Ptolemæo, idem Varro membranas Pergami tradidit repertas. Plin. Nat. Hist. l. 13. c. 11.

[d] Genial. Dier. l. 2. c. 30.

it

it was found out, the use of it became very common[a]; although I rather incline to think, Varro's story not to be true, as to the time, as Polydore Vergil has well observed[b]; and Dr. Edwards[c], and after him Dr. Prideaux[d] have more largely proved.

2. When they had wrote upon these skins of parchment, *they were wont to fasten them together, and roll them up.* They did not cut the parchment into small pieces, as we now do our books; but all the book was wrote on one long continued page, consisting of several skins fastened together. To the end of the skins was fastened a large staff or stick, round about which they rolled up the skins: this, when so rolled up, they called *Volumen, a volvendo,* i. e. a *volume* or *roll,* and the staff about which it was rolled, they called *Umbilicus.* And hence we so frequently in the Roman authors meet with *Membranæ,* for the material on which they wrote, *Volumen,* for the book itself when wrote, and *ad Umbilicum ducere,* to come to the end of the book[e]. So Martial, in the last epigram of his fourth book, speaking to his book, says,

Ohe jam satis est, ohe Libelle,
Jam pervenimus usque ad Umbilicos.

And, in another place[f], says of his book,

Pictis luxurieris Umbilicis.

So also when he is speaking to a plagiary, that had stole his poems, he tells him[g], he should have rather made choice of a more obscure book;

Nec Umbilicis cultus atque Membrana.

I will

---

[a] Postea promiscue patuit usus rei, qua constat hominum immortalitas. Plin. ibid.

[b] Verum ego affirmarem membranas, multo ante quam tradit Varro, esse repertas. De Inventoribus Rer. l. 2. c. 8.

[c] Of the Authority and Style of the Holy Scriptures, vol. 2. c. 3.

[d] Connect. of the History of the Old and New Testament, vol. 1. b. 7.

[e] Veteres enim non solum Hebræi, sed et Ethnici, scribere solebant in membranis aut chartis, quæ in rotundum complicabantur—Apud Ethnicos voluminum fuisse usum satis indicat proverbium illud, *Ad Umbilicum ducere.* Erat enim Umbilicus lignum, circa quod chartæ descriptæ convolvebantur. Jansen. ad Psal. xxxix. 11.

[f] Lib. 3. Epig. 2.

[g] Lib. 1. Epig. 67.

[h] *Nec Umbilicis cultus,* i. e. cujus Umbilicus, is est bacillus cedrinus, buxeus, cupressinus, &c. extremæ paginæ, absoluto jam opere, assutus;

I will not be at the pains to collect any more inftances, for the proof of this matter. It is fufficiently known to thofe, who are verfed at all in antiquity, and will more fully appear, when we confider,

3. *That the Jews, long before our Saviour's time, did write their books after this manner.* There cannot be the leaft doubt, but the Jews, as well as other nations, did make ufe of the fkins of feveral animals to write upon, long before that period we mentioned; for Arifteas, in his Hiftory of the Tranflation of the Bible by the Seventy, tells us[a], that Ptolemy fent meffengers to Eleazar the high-prieft for the Jewifh Law, *becaufe they had it wrote in fkins, or parchment, in Hebrew letters.* Jofephus alfo, who relates the fame hiftory, tells us, that when the feventy-two elders were come down to Egypt, they came with prefents to the King, and the parchments, in which they had the Law, wrote in letters of gold; that when they were unfolding the books, and fhewing them to the King, he was furprized at the finenefs or thinnefs of the parchment, and that they were fo fewed or faftened together, that it was impoffible to perceive the feams, or the place where one fkin was faftened to another[b]. Whether the hiftory of Arifteas, and this chapter of Jofephus, be true or not, I need not enquire; the world has been fufficiently troubled with that difpute already. There have been fome, who have even made the place of Jofephus now cited, an argument againft this hiftory. Rivet, for inftance[c], would perfuade us, that the Jews never would write their Law in golden letters: and the very learned Chamier[d] calls the ftory of Ptolemy's ad-

---

affutus; vel umbilici extremita⸱es, quæ, complicatis in volumen membranis, utrinque apparent, cornua appellantur, ebore, argento, vel auro ornantur. Farnab. ad loc. See alfo l. 5. Epig. 6.

[a] Διὰ τὸ γράφεσθαι παρ' αἰτοῖς ἐν διφθέραις, Ἑϐραικῖς γράμμασιν. In init.

[b] Τῶν διφθερῶν, αἷς ἐγέγραμμένως εἶχον τὸς νόμως χρυσοῖς γράμμασιν—ὡς δ' ἀποκαλύψαντες τῶν ἐπιλημάτων ἐπίδιξαν αὐτῷ, θαυ-

μάσας ὁ βασιλεὺς τῆς ἰσχνότητος τὸς ὑμένας (I think it would be better to read τὸ ὑμένος), καὶ τῆς συμϐολῆς τὸ ἀπερίγνωςον, ὅτω γὰρ ἥρμοςο, &c. Antiq. Jud. lib. 12. c. 2. §. 10.

[c] Ifagog. ad Script. Sacr. c. 10. For this his opinion, he depends only upon a fable of the Rabbins, that the Law was to be wrote only with ink of fuch a fort.

[d] Panftrat. Cathol. vol. 1. l. 13. c. 4. §. 11.

miring

miring the finenefs of the parchment, a λιπτολογία or μικροφιλο-
τιμία; he means that it is an idle ftory, which deferves no
credit. But, as I faid, I need not difpute the truth of the
ftory; I take it for granted that Ariftæas, or whoever he was
that was the author of that hiftory under his name, lived before our Saviour's time. Dr. Hody [a] himfelf owns it, and has
endeavoured to prove it; and if fo, let the hiftory be fuppofed
never fo falfe, yet it cannot be fuppofed a perfon would write
of a cuftom, which never had been. The fame may be faid
alfo of the paffage cited out of Jofephus; viz. that he believed
this was the method of writing among the Jews, in the reign
of Ptolemy Philadelphus, almoft three hundred years before
our Saviour's time. It is worth our obferving, that the moft
antient Jews, as well as Jofephus, were of this opinion, that
the old way of writing the Law was upon parchment; hence
the Chaldee Paraphraft, fuppofed by the Jews to be Jonathan
(who wrote the Targum on the Prophets, and lived in or before our Saviour's time), fays in his tranflation of thefe words,
Deut. xxxi. 24. that Mofes wrote the Law ספרא על *upon parchment.* Whether this be fo or not, is very uncertain. Dr. Prideaux [b], it feems, is of the fame opinion; " It muft," fays he,
" be acknowledged, that the authentick copy of the Law,
" which Hilkiah found in the Temple, and fent to King Jo-
" fiah, was of this material, none other ufed for writing being
" of fo durable a nature, as to laft from Mofes's time till then,
" which was eight hundred and thirty years." However the
matter of fact be, I will not now enquire; only obferve, by
the by, the infufficiency of the Dean's argument; for

1. It is far from being evident, that the book, which Hilkiah found, was that which was wrote by Mofes. We are
told exprefsly, that when Solomon, at the dedication of the
Temple, brought up the ark, there was nothing found in it,
but the two tables of ftone, which Mofes had put there, 1 Kings
viii. 9.

2. Suppofe it was the book wrote by Mofes, it does not fol-

---

[a] Contra Hiftor. Arifteæ de   [b] Connect. of the Hift. of the
LXX. Interpret. cap. 20.   Old Teft. Part 1. b. 7. in fin.

low that it was of parchment, becaufe it lafted fo long; for the other materials of writing, made ufe of by the antients, were no lefs durable than this. A deep incifion into brafs, lead, ftone, or perhaps wax, was, if duly preferved, likely to laft as long as any fort of ink on parchment. Mofes's tables of ftone, we are affured, were in being at the dedication of the Temple, 1 Kings viii. 9. (which was the fpace of almoft five hundred years), and very probably continued to the deftruction of it; and other monuments of antiquity have continued legible a much longer time.

But to return, it is evident from what has been faid, that the Jews before our Saviour's time did write upon parchment, or the fkins of animals. I am now further to fhew, that they made their books after the manner that has been defcribed, viz. by rolling the fkins upon a ftaff, when they were faftened together. Now inafmuch as we have few (if any at all befides the Canonical ones of the Old Teftament) of the books of the Jews, that were wrote before our Saviour's time, it is impoffible to give fo clear an account of their way of writing, as of the Heathens, whofe books we have. Befides thofe teftimonies of Jofephus, Ariftæas, and Jonathan, I know not any. Some intimations of this matter in the Old Teftament indeed there are, which, if duly confidered, will evidence to us the manner of their writing. For inftance, it is apparent that the Jewifh books were rolled up, from the name given them in the Old Teftament: as the Romans made ufe of the word *volumen* (*a volvendo*, from its being rolled up), to denote a *book*; fo the Jews made ufe of the words מגלה and גליון, which fignify the very fame as *volumen*, derived from גלל *to roll*. The laft of thefe words we find, Ifai. viii. 1. God commands the Prophet to take גליון גדול, *a large roll*, and write therein, &c. The former we meet with feveral times in the Prophets[a], fometimes joined with the word ספר, *a book*, and fometimes not. It occurs once in the Pfalms, viz. xl. 7. *as it is written concerning me in the volume of thy book,* ספר במגלה, i. e. *in convolutione libri*, or according to a very com-

---

[a] Jer. xxxvi. 2. 14. 20, &c. Ezek. ii. 9. and iii. 1, 2, 3. Zech. v, 1, 2.

mon

mon and known Hebraifm, *in libro convoluto,* i. e. *in the book that is rolled up,* as the book of the Law then was. This interpretation is plain, and I need not be at the pains to cite the criticks and commentators, to fupport it; I think they almoft all agree, that this word was made ufe of to fignify a book [a], becaufe their books were rolled up, and fo we have traced this cuftom as far as David's time. I muft not omit obferving here, that the Seventy feem to have underftood this place otherwife, when they tranflate it, ἐν κεφαλίδι βιβλίου, and that the old Latin tranflator after them renders it, *in Capite libri;* which has made fome Popifh commentators believe, that we are to underftand, *the fum of the book.* But it does not much concern us, how the Seventy have rendered it, nor indeed fhould I have mentioned it, if St. Paul had not feemed to juftify their tranflation, by making ufe of their words, ἐν κεφαλίδι βιβλίου, &c. Heb. x. 7. I faid, *feemed to juftify;* for though St. Paul, and other writers of the New Teftament, did undoubtedly make ufe of the Septuagint, or fome Greek tranflation, in citing out of the Old Teftament; yet their ufing it, does not always juftify it, as though it were a juft tranflation of the original. It is certain the writers of the New Teftament made ufe of the Greek verfion fometimes, where the tranflators plainly miftook the words they tranflated; and the reafon why they thus followed them in their miftakes, was, becaufe they wrote to, and for thofe, who made ufe of thefe Bibles; and it might probably have been of very bad confequence, had they gone about to correct or alter them [b]. But perhaps after all, מגלת ספר may be juftly tranflated by the Seventy, κεφαλὶς βιβλίου, and κεφαλὶς may fignify the very fame thing as *volume.* So our learned countryman, Mr. Fuller, has by an ingenious criticifm endeavoured to prove [c]. I would only obferve further here, that Aquila and Symmachus tranflate this word in its juft fenfe, *a roll,* and fo Theodoret under-

[a] Vid. Janfen. Genebrard. &c. ad loc. Sixt. Senenf. Biblioth. Sanct. l. 2. ad voc. Volumen. Caftell. Buxtorf. et Schindler ad כלל See Ifai. xxxiv. 4.

[b] See concerning this matter Rivet. Ifagog. in S. Script. c. 10. and Flacc. Illyric. Par. 2. Tract. 1. de Evangelift.

[c] Mifcell. Sacr. l. 2. c. 10.

ſtood it ª, and the Seventy themſelves have very frequently
tranſlated this word χαϛίον ᵇ. I ſhall take it then for granted,
that the word מגלה proves, that the Jews before our Saviour's time were wont to roll up their books. I add,

4. That the Jews uſually wrote thus *about the time, when
St. Matthew wrote his Goſpel.* That it was thus in our Saviour's time, ſeems to be very evident from thoſe words,
Luke iv. 17. *And when he had opened the book, &c.* and ver.
20. *And he cloſed the book, &c.* The two Greek words,
ἀναπτύξας and πτύξας, tranſlated *opened* and *cloſed*, do evidently
intimate to us, what ſort of a book it was in which our Saviour read. They ſignify to *unfold*, and to *fold up again*, or (if
I may uſe the word) to *unroll* and to *roll up again*, as every
body knows who has met with theſe words in the Greek authors; and ſo here ἀναπτύξας τὸ βιϹλίον meaneth his taking the
parchment off the roll, and drawing it out in length to read it,
and πτύξας τὸ βιϹλίον means his rolling it up again round the
ſtaff. " The word ἀναπτύσσω," ſays a learned critick ª, " re-
" fers to the manner of writing among the Jews, which was
" not in parchment or paper ſewed together, as we now uſe;
" but in one continued page or long roll, and that folded up,
" to ſave it from duſt or other harm." In this ſenſe alſo the
word is uſed by the LXX. 2 Kings xix. 14. Hezekiah re-
çeived the letter, or *little books,* τὰ βιϹλία (as the LXX tranſlate
the word הספרים), καὶ ἀνέπτυξεν αὐτὰ, *and ſpread them,* or *laid
them open.* Hence it was well obſerved by Grotius, that theſe
two words anſwer to the Latin ones *evolvere* and *convolvere,*
i. e. *to fold* and *unfold* ᵈ; and I would obſerve, that the Greek

---

ª Τὴν κεφαλίδα εἴλημα εἰρήκασιν
Ἀκύλας καὶ ὁ Σύμμαχος· ὅτω δὲ
τὰς θείας γραφὰς μέχρι ᷉ τήμερον
Ἰουδαῖοι κατασκευάζειν εἰώθασι.
Theodoret. ad Pſal. xl. 8. Idem, in
Ezek. iii. κεφαλίδα καλεῖ τὰ εἰλητὰ
βιϹλία. Apud Suicer. in Theſaur.
ad κεφαλίς. Vid. et Var. Lect. et
Schol. in LXX. Hence Suidas alſo,
at the word Κεφαλίς· Τὴν κεφαλίδα, ὅπερ τινὲς εἴλημά φασιν.

ᵇ Jer. xxxvi.

ᶜ Dr. Hammond on Luke iv. 17.

ᵈ Ἀναπτύσσειν βιϹλίον eſt *evolvere,* πτύσσειν *convolvere.* Jam
Hebræorum, ut et Latinorum, libri
erant volumina; hinc *evolvere li-
brum* apud Ciceronem, atque alios:
idem eſt *revolvere* Livio et Marti-
li, quâ voce et hic uſus eſt recte La-
tinus interpres. Grot. ad loc. See
Beza, Chemnit. Cornel. ad Lapid.
Le Clerc, Whitby, &c. ad loc.

word

word πτύσσω was fo very commonly ufed for this fort of *fold-
ing* and *rolling up* their books ; that, as the Jews called their
books נכלה, from their being thus rolled up, and the Romans
called theirs *volumina* for the fame reafon ; fo, upon the very
fame account, the Greeks formed the words πτῦγμα and
πτυκτίον, πυκτὶς and πυκτίον, to denote a book, or a writing on
parchment, that was thus folded or rolled up[a]: hence Θεἷα
πυκτὶς is often ufed by the Greek Fathers for the facred Scripture[b].   From all which I think it is very fair to conclude,
that the book which our Saviour read in the fynagogue at Nazareth, was of that fort which has been defcribed, viz. a *volume of parchment.*

The matter I am upon, may receive fome confirmation
from St. Paul's charge to Timothy[c] ; *The cloak that I left at
Troas with Carpus, when thou comeft, bring with thee, and the
books, but efpecially the parchments.*   I will not now enquire
whether the word φαιλόνη, which we have tranflated a *cloak,*
fignifies a parchment roll or not.   According to Phavorinus
it does[d] ; and I can fee no reafon why our tranflators fhould
render it a *cloak,* but becaufe Beza (whom they continually
followed, and often even in his miftakes) had done fo before
them.   Whether this fignifies a parchment roll or no, there
can be little reafon to doubt but μιμβράνας does.   Dr. Edwards has fomewhere told us, that he fuppofes the parchments
here mean the fkins, which the Apoftle made ufe of in his
trade of tent-making ; but there is not the leaft foundation for
this fancy.   It would feem indeed at firft, that the parchments
and books, which St. Paul defires him to bring, were diftinct
things ; but there is no need at all of fuppofing fo.   The
Apoftle feems here to make ufe of a form of fpeech, very common in the Scriptures and all language ; viz. repeating the
fame thing in different words ; *Bring the little cheft* (or

---

[a] Πυκτίον, τὸ βιβλίον, Suid. ad
voc.

[b] Sacra Scriptura hac voce (fcil.
Πυκτὶς) fæpe defignatur. Suicer.
Thefaur. Ecclef. ad voc.

[c] 2 Tim. iv. 13.

[d] Vid. Heinf. Exerc. Sacr. ad
loc. and Dr. Hammond, who alfo
takes it in this fenfe. Jerome alfo
tells us, that fome in his time underftood by φαιλόνη, Volumen Hebraicum. Ad Damaf. Quæft. 2.

fatchel,

fatchel, for so I take the word φαιλόην), *which I left at Troas and the books ; but especially the parchments,* i. e. *the books.* The old Syriack interpreter translates the word φαιλόην, which we translate a *cloak,* בית כתבא i. e. *a chest of books or writings,* and μεμβράνας, which we translate *parchments,* he renders כרכא דמגלא i. e. *a bundle of parchment rolls.* The Syriack word here is the very same with the Hebrew one, of which we have spoke already ; so that, whether St. Paul here meant *parchment rolls* or not, it is certain the Syriack interpreter, who lived about that time (as will be hereafter proved), thought he did ; which is sufficient to my present purpose.

Another place of the New Testament, from whence we may conclude that to have been the method of writing in use among the Jews, which has been described, viz. on parchment rolls, is that, Rev. vi. 14. *The heaven departed as a scroll, when it is rolled together,* &c. The original word, which we have translated a *scroll,* is βιβλίον, a *book* ; and so here is a manifest allusion to the custom of rolling up their books or parchments, on which they wrote at that time [a].

I shall not seek for any farther proofs of this matter, only would observe, that there is a passage in Polycarp's Epistle to the Philippians, which if it do not prove the point in hand, yet may itself be explained from what has been said. In the close of his Epistle, he tells the Philippians, that the Epistles of Ignatius ὑποτεταγμέναι εἰσι, were annexed or subjoined (*subjectæ sunt* according to the old Latin Version) to his own Epistle. This seems capable of no other meaning, than *that at the end, or bottom of the roll, on which his Epistle was wrote, were fastened together the skins, on which Ignatius's were wrote.*

And thus I have largely considered, what the method of writing was among the Jews before our Saviour's time, and about that time when St. Matthew wrote ; and now, I think, I may justly draw my conclusion, that St. Matthew did not write his Gospel on small scraps or scrolls of paper. Why should he write in a method so very different from all his cotemporaries ? If every one else wrote on large skins of parch-

---

[a] There is the very same allusion or comparison, Isai. xxxiv. 4.

ment,

ment, is it credible that he would write upon fmall fcraps of paper, or of any other material whatfoever ? As for the Egyptian paper, it is a very great queftion, whether it was ever in ufe among the Jews at all.   I have not yet feen any reafon to believe that it was ; there is not, that I know of, the leaft intimation of any fuch thing, either in the Old or New Teftament, or Jofephus.   But let us take it for granted, that the Jews, as well as other nations, did make ufe of this fort of paper; it will not follow, that St. Matthew had any need to write his Gofpel on fmall pieces or fcraps of it.   I am very apt to think, that the fize of this paper was as large, as that which we now ordinarily make ufe of.   We read feveral times in antient writers, of fhips or boats made of this papyrus ; *They make boats of papyrus, and fails of its bark,* fays Pliny [a] ; and in another place, he mentions *naves papyraceas* [b], *fhips made of papyrus :* Plutarch alfo talks of παπύρινα σκάφη, *boats of papyrus* [c]. I cannot omit mentioning here the opinion of feveral learned men, that the ark or boat, into which Mofes was put on the river in Egypt, was made of this papyrus.   So Grotius, *fifcellam fcirpeam,* i. e. *ex papyro* ; and, to confirm his interpretation, he cites this verfe of Lucan, lib. 4. v. 136. [d]

Conferitur bibula Memphitis cymba papyro.

This opinion feems to be confirmed from thofe words of the prophet, Ifai. xviii. 1, 2. *Wo to the land fhadowing with wings, which is beyond the rivers of Ethiopia ; that fendeth ambaffadors by the fea, even in veffels of bulrufhes upon the waters.* Here we not only read of veffels made of bulrufhes, in or near Egypt ; but what is very obfervable, the fame word is put here, to denote that of which thefe veffels were made, בכלי נמא, which is ufed to denote that of which Mofes's ark was made, תבת נמא, Exod. ii. 3.   So then, if the Egyptian papyrus was thus large, though the Jews did ufe it, yet it is not at all

[a] Ex papyro navigia texunt, et e libro vela.   Hift. Natut. l. 13. c. 11.
[b] L. 6. c. 22.
[c] In Lib. de If. et Ofir. apud

Doughteium in Analect. Sacr. Excurf. 156. where other like inftances are produced.
[d] Annot. ad Exod. ii. 3.

likely

likely St. Matthew would write upon fmall fcraps and fcrolls ; efpecially if we confider, how *very fmall, and many* thefe fcraps and fcrolls were ; which fhall be the fubject of the following chapter.

After all that has been faid in this chapter, I confefs there might have been fome other methods of writing in ufe among the Jews, in our Saviour's time. There is another way mentioned by St. Luke, chap. i. 63. *And he afked for a writing-table, and wrote,* &c.' What fort of writing-table this was, and what the proper meaning of the word Πιναξιδιον here is, feems not very eafy to be told. Tertullian [a], and after him feveral others [b], fuppofe it to be a *wax-table :* whether this opinion be true or not, I cannot determine. The Romans were wont to write their letters, and other fmaller matters, on fuch tables; perhaps Zacharias might write on fuch a one, and perhaps it might be on a little thin ftone table, fuch as we now commonly ufe. Yet neither of thefe was the material, of which their books were compofed ; and I remember, Tully mentions *the transferring the contents of thefe fort of tables into books* [c]. Their books and their tables were therefore different. Befides this, I do not find there is in the facred writings, or any where elfe, any intimation of another method of writing, in ufe among the Jews about this time ; and therefore, fince it has been proved to be the ordinary method of the Jews to write their books on long rolls of parchment, I conclude St. Matthew alfo wrote his Gofpel fo, and not, as Mr. Whifton fays, upon fmall pieces of paper ; which will more fully appear in the following chapter.

---

[a] At enim Zacharias temporali vocis orbatione mulctatus—manibus fuis a corde dictat, et nomen filii fine ore pronuntiat ; loquitur in Stylo, auditur in Cera, &c. Lib. de Idololat. c. 23.'

[b] Erafmus, Gualtperius, Heinfius, et alii, ad loc.

[c] Literæ, lituræque omnes affimulatæ, expreffæ, de tabulis in libros transferuntur. Orat. vii. in Verrem, verf. fin.

CHAP.

CHAP. XVI.

Mr. Whiston's strange Suppofition, of St. Matthew's writing this Part of his Gofpel on fmall Pieces of Paper, confuted from the Confideration of their Number and unequal Size. A Table of them, by which it appears that they were at leaft twenty in Number, of very different Sizes. Some contained feveral Chapters, others but a few Verfes, others but one Verfe. The Improbability of St. Matthew's writing thus. The Size of the Parchment Rolls, on which the Jews wrote.

THE improbability of St. Matthew's writing his Gofpel upon fmall pieces of paper (as Mr. Whifton fuppofes he did), will appear much greater, if we confider the *number and fize of thefe feveral papers.*

It is an old and true faying of the philofopher, Ἑνὸς ἀτόπȣ δοθέντος, πολλὰ ἀναγκαῖȣ ἰσι συμβαίνειν; *One abfurdity advanced, neceffarily leads a perfon into many others to maintain it.* For as truth needs not to be, nor indeed can be, fupported by that which is falfe; fo that which is falfe, cannot be fupported by any thing which is true. A ftrange fondnefs to be reputed the authors of fome new difcovery, and a great unwillingnefs to be of the fame opinion with the greateft part of the world, often betrays very learned men into thofe abfurdities, which elfe they would never have fallen into or maintained. I do not fay, nor do I believe, this was the cafe with Mr. Whifton; and yet I cannot but think, that it was a too great zeal for his new opinion, which hindered him from feeing the confequences of it: nothing elfe could have prevented a genius fo penetrating, from difcovering thofe confequences of his opinion, which I am now about to obferve.

His hypothefis (as has been faid already) is, *that the feveral parts or periods of this former part of St. Matthew's Gofpel, were written at firft feparately, and upon feveral diftinct papers; which were put together in their prefent order by thofe,*
who

who did not perfectly know the true series of the history. So then every one of the transposed and misplaced branches, be it larger, or lesser, was written on a distinct separate piece of paper. Now there can be no better argument to confute this hypothesis, than the consideration of the *size* and *number* of these papers. Upon due examination we shall find the number to be no less than *twenty*, in this small part of the history, of *very different and unequal sizes*; as will appear by the following table, made out of Mr. Whiston's Harmony.

A Table of the several distinct papers, on which, according to Mr. Whiston, St. Matthew at first wrote his Gospel, with the number of verses, of which each part or paper did consist.

N. B. I have in this Table observed the order of Mr. Whiston's Harmony.

The papers on which St. Matthew wrote, since misplaced.	The number of verses, of which each paper did consist.
1. Ch. viii. 14—17.	1. Four verses.
2. viii. 2—4.	2. Three verses.
3. ix. 2—17.	3. Sixteen verses.
4. xii. 1—21.	4. Twenty-one verses.
5. iv. 23—25. and v. 1.	5. Four verses.
6. viii. 1.	6. One verse.
7. v. 2, &c. vi and vii.	7. A hundred and ten.
8. viii. 5—13.	8. Nine verses.
9. xi. 2 to the end.	9. Twenty-nine verses.
10. xii. 22—50. and xiii. 1—53.	10. Eighty-one verses.
11. viii. 18.	11. One verse.
12. viii. 23—34. and ix. 1.	12. Thirteen verses.
13. viii. 19—22.	13. Four verses.
14. ix. 18—34.	14. Seventeen verses.
15. xiii. 54—58.	15. Five verses.
16. ix. 35—38. and x. and xi. 1.	16. Forty-seven verses.

These

These are the several parts of St. Matthew's Gospel, which Mr. Whiston supposes misplaced ; besides these, there is also another branch in the former part of this Gospel; which he has in his Harmony placed contrary to the order of our present copies ; and consequently, must according to this hypothesis be misplaced, and so also be wrote upon a separate and distinct piece of paper.   That which I mean, is the account of our Lord's temptation by the Devil in the mountain, chap. iv. 8, &c.   This evidently implies the dislocation of two other branches, and consequently their being wrote also on separate pieces of paper.   These papers, and the number of verses are,

17. Ch. iv. 8—11.	17. Three	
18. and ver. 5—8.	18. Three	} Verses.
19. and ver. 12—22.	19. Twelve	

Thus it is evident, that, according to Mr. Whiston, St. Matthew must have wrote this former part of his Gospel *upon twenty several pieces of paper* ; although we suppose that the three first chapters, and the four first verses of the fourth, were all wrote upon one.   But is this a thing credible ? especially if we look upon the foregoing table, and see of what very different sizes these papers were, some to contain *two or three long chapters*, others only *two or three short verses*, and others only *one*.   What reason can possibly be assigned, why this inspired Apostle should write after this manner ? I remember Diogenes Laertius, in the Life of Cleanthes, tells us [a], that that philosopher " being poor, and wanting money " to buy paper, was wont to write the lectures and discourses " of his master Zeno on small shells or bones of oxen." But however poor our Saviour's Apostles were, we can hardly suppose them forced to any such necessity as this : St. Matthew certainly was able to procure a few skins of parchment to write his Gospel upon ; and, if he was, nothing can excuse

---

[a] Τѯτόν φασιν εἰς ὄϛρακα καὶ ὥϛε ὠνήσασθαι χαϛία.   Diog.
Ϭῶν ἐμπιπλάτας γράφειν, ἄπιρ ἤκει   Laert. in Vit. Cleant. §. 174.
ταρὰ τᾶ Ζήνωιος, ἀπορίᾳ κιμμάτων

him

him for writing it as Mr. Whifton fuppofes. He could not
but forefee his Gofpel fo wrote, muft be liable to confufion
and diflocation; and can it be fuppofed, that an infpired writer
would have no more regard to that which was dictated to
him by God's holy Spirit? Would he be fo unaccountably
carelefs in writing that which was defigned for the benefit of
mankind in all ages of the world? A perfon of an ordinary
capacity, in writing a common book, cannot be fuppofed to
have wrote after fuch a manner, and much lefs *an accurate*
writer under the conduct of divine Infpiration (as Mr. Whifton
allows St. Matthew to have been), in writing one of the moft
ufeful books, and of the moft important confequence to the
world, that ever was wrote.

The foregoing reafoning may (if indeed it needed any) receive fome confirmation, from the confideration of St. Matthew's character; *he was a Publican,* and therefore more
likely to be exact and accurate in his writing, than others.
The Publicans were cuftom-houfe officers, whofe bufinefs
was to take an account of the importation and exportation of
goods, and to collect the money or duty which was laid upon
them. For this purpofe they had (as Cicero tells us [a]) their
tabulas accepti et expenfi, which were very exact *accounts of*
what they expended, and what they received, and were upon
proper occafions (if not always) *transferred into books, and*
tranfmitted to Rome [b]. Of this occupation was St. Matthew,
one whofe bufinefs was writing; and is it at all probable, that
fuch a one would write after the manner Mr. Whifton fuppofes? If he was no more careful in the keeping of his accounts, than this fuppofes him to be in writing his Gofpel,
truly he was but a very bad officer.

It may not be improper, before I conclude this argument,
to fhew fomewhat of the *fize of thefe parchment rolls, on which*
the Jews were wont to write; that fo comparing thefe with
thofe pieces of paper, on which Mr. Whifton fuppofes St.
Matthew to have wrote, that fuppofition may appear the more
unreafonable.

[a] Orat. in Verr. vii. §. 186.   [b] Cicer. ibid. verf. fin.

It

It is very certain thefe rolls were of very different fizes; the prophet Ifaiah was commanded to prepare *a great roll*, chap. viii. 1. and Jeremiah prepared fuch a one, as contained *all the prophecies God had fpoke by him againſt Ifrael and Judah, from the days of Joſiah unto that time*, chap. xxxvi. 2. i. e. as many as he had received in the fpace of *twenty-three years*, as appears by the chronology, and chap. xxv. 3. Jofephus, when he had finifhed his hiftory of the Jewifh Antiquities, fays, it was βιϐλίοις μὲν εἴκοσι περιειλημμένη, *folded up in twenty volumes or books*. The expreffion (if I do not miftake it) feems to imply, that each of thefe books was a diftinct volume; and fo every one of them was of a larger fize, than the whole of St. Matthew's Gofpel would have made. He adds further, that thefe twenty books contained fixty thoufand ϛίχοι or *lines*; and fince thefe books were moft of them contrived by the author to be pretty near of a fize, we may conclude that, one with another, each of thefe volumes contained about three thoufand lines; and fuch volumes muft needs [a] contain a great many fkins of parchment.

Maimonides out of the Talmud tells us, that the parchments, on which the Jews wrote their bibles, were to be fix hands in breadth, and fix in length [b]; and fo the prefent Jews, retaining the old cuftom of their nation, write the law which they ufe in their fynagogues, in one fuch large volume [c]. And if Father Simon is to be believed, the Jews have not altered the antient cuftom, but have juft fuch volumes in their fynagogues now, as formerly they had. There is a controverfy between that Father and the learned Ifaac Voffius on that head; the former contending, that " the Pentateuch, or five " books of Mofes, did all make but one volume;" the latter, " that they were as many volumes as books." The former

---

[a] After a computation of the number of lines in one of the cloſeſt of our printed editions in folio, in which the Greek taketh the whole breadth of the page, I find the number of lines in the print, does not amount to very much above a third part of the number of lines, that were in Jofephus's own manuſcript.

[b] Vide Leufden. Diſſert. 34. de Pentateuch. Manuſcriptis, p. 399, and Dr. Prideaux's Connection of the Hift. of the Old and New Teft. Part 1. b. 5.

[c] Vid. Leufden. loc. cit.

aſſerts,

afferts, " they were one volume in the time of Chrift ;" the latter fays ; " the contrary is evident from the hiftory of Ari-" ftæas, which mentions the law as written in feveral vo-" lumes ;" and adds, " that of the infinite number of books " there are in the world divided into volumes, there is not " one in all antiquity which can be evidenced to have been " as big a volume, as half the Pentateuch would have made." He concludes afferting the prefent fynagogue books to be *more for fhew, than for ufe,* &c. * It does not feem very material, which of thefe learned gentlemen was in the right : either of their opinions being fuppofed true, fufficiently evidences the abfurdity of imagining St. Matthew to have wrote fo fmall a part of his Gofpel, on fo many pieces of paper as have been mentioned.

Thus I have endeavoured to fhew the unreafonablenefs of fuppofing St. Matthew to have wrote after that manner, which Mr. Whifton fuppofes : after the clofeft confideration of the matter, I am not able to conceive of any thing, which could be the motive or reafon of St. Matthew's writing thus. Perhaps it may be faid, he wrote down his accounts of matters as they came to pafs, left they fhould flip his memory ; but this fuppofition is upon many accounts groundlefs and falfe, feveral of thefe things having come to pafs before St. Matthew was called, and almoft all the parts or periods fo introduced, as to imply a connection (though not in point of time) with the preceding and following parts of the hiftory. But a fuller anfwer to this opinion I do not think myfelf yet obliged to make ; only would refer the reader to the foregoing table.

As to the hints, which Mr. Whifton propofes, to reftore thefe difordered parts to their true order again, I cannot think, that, befides what has been already faid, they require any particular confideration. I would only make this one remark

---

* Cum infiniti fuperfint libri in volumina diftincti, vel unum in tota antiquitate oftendatur volumen, quod ad tantam excrefcat molem, ut vel dimidiam librorum Moyfis partem exæquet. Voff. Refponf. ad iterat, P. Simon. Object. p. 371, et ejufdem Refponf. ad tertias Simon. Object. p. 95.

from them, viz. that he, who did tranfpofe them, muſt be one
that was very well acquainted with the Goſpel hiſtory; and
ſuch a one could not poffibly make ſuch blunders as theſe.
But I leave this, and the more particular confideration of this
matter, to thoſe who ſhall judge it neceſſary.

C H A P. XVII.

*Mr. Whiſton's Obſervation, that our preſent Greek Copies of
this Goſpel are a Tranſlation out of Hebrew, and for that
Reaſon more liable to the Diſorder, which he ſuppoſes, confidered. St. Matthew did not write his Goſpel in Hebrew,
though it is aſſerted by all the Fathers. The Fathers have
frequently (one after another) fallen into the ſame Miſtake in
Matters of Fact. How they came to fall into this Miſtake,
viz. by taking the Goſpel of the Nazarenes and Ebionites for
the true authentick Goſpel of St. Matthew. The Fathers
were under a Sort of Neceſſity of believing this Miſtake.*

THE remaining part of what Mr. Whiſton ſays, to eſtab_
liſh his propoſition, confiſts of an obſervation or two,
which he imagined would make it appear more probable, and
give ſome light in this matter to ſome future inquiries; and
a vindication of himſelf *from ſuch cenſures, as the ſtrangeneſs of
the propoſition would occaſion* [a].

The two obſervations which Mr. Whiſton makes, are, he
ſays, inſtead of ſome conjectures which he once deſigned to
have offered, how theſe ſections came to be ſo ſtrangely tranſpoſed. It is to be lamented, that any thing ſhould have been
the unhappy means of preventing ſo good a deſign. Mr.
Whiſton's zeal for truth, and his indefatigable endeavours to
find it out, perſuade me, that nothing but the impoſſibility of

[a] Pag. 111.

accompliſhing

accomplishing his design, would have prevented him in pursuing it. For my part (as I have already said) I cannot see any other way of accounting for the disorder, than that which Mr. Whiston and Mr. Toinard have taken, and which has been considered in the two foregoing chapters.

I proceed now to consider Mr. Whiston's two observations; the first is this, viz. " The present copies of St. Mat-
" thew are only a translation from the Hebrew (in which lan-
" guage all antiquity affirm that Gospel was written), and
" may therefore more probably have been subject to some
" confusion and disorder than any of the rest, whose own co-
" pies we still have in the same language wherein they were
" originally written by their authors."

This observation of Mr. Whiston's will appear to be no support to his hypothesis, when the two following propositions are duly considered.

1. *That St. Matthew's Gospel, in our present copies, is not a translation out of Hebrew, but the original Greek itself, in which that Evangelist wrote.*

2. *Supposing our present Greek copies are a translation out of Hebrew, yet they were not, for that reason, at all the more likely to suffer any such dislocations or disorder, as Mr. Whiston supposes.*

1. *St. Matthew's Gospel, in our present copies, is not a translation out of Hebrew, but the original Greek itself, in which that Evangelist wrote.* I own indeed with Mr. Whiston, *that all antiquity hath affirmed this:* I cannot find, that so much as any one of the antients did believe this Gospel originally wrote in Greek. Papias [a], Irenæus [b], Origen [c], Jerome [d], Austin [e], Eusebius [f], Theophylact [g], and several others [h], do all agree

---

[a] Apud Euseb. Hist. Eccl. l. 3. c. 39.
[b] Adv. Hæref. l. 3. c. 1.
[c] Apud Euseb. Hist. Eccl. l. 6. c. 25.
[d] Proem. in Comment. Sup. Matth. et in Catalog. Scriptor. Eccl. ad voc. Matth.

[e] De Consens. Evang. l. 1. c. 2.
[f] Hist. Eccl. l. 3. c. 24.
[g] Præfat. in Matth.
[h] There are several others, (viz. Cyril of Jerusalem, Chrysostom, &c.) cited by Du Pin in his Hist. of the Canon of the New Test. vol. ii. c. 2. §. 3. but I have them not.

to affure us, that this Gofpel was originally wrote in Hebrew. I fhall not go about particularly to confider each of thefe teftimonies ; Dr. Whitby has already done this, as to the moft confiderable of them [a], *in his Prefatory Difcourfe to the Four Evangelifts :* inftead of this, I will make a few obfervations, which may help to give fome light into this matter.

1. It is certain, that a great many of the Fathers have fallen into the fame miftake, not only in matters of mere fpeculation (which was very common), but alfo in matters of fact. Every one, who is at all acquainted with the Popifh controverfial writings, will eafily admit this obfervation to be true. It is common in them to meet with a great body of Fathers, cited to fupport the moft apparent falfehoods. A perfuafion that the Scriptures of the Old Teftament were corrupted by the Jews, prevailed very much among the Fathers, though a notorious falfehood : and Dr. Whitby, in his Treatife of Traditions, has fhewed, that " the Fathers have been " impofed upon by the Jews, in other things, received from " them by tradition, and afferted by more teftimonies of an " tient Fathers, than are vouched to prove that the Gofpel " according to St. Matthew was firft written in Hebrew. " So, for inftance, they do a great many of them relate the " ftory, of the feventy tranflators of the Greek Bible making " their tranflation in fo many cells, which is a mere fable." For a further confirmation of this matter, I fhall think it fufficient to refer the reader to that excellent treatife of Mr. Daillé, *Concerning the Right Ufe of the Fathers* [b].

It may here be objected, that I myfelf have made ufe of their teftimony, to prove the manner in which St. Mark's Gofpel was wrote [c].

To this I only anfwer, that in fuch cafes, where there can be no objection made againft any particular teftimony, nor any probable reafon affigned, why they fhould fall into fuch miftake, we ought certainly to believe them. The former was the cafe in refpect of the writing of St. Mark's Gofpel ;

---

[a] Sect. 5.
[b] See efpecially Part II. c. 3.
[c] P. 50.

the latter is the cafe in the matter now under confideration, as will appear by what follows,

2. Though we fuppofe it a miftake that St. Matthew wrote his Gofpel in Hebrew, it was almoft impoffible that a great number of the fathers fhould not fall into it. Although it was originally wrote in Greek, it had been very ftrange if many of the Fathers had not believed it to be wrote in Hebrew. However like a paradox this may feem, I doubt not but to make it appear very probable by the following obfervations.

Obf. I. That the Nazarenes or Ebionites, two very early fects among the Chriftians, had a Gofpel which they made ufe of, called The Gofpel according to the Hebrews [a]. Though they were certainly two different fects (and *not the fame perfons,* as Mr. Toland, according to his old way of blundering, would have them to be [b]), yet the difference between their Gofpels was not very great: fome difference it feems there was, for the Gofpel of the Nazarenes *was moft full and entire in Hebrew,* but the Gofpel of the Ebionites was *adulterated and imperfect,* if Epiphanius be to be credited in this matter [c]; but according to Jerome, they feem to have been the fame Gofpel [d], for he fpeaks of the Gofpel of the Nazarenes and Ebionites as *one, which,* fays he, *I tranflated into Greek.*

[a] Ἔχουσι δὲ (fcil. Nazaræi) τὸ κατὰ Ματθαῖον Εὐαγγέλιον πληρέστατον Ἑβραϊστὶ, Epiphan. Hæref. 29. §. 9.
In Evangelio juxta Hebræos— quo utuntur ufque hodie Nazareni. Hieronym. adv. Pelag. l. 3. c. 1. Εὐαγγελίῳ δὲ μόνῳ τῷ καθ᾽ Ἑβραίους λεγομένῳ χρώμενοι, fcil. Ebionæi. Eufeb. l. 3. c. 27.
[b] In his late pamphlet called Nazarenus, c. 9.
[c] Epiphanius's account of the Gofpel of the Nazarenes, fee in Hæref. 29, §. 9. juft now cited. Of the Gofpel of the Ebionites, Hæref. 30. §. 3. he fays they call it the

Gofpel according to the Hebrews; and §. 13. he fpeaks thus of it; Ἐν τῷ γὰρ παρ᾽ αὐτοῖς Εὐαγγελίῳ κατὰ Ματθαῖον ὀνομαζομένῳ, οὐχ ὅλῳ δὲ πληρεστάτῳ, ἀλλὰ νενοθευμένῳ καὶ ἠκρωτηριασμένῳ, Ἑβραϊκὸν δὲ τοῦτο καλοῦσιν, &c. i. e. *in the Gofpel which the Ebionites ufe, called the Gofpel according to St. Matthew, not entire, but imperfect and corrupted.*
[d] In Evangelio, quo utuntur Nazareni et Ebionitæ, quod nuper in Græcum de Hebræo Sermone tranftulimus. Comment. in Matth. l. 2. c. 12.

2. This

2. This their Gofpel was wrote in Hebrew, or rather, that which was then the language of the Jews, Syriack or Syro-Chaldaick. This is evident from the paffages in Jerome and Epiphanius juft cited. The former of whom tells us in another place, " that there was a Hebrew copy even in his time " in the library at Cæfarea;" and adds, " that he himfelf had " the liberty granted him by the Nazarenes that lived at Be-" rea, to tranfcribe their copy." It is thought by fome that the Hebrew copy, which was at Cæfarea, was judged by Jerome to be St. Matthew's own manufcript; but there is not any foundation for this opinion in that Father's words [a].

3. This Hebrew Gofpel, which the Nazarenes and Ebionites made ufe of, they believed, and confequently declared, to be the true Gofpel, which St. Matthew wrote. This is evident by their putting fo great a value upon it, *as to rejeƈt all the others, and to make ufe only of this* [b]. Hence Eufebius tells us [c], " that thofe Jews, who had received the faith of " Chrift, were extremely fond of this Gofpel according to " the Hebrews." By thefe Jews it is impoffible (as Valefius has obferved) to underftand any but the Nazarenes and Ebionites.

4. *This opinion, which the Nazarenes and Ebionites had of their Gofpel, prevailed fo far, as to be believed by a great many, if not by moft.* Jerome exprefsly tells us, that, in his time, *it was believed by moft to be the true and authentick Gofpel of Matthew* [d]. And Eufebius tells us, that *it was acknowledged to be a genuine book, by moft in his time, and that it was rejeƈted only by fome.* His words are ; " Among thefe, viz.

---

[a] Porro ipfum Hebraicum habetur ufque hodie in Cæfurienfi bibliotheca, quam Pamphilus Martyr ftudiofiffime confecit. Mihi quoque a Nazaræis, qui in Beroea, urbe Syriæ, hoc volumine utuntur, defcribendi facultas fuit. Catalog. Script. Ecclef. ad Matth.

[b] Τῶν λοιπῶν Εὐαγγελίων σμικρὸν ἐποιεῖτο λόγον. Eufeb. Hift. Eccl. l. 3. c. 27.

Τὸ καθ' Ἑϐραίους Εὐαγγέλιον —ᾧ μάλιϛα Ἑϐραίων οἱ τὸν Χριϛὸν παραδιξάμινοι χαίρουσι. Hift. Eccl. l. 3. c. 25.

[d] In Evangelio, quo utuntur Nazareni et Ebionitæ, quod nuper in Græcum de Hebræo fermone tranftulimus, et quod vocatur a plerifque Matthæi authenticum. Comm. in Matth. lib. 2. c. 12.

" the

" the spurious books, some place the Gospel according to the
" Hebrews." His using the word τινὲς, and saying they were
only *some*, who looked upon this Gospel as spurious and Apocryphal, is a plain intimation, that *a great many believed it to
be genuine* [a]. It is not at all strange, that the Nazarenes
should endeavour to persuade the world, that their Gospel was
the true one; and should gain credit with those, who were not
able to contradict them.

5. *This current and commonly received opinion was most certainly false.* Here I must take it for granted, that our present
Greek copies are authentick and true, I mean only so far as
to contain all that St. Matthew wrote; and if so, it is certain
the Gospels of the Nazarenes and Ebionites were spurious,
for they contain a great many idle fables, which are not in
ours. These interpolations or additions are in part collected
by Grotius [b], Father Simon [c]; and others; but very fully, and
set down at large, by the learned and laborious Fabricius, in
his useful book, intitled, *Codex Apocryphus Novi Testamenti,*
&c. [d] Any one, who will be at the pains to consult the
places referred to, will soon perceive, that *the Gospel of St.
Matthew according to the Hebrews, which the Nazarenes and
Ebionites made use of, was very different from our present Gospel of St. Matthew.* The same may be undeniably proved
from Jerome's translating it into Greek; had it been the
same, or had there been only some little difference between
this Hebrew Gospel, and the true Greek copies, which were
received into the Canon of the Church, it had been very absurd for Jerome to have translated it out of the Hebrew into
Greek, as he says he did. Now from the foregoing observations it is very easy to perceive, how it came to pass that so
many of the antient Fathers were imposed upon, and made to
believe that St. Matthew wrote his Gospel in Hebrew. There
was a Gospel in the world, which went under St. Matthew's

---

[a] Ἤδη δ' ἐν τούτοις (sc. λόγοις)
τινὲς καὶ αὐτὸ καθ' Ἑβραίους Εὐαγγέλιον κατέλεξαν. Loc. jam cit. Τινὲς,
i. e. a paucis quibusdam. Vid.
Millii Proleg. in N. T. §. 40.

[b] In Titul. Matth.
[c] Critic. Hist. of the New Test.
par. 1. c. 7. p. 68, &c. Du Pin,
vol. 2. c. 2. §. 3.
[d] From p. 356 to p. 371.

name, wrote in Hebrew, and declared by those, who used it, to be the original of St. Matthew; the credulous multitude believed as the Nazarenes did, and so the mistake was spread in the world. It is not possible but the Nazarenes would gain credit with some; nay it has been proved, that the generality did believe it; and therefore it can be no wonder, that so many have asserted it.

C H A P. XVIII.

The Fathers fell into the Mistake that St. Matthew wrote in Hebrew, because none of them, except Origen, Jerome, and Epiphanius, understood that Language. They were, upon that Account, unable to compare the Gospel of the Nazarenes with their own Greek Copies, and discover its Spuriousness. This confirmed by a Remark, that none of the Fathers, who assert St. Matthew wrote in Hebrew, have cited the Gospel of the Nazarenes, except the three mentioned, who understood that Language. The Reasons assigned, why they (Epiphanius, Jerome, and Origen) fell into the same Mistake. Papias, the first Christian Writer who asserts this, was a very fabulous and credulous Person, yet was followed by many of the Fathers in his Mistakes (as Eusebius observes), by reason of his Antiquity. His Testimony in this Matter proved by one part of it to be false.

IT will very much add to the probability of the foregoing account, that of all those Fathers, who have fallen into this mistake, there were none that were able to prove it to be so, except Origen, Epiphanius, and Jerome. They did not any of them understand the Hebrew language, and consequently not being able to compare the Gospel of the Nazarenes with their own Greek copies, could not perceive its interpolations and additions, and so were under a sort of necessity of believing the common report. Had they been able to have read

this

this Hebrew Gospel, and fo to have perceived the difference between it and their own, they would certainly have rejected it, as not agreeable to St. Matthew's original, and confequently have loft the foundation of their opinion, that St. Matthew wrote in Hebrew.

To fupport this, I have made the following remark, viz. *That not one of all thofe Fathers, who have afferted the Gofpel of St. Matthew to be originally wrote in Hebrew, have made any ufe of the Gofpel of the Nazarenes in their writings, except the three above-mentioned, who underftood Hebrew.* There is not the leaft evidence that either Papias, Irenæus, Eufebius, Auftin, Chryfoftom, Cyril, or Theophylact, ever faw, or made ufe of, this Gofpel. It is not fo much as once referred to in all their writings [a]. This could only be, becaufe they did not underftand the language in which it was written: had they underftood Hebrew, no doubt fome of them would have ufed it, as well as thofe three Fathers who did. Indeed it has been thought by feveral learned men, that Papias made ufe of this Gofpel, and cited the ftory of the adulterous woman out of it. So Father Simon ; " Papias faith, that the hiftory of " the woman, who was accufed of many fins before our Sa- " viour, is to be read in the Gofpel that was called *According* " *to the Hebrews.*" But this is a very great miftake, which this and other learned men are fallen into, for want of carefully obferving Eufebius's words ; he does not fay that *Papias took this out of the Gofpel according to the Hebrews* ; but that this ftory *was among Papias's works,* and then adds in his own words, *that this hiftory is in that Gofpel* [b]. From whence it does not follow, that he, any more than Papias, had read this Gofpel. If then none of thofe, who affert St. Matthew to have wrote in Hebrew, did underftand Hebrew, and if none of them did fee the Gofpel of the Nazarenes ; no wonder they fell in with the common report of the Nazarenes, that their Gofpel was the true original one of St. Matthew. Thus I

---

[a] The ground of my afferting this, is Fabricius's collection of the fragments of it, among which there is not one cited out of any of thofe Fathers.

[b] Eufeb. Hift. Eccl. l. 3. c. 29.

have

have fhewn, how very likely it was, the Fathers fhould fall into this miftake.

This is fo far from being a precarious fuppofition, that it may be made very evident by that which Epiphanius tells us; viz. " That the Nazarenes, in his time, had the Gofpel of " Matthew very complete in Hebrew; for without doubt it " is preferved by them till this day, as it was at firft written " in Hebrew letters; but I cannot tell whether they have " taken away the genealogies from Abraham to Chrift, or " not [a]." Now from thefe words it is evident,

1. That he never faw the Gofpel of the Nazarenes; and fo,

2. He thought it to be the very fame with that which St. Matthew wrote; wherefore,

3. He could not but believe St. Matthew wrote his Gofpel at firft in Hebrew.

This was the cafe with Epiphanius; and if it was fo with one that was a native of Paleftine, that underftood the Hebrew language; if, I fay, he was thus impofed upon by the Nazarenes, how much more eafily would thofe be impofed upon, who lived in diftant countries, and knew nothing at all of the language.

It feems indeed a little ftrange, that Origen and Jerome, who both underftood the language, and faw the Gofpel of the Nazarenes, fhould fall into this error. They compared frequently the Gofpel of the Nazarenes, and the Greek copies together, and cite them very often in their works; nay, and Jerome tranflated this Gofpel into Greek and Latin: they could not therefore be deceived, and think it the original of St. Matthew, and therefore conclude that St. Matthew wrote in Hebrew.

This indeed feems to be a very confiderable objection,

---

[a] Ἔχυσι δὲ τὸ κατὰ Ματθαῖον Εὐαγγέλιον πληρίτατον Ἑβραΐςί· ῶας᾽ αὐτοῖς γὰρ σαφῶς τῦτο, καθὼς ἐξ ἀρχῆς ἐγράφη Ἑβραϊκῖς γράμμασιν, ἔτι σώζεται. Οὐκ οἶδα δὲ, εἰ καὶ τὰς γενεαλογίας τὰς ἀπὸ τῦ Ἀβραὰμ ἄχρι Χριςῦ ῶεριεῖλον. Hæref. 29. §. 9.

which

which has not, I think, been at all taken notice of yet. In anſwer to it, I obſerve;

1. As to Origen, that he does not deliver it as his opinion, that St. Matthew wrote in Hebrew, *but only as what he received by tradition*; unleſs he mention it ſomewhere elſe in his writings, beſides that place cited by Euſebius[a]. But,

2. Suppoſe both Jerome and he had aſſerted this, it might perhaps proceed *from a too great reſpeƈt to ſo univerſal a tradition.* They found it was aſſerted by every body, and therefore they believed it: it is well known, how very little ſuſpicious the firſt Chriſtians were of the traditions of the Church. But,

3. This will appear more probable, if we conſider, *who among the Gentile Chriſtians was the firſt author of this opinion.* As far as we can trace it, it owes its original to Papias, Biſhop of Hierapolis[b]; who, though a perſon of a very weak genius, both credulous and fabulous, was very likely to be believed, even by Jerome and Origen. He was cotemporary with the Apoſtles, and paſſed under the ſpecious charaƈter of being *a hearer of St. John, an intimate of Polycarp, and a man of the greateſt antiquity*[c]; and this poſſibly might, in ſome meaſure, influence theſe two learned men to give into the received opinion, without making themſelves a ſtriƈt inquiry thereinto.

4. This conjeƈture is very much confirmed by a remark, which Euſebius has made concerning this Papias[d], viz. " That he has related a great many fabulous ſtories of our " Saviour, particularly that he ſhould reign corporally on " earth, for a thouſand years after the reſurreƈtion. Theſe

<hr>

[a] Ὡς ἐν παραδόσει μαθὼν περὶ τῶν τισσάρων Εὐαγγελίων. Hiſtor. Eccl. l. 6. c. 25.

[b] L. 6. c. 39.

[c] Ταῦτα δὲ καὶ Παπίας Ἰωάννυ μὲν ἀκουςὴς, Πολυκάρπυ δὲ ἑταῖρος γιγονὼς, ἀρχαῖος ἀνήρ. Iren. adv. Hæreſ. l. 5. c. 33. Concerning Papias's age, and this teſtimony of Irenæus, ſee the learned Mr. Dod-

well's Diſſert. in Iren. 1. §. 3, &c.

[d] Σφόδρα γάρ τοι σμικρὸς ὢν τὸν νῦν, ὡς ἂν ἐκ τῶν αὐτοῦ λόγων τεκμηράμενόν εἰπεῖν, φαίνεται· πλὴν καὶ τοῖς μετ' αὐτὸν πλείϛοις ὅσοις τῶν ἐκκλησιαϛικῶν, τῆς ὁμοίας αὐτῷ δόξης παραίτιος γίγονε, τὴν ἀρχαιότητα τ' ἀνδρὸς προϛεϛελημίνοις. Hiſt. Eccl. l. 3. c. 39.

" things,

" things, fays Eufebius, he imagined, miftaking the Apoftles'
" meaning—for he was a perſon of a very mean genius, as
" appears from his works; yet almoſt all Ecclefiaſtical wri-
" ters were led by him into this miſtake, influenced by the
" antiquity of the man; or as Valeſius renders it, *hominis*
" *vetuſtate ſententiam ſuam tuentibus,* i. e. defending · their
" opinion by the argument of its author's antiquity." This
now makes it more probable, that Origen and Jerome, who
were able to confute it, ſhould yet receive this common tradition.

Having here had occaſion to mention Papias, as the firſt
who publiſhed this opinion of St. Matthew's being written
originally in Hebrew, I cannot but take notice of *one thing in
his teſtimony, which ſeems to invalidate it, or at leaſt to make
it very dubious and uncertain.* What I mean is this: he ſays[a],
that St. Matthew wrote his Goſpel in Hebrew, and that *every
one interpreted it as they were able,* ἡρμήνευσι δ᾽ αὐτὰ ὡς ἠδύνατο
ἵκαςος. Now hence it follows, that in his time there was no
authentick Greek Verſion made, if there was any at all. This
Father Simon (though it be to ſerve a bad purpoſe) does
juſtly infer[b]; " If," ſays he, " there had been in his time
" (viz. Papias's) a Greek Verſion of the Goſpel of St. Mat-
" thew, which had been made by ſome Apoſtle, he would not
" have failed to have told us of it." But notwithſtanding
this aſſertion of Papias, there ſeems to be very good reaſon to
believe the contrary; for all the writers of that age, cotemporaries with Papias, and ſome of them older than he, when they
cite this Goſpel, do cite it as it is in our preſent Greek
copies. Clemens Romanus, Ignatius, Barnabas, Polycarp
(an acquaintance of Papias's[c]), Irenæus (an acquaintance of
Polycarp's[d]), and Juſtin Martyr, do cite this Goſpel in ſuch
a manner, as undeniably evidences, not only that they made
uſe of the ſame copies, but alſo the ſame with our preſent
Greek ones. This I aſſert upon a ſtrict examination of this

[a] Eufeb. Hiſt. Eccl. l. 3. c. 39.　　[c] Iren. Adv. Hæreſ. l. 5. c. 33.
[b] Critic. Hiſt. of the New Teſt.　　[d] Eufeb. Hiſt. Eccl. l. 5. c. 20.
Part 1. c. 9. p. 79.

matter

matter in each of thefe authors.   Now this could not poffibly have been, if, according to Papias, every one tranflated as they were able, and there was no common verfion.   Nothing can be more abfurd than to fuppofe, that they fhould all happen to make ufe of the fame Greek words.   Befides, none of thefe Fathers, except. Barnabas, did underftand, or were able to tranflate at all out of the Hebrew.   There muft therefore (fuppofing St. Matthew to have wrote in Hebrew) been fome common verfion at this time into Greek, and confequently Papias muft be miftaken in this part of his teftimony; and if fo, it feems very reafonable to conclude, he was miftaken in the other part alfo.   And thus I think we have fet afide the firft and moft antient teftimony, that St. Matthew wrote in Hebrew, and that which, together with the tradition of the Nazarenes, feems to have led fo many of the Fathers into this miftake.

Upon the whole, this is what I judge to be clear from what has been faid : the Nazarenes made very early a tranflation of St. Matthew's Gofpel into Hebrew, for the ufe of the Jews, with feveral additions ; this they ftill called, *The Gofpel of St. Matthew,* and declared to be his original ; Papias, a filly and credulous writer, believed them ; and fo, in fucceeding ages, the Nazarenes ftill declaring the fame, the opinion paffed from one to another without any contradiction .

---

* Les Nazaréens écrivèrent leur Evangile fur les inftruétions ou Memoires de S. Matthieu, et ils en parlèrent comme de l'Evangile de S. Matthieu. Papias les crut de bonne foi, et cette opinion paffe ainfi de main en main.   Mr. L'Enfant, Chaplain to the King of Pruffia, in his Remarks upon Dr. Mill's Teftament, in a Letter to Mr. Le Clerc, Biblioth. choifie. Tom. 16. Art. 5. p. 292.

C H A P. XIX.

Several Arguments, by which it appears probable, that St. Mat-
thew did not write his Gospel in Hebrew. The Greek was
the most common Language, and for that Reason that Gospel
was most likely to be useful therein. The Supposing it a Trans-
lation makes its Inspiration dubious. It is not probable, that
the Original Hebrew would ever have been lost. The He-
brew one we have now, is certainly a Translation out of
Greek.

THOUGH there is not, that I know of, any one considerable argument to prove, that St. Matthew wrote
in Hebrew, besides the testimony of the Fathers; yet very
great numbers of learned men have thought that of itself sufficient. The Papists almost all, and a great many among the
Protestants (viz. Casaubon, Grotius, Dr. Cave, Vossius, &c.),
have submitted to the authority of the Fathers in this matter.
On the other hand, the warmest advocates for the Reformation (viz. Calvin, Chemnitius, Chamier, Whitaker, Mich.
Waltherus, &c.) contend, that our present Greek copies are
the original in which St. Matthew wrote.

Having in the foregoing Chapter endeavoured to shew,
how it came to pass, that the Fathers so universally fell into
the mistake of St. Matthew's being wrote in Hebrew, I would
now offer two or three other arguments, whereby it will appear, this Gospel was originally written in Greek, and not in
Hebrew.

1. *The Greek was the most proper language for St. Matthew*
to write in, in order to answer the ends and designs of his writ-
ing. Here I must take it for granted, that St. Matthew's
design in writing, was the same as that of the other writers of
the New Testament, viz. the propagating the history and
doctrines of Christ, to as great a part of the world as possible.

For

For though St. Matthew (as well as St. Mark, and perhaps all the sacred writers of the New Testament) was more immediately influenced by some particular occasion to write; yet there can be no doubt but that he would write his Gospel, so that it might be of the most extensive usefulness. It is hard to suppose him under the conduct of divine inspiration, and not suppose him to write so, as his Gospel should be most useful and beneficial to the world; and if so, then it was necessary he should write in Greek. The Hebrew language was then but very little known and used, in comparison of what the Greek was. Nay the Latin, the language of the empire, was not at that time, when St. Matthew wrote, near so much in use as the Greek : *the Greek language is read in all nations, but the Latin is confined within very narrow limits,* says Cicero[a]. Hence it is observable, that St. Paul, though he wrote to the Jews or Hebrews, yet, for the more extensive usefulness of that inspired Epistle, wrote in Greek. And so also did St. Peter and St. James, although their Epistles were immediately designed for, and directed to, the Jews.

2. Our present Greek copy of St. Matthew is not a translation out of Hebrew, *because the supposing it to be so, makes its authority very precarious and uncertain.* This argument is founded upon the supposition of this (as well as other historical books) being wrote by the influences and inspiration of the Holy Spirit. Now the supposing it a translation, is inconsistent with that authority and esteem, which every inspired book does necessarily demand. This is evident, because we have not the least evidence of the inspiration of the translator, nor the least reason to conclude the translation is just. The Fathers, who were imposed upon to believe it originally wrote in Hebrew, found themselves under a necessity of imputing the translation to some inspired person, though they can by no means agree who the person was. The Author of the Synopsis which goes under Athanasius's name, says; *It was translated by James, the brother of our Lord, according to the*

---

[a] Græca leguntur in omnibus fere gentibus, Latina suis finibus, exiguis sane, continentur. Orat. pro Arch. Poet. §. 23.

flesh.

flesh [a]. Theophylact attributes it to St. John the Evangelist, according to the tradition that was current in his time [b]. Anastasius Sinaita says it was done by St. Luke and St. Paul jointly [c]. Nicephorus ascribes it to Barnabas [d]. Such was the diversity of opinions among the antients in this matter; but in this they all agree, that it was necessary it should be done by an inspired person. So also the more modern writers, especially the Protestants, who believe it a translation (though few, I think, except Dr. Mill [e] pretend to fix the person), all find it necessary to conclude it done by an inspired person. So Casaubon [f] and many others; but the truth is, they have no just foundation for saying so: Jerome honestly confesses, *it was very uncertain, who translated it out of Hebrew into Greek* [g]: and if so, it is impossible it should have equal authority with the other books. For all we know to the contrary, it may be a very false and corrupt translation; it may be done by a person no way qualified for such a work; and does not this now make its authority dubious and uncertain? For my part I freely own, if I believed it to be a translation made by a person I know nothing of, I could not yield it that same respect, and have that same value for it, as the other parts of the sacred writings. The Papists, who are always endeavouring to lessen the authority of the Scriptures, that so they might make them depend upon their church for their authority, were very well aware of this; and hence there is not, I think, above one or two of them (viz. Cajetan, and Erasmus, if he be to be called a Papist), but have fallen in with the common error of the Fathers. Baronius, Father Simon, Du Pin, and the

---

[a] Ἑρμηνεύθη δὲ ὑπὸ Ἰακώβε τε ἀδελφε τε Κυρίε τὸ κατὰ σάρκα. Vid. Casaub. ad Baron. Annal. c. 16. §. 115.

[b] Præfat. in Matth.

[c] Apud Casaub. ibid.

[d] Hist. Eccl. l. 16. c. 37.

[e] Prolegom. in Nov. Test. §. 66.

[f] Quæ diversitas sententiarum, ut de vero auctore certo pronuntiare nos vetat, ita illud certissime de-monstrat, ipsis Apostolorum temporibus, ab uno illorum, aut illorum auspiciis, vel potius Spiritus Sancti, cujus ipsi erant organa, Græcum textum ex Hebraico esse confectum. Exercit. ad Baron. Annal. c. 15. §. 12.

[g] Quod quis postea in Græcum transtulerit, non satis certum est. Catal. Eccles. Script. in voc. Matth.

rest

reſt of the Popiſh writers, have been of this opinion, and being ſo, have not failed to draw the conſequence I am now ſpeaking of, from it, viz. *that our preſent Greek copies are of very dubious authority.* "I affirm it," ſays Baronius [a], "that "the authority of the Greek text is very uncertain, unleſs we "had the original Hebrew to compare with it." The learned Caſaubon in his anſwer to Baronius (though he believed St. Matthew wrote his Goſpel in Hebrew) was very unwilling to allow the Cardinal's conſequence; "If," ſays he, "the Greek "text of this Goſpel depends upon the Hebrew, then this "Goſpel, as we have it now, is of no authority;" and adds a little after; "then the faith of the true Catholick Church muſt "depend upon the faith or credit of Hereticks *(he means the* "*Roman Church),* which God forbid [b]." To this Father Simon anſwers, heartily eſpouſing the cauſe of Baronius, and ſays in ſo many words; "There is nothing, but the authority "of the church alone, that gives authority to this Verſion, and "that can oblige us to prefer it before the Hebrew or Chal-"daick copy of the Nazarenes [c]." However Caſaubon and other Proteſtants may ſeem to ſhuffle off, and elude theſe conſequences, they ſeem to be inevitable. Hence it was juſtly remarked by Mr. L'Enfant in his letter to Le Clerc [d]; "It "appears to me very probable, that St. Matthew wrote his "Goſpel in Greek, as the other Apoſtles did, and with the "ſame deſign. For I can think of nothing that ſounds more "like a Papiſt, than to talk of the work of an Apoſtle tranſ-"lated into Greek, by I do not know who, nor I do not know "how." As we would therefore avoid this conſequence of

---

[a] Dico, quod Græcus textus cujus fidei ſit, niſi collato cum Hebræo originali, affirmare non poſſumus. Apud Caſaubon. Exercit. c. 16. §. 115.

[b] Si auctoritas Græci textus pendet ab Hebraico textu; quum Hebræa dudum perierint, neque uſquam extent hodie; ſequitur neceſſario, nullum hodie ejus Evangelii debere eſſe pondus, nullam auctoritatem—Adde quod hæc ſententia fidem Catholicæ Eccleſiæ fa-

cit pendere (nefas dictu) ab hæretticorum fide. Caſaub. ibid.
Critic. Hiſt. of the New Teſt. Par. 1. c. 9.

[d] Il me paroit fort vraiſemblable, que St. Matthieu écrivit ſon Evangile en Grec, comme les autres, et dans le même deſſein. Car je ne trouve rien, qui ait plus l'air d'un Romain, qu'une Verſion Gréque d'un ouvrage d'un Apôtre, faite par je ne ſais qui, ni comment. Biblioth. Choiſie, tom. 16. Art. 5. p. 292.

making the authority of this Gofpel uncertain, we muft conclude it not to be a tranflation.   I would only add further on
this head, that not only the Papifts, but the Jews, and other
enemies of Chriftianity, will be very likely to improve this
affertion to the difhonour of this Gofpel, fo far as to make
them rejeɛt as uncertain one of the moft valuable parts of facred Hiftory.   This is not only what might be reafonably ex-
peɛted, but what has been really matter of faɛt [a].   So the
learned Jew, with whom Limborch difputes, argues againft
this Gofpel ; " They fay," fays he, " that Matthew wrote in
" Hebrew, but the original is loft ; afterwards his Gofpel ap-
" peared in Greek, but no body knows who tranflated it [b].

3. St. Matthew's Gofpel was not wrote originally in Hebrew, but in Greek ; becaufe, if fo, the original Gofpel is entirely loft, which cannot be fuppofed.   If it was wrote in Hebrew, it is very certain that which we now have in that language under St. Matthew's name, is not it.   For this was
firft publifhed by Munfter, and he owns he received it from
the Jews *tattered, torn, and very imperfeɛt*, and *that he himfelf
added what he thought neceffary :* fo that it is very ftrange,
that Quinquarboreus, in his preface to this Hebrew Gofpel [c],
fhould imagine it to be the very fame Gofpel which St. Matthew wrote, although he had obferved what Munfter faid.
I need not be at the pains to confute this opinion : it is evidently a Verfion of our prefent Greek ; it has here and there
a few words added, and fometimes a few omitted ; yet it is (as
far as I have obferved) a pretty good Verfion, though I dare
affirm it is but a late one.   If St. Matthew therefore wrote in
Hebrew, the original is loft ; but this cannot be fuppofed,
without alfo fuppofing the firft Chriftians and primitive
churches guilty of unpardonable negligence.   Is it likely a
treafure of fo much value, would be no more regarded ?   If it

---

[a] Vid. Sixt. Senenf. l. 7. de
Evang. Matth. Hæref.

[b] Matthæus fertur Hebraico i-
diomate fcripfiffe ; fed quod, eo
autographo deperdito, Græco fermone poftea tranflatum apparuit, ab
incerto autore ea lingua donatum.

Limborch. de Verit. Chrift. Relig.
quæf. 4. num. 8.

[c] Quod autem hoc ipfum fit E-
vangelium, quod D. Matthæus
Hebraice fcripfit, ambigere quis
poffit. Edit. Parif. A. D. 1551.

was

was wrote in Hebrew, it was wrote for the Jews, and the Jews were not wont to be so careless of their sacred books. The Bishop and Church at Jerusalem would, no doubt, have safely preserved a book so valuable. " Surely," says Chamier [a], " the negligence of the Universal Church, or even the " Church at Jerusalem, would not be so great as to let the " original of St. Matthew be lost, that there is not the least " of it to be found; nay that it should not only now be not " extant, but even utterly unknown in the second century." There were, no doubt, copies of this Gospel taken as soon as it was published, and spread among the Jews every where; and is it likely that all these copies should be so entirely lost? This is hard to be conceived, and therefore it is very improbable that St. Matthew wrote first in Hebrew.

CHAP. XX.

Though St. Matthew's Gospel be supposed a Translation out of Hebrew, yet it was not for that Reason more liable to Dislocation or Disorder.

AS it is probable, that our present Greek copies of St. Matthew are not a translation out of Hebrew; so

2. It is certain that if they were, they would not have been at all upon that account more liable to the confusion and disorder Mr. Whiston supposes. I confess I am not able to guess, how the translation (supposing it to be so) could any way influence, or occasion these dislocations. It were to be wished that Mr. Whiston had told us, how the translating it could have had this bad influence, or that he had produced one single instance of any one book in the world, that has thus suffered by its being translated. Of the vast number of Versions, that have

[a] Non fuisse tantam sive Ecclesiæ Universalis, sive etiam Hierosolymitanæ, negligentiam, ut ejus Editionis nullum sit omnino vestigium conservatum, &c. Panstrat. Cathol. l. 11. c. 8. §. 8.

been made of the Old, and the other parts of the New Teſtament into all languages, not one has produced this bad effect ;
neither the Seventy, nor Jonathan, nor Onkelos, nor any other
of the Greek or Chaldee tranſlators, diſordered the Old Teſtament by their Verſions; neither the Syriack, nor Arabick,
nor any of the many Latin tranſlators of the New Teſtament,
did occaſion any ſuch diſlocations in it; and is it then to be
credited, that the tranſlator of St. Matthew ſhould be the occaſion of ſo many diſlocations in this part of his Goſpel?
When not one of all the Verſions in the world has occa-
ſioned ſo much as one ſingle diſorder, is it likely the tranſlator
of St. Matthew ſhould occaſion about twenty, in ten ſhort
chapters?

But to ſhew the abſurdity of this ſuppoſition, I would argue in the following manner:

If the tranſlation of this Goſpel be ſuppoſed to influence,
and cauſe the tranſpoſition and diſorder of theſe ſeveral parts,
then it is plain theſe parts were not tranſpoſed or miſplaced before the tranſlator began his work, and conſequently the diſorder muſt happen either *in the time of tranſlating*, or *afterwards*. It was not likely to be done *in the time of tranſlating*;
for why ſhould a perſon's reading a book with a deſign to
tranſlate it into another language, any more occaſion a diſorder in it, than if he had read it with no ſuch deſign? If it was
in its right order *then* (according to the ſuppoſition), it is
much more reaſonable to ſuppoſe the tranſlator would endeavour to keep it ſo, than by any means miſplace it. Thus it
was not done in the time of tranſlating; and it is very evident the tranſlation could not influence the diſorder *after it
was made*, but would rather be a good means to prevent any
ſuch diſorder happening to the original, if there had been any
danger of it.

The other remark, which Mr. Whiſton makes, is, that
*this diſorder concludes, and the true order begins to be obſerved,
at a very remarkable period, viz. the death of St. John the Baptiſt, and the commencing of our Saviour's ſingle miniſtry thereupon* [a]. To this I think it ſufficient to anſwer, that there are

[a] P. 111.

ſeveral

feveral other periods of the Gofpel hiftory, as remarkable as th.s, where no diforder has happened.

CHAP. XXI.

Several Arguments to prove, that our prefent Greek copies of St. Matthew are not at all tranfpofed or difordered, fince that Evangelift's firft writing. No Book ever was thus difordered. It does not feem agreeable to the Care, which Divine Providence always exercifed towards the facred Books, to permit this to have happened to St. Matthew's Gofpel. No other Part of St. Matthew's Gofpel difordered, and therefore not this. The Diflocations, which Mr. Whifton fuppofes, could not happen to this Gofpel in the Apoftles' Time.

HITHERTO I have been confidering what Mr. Whifton offers in defence of his propofition, and by many ways fhewing how unreafonable it is, to affert this Gofpel fo tranfpofed and mifplaced, as he does. All that I fhall do further, fhall be only to add three or four other arguments, by which it will appear, that *our prefent copies of St. Matthew have not fuffered any diflocations, but are in this refpect the very fame, as when St. Matthew at firft wrote.* In order to which I obferve;

1. That there never has yet been difcovered or proved an inftance of any fuch tranfpofitions and mifplacings, in any writings facred or profane, in any language, by any means whatfoever. It is indeed very difficult to affert and defend an univerfal negative propofition, and to fay fuch a thing *never has been,* unlefs the being of it be impoffible, and imply a contradiction to fome certain and well-eftablifhed truth. Though indeed fuch a diforder as Mr. Whifton fuppofes, be not a thing in itfelf abfolutely impoffible to have happened either to this, or fome other book ; yet I will venture to affert, it is fuch a diforder, as never has happened to any one whatfoever. If

ever

ever fuch a thing did happen, it was moft likely to have been before the art of writing was brought to that perfection, and had received thofe improvements, which it had in St. Matthew's time: inftead of this, not one of the books of the Old Teftament, nor Homer, Hefiod, Demofthenes, Ifocrates, &c. who wrote long before St. Matthew's time; nor any of the books of the New Teftament; nor Cicero, Ovid, Horace, nor any of the Roman poets or hiftorians, who wrote about his time, have fuffered any fuch misfortune, as Mr. Whifton fuppofes this Gofpel to have done. It is true indeed, Spinoza, and after him Father Simon, and Mr. Whifton, *have imagined fome fuch diflocations to have happened to fome parts of the Old Teftament* (as has been faid in the Preface). But after the clofeft examination of what they have faid, I can find little more than bare affertions; and therefore till fome further proof, than yet has been, be made, I muft conclude their opinion falfe.

2. It does not feem confiftent with that care, which Divine Providence always did exercife, and may be reafonably fuppofed always would exercife, towards the books of infpiration, to fuppofe this Gofpel fo confufed and difordered as Mr. Whifton does. Every one, who is at all acquainted with the hiftory of the Jewifh nation, muft needs acknowledge, that a remarkably kind Providence has always concerned itfelf in the prefervation of the books of the Old Teftament. In the moft degenerate ftate of that unhappy nation, in the times of their ignorance and idolatry, their flavery and captivity, the books which were given them by God, and received into the Canon of their Church, were preferved fafe and uncorrupted, notwithftanding the malicious efforts of their enemies to the contrary. It does not appear that any one of all thefe books has been loft [a], though their conquering enemies endeavoured to the utmoft to deftroy them. A remarkable inftance of this Jofephus tells us [b]; viz. that *Antiochus Epiphanes, when he*

---

[a] Vide Turretin. de Scrip. Quæft. 7. et Spanhem. Dub. Evang. Par. 2. Dub. 88.

[b] Ἡφανίζιτο δὲ, ἴ πυ βίβλος εὑρεθείη ἱερὰ, καὶ νόμος, καὶ παρ᾽ οἷς εὑρεθείη, καὶ ὅτοι κακοὶ κακῶς ἀπώλοντο. Antiq. Jud. l. 12. c. 5. §. 4. The fame account we have 1 Macc. i. 56, 57.

bad

had fubdued *Jerufalem, tried all poffible methods to abolifh the religion of the Jews; and, in order to that, made particular fearch after the facred volume, deftroying it wherever it was found, and punifhing with death all thofe in whofe poffeffion it was.* But he, who was the author of them, took care of them, and preferved them not only from being loft, but from being in any remarkable degree corrupted. It is true indeed, there are fome flight corruptions crept into the text, both of the Old and New Teftament, through the carelefsnefs of tranfcribers; there are a great number of various lections in both; but thefe are fuch as without a conftant miracle could not but happen, and are to be found in as great, or greater number, in feveral of the profane authors (as the learned Dr. Bentley has very well obferved *), and are for the moft part fuch, that it is not much matter which reading we choofe. But the corruptions, which Mr. Whifton fuppofes in St. Matthew, are of another nature : thefe are fuch as render the text of the Gofpel very precarious, and make it depend upon the judgment and fancy of every one, who pleafes to alter it. And is this now confiftent with the care of Divine Providence? Is it likely God would permit this ufeful Gofpel to be thus confufedly put together by fuch a blunderer, who out of twenty parts could not put but *one* in its proper order? This fure can never be believed by any, who acknowledge a divine Providence to have concerned itfelf at all about the facred volume.

3. It is very improbable this part of St. Matthew's Gofpel fhould be fo difordered and confufed; becaufe all the other part of it is exactly in the order, in which the Evangelift wrote, without the leaft tranfpofition. Mr. Whifton's hypothefis, by which he accounts for the diflocation of the feveral periods of the former part of this Gofpel, is, that they were wrote upon *feparate and diftinct* pieces of paper : now upon this hypothefis I argue thus;

Either St. Matthew wrote the other parts of his Gofpel on fmall pieces of paper, or he did not. If it be faid, he did not, then it is yet more unaccountable, that he fhould write this for-

* Anfwer to the Difcourfe of Free Thinking, Part I. p. 64, &c.

　　　　　　　　　　　mer

mer part fo : it is incredible, that thefe fourteen chapters fhould be written on twenty feveral pieces of paper, and the other fourteen on one large roll. If on the other hand it be faid, that St. Matthew wrote the latter part of his Gofpel, as he did the former, on many pieces of paper ; then it is no lefs incredible, that none of thefe pieces fhould have the fame misfortune to be difordered and mifplaced, as the former. How can it be fuppofed poffible, that every one of the papers in the latter part fhould be in its right and due order, and not fo much as one of the former but is mifplaced, except the firft ? I conclude therefore, that the former part of this Gofpel is not mifplaced.

4. The improbability of this part of St. Matthew's Gofpel being mifplaced, will appear, if we confider that there has been no time ever fince St. Matthew wrote, in which there were not fome circumftances, which would prevent fuch a diforder. To evidence this, I argue thus ; If this part of St. Matthew's Gofpel be mifplaced, either the diforder happened in the Apoftles' time, or not till after their deceafe. But as it is improbable that it happened in their time, fo it is morally impoffible that it fhould have happened afterwards.

I. It is not probable, that this diforder could happen in the time of the Apoftles; for if it had, they would, no doubt, have rectified it. Many reafons would oblige them, not to fuffer fo great a diflocation to remain in the Gofpel hiftory. They would never recommend a book to the perufal of their converts, which they knew juftly chargeable with fuch notorious corruptions. It is much more reafonable to fuppofe, that, if this Gofpel was then mifplaced and out of order, they would reftore it to its proper order, and take care that fome copies fhould be made, in which the hiftories fhould be placed in the fame order in which the Evangelift wrote. Now if they did this, it is ftrange none of thefe copies fhould have others made from them, but all the books in the world fhould proceed from one difordered copy, made in the Apoftles' time.

It may perhaps be faid, that this diforder might happen in the Apoftles' time, and they be ignorant of it. This indeed is poffible, but very improbable. The office and bufinefs of an Apoftle was to preach the doctrine, and publifh the miracles,

racles, of Jefus Chrift. Now St. Matthew having, by the influences of the Holy Spirit, collected a very early, full, and authentick account, both of the doctrines and miracles of Chrift, there can be no doubt but the Apoftles would make ufe of it themfelves, and recommend it to the ufe of others. Not to have done this, would have been to caft that contempt upon the work of one infpired Apoftle, which we cannot fuppofe another would do; befides not to have made ufe of this, would have been to neglect one likely means of obtaining the ends of their apoftlefhip. Hence Eufebius [a] tells us, that when the pious Pantænus (who lived in the time of Irenæus and Origen) *went to preach the Gospel to the Indians, where St. Bartholomew had been preaching the Gospel before him, he found there the Gospel of St. Matthew.* No doubt the Apoftles, when they went abroad to preach the Gofpel, did take both this and the other Gofpels along with them, and left copies of them, when they were gone, for the ufe of their converts, as I fhall fhew more fully hereafter. Hence it feems very reafonable to conclude the Apoftles made ufe of this Gofpel; which if they did, they being eye-witneffes to the hiftory, could not but perceive fuch diflocations and mifplacings, as thofe which we are treating of, and fo, no doubt, would have corrected them. This argument is abundantly confirmed by a teftimony of Eufebius [a], viz. *that the three former Gospels were perused by St. John, and that he approved them.* Now if St. Matthew's Gofpel had been fo confufedly fet together, as Mr. Whifton fuppofes, St. John would certainly never have approved of it. Mr. Whifton cannot queftion this teftimony of Eufebius, having himfelf ufed it on another occafion [c]. I conclude therefore, that this diforder did not happen to this Gofpel in the Apoftles' time.

---

[a] Hift. Eccl. l. 5. c. 10. Vid. Valef. ad loc.

[b] Τῶν προαναγραφέντων τριῶν εἰς πάντας ἤδη καὶ εἰς αὐτὸν (fc. Ἰωάννην) διαδιδομένων, ἀποδέξασθαι

μὲν φασὶν, &c. Hift. Eccl. l. 3. c. 24. The fame is related by Theophylact. Præfat. in Matth.

[c] P. 132.

CHAP. XXII.

The Diforder Mr. Whifton fuppofes in the former Part of St.
Matthew's Gofpel, could not poffibly happen after the Apoftles'
Time; becaufe of the great Number of Copies, that were
fpread abroad in the World in their Time. The Time when
St. Matthew wrote, and the Diftance between that Time and
St. John's Death, confidered. That the Gofpels were very
much difperfed in the Apoftles' Time, largely proved. Mr.
Hobbes, Mr. Toland, and Mr. Dodwell's Notion of the Gof-
pels being a long while unknown and concealed, confuted by
feveral Arguments.

II. AS this diforder did not happen in the time of the
Apoftles, fo it neither did nor poffibly could happen
afterwards. Mr. Whifton does not any where hint to us, at
what time he fuppofes thefe diflocations made ; nor does Mr.
Toinard fay any more in this refpect, than that they were
done, *antiquiffima fchedarum tranfpofitione, by a very antient.*
confufion of the papers, on which they were wrote. It was
not without reafon that they thus left the time undetermined,
being well aware of the difficulties that would attend their
hypothefis, if they had determined it. As fuch diflocations
could not happen in the Apoftles' time, fo it was morally impoffible they fhould have happened afterwards : to mention no
other arguments, this will fufficiently appear by the two following confiderations.

1. That there were a very great number of thefe Gofpels,
fpread up and down in the world before the Apoftles' death.

2. The Syriack Verfion, which feems to have been made
in the Apoftles' time, has the feveral branches or periods of this
hiftory in the fame order with our prefent Greek copies.

1. The diforder or diflocation, which Mr. Whifton fuppofes in St. Matthew's Gofpel, could not poffibly happen after
the Apoftles' death ; becaufe between the firft writing of it
and

and that time, there were a very great number of true copies
spread in different parts of the world, which would certainly
prevent it.   It is not very easy, indeed, precisely to determine
the time, in which either this, or any of the Gospels, was
wrote.   The most antient account, which I have met with,
about the time of St. Matthew's writing, is in Irenæus, viz.
*that he wrote it, when St. Peter and St. Paul were preaching
the Gospel at Rome* [a].   When St. Peter was at Rome is not
very certain; Irenæus tells us here, it was the same time that
St. Paul was there, viz. in the third year of Nero (according
to Eusebius, in his Chronicon), and the fifty-ninth of Christ;
and to this most chronologers [b] agree.   Now according to this
account, this Gospel was not written till about twenty-six
years after our Lord's ascension.   But this seems very improbable, because the Christian converts cannot be supposed to
have been so long a time destitute of any written account of
our Saviour's miracles and doctrines.   It is much more likely,
that this Gospel was wrote at the time, when Eusebius has
placed it in his Chronicon, viz. in the third year of Caligula,
and the forty-first of Christ.   To this agrees the account of
Theophylact [c], that St. Matthew *wrote his Gospel about eight
years after our Lord's ascension.*   The same is affirmed at the
end of several antient manuscripts.   So, for instance, in that
of Beza (which he gave to the University of Cambridge, and
is reputed the most antient manuscript of the Gospels in the
world), there is written [d]; *The Gospel of St. Matthew was
published eight years after our Lord's ascension.*   The same is
written at the end of an antient manuscript [e] in Mr. Colbert's
library.   To the same purpose, at the end of the old Arabick
Version of this Gospel, it is written [f]; *St. Matthew wrote
eight years after our Lord ascended, in the first year of Clau-*

---

[a] Ὁ μὲν δὴ Ματθαῖος—γραφὴν
ἐξήνεγκεν Εὐαγγελίου, τῷ Πέτρῳ καὶ
τοῦ Παύλου ἐν Ῥώμῃ εὐαγγελιζομένων. Adver. Hæref. l. 3. c. 1.
[b] Helvicus, Petavius, Spanheim,
Tallents, Dr. Lightfoot, &c. Vid.
et Lactant. l. 4. c. 21.

[c] Præfat. in Matth.
[d] See Bez. ad Matt. xxviii. ult.
[e] See Father Simon Crit. Hist.
of the New Test. Par. 1. c. 11.
[f] Vid. Lud. de Dieu, ad Matt.
xxviii. ult.

dius [a]. Now if we take this laſt account, and reckon from St. Matthew's writing eight years after our Lord's aſcenſion (in the laſt years of Caligula, or the firſt of Claudius) to the death of St. John, we ſhall find the intervening ſpace to be about ſixty years ; for St. John lived till the reign of Trajan, as Irenæus [b], who lived not long after him, and Clemens Alexandrinus [c], inform us. Now Trajan, according to Euſebius [d], began his reign in the year of Chriſt 101; ſo that from St. Matthew's writing in the year of Chriſt 41 to the death of St. John in Trajan's reign, muſt be at leaſt ſixty years ; and, in this long interval, there were undoubtedly great numbers of copies of this Goſpel diſperſed in all thoſe diſtant countries, where the Goſpel was preached. Very probably many thouſand copies were made, and ſent into all thoſe places, where Chriſtianity prevailed. Euſebius [e], ſpeaking concerning the Evangeliſts in the apoſtolick times, ſays, *They travelled up and down in the world, preaching the Goſpel, and very induſtriouſly endeavoured,* τὴν τῶν θείων Εὐαγγελίων παραδιδόναι γραφήν· i. e. *to diſperſe abroad copies of the holy Goſpels.* And in another place [f] he aſſures us, that, *before St. John wrote his Goſpel, the other Goſpels were in the hands of all men.* If this be true, is it a thing credible, that of all the copies that have been known in the world, not one ſhould be derived from any of thoſe vaſt numbers of copies that were made, and ſpread abroad in the world, in the Apoſtles' time ? Can it be imagined, that all the manuſcripts in the world are derived from one confuſed, miſplaced copy, that was made after the Apoſtles' time ; and not ſo much as one from any of thoſe innumerable copies, that were in their right order till the Apoſtles' death ? This, I think, cannot without manifeſt abſurdity be ſuppoſed.

---

[a] This does not differ above half a year from the above-mentioned account out of Eufebius, of its being written in the third year of Caligula ; for he reigned but three years and ſome months, and Claudius ſucceeded him.

[b] Adv. Hæref. l. 2. c. 39. in fin.

[c] Apud Eufeb. Hift. Eccl. l. 3. c. 23.

[d] In Chronic.

[e] Hift. Eccl. l. 3. c. 37.

[f] Τῶν προαναγραφέντων τριῶν εἰς πάντας ἤδη — διαδιδομένων. l. 3. c. 24.

It

It will not be at all foreign to my present purpose, to consider a little more particularly, what a great number of copies
of the Gospels, and particularly of St. Matthew's, were spread
abroad in the world in the Apostles' time, at least before the
death of St. John. I am the more inclined to consider this
matter, because, I find, a very learned writer has taken some
pains to persuade the world, *that the Gospels, and other writ-*
ings of the New Testament, lay for a long time concealed and
unobserved in the world. The person I mean is Mr. Dodwell, who in his elaborate Dissertations upon Irenæus [a] tells
us, *That the Canonical writings of the New Testament lay con-*
cealed and unknown in the coffers of some private churches, or
perhaps some private persons, till the later times of Trajan, or
perhaps of Adrian (i. e. till the year of Christ 120, or perhaps
130.); *so that they were not at all known by the Catholick*
Church. He proceeds for a page or two, in saying things
much to the same purpose. Mr. Toland, observing how
much this passage would serve his purpose, *to render the Canon*
of Scripture uncertain, transcribes it at large in his Amyntor,
and declares his assent to the truth of it [b]. Mr. Hobbes, in
his Leviathan, is very much of the same opinion; he says [c],
The copies of the books of the New Testament were, not many—
That the Council of Laodicea is the first we know of, that re-
commended the Bible to the then Christian Churches—That the
copies of the books of the New Testament were then only in the
hands of the ecclesiasticks, &c. I do not design particularly to
discuss this whimsical and groundless opinion. Mr. Nye,
in his Answer to Amyntor [d], Mr. Le Clerc, in his Reflections
on these two Sections of Mr. Dodwell [e], and Archbishop Te-
nison, in his Answer to Leviathan [f], have sufficiently done this
already. I shall only endeavour by two or three arguments to

---

[a] Latitabant enim usque ad re-
centiora illa, seu Trajani, seu etiam
fortasse Hadriani tempora, in priva-
tarum ecclesiarum, seu etiam hominum scriniis Scripta illa Canonica,
ne ad Ecclesiæ Catholicæ notitiam
pervenirent. Dissert. 1. §. 38.

[b] Pag. 78.
[c] Leviath. Par. 3. c. 33.
[d] P. 41.
[e] In his third Dissertation annexed to his Harmony of the Gospels.
[f] Hobbes's Creed, Art. 9.

evidence,

evidence, that the Gofpels were fo much difperfed abroad in the world, that no fuch confufion could happen to St. Matthew, as Mr. Whifton fuppofes. This will appear;

1. If we confider the defign and end, for which thefe facred books were written. They were not written for the ufe of any one private particular perfon, but for the benefit and inftruction of all mankind. They were books of a more large and extenfive importance, than any which had ever yet been publifhed in the world; they were fuch in which the prefent and future happinefs of all men was nearly concerned. And is it likely, fuch books fhould lie concealed in private chefts or coffers, fome for forty, others for fifty, fixty, feventy, or more years? The zeal of the Apoftles and firft Chriftians, for propagating Chriftianity, was not fuch as it is reprefented, if they would be fo negligent as this. If this be fuppofed, it follows, that they flighted one of the moft likely means to make men converts to their new religion. Whatever others did, one would imagine the penmen of thefe facred books fhould themfelves have taken care to diftribute and difperfe them. If they did not thus, it will follow, that they had not very juft regards to that holy Spirit, who influenced them to write. Befides Chriftianity, in its very infancy, made a very great noife in the world: the doctrines of it were new and furprifing; vaft numbers continually embraced it: one would think therefore, that, had there been nothing elfe, men's curiofity would have influenced them to procure thofe authentick accounts, which the Gofpels contain; that fo they might know the hiftory of a perfon's life and doctrines, who had been fo remarkable, and made fo great a figure in the world. I remember Jofephus [a] tells us, that when he had finifhed his Hiftory of the War of the Jews, *he immediately fold great numbers of his books to the Romans, Jews, and others, who underftood the Greek language.* And can it be fuppofed that this,

---

[a] Πολλοῖς μὲν Ῥωμαίων τοῖς συμπεπολεμηκόσι, πολλοῖς δὲ τὶ ἡμετέρων ἐπίπρασκον, ἀνδράσι καὶ τῆς Ἑλληνικῆς σοφίας μετεσχηκόσιν. Contra Appion. l. 1. §. 9.

the

the most useful and remarkable history that ever was in the world, should lie in private coffers, quite concealed and unknown, for so long a time as has been mentioned.

2. It will appear, that copies of the Gospels were dispersed in the Apostles' time, into distant countries, and did not lie in the coffers or chests of any private persons ; if we consider, that they are made use of, and referred to, by all those, who are reputed to be writers of the apostolick age, except Hermas, whose design did not at all lead him to cite them. The writers I mean (which are indeed the only ones we have), are Clemens Romanus, Barnabas, Ignatius, and Polycarp ; each of which (though they lived in very distant countries) had, and made use of, those Gospels, which were published when they wrote their Epistles. I mean the Gospels of St. Matthew, St. Mark, and St. Luke ; for, as far as I have observed, they do none of them cite, or so much as refer to, any thing which is in St. John's Gospel ; which, by the way, seems somewhat like an argument, that these Epistles were written before that Gospel.

Mr. Dodwell, in the Dissertation just now mentioned, would persuade us, that the writers of the apostolick age have made no use, in their books, of the Gospels, or other writings of the New Testament. This is most apparently false, as any one may easily perceive, who will read those books with this view. It is sufficient to my present purpose, to shew that St. Matthew's Gospel is cited by these writers.

A Table of places, cited out of St. Matthew's Gospel by the Apostolick Fathers.

I. Clemens Romanus, in his Epistle to the Corinthians, ch. xiii. advises them to remember several of our Lord's sayings, which are recited by St. Matthew, chap. vi. 14. and vii. 1, 2, 12.

II. Barnabas, ch. iv. cites Matth. ch. xx. 16. and xxii. 14.

Ch. v. he refers to Matth. ix. 13.

Ch. v. he cites a prophecy out of Zechariah, ch. xiii. 7. in words different both from the Hebrew, and the Septuagint,

tuagint, but exactly the same with our Saviour's words, as related by St. Matthew, ch. xxvi. 31.

Ch. vii. he cites Matth. xxvii. 54.

Ch. xix. he refers to Matth. v. 42.

III. Polycarp, in his Epistle to the Philippians, ch. ii. cites Matth. vii. 1. and v. 3, 10.

Ch. vi. he cites Matth. vi. 12, 14.

Ch. vii. he cites Matth. vi. 13. and xxvi. 41.

IV. Ignatius, in his Epistle to the Smyrneans, ch. i. cites Matth. iii. 15.

In his Epistle to Polycarp, ch. ii. he cites Matth. x. 16.

In his Epistle to the Ephesians, ch. xiv. he cites Matth. xii. 33. These are reckoned among his genuine Epistles.

By a careful observing of these writings with this view, perhaps there may be found several other places of this Gospel referred to in them. Those now cited are sufficient to prove, that this Gospel was widely dispersed in the Apostles' time, and made use of in very distant countries; for Clemens wrote his Epistle from Rome, Barnabas from Cyprus, Polycarp from Smyrna, Ignatius from Antioch; and these were places widely distant from each other. If then these Gospels were thus in the hands of all those of that age, whose writings we now have, it is very reasonable to suppose, they were also in the hands of innumerable others.

I would only add, that in the Constitutions, which Mr. Whiston supposes to be *the Apostles'*, and collected by Clemens, this Gospel is frequently cited, and recommended, among the other sacred Gospels, to the perusal of all Christians; which would have been very absurd, if the Gospels were not dispersed, and spread abroad in the world.

3. This matter will be further confirmed, if we consider, how much it was the practice of the first Christians to read the Scriptures. St. Paul's Epistles were wont to be publickly read in the churches, to which they were written, and other churches too, as is plain from those words, Col. iv. 16. *And when*

when this *Epiftle is read among you, cause that it be read alfo in the church of the Laodiceans; and that ye likewife read the Epiftle from Laodicea.* Timothy has this character given him by St. Paul, *that he from a child had made the Scriptures his ftudy,* 2 Tim. iii. 15. It feems to me very probable, that he means here both the Scriptures of the New and Old Teftament ; for he gives them this character, *that they were able to make him wife unto falvation;* which character at that time did moft properly belong to the books of the New Teftament, which were then written. Polycarp, in his Epiftle to the Philippians, tells them, *he did not doubt but they were converfant with the facred Scriptures.* The laft Canon of the Apoftles obliges all Laity and Clergy, *to procure the facred books, both of the Old and New Teftament;* and b. i. c. 5. the Chriftians are required *diligently to read the Gofpels* [a]. This is authority, which Mr. Whifton will not difpute. If then the Chriftians did, and were obliged to read the Gofpels, they did not lie concealed and unknown till the times of Trajan or Hadrian.

I would only add here, that reading the Gofpels was one part of the public fervice of the primitive Chriftians, in their religious affemblies. It is certain that a great part of the Jewifh worfhip in their fynagogues, confifted in reading of the Law [b]. Jofephus tells us, that *they did this in obedience to the command of Mofes* [c]. Now it is well known, that the Chriftians conformed themfelves very much in their worfhip to the cuftoms of the Jews. Juftin Martyr [d], who lived but a little while after the Apoftles' time, tells us, " That on the day " which is called Sunday, there was an affembly of all, that " lived (near) in town or country, in the fame place ; and

---

[a] Διέρχη ἐπιμελῶς τὸ Εὐαγγέλιον.

[b] Luke iv. 16, 17. and Acts xv. 21.

[c] Ἑκάστης ἑβδομάδος τῶν ἄλλων ἔργων ἀφεμένες, ἐπὶ τὴν ἀκρόασιν τῶ νόμου ἐκέλευσε (fc. Mofes) συλλέγεσθαι. Contra Appion. l. 2. §. 17.

[d] Καὶ τῇ τοῦ ἡλίου λεγομένῃ ἡμέρᾳ, πάντων κατὰ πόλεις ἢ ἀγρὲς μένοντων ἐπὶ τὸ αὐτὸ συνέλευσις γίνεται, καὶ τὰ ἀπομνημονεύματα τῶν ἀποστόλων, καὶ τὰ συγγράμματα τῶν προφητῶν, ἀναγινώσκεται. Apol. 2. p. 98.

" the

" the hiſtorical memoirs of the Apoſtles (i.e. the Goſpels) and
" the writings of the prophets were read."

Now from all this I think it is evident, a great number of
copies of this Goſpel were ſpread abroad in the world, in the
Apoſtles' time. Theſe, as has been proved, were in their
right order, in which St. Matthew wrote; and ſince it is impoſſible but ſome of thoſe copies that are in the world, muſt
be derived from ſome of theſe, and ſince all the copies that
are in the world, are in the ſame order with our preſent copies; it neceſſarily follows, this part of St. Matthew's Goſpel
has not been miſplaced or diſordered ſince the Apoſtles' time.

C H A P. XXIII.

*St. Matthew's Goſpel, in our preſent Copies, was not diſordered
and miſplaced ſince the Apoſtles' Time; becauſe the Syriack
Verſion, which was made in the Apoſtles' Time, is in the ſame
Order with our preſent Copies. An Attempt to prove, that the
Syriack Verſion was made in that Time. Syriack was the
Language of the Jews in the Apoſtles' Time. Great Num-
bers of Jews were converted to Chriſtianity, and therefore
needed a Verſion in that Language.*

BY what has been ſaid in the foregoing Chapter, it is evident St. Matthew's Goſpel was not miſplaced ſince the
Apoſtles' time: the ſame will be further proved, if we conſider;

2. That the Syriack Verſion, which ſeems to have been
made in the Apoſtles' time, is exactly in the ſame order in this
part of St. Matthew's Goſpel, with our preſent copies. This
is an argument, which undeniably proves the point I am contending for, if it can be made appear, that this Verſion was
made in that time. It is not to be expected, we ſhould have
as clear evidence of this, as we have of ſome other matters of

fact

fact in the Apostolick times; because, of the vast number of Jews, who were at first converted to Christianity, and who made use of this Version, there is not one (except the Apostles), who has wrote any thing which is come down to our present time. Nevertheless, I hope to make it at least probable, that this Version was made in the time of the Apostles. In order to which, I will shew;

1. That Syriack was the language in use among the Jews, in our Saviour's and the Apostles' time.

2. That it was very necessary a Version should be made, and very likely a Version was made, of the New Testament into this language in the Apostles' time.

3. That it is probable this Version, which we now have, is the same which was then made.

1. The Syriack was the language in common use among the Jews, in the time of our Saviour and his Apostles. Till the Jews were carried captives to Babylon, they undoubtedly retained their own language, viz. the pure Hebrew, and understood not Syriack, as is plain from 2 Kings xviii. 26. and Jer. v. 15. Being at Babylon for seventy years, they learnt the language of the country, which afterwards they never lost. *This was a place* (says the great Bochart[a]), *always fatal to the Hebrew language.* That which they learnt, was not very much different from the Hebrew, though it went under a different name, and was called sometimes Chaldee, and sometimes Syriack: so Dan. i. 4. it is called ולשון כשדים i. e. *the tongue of the Chaldeans*; and ch. ii. 4. the same is called Syriack; *the Chaldeans spake to the King* ארמית i. e. *in the Syriack tongue.* It was this (perhaps a little altered), in which our Saviour and his Apostles conversed[b], and the Jews generally, in their time:

for

---

[a] Eadem Babylon, ubi cæteræ linguæ natæ sunt, semper Hebraicæ fuit fatalis, semel in confusione Linguarum, et rursus cum Judæi ibi captivi patrium sermonem didicerunt. Phaleg. l. 1. c. 15.

See to the same purpose Dr. Prideaux Connect. of the Hist. of the Old and New Test. Par. 1. B. 5. and Par. 2. B. 8.

[b] Is vero Syrorum Sermo, Christi et Apostolorum temporibus, propter diuturnam illam in Babylone captivitatem, et Assyriorum contra in Judæam translationem, genti Hebraicæ popularis fuit et vernaculus, adeo ut nulli tunc scirent Hebraice, nisi qui singulari studio ex libris didicissent. Quamobrem Christum quoque et Apostolos eodem sermone popu-

popu-

for the proof of this, I ſhall only alledge a few places out of the New Teſtament; the great number of Syriack words, that are to be found therein, do ſufficiently prove it, viz. ſuch as *Talitha Kumi* [a], *Ephphatha* [b], *Eloi Eloi lama ſabachthani* [c], *Be-theſda* [d], *Golgotha* [e], *Gabbatha* [f], *Raca* [g], *Cephas* [h], *Aceldama* [i], *Boanerges* [k], *Maran-atha* [l], *Bar-Jona* [m], *Abba* [n], &c. Theſe are all evidently Syriack words (as they know who are ac-quainted with this language); which were uſed by the Jews in and about our Saviour's time. I would only obſerve con-cerning one of theſe Syriack words, viz. the word *Aceldama*, that it is ſaid to be ἐν τῇ ἰδίᾳ διαλέκτῳ αὐτῶν, i. e. *in their own dialect or language.* It is true indeed, that two or three of theſe words are called Hebrew, ſo John v. 2. ἡ ἐπιλεγομένη Ἑβραϊςὶ Βηθεσδὰ, *which is called in Hebrew Betheſda,* and John xix. 13. Ἑβραϊςὶ Γαββαθὰ, i. e. *in Hebrew Gabbatha.* But it is a very trite and common obſervation, that Syriack and Chal-dee are frequently called Hebrew; whence Nonnus in his Greek Paraphraſe on John, tranſlates Ἑβραϊςὶ, Σύρῳ μύθῳ, in the laſt place cited; and ver. 17. he renders the ſame word Σύρῳ ςόμα. So Philo [o] and the Fathers commonly call Chaldee and Syriack, Hebrew. Nor is this ſtrange, when we conſider that Hebrew was the old language, from which theſe two dialects (very little different from it) are derived.

The old Hebrew was ſo far from being the language of the country at this time, that they had now, and for a long time before had, an officer in the ſynagogues, called מְתֻרְגְּמָן, whoſe buſineſs it was, when the Old Teſtament was read, to tranſlate the Hebrew, and give the people the ſenſe of it, period by period, in Chaldee, or Syriack [p]. Hence alſo it was, that

---

popularibus ſuis locutos fuiſſe, cum ipſa ratio, tum in Græco relictæ voces Syriacæ, ſatis evincunt. Tre-mell. Præfat. in Teſt. Syriac.

[a] Mark v. 41.
[b] Mark vii. 34.
[c] Mark xv. 34.
[d] John v. 2.
[e] Matt. xxvii. 33.
[f] John xix. 13.
[g] Matt. v. 22.

[h] John i. 42.
[i] Acts i. 19.
[k] Mark iii. 17.
[l] 1 Cor. xvj. 22.
[m] Matt xvi. 17.
[n] Mark xiv. 36.
[o] Vid. Caſaub. ad Baron. An-nal. c. xvi. §. 11.
[p] Dr. Lightfoot Harm. of the Goſpels, Year 31. §. 23.

the חרגומים i. e. *the Chaldee tranſlations* of the Old Teſtament were made in, or before, our Saviour's time.

- There has been a controverſy between the learned Mr. Voſſius, and Father Simon, concerning the language the Jews ſpake at this time. The former pretends, that Greek was then the language of the Jews; but Father Simon has ſufficiently[b] ſhewn the weakneſs of his arguments[b]. It ſeems to me very evident, the common Jews did not at all underſtand Greek. It was indeed the language moſt known in the world (much more perhaps than either Latin or French are now); and for that reaſon, as has been ſaid, the books of the New Teſtament were wrote in it: but the common Jews were not acquainted with it; and therefore St. Paul, when he was apprehended at Jeruſalem, though he ſpake to the officer (who perhaps was a Roman) *in Greek* (Acts xxi. 37.); yet, when he made his ſpeech to the people, he ſpake εβραιδι διαλεκτω, *in the Hebrew tongue*, or, which is the ſame (as has been proved), *in the Syriack*. He knew the people could not underſtand him in any other; and ſo we find, that, when he ſpake no more Greek, but in their own language, they diligently hearkened to him, ch. xxii. 2. Hence Joſephus tells us, that he wrote his Hiſtory firſt in Hebrew, or Syriack, for the uſe of his countrymen; but afterwards, that it might be of more extenſive uſe, tranſlated it into Greek: though (as he ſays a little after) he was very backward to that work, *becauſe it was a language very different from that of his country*[c].

2. This being the language of the Jews in our Saviour's time, it was very neceſſary a Verſion ſhould be made, and conſequently, likely a Verſion was made, of the New Teſtament into this language, before the Apoſtles' death. Although the body and greateſt part of the Jews rejected Chriſtianity, yet there were very conſiderable numbers of them that embraced it. We read, Acts xxi. 20. of many (μυριαδες) *ten thou-*

---

[a] Voſſ. Reſponſ. ad iterat. P. Simon obiect.
[b] Critic. Hiſt. of the New Teſt. Par. 1. c. 6.

[c] Εἰς ἀλλοδαπην ἡμιν και ξενης διαλεκτω συνθηκην. Praefat. in Antiq. Jud. §. 2.

ſands

fands of Jews that believed, and received the doctrines of Chrift. There can be no reafonable doubt, but that great additions were made to their number continually, both at Jerufalem, and other parts of Judæa. And now can it be fuppofed, that fo many thoufand converts fhould be left fo long without thofe infpired books, which contained the foundation of their religion? Here, and here only, they could have a particular, exact, and authentick account of the doctrines of that religion, which they had embraced; and is it not likely they would endeavour to get thefe books tranflated into their own language? Either the Apoftles, or themfelves, certainly would take care to have a Verfion made.

1. It may reafonably be fuppofed, that the Apoftles, who were fo much among the Jews, would take care to have the Gofpel Hiftory and their own writings publifhed among them, in their own language. Their zeal for the intereft of Chriftianity (which was in all refpects fo very great) would undoubtedly influence them to take this probable method of advancing it. Add to this, the particular fondnefs and affection, that appeared in feveral of them, towards their own countrymen. Nothing lefs than a revelation from heaven, would ferve to convince Peter, that he might leave them, and go to preach to the Gentiles[a]. The concern St. Paul had for them and their intereft, was fo tender and paffionate, that he was even ready *to wifh himfelf accurfed from Chrift,* if fo be they might be happy[b]. And now, would not all this their zeal for Chriftianity in general, and their particular love to their countrymen, excite them to procure a Verfion of thefe facred books for their ufe? Nothing can be fuppofed, which would prevent the Apoftles from doing this, unlefs we fuppofe they were of the fame mind with the Papifts, viz. that the Scriptures ought not to be tranflated into the common languages, for the ufe of the people. But the Apoftles were of a different opinion in this matter from their pretended fucceffors, who for intereft have made it religion, to keep the people in ignorance. Their grand employment was, to inftruct men in

[a] Acts x. 9, &c.   [b] Rom. ix. 3.

the

the hiſtory and doctrines of Chriſt; and now was any way more likely to do this, than giving them the Scriptures in their own language? The ſame reaſon, which put each of them upon writing in Greek, for the univerſal benefit of mankind, would very probably influence thoſe of them, who were at Jeruſalem, to tranſlate their books into the language we are ſpeaking of. Well does Tremellius argue on this head [a]; " It " is altogether probable" (he is ſpeaking of the Syriack Verſion), " that it was made in the very beginning of Chriſti-" anity, either by the Apoſtles or ſome of their diſciples; un-" leſs we will chooſe rather to believe, that in writing, they " had regard only to thoſe of other nations, and very little, or " none at all to thoſe of their own."   But,

2. If we ſuppoſe the Apoſtles thus negligent of the intereſt of the believing Jews, and not to have done this for them, we may with a great deal of reaſon ſuppoſe, that they would take care to have it done themſelves. Every body knows, how prodigiouſly fond the Jewiſh nation was of the ſacred books of the Old Teſtament, *becauſe they came from God*; and would not the converted Jews be likewiſe fond of the books of the New Teſtament, *which they believed alſo came from God?* They were careful enough to get the Hebrew of the Old Teſtament tranſlated into Chaldee, and may be as reaſonably ſuppoſed (I mean they who were converted) to get the Greek of the New Teſtament tranſlated into Syriack. Upon the whole, I think it fair to conclude, that a Verſion of the New Teſtament was made into this language in the time of the Apoſtles.

[a] Præfat. in Verſ. Syr.

C H A P. XXIV.

The Syriack Verſion, which we now have, is the ſame which
was made in the Apoſtles' Time. This proved by three argu-
ments. The Syrians, from whom we had it, believed it to be
the ſame. It is improbable the Antient Verſion ſhould be loſt.
It wants the Parts of the New Teſtament, which were laſt
written.

I HAVE attempted in the foregoing Chapter to ſhew, that
a Verſion of the New Teſtament was made into Syriack
in the time of the Apoſtles; I ſhall now endeavour to prove,

3. That the Syriack Verſion which we now have, is the
ſame which was then made. In order to which, I obſerve;

1. That it was conſtantly and univerſally believed by the
Syrians, from whom we had this Verſion, that it was made by
St. Mark the Evangeliſt. The truth of this depends upon the
teſtimony of Poſtellus[a], a learned man, who aſſiſted Widman-
ſtadius in his firſt edition of this Verſion; and avers, that he
received this account from the Syrians themſelves, when he
travelled among them, to acquire the knowledge of their language and cuſtoms.

2. Whether this Verſion was made by St. Mark or not, it
is very improbable that the Church at Jeruſalem or Antioch,
or any other Church, for whom the Syriack Verſion was firſt
made, would ſuffer it to be loſt. There was no more probability of the Syrians loſing their tranſlation, than of the Greek
Churches loſing their original. A Church of Chriſtians, who
were in poſſeſſion of ſo valuable a treaſure, would be continually uſing it; its copies would be daily multiplying amongſt
them, and ſo they cannot reaſonably be ſuppoſed to have loſt
it; they looked upon it as the word of God, though not in
the language in which it was originally written, and therefore

------

[a] Guid. Fabrit. Præfat. in Syr. Teſt.

would

would be careful in preserving it. Every one knows, how exceeding fond the Jews were of their Chaldee Verfions of the Old Teftament. Galatinus tells us [a], they *paid the fame refpect to them, as to the original itfelf:* and is it not likely the Chriftian Jews would be as careful of their tranflations of the New Teftament, as the others were of the tranflations of the Old?

3. The Syriack Verfion, which we now have, is the fame which was made in the Apoftles' time, becaufe it has not in it thofe books of the New Teftament, which were laft written, viz. *The fecond Epiftle of Peter, the fecond and third of John, the Epiftle of Jude, and the Revelation.* Thefe indeed have been added, fince this Verfion was brought into Europe, viz. the four Epiftles by Mr. Pocock, and the Revelation by De Dieu; but it is, I think, agreed by every body, even the editors themfelves, that thefe are but modern tranflations. Now there can be but two probable reafons affigned, why they were wanting in the copy brought by Mofes Meridinæus into Europe, and the other antient Syriack copies; viz. either,

1. Becaufe they were not received into the Canon, and judged authentick, when this Verfion was made. It is certain thefe books were not at firft received by all, but for a long time rejected by many, as Eufebius tells us [b]: or

2. They are not in the Syriack copies, becaufe they were not written when the Syriack Verfion was made; and this indeed feems moft probable; for had they been written then, thofe fo ufeful Epiftles would have been tranflated, for the fame reafon as the others. This was the argument, which, among others, convinced Tremellius [c] and the learned Bp. Walton [d], that this Verfion was made in the Apoftles' time. I conclude therefore, fince this Verfion has the feveral periods of St. Matthew's Gofpel, in the fame order with our prefent copies, that they never have been diforderd or mifplaced.

[a] De Arcan. Cathol. Verit. l. 1. c. 6.
[b] Hift. Eccl. l. 3. c. 24, 25. & l. 6. c. 25. & l. 7. c. 25.
[c] Præfat. in Nov. Teft. Syr.
[d] Prolegom. in Bibl. Polyglot. xiii. §. 15.

I N D E X

A

BENT-

END OF VOL. III.

ERRATA IN VOL. III.

P. 57. l. 2. for *Hypotopofes* read *Hypotypofes*
72. l. 6. after *Romans* place a comma
In the Vindication.
25. l. 7. for *word* read *words*
52. l. 13. for *of* read *off*

www.ingramcontent.com/pod-product-compliance
Lightning Source LLC
Chambersburg PA
CBHW060524030726
47498CB00004B/1063